P9-DBO-468

THE
BUILDING
A BIOGRAPHY OF THE PENTAGON

THE
BUILDING
A BIOGRAPHY OF THE PENTAGON

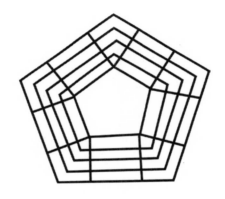

DAVID ALEXANDER

ZENITH PRESS

First published in 2008 by Zenith Press, an imprint of MBI Publishing Company, 400 First Avenue North, Suite 300, Minneapolis, MN 55401 USA

Copyright © 2008 by David Alexander

All rights reserved. With the exception of quoting brief passages for the purposes of review, no part of this publication may be reproduced without prior written permission from the Publisher. The information in this book is true and complete to the best of our knowledge.

Zenith Press titles are also available at discounts in bulk quantity for industrial or sales-promotional use. For details write to Special Sales Manager at MBI Publishing Company, 400 First Avenue North, Suite 300, Minneapolis, MN 55401 USA.

To find out more about our books, join us online at www.zenithpress.com.

ISBN-13: 978-0-7603-2087-7

Printed in the United States of America

Library of Congress Cataloging-in-Publication Data

Alexander, David S.
  The building : a biography of the Pentagon / David Alexander.
    p. cm.
  ISBN-13: 978-0-7603-2087-7 (hardbound)
  ISBN-10: 0-7603-2087-X (hardbound)
  1. Pentagon (Va.)--History. I. Title. II. Title: Biography of the Pentagon.
UA26.A727A54 2007
355.709755'295--dc22
                                        2006022063

Designer: Jennifer Bergstrom

Printed in the United States of America

This book is dedicated to the gifted people behind the Building's walls, especially those who tragically lost their lives on September 11, 2001.

*I cease not to advocate peace; even though
unjust it is better than the most just war.*

—*Cicero: Epistolae ad Atticum*, Book VII, Epistle 14

*As long as there are sovereign nations possessing great power,
war is inevitable.*

—"Einstein on the Atomic bomb," *Atlantic Monthly*,
November 1945

*We fight not to enslave, but to set a country free,
and to make room upon the earth for honest men to live in.*

—Thomas Paine, "The American Crisis, No. IV,"
September 12, 1777

CONTENTS

PREFACE

In planning, researching, and writing this book one of my principal questions was this: How is the story of the Pentagon different from the story of World War II, the Cold War, the several regional wars, including Korea and Vietnam, the war in Iraq, and the numerous "police actions" and peacekeeping missions ("operations other than war") in which the United States has been involved since the Building's groundbreaking ceremony on September 11, 1941? How do you separate the history of the Pentagon from the history of the U.S. military, the presidency, the Department of Defense (DOD), and Congress—for that matter, the histories of enemies and allies where these touch on the story—between then and now? This was a central question and a test of the underlying validity of the book. It was a difficult one to sort out, because the short answer seemed to be that, in fact, the story, let alone the history, of the Pentagon was essentially indistinguishable from the history of the wars in which America has been engaged since, and immediately preceding, the Pentagon's establishment. Such being the case, the concept of the Pentagon's biographical history had no validity, and the only story that could be told, per se, would have been one that merely involved the details of the Building's planning and construction and the nuts-and-bolts of how the Pentagon works.

While these aspects are interesting enough in their own right, there have already been several good books published on them, and besides it wasn't what I set out to write. The Building's "biography" would have to encompass what might be called a "third dimension" of narrative to fulfill its vision and justify its creation. Fortunately as my investigations into the subject developed and deepened I discovered that this third dimension was, in fact, an element of the ground truth all along, and that I'd zeroed in on it in the conceptual stages of chronicling the Pentagon's story.

The Pentagon is much more than a Goliath of a building that houses one of the most sprawling government bureaucracies on earth; yes, it's certainly a symbol, too, and one of the most iconic symbols for anyone's military in the world. Say "the Pentagon" and you've spoken a mantra for the U.S. military establishment. Say "the Pentagon" and you've instantaneously evoked a

Medusa-headed mixed metaphor that shoehorns a dozen concepts into one compact phrase-word. Say "the Pentagon" when you want to refer to either the U.S. military, the U.S. Department of Defense, the U.S. Joint Chiefs of Staff, the defense budget for any given fiscal year, the Office of the Secretary of Defense, or the organizing principle behind any current military enterprise in which the United States is involved, and you've noted all these things at once.

Consequently, say "the Pentagon" and you've chanted a powerful mantra that is immediately synonymous with the most sinister of forces to antiwar activists, pacifists, and their ideological collaborators as the quintessence of warmongering; in fact the Yippies and the Fugs rock band did precisely this during the 1967 March on the Pentagon, as part of an "exorcism" of what they deemed America's satanic militarist zeitgeist of the era, and during an attempt to levitate the Pentagon some ten feet off the ground (which adherents and disciples later maintained actually happened, though allowing, tongue-in-cheek, that it had probably not been by the full ten feet).

In short that third dimension of narrative exists because the Pentagon is more than building, symbol, or icon; from almost the first moment of its construction—before even the first of its five wedges and five floors was completed—it became one of the most important centers of power in the world, and also from almost the first moment, the decisions that were made within it had an effect on the history of the world as profound as any that originated across the Potomac at 1600 Pennsylvania Avenue, 10 Downing Street in London, or Red Square in Moscow—or, for that matter, anyplace else on the planet.

The Pentagon continues to this day to be the physical embodiment of this power, which is a combination of the military and political arms of the United States and is personified in the physical arrangement of the Building itself. As a general rule, the fourth floor contains the offices of the Joint Staff and the third floor those of the Department of Defense, while the many offices between the "E" or outer ring of the Building and the main corridor or "A" ring are staffed by both civilian and military personnel—some twenty-five thousand of them, in fact, on any given business day and perhaps a quarter of that on weekends. There are also a number of command centers and operational areas located throughout the huge edifice.

In World War II, the Pentagon became the centralized location for the then War Department of the United States, which was established in

1789 to organize, conduct, and oversee the operation of American military forces. (A separate Department of the Navy was created in 1798.) Such a central headquarters was a necessity. Between the end of World War I and the early years of World War II (before and after U.S. entry into the conflict in Europe) the War and Navy departments were scattered across the District of Columbia and in adjacent communities, such as Arlington, Virginia. Their staffs conducted operations in an ad hoc assortment of buildings—some accounts give seventeen as the number, others twenty-one; the precise quantity can't be exactly known—that included at least one rented garage.

As the new face of industrialized total war became manifest in Europe, it became apparent that old arrangements were not working any longer. In order to meaningfully and effectively project its military might against enemy forces that were hedging it round in those perilous days, the United States needed to restructure its forces, and do it with unprecedented speed. The Pentagon, coupled with the repeal of congressional acts mandating disarmament signed into law after the armistice that ended World War I, answered this need in most regards. It was completed in a record sixteen months, with the War Department taking occupancy before the final finishing touches—such as the decorative facing of slabs of a unique, pale Indiana limestone—were put in place.

From its location at a former crossroads not far from the west bank of the Potomac River, the Pentagon became a central organizing principle behind the deployment of U.S. and Allied forces in every theater of this new, mechanized, global war. Its staff was involved in every detail of the procurement, planning, and mobilization process in virtually every action of that far-flung conflict, from the steaming jungles of Burma, where Stilwell was engaged against Japanese forces to build the Burma road, to the beachheads of Anzio, Normandy, and Tripoli, where U.S., British, and other Allied troops were landing in the first modern amphibious assaults on a massive scale.

Its presence reached out to the epochal tri-power conferences, such as the Casablanca Conference, between the Allied powers in which the central policy and plans for the war were made, and it coordinated the critical planning on both sides of the Atlantic and between SHAEF, the Supreme Headquarters of the Allied Expeditionary Forces, located in London, and the White House and State Department in the District. The Pentagon was an unseen adjunct to every soldier in every theater of combat during the war, and it was there with Truman when he signed the orders that were to drop two atomic gravity bombs on two cities in Japan in 1945.

After the war ended, the Pentagon's importance was not eclipsed; on the contrary, in a world that grew increasingly complex nationally and internationally, internally and externally, with every passing year, the Building began playing an ever-increasing role in global affairs. Between 1945 and the end of the immediate postwar era, and 1950 and the start of the Cold War's burgeoning game of nuclear brinkmanship and brushfire wars, a series of defense and security enactments only matched by those that took place in the aftermath of September 11, 2001, transformed the defense and security structure of the United States.

Among these significant developments was the joining of the War Department (with its name changed to the Department of the Army) and the Department of the Navy with the newly created Department of the Air Force under a defense department headed by an entirely new cabinet post: secretary of defense. Also established was a restructuring of the U.S. military that saw the newly created billet of chairman to head the Joint Chiefs of Staff.

Throughout the Cold War, during the Gulf War, in war-torn Yugoslavia, in the Iraq War, and the global war on terrorism, the Pentagon has continued to change and play an ever-increasing role. Throughout these years, also, it has not escaped controversy. During the 1980s the Pentagon was the nucleus of a series of budget and procurement scandals that sent at least one high official to prison and might have put many others in government and defense corporations behind bars had they not cut separate deals and gained amnesty; more recently Secretary of Defense Donald Rumsfeld resigned under fire. Small wonder that the Building is commonly known as "the Puzzle Palace."

Yet the story of war is as central to the story of the Building as that of the Pentagon is to the history of modern wars. The war on terror has been called a second Cold War by some, but I tend to disagree. In thinking about the Pentagon I tend to believe that what is happening today is more like a second World War II; during that time an isolationist America that was content to remain detached from the turmoil of other nations found itself the center of building hatred and enmity from other nations.

Imperial Japan, Nazi Germany, Fascist Italy, and their allies all saw in the United States the antithesis of authoritarian regimes whose sole claim to power was based on the hegemony of force, the threat of punishment, and rule based on fear rather than democratically enacted laws. The United States stood for everything that threatened the power of the tyrants who had come to power in these countries and who thrived only in the fertile soil of discord which they'd sowed. This made the United States their target and principal foe, for as long as America existed their own existences were precarious. This is much like the threat the United States faces today, except for the chief differences that our enemies now are frequently not nation states but transnational cellular groupings, and that the forces they command pose an amorphous, asymmetric threat to our national existence.

The Cold War, by comparison, was a largely bipolar confrontation between established world powers. It was a contest in slow motion between two massive, industrialized giants and their respective political systems for hegemony in the world. World War II was a Texas Death Match; the Cold War was the proverbial dance with a 300-pound gorilla. I leave the reader to draw his or her own conclusions about which metaphor is closer to what we face today against global terrorism.

Talk of metaphors—rich in history, sometimes rocked by conflict and controversy, a potent symbol of the arsenal of democracy, hated by some, revered or feared by others, the Pentagon is like the proverbial elephant touched by the three blind beggars—it is more known by one or several of its constituent parts than as the multifaceted whole that it actually is. The purpose of this book is to shed light on trunk, tail, legs, tusks, and belly of this leviathan of defense.

In doing so I have taken an integrated approach to chronicling the history of the Building from its inception during the tumultuous days before and during World War II, continue through the Cold War and the post-Cold War era until the attacks of 9/11, and conclude with a final section on the Pentagon in the first decade of the twenty-first century.

In writing the book my aim is to combine documentary sources with accounts derived from firsthand research at the Pentagon and at many of the scenes of the historic events in which it has played key roles, as well as with the principal actors in the story. Nothing less than this can do justice to an institution as large and as significant, as feared and as respected, as misconstrued and as quintessential as is the edifice, organizations, and set of concepts collectively known as the Building.

ACKNOWLEDGMENTS

A great many individuals have assisted me in the course of writing this book in ways large and small. They know who they are. More importantly, they'll know it's them I mean—thanks to all of you for your support and understanding. D. A.

BOOK ONE

A RENDEZVOUS WITH DESTINY

The American Military Establishment Between World Wars

There is a mysterious cycle in human events. To some generations much is given. Of others much is expected. This generation of Americans has a rendezvous with destiny.

—President Franklin Delano Roosevelt,
Philadelphia speech, June 1936

CHAPTER ONE

THE WINDS OF CHANGE

Vie victus!—"Woe to the conquered!"
—Old Roman proverb

I t may be ironic that some of the most classically heroic architecture
in the United States arose out of some of the worst building sites
imaginable. Both the District of Columbia and the site of the Pentagon
were originally areas of malodorous swampland. The District, a corner of
northwestern Maryland and southeastern Pennsylvania, was set aside for
the seat of the U.S. government mainly because it was deemed to have no
value for farming—at a time when farmland took up about 46 percent
of all acreage in the United States this was tantamount to saying it was
hell's little acre. Indeed it could justly be claimed of the seat of America's
government that it emerged from the primeval swamp like some new
species of luxuriant, complicated flora.

But then, D.C. is a place of curiosities, from a vast natural history
museum whose establishment was funded by a bequest from a man named
Smithson who had never set foot in the United States, to the plate-glass and
steel skyscrapers that tower over neo-Romanesque buildings reminiscent
of the Forum of the Caesars, Washington has an ambiance unique among
cities and a place unique among the capitals of the world.

For one thing, the District of Columbia, unlike most other capitals,
is not synonymous with a capital city. London may be the capital of

Britain, Paris may be the capital of France, Rome may be the capital of Italy, and Moscow may be the capital of Russia, but it's not New York, L.A., or Chicago that claims the same distinction in the United States. Indeed, the closest analogs to the District are, curiously, religious ones. The holy cities of the Vatican and Mecca, for example, specially cordoned off and invested with great and ennobling works, seem closest in tenor to the shrines to American political tradition found in the District of Columbia.

Few, if any, places in the United States have been laid out with as deliberate a plan to inspire precisely this awe in those who pass through its thoroughfares, nor have many American municipalities undertaken programs of vast public works over the course of many decades and political administrations. There is a symmetry to greater Washington, D.C., that is marred by a single exception—that exception happens to be the largest government office building in the entire world, perhaps the largest office building of any kind, government or otherwise. The name by which it's known—not to be confused with the name it was originally given— is the Pentagon.

The Pentagon did not evolve with the same deliberateness as many if not most of the District's other landmarks. It sprang almost spontaneously into being, like Minerva from the brow of Zeus. It was, in fact, planned as a temporary military headquarters only, like an earlier Army-Navy headquarters complex in metropolitan D.C. that will be looked at shortly. To use a less heroic metaphor, it mushroomed from the swamps of a place called Five Points, inventing itself as it rose from cement piles steam-hammered into the soggy ground that were its concrete roots. From its inception, the Pentagon was an oddity and a paradox, an institution that defied tradition and a breeding ground for iconoclasts presided over by an arch military iconoclast named George Marshall whose brief from his boss, Franklin Delano Roosevelt, was to shake things up and shake them up hard.

The Pentagon's name, too, was completely impromptu. It was to originally have been called simply the War Department Building, but common usage quickly dubbed it the Pentagon. The origins of this usage depend on who's telling the story. One version has it that the chief opponent of the new U.S. military headquarters, one Gilmore David Clarke, who chaired the Washington Fine Arts Commission and opposed the massive planned construction project on the grounds that it would obscure a panoramic view from Arlington, Virginia, to the White House—decried the pentagonal building in a meeting with FDR in the Oval Office.

The New York City–born Clarke and Franklin Delano Roosevelt, the former governor of New York State and now president, were no strangers to one another. Clarke had been involved with numerous public building projects—many of them in New York City—which included the Central Park Zoo and the landscape architecture for the 1939 World's Fair; years later he would be one of the principal designers of Flushing Meadows Park, in the borough of Queens, New York, that hosted the 1964 World's Fair. He designed the fair's trademark, the huge stainless steel globe of the world called the Unisphere that still marks the site today. Clarke was also a close associate of city planner Robert Moses with whom he would help build New Jersey's Garden State Parkway. Moreover, Clarke—a former engineer with the U.S. Army Corps of Engineers—and the chief proponent of the new, pentagonal War Department building, General Brehon B. Somervell, were old antagonists who had collided years before in New York when Somervell headed the crews building La Guardia Airport.

Clarke, in short, was no mere tyro or local fuddy-duddy; he was every inch a match for the redoubtable "Bill" Somervell and an architect and engineer whose traction with Roosevelt was of a high order of magnitude. Nevertheless, the former New York governor was said to have replied in his most patrician tones that, "I for one rather like the idea of a pentagon," weighing in on Somervell's side for all the formidable prestige that Clarke and Delano mustered against the Pentagon building project.

But there are other versions of the story. Probably it was simpler to use a single three-syllable word that succinctly described the new War Department Building than three polysyllabic words that said the same thing. Whatever the reason, it could just as correctly be said that the five-sided building became the Pentagon by sheer force of personality as it pushed its way out of the swampy bottom of Five Points.

There is more than mere metaphor behind this statement, too— the Pentagon drew into its substance the very sand at the bottom of the nearby Potomac River. Some thirty million tons of sand were dredged

5

from the river to form the matrix of the seven hundred million tons of cement from which its walls were fashioned, turning it into a sort of man-made fossilized riverbed.

From the outset the Pentagon was an anomaly, but it was more than that. Unknown to even its planners and builders the Pentagon was a presaging of a future full of both terror and promise. It was a break in time made manifest on the eve of America's entry into a global conflict that was to be, before it was over, like no other war that humanity had ever fought, a gigantic stone mile marker on the road to the America of the twenty-first century.

No one suspected this at the time—no one could have intimated it—yet in hindsight this shadow cast by futurity upon the present was there all the while. Like the proverbial white elephant in the room, everybody saw what had entered the picture, only nobody was prepared to acknowledge the truth of its presence amid the willfully blind.

* * *

The Pentagon's construction began at the nether cusp of an interwar period that spanned the years between the end World War I to the eve of U.S. entry into World War II. Its five-sided architectonic expression was archetypal. Throughout the history of warfare, the pentagonal structure—star-sided, angular, affording natural defensive works while trapping attackers, rising low on the landscape, with massive walls—has been the model on which fortresses have been based.

On the peaks of steep hills throughout central Italy one encounters such buildings and wonders how any forces armed only with muscle-power weapons such as pikes, staves, swords, and crossbows could have ever taken them; and even the next thought, that they were conquered by siege, seems hard to fathom when confronted by such mighty edifices. The Pentagon, though officially conceived as an office building to house the large military and civilian staff of the U.S. War Department during a fragile interwar peace that was expected to burgeon on America's almost inevitable entry into the European conflict, was built to resemble nothing less than a mighty fortress on the bank of the Potomac.

Symbolically, perhaps unconsciously, it was a statement in steel-waffled concrete that America was about to harden itself against adversity, to temper its sinews for a fight to the finish against a Satanic adversary. Herodotus reports in his *History of Herodotus* that the Persian monarch Darius asked for gifts of earth and water from his far-flung satrapies as symbols of obeisance; these elements are deeply rooted in a sense of homeland, as deep to a nation as flesh and blood is to the individual.

Whether it escaped the planners and builders or not, the massive amounts of sand and water taken from the Potomac to fashion the Building was a token that America had put the hidden marrow of its soul into this mighty edifice, one such as it had never before seen fit to build. It was to be, as one observer put it during the Vietnam era, "a vast concrete and limestone materialization of the military mind."

The old War Department Building that preceded the Pentagon was everything that the new seat of American military power was not—almost a negative doppelganger. It bespoke a world of finite limitations in war, peace, and commerce that marked the nineteenth century's culminating Belle Epoch. The Pentagon bespoke the streamlined face of emerging warfare, what came eventually to be called "industrial" warfare.

It resembled a factory or a prison as much as it did a fortress, albeit of gargantuan dimensions, and it harbingered the military-industrial complex later vilified by World War II's supreme military commander turned U.S. president. This concrete juggernaut presaged the military juggernaut that the U.S. was to become in the twentieth century, but nothing presaged the cataclysmic developments of the global war that was soon to enmesh the United States and transform it in the course of battle. Nothing could.

* * *

The seeds of impending conflict were sown in a railway car parked on a siding on the outskirts of Versailles, France, after the surrender of Germany in November 11, 1918. It was a treaty of vengeance, intended to weaken Germany to such an extent that it could never again pose a military threat to the security of Europe. The treaty was more than successful at this but its draconian requirements also weakened Europe. The Great

CHAPTER ONE

War had left behind a dazed and distressed continent whose attempts to return to normalcy were met with almost insurmountable challenges at every turn. Not even the peace settlements of 1919 or subsequent bailouts of Germany by the United States and Great Britain could offset these trials.

The cataclysm of war had struck mankind a hammer blow that knocked the world off its axis. Its shock waves rocked the old order from the depths of its foundations. They came one after another, blasting away at the tottering vestiges of the old nineteenth-century global power structure like Odin's bowling balls thundering down Ragnarok alley, casting down the disarrayed remnants of a once neat and systematic arrangement between sovereign nations. At the outset, World War I had been viewed on both sides by an outdated paradigm. Neither London nor Berlin nor Paris had expected the conflict to last longer than a matter of months at most. Since the Battle of Waterloo of 1815, and much like it, successive European conflicts were relatively tidy affairs settled in the manner of gentlemen on a battlefield. After the battle, winners and losers drew up treaties, territory and money changed hands, and the prevalent order continued largely undisturbed. Some commanders, like Napoleon, had leisure to draw up maxims of warfare, with the intention of applying them in the next sallying forth to the field of arms.

None of the combatants fully grasped the impact of breakthroughs in military technology that had occurred in the roughly sixty years prior to the eve of battle, nor suspected that these would have transformed warfare in utterly unexpected ways. The machine gun, the airplane, and the tank, to name but three of the key transformational technologies that also included chemical warfare, enabled industrial killing on a never-before-seen scale and sparked countermeasures that bred counter-countermeasures that spiraled into a vortex such as William Butler Yeats alluded to in his 1921 poem "The Second Coming," where he wrote:

> *Turning and turning in the widening gyre*
> *The falcon cannot hear the falconer,*
> *Things fall apart; the center cannot hold,*
> *Mere anarchy is loosed upon the world,*
> *The blood-dimmed tide is loose, and everywhere*

The ceremony of innocence is drowned;
The best lack all conviction, while the worst
Are full of passionate intensity.

The precision striking capability of World War I weaponry was, collectively, many orders of magnitude greater than that deployed in combat in the previous major war, which was the Franco-Prussian War of 1870–1871, which itself witnessed the devastating advantage of all-steel German cannonry versus the brass gunnery of the soon-to-be defeated French. The lethality of new military weaponry was enhanced all the more by the advent of aerial photo-reconnaissance to pinpoint targets and conduct after-engagement battle-damage assessments.

While dashing air aces did engage in dogfights, these were more the exception than the rule; in the main, such airborne confrontations took place to clear the skies over the battlefield so that the photo-reconnaissance planes—which carried no armament at all—could be sent in to fly over the battlefields then bring in their canisters of film for development. It was a dangerous mission, and the pilots of such planes took the full brunt of German ground-to-air fire on their low-altitude sweeps. Despite armored undersides the planes usually came back shot full of holes, but it was worth it. The photographic intelligence take they brought back enabled the British and Americans—for the Germans neglected this element of the tactical arts to their detriment—to more accurately assess the impact of their fires.

The innovations in the technology of warfare came at a rapid-fire pace, changing the face of war throughout the conflict. These innovations helped to draw it out beyond the expectations of any of the belligerents.

This entirely new kind of warfare born in the four bloody years between July 1914 and November 1918 was a prelude to the post-armistice breakdown of the Old World Order. Like the shocks that had thundered across the battlefields from the Marne to Belleau Wood to Soissons, peace was shaken apart in a rapid-fire sequence that convulsed Europe with rioting, assassination, and civil war, a state of near anarchy. This plunged the United States into the worst depression it had ever suffered and paved the way for totalitarian dictatorships to arise in Russia, Germany, and Italy.

9

Worse yet, perhaps, than even economic and political crises was a crisis of faith that had been anticipated by Friedrich Nietzsche when he wrote about the Superman, the Antichrist, and the transvaluation of values a generation before.

Now, unlike in Nietzsche's day, the crisis was not about religion versus science so much as pragmatic nihilism versus everything else. Intellectuals, artists, and writers shared the mounting anarchic bent of the masses and mirrored it in manifestos, canvases, and cinematic productions enshrining darkness and decline. After losing his faith in religion, Western man had lost his faith in reason and progress; nothing remained but faith in himself, in action for action's sake.

Iconic in this regard was the chef-d'oeuvre of the German philosopher Oswald Spengler published in English translation as *The Decline of the West*, which preached the end not only of material progress but that of spiritual, moral, and intellectual development that harbingered a slide back into a state of barbarism. Such an atmosphere was ripe for appeals to party, class, nation, and race by demagogues and rabble-rousers.

As the 1920s and 1930s ran their course, Russian Communists, Italian Fascists, German Nazis, Chinese members of the Kuomintang, Indian members of the Congress Party, even American New Dealers, exchanged the old faith in traditional institutions with a new faith in a twentieth-century cult of what might be described as radical pragmatism.

The West might have found itself embroiled in moral dilemmas, but for the colonies of the Great Powers that emerged from the conflagration weakened and shaken to their roots, the opposite case was largely true. World War I had weakened the former imperial masters beyond their wildest expectations. The armistice signaled a clarion call to arms. One by one, the colonies that made up the empires of the major European powers began to rebel against foreign domination and control.

In China a second revolution installed the Kuomintang into power. In north and central Africa, revolt spread and nationalist movements arose, as they also did in India, in Burma, and in island nations scattered across the Pacific and Indian oceans. The vast colonial empires that had been built up over the last 200 years of exploration and conquest by European nations were disintegrating as regional flashpoints ignited and nationalist sentiments exploded into sometimes violent confrontation between colonial overlords and their hostile dependencies.

Although the United States had been spared the physical destruction that had been meted out to European territory, it nevertheless could not escape the rippling shock waves of the titanic conflict in which it had played a key role. After Germany's surrender and the signing of the armistice, President Woodrow Wilson had presided over a massive postwar program of disarmament, among whose consequences was the War Depreciation Act of 1920, which put in place a radical reduction in U.S. defense spending. Wilson also lobbied hard for the establishment of the League of Nations and a pivotal role for the United States in it. He had not reckoned with the lasting trend toward isolationism in the United States; it thwarted his efforts. The massive loans that were sanctioned by the U.S. and Britain to bail out Germany also had an impact on rising unemployment, trade deficits, and growing international monetary problems.

The United States entered the 1920s riding the boom of being the only major postwar power left intact, the last man standing in a free-for-all that had knocked the stuffing out of the Great Powers of Europe and from which they would never again fully rebound. By the mid-1920s the rippling foreshocks of a global depression were being felt across the Atlantic. When the Great Depression struck, with its full force, it hit the United States like an economic asteroid, hurling deadly fragments into almost every sector of American life.

In Germany an economic crisis fueled by the *Dolchstoss* or "stab in the back" conspiracy theory that held that the country's generals had betrayed it in World War I, paved the way to the rise of Nazism. In Italy, Fascism under Mussolini, who was given the comic-opera title of "Il Duce," had transformed the nation but also had led it astray, while in Spain, a vicious civil war between Communists and Fascists drew the attention of the world.

In Japan a growing militarism arose whose goal was the annexation and exploitation of East Asia and the Pacific Rim. In July 1937 Japan's attack on China began World War II in fact, if not in general perception. The dictators that had sprung up amid the turmoil exploited and extended the collapse while the British and French looked on and tried forestalling disaster through negotiation.

In the United States, the mood of isolationism flew in the face of the sinister reality of war clouds looming on the horizon. Franklin Delano Roosevelt, a protégé of his thrice-removed predecessor Woodrow Wilson, was elected president of a nation mired in the depths of a world depression. The solution of internal economic problems, not intervention in foreign conflict, was the nation's intent. Most Americans, including the country's political leadership, wanted the country to remain neutral; the stigma attached to neutrality today largely didn't exist back then.

Roosevelt's New Deal sought to stimulate the economy and put America back on its feet. At the same time the president also understood that the United States might be called upon to fight another war in Europe against a much more formidable enemy than it had faced before. In 1934, Roosevelt, a former assistant secretary of the navy, authorized the rebuilding of the U.S. Navy, and in 1937 construction of the battleship *North Carolina* began.[1]

In that same year, FDR made his famous "quarantine speech," in which he proposed that the "90 percent" of the peace-loving nations act to isolate and quarantine the "10 percent" who wanted war. By 1940, after FDR's reelection to a third term in office, it had become a lamentably self-evident truth that the United States would enter the war, and that more pressing changes needed to be made in order for this to happen. One of the answers was the consolidation of the War Department into a new headquarters that would house the expanded military staff and civilian personnel committed to the Promethean task of restructuring America's armed services into a combat-ready fighting force for a war that would probably be fought on two widely separated fronts.

In July 1937, nineteen years after the armistice that ended World War I, as Western Europe was going to hell in a hurry, a column of Japanese troops crossed a bridge in China. It wasn't a shot heard around the world, but it should have been. Although the European powers and the United States would not recognize that World War II had started until a little more than two years later, it had in fact begun. The name of

---

1. Revisionist historians have proposed that FDR, convinced that American involvement in a coming second world war was inevitable, actively sought to break U.S. neutrality via the "back door," and that, by initiatives such as Lend Lease and the convoy system established to aid the British, Roosevelt hoped the United States would become drawn into the war in Europe.

the bridge was that of a European mariner who had rediscovered China after the European dark ages: Marco Polo. No one noticed anything ironic in this development either, at least at the time.

As the crunch of hobnailed foot soldiers' boots echoed across the verdant Asian hillsides, as demolition charges blew the city gates clean off their hinges and the column of troops spread through the city of Beijing that lay behind it, the war clouds that had gathered for almost two decades began to pour forth their black rain of mass death on the world. The garrison of Chinese soldiers didn't hold out long. Within a matter of weeks Imperial troops had forced the ancient city to surrender.

Here was a spark that could ignite dry tinder as not even the Spanish Civil War, that had been raging since 1936, could do. For this was China: The northeastern borders of Soviet Russia were not far away, and Stalin, the self-styled "Iron Man" who ruled his vast domain with an iron fist, knew that Hitler had signed the Anti-Comintern Pact with Japan the year before. Soviet personnel and war machinery, including the bomber aircraft whose unleashed devastation on civilians caught in the conflict would give rise to Picasso's cry of mass suffering on canvas, *Guernica*, were already figuring in the Spanish Civil War. With the Japanese in control of the Chinese capital, the mechanisms of global war began to ratchet up one lethal notch toward the lightning strike of armed conflict. World War II was now virtually inevitable, and this fact had not been lost on those in charge of the American political and defense establishments.

* * *

In the years between the two world wars, and despite Wilsonian reductions in military spending, the U.S. War Department began to grow both physically as well as in the scope of its mission. The seagoing troop transports that had originally shipped U.S. soldiers across the Atlantic to Europe to fight the Great War had all come home by now, and the vast infrastructure of waging war had either been returned to warehouse stockpiles, mothballed, or sold for scrap; but the role of the United States as a world power had increased.

For the first time—but not the last—the United States had demonstrated its uncanny ability to rapidly and continuously produce an array of munitions, armaments, and war materiel of all kinds that seemed almost limitless from the standpoint of Old World productivity levels. War-torn European Great Powers, on the contrary, found themselves depopulated by the conflict, drained of natural and material resources, and either embattled by the independence-bent indigenes of their subject foreign holdings or bereft of their colonial empires entirely.

America, on the other hand, had emerged not only for the most part unscathed but found itself, largely by default, and like it or not, to be the inheritor of much of European and world problems. U.S. President Woodrow Wilson was partly responsible for this development; seeing himself as a world messiah and having championed the role of the United States in the same messianic terms for decades, he now found a ready-made cause in the rebuilding of ruined Europe. Between the Wilson and Roosevelt administrations, two one-term presidents, Harding and Coolidge, though both isolationist in political outlook and world view, presided over a continuing growth of America at home and as a preeminent power on the world stage, and even Hoover, whose administration ushered in the Great Depression, began his single term in office amid postwar prosperity.

In the aftermath of war the United States had changed radically. It had emerged from the conflict not only as the international economic powerhouse that it had been prior to 1917, but it was now a military juggernaut that simultaneously challenged the ancient hegemony of the great European land powers and the armed might of Britannia on the high seas.

Having entered the war as a junior partner to the British Empire, the United States had proven its mettle on the battlefield and astonished the Old World powers with its prodigious industrial output and the courage and skill of its troops in combat.

* * *

The city of Washington, D.C., was growing as well, and its growth also burgeoned forth on several levels simultaneously. Architecturally and materially, the city became the scene of new public works that were to collectively transform it within a short period of time into one of the world's premier global capitals. Fiscally, the federal government of the United States had begun a process of postwar expansion that exponentially increased its need and stoked its hunger for fresh administrative office space. The new array of responsibilities both at home and abroad faced by America in the long armistice between the two world wars—and indeed long afterward—required an ever-expanding infrastructure in order to function effectively.

Public works on a grand scale were changing the architectural landscape of the nation's capital. Downtown Washington was experiencing a wave of new building in the corner of the district southwest of the Ellipse known as the Federal Triangle. In the vicinity of the White House, a bold new program of building to complement this part of the city was now in its latter planning stages. It was to be called the Northwest Rectangle. Its centerpieces were to be a cluster of departmental office buildings that would offset the concentration of architecture that had been built in the grand *fin de siecle* style that lined the Mall and had the Capitol building as its centerpiece.

The plan for the Northwest Rectangle dated back to the mid-1920s. At that time the National Capital Park and Planning Commission first envisioned a bold plan for a complex of buildings situated at Foggy Bottom. The Rectangle would complement the Triangle both visually and administratively. Its miles of new office space, European-style grand boulevards, and tree-lined public parks would both relieve the burden of space needed to house the rapidly multiplying administrative apparatus of the federal government and make communication between the Capitol's other main power center, situated on the east side of town, an easy cross-town shuttle.

The Federal Triangle was then, as it is now, not only the center of administrative power in the capital but also its judicial and intellectual nexus; both the august Supreme Court building and the several buildings that collectively make up the Smithsonian Institution flank the Mall with the tiers of marble stairs that lead to the bicameral houses of Congress at the end of the stately, verdant promenade.

Architecturally, the District was viewed as being bottom-heavy at one end and far too light at its other main visual anchor point. True, the White House, fronted as it was by the Ellipse and flanked by buildings as august in their own right as many found in the Federal Triangle, was both the architectural and symbolic equal of the Capitol. Nevertheless, for sheer visual presence the Federal Triangle was overpowering. Not only would full realization of the Northwest Rectangle building program balance the architectural scales, it would also provide additional space for the ever-swelling ranks of personnel that made the wheels of government turn.

By the late 1930s, planning for the Northwest Rectangle was well advanced. Architectural plans were spread and ready on drawing boards. Federal funds had been allocated, building sites had been selected, and preliminary spadework done by construction contractors. Nevertheless, nothing, or very little, ever came of the project's great expectations and exalted ambitions. Some dirt was turned, but not a whole lot. Only two buildings were ever completed under the herculean civic construction program. These were the Interior Department Building and the War Department Building. Both buildings still stand as familiar landmarks to Washingtonians, but the latter, unlike the former, no longer bears its original name or even now serves its original purpose.

The War Department Building is known today as the Harry S. Truman Building, its large metal letters spelling out "State Department" familiar to denizens of the District since 1951, when they were first mounted over the Twenty-First Street entrance door of what was then called the State Department Building.[2]

The rectangular cement building of cream-hued frontage, with its clean mid-twentieth-century lines, had been put up between 1939 and 1941. It was to be the first in a group of futurist office towers planned to replace the State, War, and Navy Building, the nation's first modern headquarters of the military, which had been built immediately following the Civil War between 1871 and 1888.

2. The building was officially named after the thirty-third U.S. president in 2000 and was previously also called the "Main State" Building until the early 1960s when a sizeable addition was added to the original structure. Washingtonians then fell into the habit of referring to the original building as "Old State" and the new wing as "New State." With the addition of the new wing the building became the largest federal building in the Washington, D.C., metropolitan area, a distinction it holds today.

This earlier building, which is today officially known as the Dwight D. Eisenhower Executive Office Building, but colloquially referred to as the Old Executive Office Building (commonly abbreviated as the OEOB to Washingtonians), is a District landmark that stands out architecturally like a wedding cake in a bakery display case amid an assortment of handsome, if far less ornate, creations. The State, War, and Navy Building was constructed from a design by English-born architect Alfred Bult Mullet who was supervising architect of the Treasury Department from 1866 to 1874; Mullet also designed the Greek Revival Treasury Building that flanks the White House on the other side of the OEOB.

Mullet's design for the State, War, and Navy Building was unlike his previous success; in fact it was almost the diametrical opposite of the architect's *chef d'ouevre*. Mullet envisioned an elaborate Second Empire design that harked back to the nobly raised chateaus and boulevards grandes that cut broad, stately swathes through the spiraling *arrondissements* of Paris that George Eugene Haussmann designed at the behest of Napoleon III in the 1850s. In 1889, Mullet's design was selected by a congressional commission convened to select a site and prepare plans and cost estimates for a new building to house the Department of State and the War and Navy departments.

The building, lavish with cast-iron fixtures, resplendent with fanciful ornamentations of polished brass and rococo appurtenances that even a Napoleon would have found tailor-made to his imperial tastes, is beautiful even today. Indeed—little known to most viewers of high-level Washington affairs from presidential news conferences to state receptions—it has over the years been the scene of many televised events, as well as the location of the working offices of several presidents.

The Indian Treaty Room, for example—originally the navy's library and reception room—cost more per square foot than any room in the building because of its rich marble wall panels, 800-pound bronze sconces, and exquisitely detailed gold leaf ornamentation. The room has been the scene of many presidential news conferences and is frequently, indeed continually, used for conferences and receptions attended by the president; this was true for the Clinton administration and for that of George W. Bush.

In between Mullet's triumph and what Washingtonians once mocked as "Somervell's folly," the increasing complexity of warfare manifested an exponential increase in the manpower and specialization necessary to wage it effectively and win it decisively. Almost four decades had elapsed since the turn of the century; now first-generation armies dependent on horse cavalry, primitive automatic weapons, fly-by-the-seat-of-your-pants aviation, and crude submersible vessels had given way to second-generation forces capable of waging war on land, sea, and air and in what today is called a "fifth dimension" of invisible wavelengths, including radio and radar transmissions.

During the war years between 1914 and 1918 the United States had stepped into the role of a global military power to rival that of the great European nations. During the 22-year interwar period between 1918 and 1942, when America would officially intervene in World War II, the United States had entered a new phase of physical, economic, and industrial growth. In part, this surge of national power had been directed toward a preparedness to fight on the Allied side in a conflict that rational leaders knew could not be evaded indefinitely.

While isolationism was the dominant political modus throughout the 1920s and 1930s, those more farsighted strata of American society grew to view a new second war as inevitable. The pace of military reorganization, if growing by fits and starts under the fire of isolationist forces, grew steadily until, by 1939, when war had finally come to Europe, it had taken on something of the quality of an arrow nocked within the flexed arc of a tautly drawn bow.

* * *

The War Department Building, constructed at a cost of around $9 million—a vast sum by the standards of the era—on Virginia Avenue near Constitution Avenue, in the heart of Foggy Bottom, was viewed as one of the answers to an impending global military crisis.

The offices of the U.S. military had, by the middle years of the interwar period, spilled over from the rococo elegance of the palatial edifice designed by Mullet into an assortment of often incongruous spaces that were scattered haphazardly across the length and breadth of the District and across the Potomac River in Arlington, Virginia. The U.S. Army's staff was alone billeted in, by some accounts, seventeen, by other accounts, twenty-two, buildings, which included the Social Security and Railroad Retirement building and rented garage space in their sometimes motley ranks.

The main cluster of offices, however, and the central hub of staff activity in the years before the Pentagon was constructed, was the army's Munitions Building, which dated back to 1918 when it was built as temporary office space for World War I military staff. As World War II loomed, it was described by contemporaries as a dark "rabbit warren" of offices and corridors built helter-skelter as the need arose. Like Stimson and many others, newly appointed Army Chief of Staff General George Marshall had his office there.

The War Department's new Virginia Avenue headquarters building, which officially opened for occupancy in June 1941, that was to consolidate these offices into a single location was to be a modern masterpiece, as different from the old State, War, and Navy Building as a powdered wig from a two-piece business suit, and a Second Temple compared with the Sodom and Gomorrah of the purportedly seedy Munitions Building. Actually, the use of the word *building* is a misnomer. The War Department's headquarters was planned to eventually consist of several buildings that would occupy a sizeable tract of land next to the Naval Hospital and house what one contemporary newspaper article termed the "24,000 clerks [which] infest office buildings in every nook and cranny of the nation's capital." While the first of these buildings was completed, the others were never built.

This new seat of America's military infrastructure was designed between 1938 and 1939 by consulting architects Gilbert S. Underwood and William Dewy Foster under Louis Simon, supervising architect of the treasury. This was an era marked, if not distinguished, by Futurism and Art Deco, which has spawned a host of modern buildings in the United States and Europe, including the Chrysler Building in midtown Manhattan. Representative of these new architectural trends were the Trilon and Perisphere of the 1939 New York World's Fair that formed the centerpiece of an exposition whose theme was nothing less than Futurity itself.

In Europe, the newly minted Fascist state of Italian *duce* Benito Mussolini had also embarked on architecture that was starkly twentieth century. In the Rome Exposition of 1932, dubbed *La Mostra Delle Revoluzione Fascista*, Futurism proved the basis for a similar architecture based on streamlining, functionalism, and the use of new building materials such as reinforced concrete, plate glass, and structural steel. As the twentieth century raced heedlessly to its midpoint at breakneck velocity, it seems in hindsight almost as if magnetic lines of gathering speed and force transformed themselves into a sometimes austere, yet undeniably bold architecture that crossed and broke through political, ideological, and cultural barriers on both sides of the Atlantic.

Be that as it may, and despite several reviews and changes, the War Department Building was every inch a manifestation of this onrushing future that so starkly contrasted to the immediate past. By the time the new headquarters for the War Department was completed, it was intended to incorporate the latest in office design technology. These innovations included central air conditioning, fluorescent lighting, banks of passenger elevators, and acoustical ceiling tiles to muffle distracting sounds. Its interior design would do away with the problems that plagued the veritable shanty-town environment that, at least by popular consensus, blighted the Munitions Building and made it a veritable medieval dungeon by comparison.

There were only two things wrong with this innovative new building, which was so far ahead of its time. One was that the consulting architect for the National Capital Park and Planning Commission, and outspoken critic of D.C. overdevelopment, Gilmore Clarke, predicted that it would be obsolete before completion due to the pace of burgeoning manpower requirements outstripping the office space allocated for them. Second, and possibly more important, a key member of the White House cabinet, and a figure who ranked with George Marshall in importance to the U.S. war effort, hated the War Department Building and, in fact, wanted it torn town. This was Secretary of War Henry Lewis Stimson.

Stimson was a Republican New Dealer who began his political career as a New York City trial lawyer at the turn of the twentieth century. He'd entered the political scene of the era with a gubernatorial run in 1910. Though his bid for governor of New York failed, Stimson had walked away from the elections to become a high-profile player in national politics. A year later, in 1911, a newly elected President William Howard Taft chose Stimson as his secretary of war. World War I began soon after Stimson returned to private law practice in New York, and Stimson enlisted in the army. He was given the rank of colonel and served in the Fifth Artillery Brigade, which saw action at Dunkirk, the Marne, and Belleau Wood. Following demobilization, Stimson served as ambassador to Great Britain and after Hoover took office was appointed secretary of state in 1929.

By the time Roosevelt occupied the Oval Office at 1600 Pennsylvania Avenue with a presidential win in 1932 and reached out to form a bipartisan New Deal coalition to implement his sweeping plans for economic and military overhaul, Stimson was seventy-three years old but still at the top of his form. In 1940—the same year he'd appointed Frank Knox as secretary of the navy and James V. Forrestal (who was to become the first secretary of defense) as Knox's administrative assistant— Roosevelt, seeking a bipartisan cabinet in tune with his New Deal policies, appointed Stimson secretary of war. Both Stimson and Knox were Republicans (Knox had been the running mate of Republican presidential hopeful Alf Landon) in a primarily Democratic cabinet, and Knox, now a Chicago publisher, had needed to be courted by FDR in a voluminous exchange of correspondence in which Roosevelt had, according to the memoirs of his secretary Grace Tully, "begged" Knox to accept the post.

Singularly important in the case of Stimson was that—as an August 25, 1941, *Time* magazine cover story on the new chief of the War Department titled "Secretary of War" put it—Stimson was that rare breed of Republican internationalist who had supported FDR's foreign policy initiatives in the face of overwhelming Republican opposition. As secretary of state of the outgoing Hoover administration in early 1933, Stimson had been one of the few exiting cabinet members who made a pilgrim's journey to the FDR White House to brief the incoming president and secretary of state.

Stimson's appointment came after the ouster of sitting War Secretary Harold Hines Woodring, whom Roosevelt had never liked. Woodring had been hastily selected for the War Department post after FDR's old

Hyde Park crony George Dern died, leaving the post vacant. The position statutorily had to be filled within 30 days. FDR had coyly confided to intimates that he could "make changes" later on if necessary. He did, after Woodring, a pro-neutrality man openly hostile to both FDR's interventionist foreign policy and the president's advocacy of military expansion at home, dragged his heels as war secretary in providing aid to a Britain beleaguered by the Axis juggernaut.

While looked at by his political enemies as an old-fashioned septuagenarian, Stimson still held considerable influence among Washingtonian elites. He was also on the short list of those with a direct channel to the Oval Office. FDR, who could drop his Hyde Park manners and turn into the stereotype of the irascible Dutchman at the drop of a hat, respected Stimson. More often than not, he'd act on Stimson's recommendations. Such was the case with Stimson's pet peeve, the brand spanking new War Department Building. Stimson's disaffection for the $9 million structure that had just been completed on Foggy Bottom's Virginia Avenue would prove fatefully catalytic to the Pentagon's genesis only a short time later.

Likening its canopied and singularly unmilitary façade to that of "a provincial opera house," Stimson viewed the building as only cosmetically superior to the Munitions Building, if that. It was a clean, well lighted place with air conditioning and reliable electrical mains, with elevator banks thrown into the bargain, and it was a few floors taller than the Munitions Building. In Stimson's view, however, it wasn't large enough, not by half, to house the beefed-up bureaucracy of an inevitable hypertrophied military that he believed would soon be engaged in the coming war, one that would dwarf the Great War in scope, intensity, and national risk.

The new war secretary opposed the plan to move his department, and the headquarters of the U.S. Army, into the War Department Building, informing the president that he would not relocate the offices and agencies that made up the War Department to the new building. Stimson preferred to keep them scattered as they presently were. In fact, the secretary of war pressed, the War Department Building should be torn down before it was even occupied and a new department headquarters constructed under the direction of a staff hand-selected by Stimson and acting on the president's personal authority. To prove he meant business, Stimson continued to work out of his humble office in the Munitions Building where direct access to Marshall and other senior officers generally meant a short walk from his office and a rap on a door.

The controversy fast developed into what was dubbed by one reporter "a sizzling row" amid Washington's political power brokers, many of whom viewed the relocation of the War Department from the 50-acre Federal Triangle between Pennsylvania and Constitution avenues as a disruption of the hoary Triangle Development plan that had its roots in the nation's hallowed past, indeed which dated back to the original celebrated plan presented to George Washington by General Pierre L'Enfant in 1791.

Nevertheless, the secretary of war made certain that all staff remained dispersed throughout the District and its Virginia exurbs until the first wedge of the new pentagonal structure occupying 35 acres on the Arlington Lowlands across the Potomac was complete. Hardly had the plaster and paint dried when, in 1944, the army officially vacated the new building in Foggy Bottom for its still newer headquarters across the river in Arlington. The building's new tenant, the State Department, began moving in throughout the 1940s.

In many respects history has been as unkind to Henry Stimson in painting his opposition to the War Department Building in purely emotional tones as it has been to the Munitions Building that Stimson preferred to it by describing it as a dank, dark "warren" of offices that was outdated and worthy of little except demolition. While even contemporary media accounts of the "sizzling row" largely give the impression that the Munitions Building was Hell's Little Acre on Constitution Avenue, the facts argue for a very different, and in the main, opposite, set of observations, and suggest that Stimson had good reason to block the War Department's move into its new headquarters. The "sizzling row" that developed over relocation plans and building projects had its roots in Washington politics, and efforts to push Stimson's department into the War Department Building went part and parcel with those politics.

The Munitions Building did not even exist as a separate structure. It was essentially one half of a far larger complex whose front façade stretched for nearly a third of a mile along Constitution Avenue's South Side a short distance from the Washington Monument, and whose other half was the Main Navy Building, often referred to as the "Navy Annex" or "Navy Department" Building, the former being a holdover from the pre–World War I era when the navy had rented a nine-story building near the corner of New York Avenue and Eighteenth Street. Eight wings of the complex were devoted to army staff housed in the Munitions Building while the navy occupied nine wings of office space.[3]

The blocks of wings were divided one from the other by what the navy describes as a "vehicle entryway" to a large rear parking lot with a five-hundred-vehicle capacity. The three-story, low-rise complex had long main corridors that ran on an east-west axis that branched at regular intervals into north-south wings. Although supposedly constructed in 1918 as a "temporary" structure to serve the expanded wartime needs of the U.S. War Department, the complex was in fact "temporary" in name only, largely because Congress, bowing to factions in the capital that coveted the land on which the complex rose for other purposes, mandated it be classified as such.

In fact, the vast Army-Navy complex, which was to see more than fourteen thousand military and civilian workers pass through its halls by the end of World War I, was anything but temporary; on the contrary, it was built to last. Constructed of poured concrete reinforced with 4,500 tons of steel bars, with floors and stairways made of the same materials, with 940,000 square feet for the navy and 840,000 for the army, the building complex devoted almost 1.5 million square feet to office space, with the five-hundred-vehicle parking lot at its rear. Far from being a gloomy warren, the complex's hundreds of offices were probably better lit and ventilated than any other building in Washington; extant photographs show long rooms with overhead electrical lighting and rows of windows facing Constitution Avenue and adjoining streets. The working environment

3. This should not be confused with a contemporary office building called the Navy Annex near the Pentagon adjacent to the Marine Corps base at Henderson Hall on Columbia Pike, about a mile from the Building; it was also used as swing space for staff displaced by the Pentagon renovation program before and after the 9/11 attack. Shades of the "seventeen" buildings!

was also considered user-friendly not only by Stimson and Marshall, but by most of its many inhabitants over the course of its existence.[4]

Indeed, the huge Army-Navy complex, judged on the basis of historical photographs, its architectural design and pale color of its facade, its spacious parking lot, the building techniques that put it up, the rapidity of its construction, and many other factors, including the original intent to build it as a "temporary" structure, shows it to be nothing less than a prefiguring of the Pentagon itself, whose five-sided structure was more an accident of its location at a crossroads in Arlington than a deliberate aim of its designers and builders, and which was originally conceived to be a low-rise building very much on the same plan as the Munitions and Main Navy Buildings. Small wonder, then, that Stimson disapproved of the War Department Building plan, which would have seemed to him like a misguided attempt to jam a very large square peg into a very small round hole, air conditioned or not, and its then ranking as the largest federal office building in the United States notwithstanding.

The high command of the U.S. Navy remained at Main Navy throughout the course of World War II, and the navy did not completely move to the Pentagon until after the war's end pursuant to federally mandated unification of the armed services under the National Security Acts of 1947 and 1949, most of whose provisions the navy hotly contested. Indeed, this mass refusal to move in left large portions of the Building comparatively deserted, including spacious office suites that had been intended to be occupied by the U.S. Navy's top brass; this state of affairs resulted, in at least one case, and with Somervell's probable connivance, in a wryly ironic development a few years down the line, as will be seen later.

In fact, to state that the construction of the Pentagon was largely an army project, championed by Henry Stimson who, like Bill Somervell, was an old army hand, and that the navy would have been perfectly content to conduct its staff work at its Constitution Avenue headquarters into the Cold War is by no means to stretch a point. So well regarded was the Main Navy Building that it was occupied by military staff offices

---

4. By contrast, the War Department Building's successor, the Truman Building, only achieved a surface area of 1.4 million square feet with its new additions of the early 1960s.

continuously until 1970, when it was finally ordered to be demolished by President Richard Nixon.

Today, the site of the complex is occupied by Constitution Gardens Park, with the Vietnam Memorial located near the western end of what had formerly been the Munitions Building.

CHAPTER TWO

A PRISONER OF DESTINY

I t was September 12, 1938. The president was sitting in his private railroad car in the Rochester, New York, stockyards. Beside him sat his protégé, Harry Hopkins. A radio was turned on in front of them. Both men frowned, and the tip of a cigarette in the white bone ivory holder that had graced so many magazine and newspaper photographs flared as Franklin Roosevelt deeply inhaled the tobacco smoke that had already filled the small enclosure with a gray-blue haze. The president had been rolling through the hustings, stumping for Democratic candidates running for office in the hopes of breaking a Republican deadlock in Congress that was hampering his New Deal plans and whose isolationism was, he felt, dangerous to American national security.

An all-too-familiar voice was blaring from the speaker grille, the guttural words sparking bouts of applause and wild cheering from his massive audience. The Nazi dictator, Adolf Hitler, was in the midst of yet another of his rabble-rousing ultranationalistic speeches to overflowing crowds at a rally in the old Bavarian city of Nuremberg, whose fifteenth-century walls, which still existed, sported some eighty siege towers.

This rally was one of the biggest yet, even though the Third Reich had made Nuremberg its official "pageant city" and Nuremberg's cobbled streets had witnessed many a triumphal parade and martial rally since the Nazis had come to power in Germany. Now, standing alone on a high platform, flanked by the stark regalia of the Third Reich and facing a capacity crowd of at least twenty thousand followers

27

that filled the immense stadium at Nuremberg, Hitler was then at the height of his powers. Notwithstanding, neither the president nor the Nazi führer could then be aware that Adolf Hitler had reached the apex of his power; that he would never again ascend to such dizzying apogees of oratory or that the easy conquests that lay immediately ahead would be a prelude to götterdämmerung greater than anything that *der Führer* found so rapturous in the Wagnerian operas he so favored as entertainment fare.

At the moment things looked considerably different, though. Screaming above the almost deafening shouts of "Sieg Heil!" from the assembled ranks of uniformed storm troopers massed at the Nazi Party Congress in Nuremberg, Hitler was whipping the crowd to a frenzy with strident accusations of the oppression of German nationals living in the Sudeten area of Czechoslovakia.

"The persecution must end!" Hitler bellowed, his voice breaking from the effort and the emotion of his half-crazed orations. "If not, the Fatherland will be compelled to rescue them!"

The president, well-traveled and coming from old Dutch New York stock, knew enough German to understand with exactitude every venomous word uttered by the shrieking Nazi dictator. Those words once again confirmed what the president and his advisors had known for some time: U.S. involvement in a European war was inevitable. The isolationism that gripped the nation would in the end ill-serve the country as the German war machine began to grind up continental Europe.

Nevertheless, unlike Hitler, who was now at the top of his form and master of all he surveyed, Roosevelt was then embattled on every side. The reason for his presence in the railway car, in fact, was the hostile Congress backed by powerful special interest groups who were vehemently opposed to his New Deal and saw a continued isolationist America as vital to their economic plans. Despite the gathering clouds of impending conflict and the sometimes unbreachable gulfs of rhetoric, politics, and Weltanschauung that separated the United States and Britain from the totalitarian dictatorships that had gained power in Germany and Italy, business cartels on both sides of the Atlantic continued their longstanding and profitable associations.

Bent on appeasement, they had hailed British Prime Minister Neville Chamberlain when he'd returned from Munich offering "peace with honor" and waving the pages of the Munich Pact like a flag of victory. The irony of Chamberlain's sellout had not been lost on a tiny Anglo-American opposition that included Winston Churchill and Roosevelt in its ranks. This minority realized that to appease Hitler was to open the door to further aggression and that the Munich Pact was the prelude to disaster, not the way to salvation touted by Chamberlain and his supporters. As to his views on suggestions from Washington to London on how best to handle Hitler, the prime minister told confidants in private, "It is always best and safest to count on nothing from the Americans but words."

Churchill, looking back in his six-volume memoirs, *The Second World War*, on Chamberlain's appeasement a decade later, and in the aftermath of World War II, termed Chamberlain's actions "the loss of the last frail chance to save the world from tyranny otherwise than by war."

Whether this was mere Churchillian hyperbole, as some have charged, or not, in the main the leaders of the British government during the interwar period evinced an unprecedented failure of nerve. Accepting Germany's exaggerated figures for the Reich's air order of battle, they were convinced that to stand up to Hitler would inevitably be to unleash the resurgent German air force, or Luftwaffe, on Britain and bomb England to ruins. As it turned out, they had bought yet another Hitlerian "big lie," but their perception, for the moment, had unfortunately become reality.

In any case, the president now realized that he must push harder to ready a U.S. war-fighting capability to meet the new world war that seemed perilously imminent. Peace, he suspected, would not survive longer than the summer of 1938. War clouds loomed ominously on the horizon.

In the euphoric aftermath of Chamberlain's triumphant return from Berlin, the Japanese had invaded China, invading Nanking at the price of a skirmish and subjecting the conquered city to an orgy of looting, arson, rape, and pillage that had not been seen since the days of Attila the Hun. Sooner or later Europe would catch fire, Roosevelt knew, and when that happened the United States would have to be prepared. As things stood the nation *wasn't*, not yet. The War Productions Act of 1920 had severely cut back on U.S. military equipment production, and so far the president had been unable to do anything to change this accomplished but unworkable fact.

On January 28, the president had asked Congress for an $800 million supplement to the 1938 defense budget for more warships. The request from the White House was met with jeers from an isolationist-controlled Senate and House whose members charged that a navy of the size FDR contemplated could not serve legitimate defensive purposes and was actually intended for offensive warfare overseas.

Newspapers, including those controlled by William Randolph Hearst, a champion of isolationism and appeasement with close ideological and commercial ties to the militant Fascist regimes in control of much of Europe, called Roosevelt a "warmonger"; some even called for his removal from office. Church groups and pacifist organizations weighed in with their own criticism. The White House was soon deluged with protests against FDR's "hysterical" rearmament policy and his "counsel of despair."

A new challenge faced Roosevelt's plan to rearm America and prepare it for the onrushing menace that he knew it must soon face. A move on Capitol Hill was then underway to limit the ability of the president to conduct foreign policy. As Roosevelt's New Deal coasted through troubled waters his opponents prepared to launch a torpedo that might sink both it and the president's ability to act in the defense of America to the bottom.

In the past eleven months there was building support for a constitutional amendment that would allow war to be declared only after a national referendum had legalized it. The proposed amendment, introduced by an anti–New Dealer Democrat from Indiana, Senator Louis Ludlow, was ultimately defeated by a narrow 209 to 188 margin, but if passed would have crippled Congress's constitutional prerogative to declare war. In any case, Ludlow and his followers were not content to let the matter drop. The Ludlow Amendment was not the last that Roosevelt would hear from the Indiana senator.

Roosevelt was in trouble over his New Deal as well. Critics had already started to call it a failure. The president's enemies scented blood in what the newspapers had begun to call the "Roosevelt recession" of 1938. The president was convinced that the forces behind the business slump that had brought on the economic turndown and the forces in business and politics eager to appease Hitler were linked or were, indeed, one and the same.

"They would really like me to be a Neville Chamberlain," Roosevelt privately confided to Harry Hopkins in the Oval Office after a particularly bad set of economic figures was released, "and if I would promise that, the market would go up and they would work positively and actively for the resumption of prosperity. But if it were done, we would only be breeding far more serious trouble four or eight years from now."

Hemmed in, the president was forced to work for rearmament and defense preparedness largely behind the scenes. In bits and pieces, fits and starts, and using a motley of chicaneries that today, in post-Watergate America, would be meat for a special congressional prosecutor, FDR cobbled together a program intended to mobilize the resources under his direct, executive control.

Among the consequences of these early and largely covert activities that were kept out of view as much as possible was to be the establishment of the Pentagon. This development was still two years away, however, and in the early part of 1938 the construction of this mammoth headquarters of the U.S. defense establishment would have been inconceivable, especially with a brand new War Department Building in the district nearing completion. Nevertheless, the president's actions started a chain of actions that would—influenced by the course of events and input from other actors on the Washington, D.C., scene—ultimately lead to precisely this development.

Among the first of these events was Roosevelt's intention to synchronize the activities of the State, Navy, and War departments. To that end FDR authorized Secretary of State Cordell Hull to establish a liaison committee tasked with starting the job of coordination. Hull was given strict orders to keep a tight lid on the operation. As little as possible was to be put on paper and all discussions were to be kept secret. Roosevelt feared that the isolationists would accuse the White House of taking a further step toward war. The hostile Congress could make things even worse for Roosevelt. Impeachment was one possibility, but there were others, including the very real prospect of a coup d'état in the offing.

Roosevelt had learned that isolationist senators had hatched a plan to remove him from the presidency and declare a World War I hero, Marine Corps General Smedley Butler, as acting president. The danger was great. The conspirators had been acting openly. Butler had gone to see the president and told him of having been approached by a group of political leaders and had named names. Fortunately for FDR the general had proven the conspirators' wrong choice. Roosevelt felt he had little alternative but to soft-pedal the issue. He allowed the story to run its course in the newspapers and fade into silence.

Hull's covert mission included top-level secret discussions with the British to explore the establishment of air bases on two strategically important islands, Canton and Enderbury. Under the plan proposed by Hull, the two islands in the South Pacific, lying between Hawaii and the Japanese Home Islands, would be used by both countries.

Japanese maneuvers in the Pacific, including one large military exercise thinly disguised as a test of new techniques for the fishing fleet of Nippon, raised new concerns about the belligerence of avowedly neutral Japan. The new Pacific bases contemplated by Roosevelt would allow refueling stops for American long-range surveillance and bomber aircraft. Hull also made clear the president's wish to lay claim to any other unoccupied Pacific island that, in the chief executive's words, "we decided we want to use."

Roosevelt's cabinet shake-ups were also intended to weed out isolationists and consolidate defense priorities. One such purge would prove vital to a new and stronger War Department that was soon to follow and critical to the course of the Pentagon's first years of organizational existence. This was the already mentioned ouster of Secretary of War Harry Woodring.

Woodring was an old Washington political hand who had been a staunch Hoover supporter and who was already serving as assistant war secretary under Roosevelt's original choice to head the War Department, George Dern. Woodring, a former Democratic governor of Kansas, was

A PRISONER OF DESTINY

an anti–New Dealer with, in FDR's considered view, a strong isolationist streak. Moreover, since his appointment to war secretary, Woodring had taken to making statements to the press that were both pro-isolation and anti–New Deal.

Republican New Dealer and internationalist Henry Stimson would be FDR's next choice to be the fifty-fourth secretary of war (he had already served as the forty-fifth war secretary during the Taft administration, which had preceded that of Wilson). Stimson was to make a critical choice as well when he appointed then Army Chief of Staff General John J. "Black Jack" Pershing's young deputy to succeed Pershing when the old campaigner retired. The deputy's name was George Marshall, and it proved to be a choice portending pivotal consequences to the outcome of World War II.

Nevertheless, the president faced fresh storms of protest when he submitted his blueprint for reorganization before the seventy-sixth Congress in February 1938. FDR's critics bluntly condemned it as a "dictator bill." One vocal opponent in the Senate even went so far as to accuse the president of "plunging a dagger into the very heart of democracy."

Indeed, the machinery of opposition to new White House policies soon began ratcheting up into higher and higher gear. Committees for "constitutional government" that seemed to arise out of thin air weighed in with mass mailings and well-planned hostile ad campaigns. On one occasion a hundred horsemen in Paul Revere outfits rode past the White House. The riders waved banners emblazoned with slogans including "No one-man rule." Roosevelt was shocked to his patrician core. He hadn't expected such a vociferous and tendentious reaction.

Nevertheless there were some victories for the embattled White House, hemmed in though it was by foes determined to hold it hostage. Among them was the passage of the Monopoly Inquiry Act of June 16. The act was Roosevelt's response to what he believed to be the perilous concentration of financial and industrial power in the hands of a few rich men while some 30 percent of the nation's populace was jobless and chronically failed to make ends meet. The act created the Temporary National Economic Committee tasked with studying the makeup of trusts, to check on pricing, profits, investment, savings, and on down

33

the line. (It is, to date, the most exhaustive examination of American economic life ever undertaken.)

All this notwithstanding, the White House was as embattled as ever on most fronts. Though Roosevelt might have succeeded in getting some concessions to his policies despite widespread hostility to them, his efforts to strengthen American defense continued to meet with open opposition on virtually all fronts. As the winter of 1938 thawed into spring, and spring bloomed into summer, the prospects for a democratic presidential win in the coming November elections began to look increasingly dim. In fact, the Democrats' prospects in the Senate and House looked equally obscure.

By mid-September, when Roosevelt sat with Hopkins on a Rochester railway siding, listening to the German führer haranguing the throngs at faraway Nuremberg, he was drained physically and emotionally from his nonstop round of campaigning. He had no idea that he, and the world, had reached a crucial turning point. September 1938 was a critical month for the prospects of peace. In that month, the world, which had tottered on the precipice between salvation and destruction, hope and despair, a troubled peace and all-out war, took the final plunge into the abyss.

On Thursday, September 15, Neville Chamberlain flew to Munich to meet with Hitler at his custom-built mountain eyrie high above the town of Berchtesgaden in the South Tyrol region of Austria. The British prime minister offered the führer what he had long demanded: the surrender of the German-occupied Sudetenland in Czechoslovakia.

Hitler accepted the surrender. The world celebrated with only a few grumblings about "peace at any price." But at a second meeting on September 22, Hitler escalated his demands. The führer insisted that the Reich occupy the Sudetenland immediately. There were to be no drawn-out negotiations this time. Chamberlain gained a small concession. Hitler would wait until October 1 until he sent in German troops.

"It's up to the Czechs now," Chamberlain said dolefully as he returned to London. Meanwhile Nazi Germany entertained separate deals with representatives of Hungary and Poland: They too wanted pieces of the Czech pie to divide among themselves. At the same time Germany secretly mobilized for a new style of rapid military assault that its general staff had dubbed *blitzkrieg* or "lightning war."

With Chamberlain's return to London, and despite the supposed "success" of his peace mission to Hitler, Britain prepared for war. Thirty-eight million gas masks were issued and experimental air raid warnings wailed from radios tuned to stations broadcasting over British Broadcasting Corporation–controlled airwaves. Workers digging zigzag trenches across London's stately parks to serve as emergency shelters from German bombs were now becoming a common sight. Four out of five London parents signed up their children for emergency evacuation to the countryside under a special government program. In a speech before Parliament on September 26, Winston Churchill declared, "If German attack is made upon Czechoslovakia . . . France will be bound to come to her assistance, and Great Britain and Russia will certainly stand by France."

British appeasers, including Chamberlain, denounced Churchill's combative speech. Britain, the prime minister announced, stood ready to concur with Hitler's demands.

As this dark September drew to a close, the president took time out from his vigorous election campaign efforts to make a last-ditch plea for peace using Fascist dictator Benito Mussolini as an intermediary to Berlin. As a result of Il Duce's efforts, Hitler grudgingly agreed to meet Chamberlain one last time. On September 29, Chamberlain flew to Munich. The pitiful outcome was an agreement that turned over Czechoslovakia to the Third Reich without a shot being fired.

"This is the second time," said Chamberlain on his return, apparently failing to see the Brobdingnagian irony of his statement, "that there has come back from Germany to Downing Street peace with honor. I believe it is peace for our time."

It was, of course, nothing like peace. On the contrary, the cowardly performance of the democracies in the face of Hitler's bluster and bluff only increased the appetites of Hitler, Mussolini, and other dictators, including Franco of Spain, for still more concessions. Chamberlain's deputation to Nazi Germany had in fact marked a prelude to the horrors of industrialized global war.

Throughout October, the pace of war preparations continued to rise. But Roosevelt's dark horse November election win gave the president a much-needed boost, if not a flat-out mandate. Though anti–New Dealers in both parties and both houses of Congress were largely still firmly entrenched in their customary and immovable power blocs, FDR himself had won reelection by a substantial popular margin. Roosevelt knew the people were behind him now. He at once began to devise plans for a new and more ambitious set of defense initiatives.

Early on in his new term of office Roosevelt summarized his objectives in a single sentence:

"I am working at the present time on two very important things— first, national defense, especially mass production of planes; and, second, the establishment of a better system of constant publicity with the idea not only of making clear our objectives and methods, but also nailing the deliberate misstatements of fact as fast as they are made."

In mid-March 1938, as Werhmacht tanks roared into Czechoslovakia's capital city, Prague, Roosevelt, with the help of War Secretary Henry Stimson, was making inroads into changing America's defense posture and building the critical defense infrastructure, including manpower, that would be necessary to fight a war against the Third Reich in Europe and, if need be, against the Japanese in the Pacific. But his efforts would still have to remain largely behind the scenes. For the time being, at least, the nation was not yet prepared to go to war in either theater.

CHAPTER THREE

A SHATTERED PEACE

Washington, D.C., at three o'clock in the morning on September 1, 1939, was silent and dark. The streets of the nation's capital were peculiarly quiet and a cool breeze, uncharacteristic for the usually muggy Indian summer, blew eastward across the Potomac from outlying Arlington, Virginia. A full moon shone down on the Great Lawn, and its ghostly white image swam in the waters of the Reflecting Pool. What cars there were had the streets pretty much to themselves; there weren't many out, though.

The district was at peace; at least it seemed so, but appearances were deceptive. In fact the peace of this night was merely the calm that sometimes settles in before the breaking violence of the impending storm. The repose of the city of Washington, D.C., this night was better likened to the "patient etherized on a table" in T. S. Eliot's poem "The Wasteland."

Elsewhere in the world, across two thousand miles of open ocean, the continent of Europe lay ill as if with a fever. In Germany, the National Socialist German Workers Party—whose acronym Nazi, derived from its initials NSDAP, was destined to leave its dark stain on the world forever—had consolidated its control of a nation that had fallen into virtually total anarchy.

The previous year, German Chancellor Adolph Hitler made himself the uncontested ruler of the Third Reich following bloody purges that completed the Nazis' rise to supremacy after the Reichstag, or German parliament building, had mysteriously burned to the ground in 1933. In Italy, a former newspaper editor named Benito Mussolini had earlier led a small army of black-shirted *Fascisti* on a march on Rome. France lay behind the protection of a line of fortifications designed by Maginot thought to be impregnable to attack, while a small island republic stood alone against the forces gathering toward a cataclysm that would rock the foundations of human society and profoundly change the system of the world order for all time.

In Washington, some expected this impending cataclysm, however. For two years, the American military establishment had been making plans for possible war with Germany and Japan, and manpower reserves for military forces had been beefed up under the Protective Mobilization Plan (PMP) of 1937 and the kindred 1939 Industrial Mobilization Plan. These war plans were based on a set of earlier color-coded war plans, ranging from Black for Germany to Yellow for China, that had been hatched on an ad hoc basis by the War and Navy departments' contingency planning staffs, and dated back to the years immediately after the First World War.

The color-coded plans included one declassified by the Defense Department only in 1974, War Plan Red, which outlined military doctrine in a hypothetical war between the United States and Great Britain, code-named Force Red. War Plan Red assumed that British forces would attack the United States via Canada, whose forces were code-named Crimson. Also drafted was War Plan White, a plan for military response to a domestic upheaval in the continental United States. Plan White, originally intended to deal with the threat of radical trade unionists like the Wobblies—maligned in the twenties and thirties as anarchists and communists—was put into effect to squelch the so-called Bonus Army, a mass movement of World War I veterans that marched on Washington to demand both payment of a postwar bonus and miscellaneous veterans' benefits in 1932 at the height of the Great Depression. The plan later formed the basis for an updated plan, Garden Plot, whose provisions were invoked in 1967 to deal with demonstrators who marched on the Pentagon and in the violent aftermath of September 11, 2001. At this writing Garden Plot is still in force as the Pentagon's plan, within the broader framework of the Homeland Security and PATRIOT acts, for actions that might call for domestic troop deployments in the wake of a terrorist attack.

Be that as it may, in 1939, subject to the PMP of 1937, a new Rainbow Plan had been placed in effect that was a consolidated, updated, and—in some cases, such as that of the British Empire—pared-down plan where former potential belligerents, such as Force Red, were no longer considered likely threats by the Department of War. Germany, however, was not one of these latter. Plans Orange and Black, the former dealing with war with Japan, the latter with armed conflict with Nazi Germany, were both in the active planning stages, with Plan Black taking precedence, for the moment, over Plan Orange. While the Japanese had gone out of their way to impress on Washington the absence of any kind of bellicose plans, the very opposite was true about Germany.

From Berlin, where the Nazis had established their beknighted epicenter of power, Adolph Hitler had issued a string of warlike proclamations. The reindustrialization of the Ruhr—a valley bowl of about one hundred square miles in which steel mills, heavy industrial factories, and munitions manufacturing plants, including that of the legendary Krupps, was located—was a fait accompli, despite the armistice provisions of the Versailles treaty. A year before, at the Nuremberg Party Rally in spring 1938, the Nazi führer had stood alone on a podium and driven the assembled thousands before him to a frenzy for war. To America's political and military leadership the imminence of global war was not a question of *if*, it was a question of *when*.

At twenty minutes to three on the morning of September 1, 1939, that *when* became *now*, when an overseas phone call came in to the White House switchboard. Russel McMullin, the night switchboard operator, was on duty, taking over from Louise L. Hackmeister, nicknamed "Hacky," who connected callers by day. McMullin had almost drifted off into a half-slumber when the flashing lights jarred him fully awake.

"This is William Bullitt," the clipped voice on the other end of the phone line said. "I'm calling with an urgent message for the president."

McMullin was a veteran operator and had put through calls from Bullitt before. He recognized the voice of the veteran U.S. ambassador. Furthermore, he knew that Bullitt was one of the chosen few who had round-the-clock access to President Franklin Delano Roosevelt. Nevertheless, the situation called for tact. McMullin was well aware that only the gravest circumstances warranted anyone being put through directly from the switchboard to Roosevelt, especially at night. He decided to wake Roosevelt's personal assistant and (as everyone at the White House knew) his present mistress, Marguerite "Missy" LeHand.

"Hold on, sir," he said, now fully awake, "I'll put you through." A surge of adrenaline coursed through McMullin. He, like everyone else at the White House, suspected the import of the call. After all, Bullitt was the U.S. ambassador to France. The call could only mean one thing: *war*.

Two stories above, in the East Wing of the executive mansion, a phone began to ring in the darkness of a silent room. The phone was on a night stand beside the bed in which Roosevelt lay striped by the same brilliant waxing moon that was casting its beams across the district. His eyes were still open. He had retired for the night only two hours before, but sleep eluded him tonight as it had a habit of doing lately.

Roosevelt, like Hitler and Churchill as well as Stalin, was an insomniac who was in the habit of conducting presidential business until late at night. FDR's sleep was never very good, especially now that he had begun to be ill. But tonight it was particularly light. He was almost glad at the jarring ringing to his left. It was an excuse to get up and do something.

"Yes?"

"This is Bill Bullitt, Mr. President," the voice said. "I'm sorry to disturb you at this hour, but this message is of the most urgent sort."

"Yes, Bill, what is it?"

"Mr. President, I regret to inform you that as of 2:17 this morning Nazi Germany has invaded Poland. Reports are contradictory, but at this point we have reason to believe that the Germans have swept aside Polish forces and are gaining ground at a rapid pace."

In his room at the U.S. embassy in Paris on the Avenue Gabriel near the Place de la Concorde, Bullit, in blue silk smoking jacket, sat and sipped at a crystal tumbler of scotch and soda just handed to him by his principal aide and protégé, Carmel Offie (who in those days might also have been openly called his "friend" or "companion"). It was close to nine in the morning local time. Offie, like Bullitt, was attired in smoking jacket and sipped a morning aperitif as he trimmed his bushy black moustache at the dresser mirror.

A little more than five minutes had elapsed since Anthony Biddle, the American ambassador to Poland, stationed in Cracow and failing to reach Washington by telephone, had managed to get through to Bullitt in Paris via an international line. Wehrmacht armor, Biddle had told him, had already forged deep into Polish territory. Bullitt, still shaken by the dreaded news, held the phone handset propped beneath his chin and shoulder and looked out the window, which faced, across the narrow Alée Marcel Proust several stories below, the grand Boulevard Champs Elysées, stretching from the Arc de Triomphe to the Place de la Concorde.

The main drag of Paris was a bustle of activity. Parisians were out in droves as usual. The air outside his balcony buzzed with a million big city noises. Everything seemed normal, yet an ineluctable dread gripped Bullitt like a ghostly hand that was squeezing his vitals. He wondered what this avenue would look like two, three, five years from now, once the war's aftermath had come. The hollow feeling in the pit of his gut was a premonition: It wouldn't be pretty, he was somehow convinced of this.

There was silence on the line. Bullitt was about to say something to break it when Roosevelt spoke up.

"Well, Bill," he said, his voice showing resignation, "it's come at last. God help us all."

"My thoughts exactly, sir," Bullitt answered.

FDR asked the U.S. ambassador to keep him posted and then set the receiver back in its cradle. He sat in the moonlit room for a few long moments, rubbing his eyes. Beneath the closed lids they were hot, swollen to the touch; the nerves in them would be red, inflamed. But he couldn't stay in bed a moment longer. He switched on the light and began to dress. Within minutes he would be at his desk in the Oval Office. A great deal was about to change. He had to be on his watch when it all happened.

Within a matter of minutes the president was back on the phone. This time he placed a call to Secretary of State Cordell Hull, Secretary of War Harold Woodring, and Acting Secretary of the Navy Charles Edison. Shaking off the final effects of fatigue, the president told each of these principal cabinet chiefs that Hitler had invaded Poland and that there would be a critical meeting that afternoon. Each cabinet head was to prepare a brief for the president on America's readiness in the face of this new and disturbing development.

These were the first, but by no means the last, telephone calls that the president would make in the early hours of September 1, 1939. Roosevelt realized that World War II had just broken out in earnest. He also realized that it would test the resolve of the free world to the maximum and that the United States would again find itself embroiled in Europe.

Sometime before dawn Roosevelt resolved to lie down again and try to sleep, but before he did he made a final call to his wife, Eleanor. At about 5 a.m., the president phoned Mrs. Roosevelt and told her, "Turn on the radio. Hitler is about to talk to the Reichstag." FDR listened to the German führer crow about the lightning-swift armored invasion. Then he turned out the light and willed himself into something resembling slumber, but very brief and very light.

* * *

At breakfast Roosevelt got a call from Joseph Kennedy, ambassador to England. Kennedy, who had irked FDR repeatedly since his appointment by proving himself a firm partisan of British appeasement factions, was at least being truthful when he declared that England was not yet ready to commit itself but that an appeal for assistance from the Poles was under consideration.

Britain's leadership still clung to the belief that war might be avoided if Germany could be persuaded to halt its advance and pull back across the Polish border. Later that day, a message counseling this from the Chamberlain government was received in Berlin. Predictably it was mocked.

Another breakfast call now came in; it was a follow-up call from Bullitt in Paris. The U.S. ambassador told Roosevelt that he had received a personal assurance from French President Daladier that France would fight the Germans should they continue their blitz on Poland. Daladier, Bullitt added, spoke for the French general staff as well as the government in making this pledge. As it turned out, Bullitt was as mistaken as the newspapers whose headlines that morning declared that the British had resolved to fight the German army.

In fact the French general staff, if resolved to anything at all at this point, was convinced that its defense forces were inadequate to stop a German assault and determined to put off a declaration of war until the absolute last possible moment. As to the Daladier government, Paris like Downing Street still clung to a desperate fantasy that Hitler could be persuaded to call off the blitzkrieg and talk peace. The French version of the illusion that beset the Anglo-French alliance was that Mussolini could mediate a negotiated truce.

Such was the state of affairs that prevailed when Roosevelt met with his cabinet later that day. Charles Edison, attending as acting secretary of the navy, recorded in his diary that Roosevelt stated that at the news of the outbreak of war he experienced a feeling of déjà vu.

"I was almost startled by a strange feeling of familiarity," the president told those assembled in the Yellow Oval Room, where he was accustomed to holding cabinet-level meetings, the sunlight streaming in through the French windows from the East Wing garden. It was, he went on, "a feeling that I had been through it all before. But after all, it was not strange. During the long years of the World War the telephone at my bedside with a direct line to the Navy Department had time and again brought me other tragic messages in the night. . . . I had in fact been through it all before."

The following day, Saturday, September 2, saw German mechanized armor rushing in a long lance of flowing steel through Polish defenses while the Luftwaffe, having cleared the skies of the little aerial resistance the Poles could throw against its fighter and bomber aircraft, now flew close air support sorties with devastating effect on the defenders. Panzer Mark IIIs hurtled pell-mell through the invasion corridor while Stuka dive bombers and Heinkel heavy bombers strafed, pounded, and smashed everything that lay in front of them.

While diplomatic efforts went on in the background without response from Berlin, the president tried to relax by playing a few hands of poker with his cronies in the Oval Office (his successor, Harry Truman, would do the same). It was a brave attempt but one destined to fail. Throughout the card game dispatches would come in from the front, every one of them bearing ever graver news.

To make matters worse, the president was losing. Those around the makeshift poker table knew that their boss took offense at being allowed to win. Roosevelt was out $35 when the last hand was played.

"War," he said, "will be declared by noon tomorrow," he announced as yet another dispatch came in.

* * *

Although war was not declared the following day, it soon came, and with it came shock waves of transformation that the United States needed to deal with.

The Pentagon was destined to play a key role in the nation's ability to adapt to the changing vicissitudes of mechanized, industrialized warfare. Indeed, it might be said that the institution of the Pentagon actually came into being because the United States and its allies found themselves confronted by enemies whose political and military organization was founded on militarism and who had experimented with often radically new forms of military technology that had been effectively, and very rapidly, transitioned into their orders of battle while America was still mired in the defense dynamics of the previous Great War.

A great deal in military tactics, doctrine, and technology had already changed since the Armistice of 1918. A new form of mobile warfare marked by a combination of rapid, mobile armor and close air support had come into being. It was called *blitzkrieg*, literally "lightning war." Among its architects had been Werhmacht Field Marshal Heinz Guderian, who would apply similar tactics in smashing the supposedly impregnable Maginot Line in a sweeping surprise attack out of the Ardennes the following year in the spring of 1940.

There were other advances in the offing, such as the advent of carrier warfare that would mark the battles fought in the Pacific Theater later in the war, but for the moment it was land war in Europe that gripped the attention of the army and the navy. The United States military establishment, like all other observers around the world, was stunned.

Moreover, as the Wehrmacht rapidly consolidated its territorial gains into a victory of staggering proportions, the deficiency of America and her allies in combating this new type of threat became startlingly clear.

The U.S. military establishment had just been presented with a display of military organization, much of which had not been anticipated. Indeed, the Nazi blitz, as metaphor of strategic speed and tactical agility, made the order of battle of friendly forces seem stolid by comparison. As the news of battle poured into the District of Columbia on the first day of September 1939, it became more and more evident that the United States defense establishment must undergo rapid changes and reorganization to meet this new threat.

At that time, the United States' military leadership was largely made up of commanders who had come of age during World War I and whose appreciation of war fighting was a product of the battles fought during that war. While the notion that the first World War was characterized by static defense lines and force-on-force infantry battles is less than accurate (World War I saw the introduction of modern aerial and armored warfare, to name but two innovations), the new emerging dynamic of mechanized warfare was not clearly understood by this generation of commanders.

Nor was the strategic vulnerability of the United States and its allies, for that matter.

As late as November 1937, General Malin Craig, who on the September morning when the German blitz began was U.S. Army chief of staff, rejected a plea for endorsement of a military air base in Alaska, stating that "the mainland of Alaska is so remote from the strategic areas of the Pacific that it is difficult to conceive of circumstances in which air operations therefore could contribute materially to the national defense."

This is not to say that there wasn't an appreciation of the danger looming in Europe and Japan or that the United States was not making preparations for a possible war. Clearly, it was. The War Department was not entirely negligent. The year 1937 saw the development, under General Craig's leadership, of initiatives such as the previously mentioned Protective Mobilization Plan. The PMP envisioned forming the Regular Army and the National Guard into an Initial Protective Force (IPF) of four hundred thousand men. The plan assumed that another seven hundred thousand men could be mobilized within eight months. Thereafter, the plans called for further mobilizations of one hundred fifty thousand men per month until an army of four million was reached. Almost all of this manpower was to be organized as infantry. The PMP called for only a single armored division among the four million troops.

It would also be unfair to charge that the U.S. government was completely surprised by war in Europe. Apart from what has been previously related in this narrative, the possibility already influenced strategic policy. In December 1937, the director of the Navy War Plans Division, Captain Royal E. Ingersoll, was sent to London to informally confer with the British Admiralty about the construction programs of both navies. The prerequisites for naval cooperation in the event of war against Japan were discussed, as was the possibility of a war with Germany. In 1938, military planners undertook a complete reexamination of American strategy in light of the growing threat of war, leading to the drafting of the Black and Orange plans against Germany and Japan, their consolidation under the Rainbow Plan, and adoption of a "Germany First" policy.

In an emergency address to Congress on January 28, 1938, Roosevelt recommended the strengthening of the country's national defense posture. The president reported with deep regret that armaments were increasing "at an unprecedented and alarming rate." He called attention to the ominous fact that at least one-fourth of the world's population was involved in "merciless devastating conflict" in spite of the fact that most people in most countries wished to live at peace.

As commander in chief of the army and navy, the president deemed it his constitutional duty to report to the Congress that the national defense of the United States was, in light of the increasing armaments of other nations, inadequate for purposes of national security, and therefore required increase. The president said that "adequate defense" meant that for the protection not only of our coasts but also of our communities far removed from the coasts, we must keep any potential enemy many hundreds of miles away from our continental landmass.

Nevertheless, despite the increasing state of military readiness of the United States, and despite the clear perception that war in Europe was not only inevitable, but that it might ultimately draw the United States into the fighting as it had done two decades before in a "war to end all wars," the events of September 1, 1939, were instrumental in revealing the deficiencies and underestimates of the American order of battle.

In the aftermath of this event, as was the case with other massive shocks to the national psyche, such as the Pearl Harbor or 9/11 surprise attacks, restructuring followed, building in tangible results at a rapid pace. One such structural reshuffling was the appointment of a new chief of staff for the U.S. Army by the president. It was a change of leadership that would have lasting consequence for America and its allies throughout the long, grueling years of global war that were to follow, as well as in the aftermath of that war.

The president needed more than laws, though. He needed more than money. He needed a right hand for defense. This he found in the person of George Marshall.

* * *

General George Catlett Marshall was sworn in as army chief of staff on September 1, 1939, the day World War II began. He replaced General Malin Craig who had served in that office for the past four years. In spring 1938, Roosevelt had chosen him to succeed Craig, who had been chief of staff to General George K. Ligget, commander of the 41st Infantry Division in World War I, and had himself succeeded Douglas MacArthur in the War Department post in 1935.

The much-decorated Craig—the 41st was a replacement division that was for a while stationed at the notorious "Saint Agony" replacement depot (troops called these "repple depples") at St. Agnese, France, before being sent into action on the western front—was by now sixty-four years old, in ill health and due to retire. Though Craig would be recalled to active duty in 1941 for a staff post as a director of army training, his career, distinguished though it was, was effectively over.

Under Roosevelt's direction during the past year, Marshall had been groomed for office by serving as Craig's deputy chief of staff. Beginning in June 1939, Marshall had been promoted to acting chief of staff toward eventually replacing his boss. Marshall's appointment flouted precedent in much the same way that Colin Powell's appointment decades later would do. Roosevelt had jumped Marshall a full rank from major general to four-star general over the heads of senior officers in the same way that Richard Cheney, as secretary of defense, jumped Powell under the elder President Bush.

In Marshall's case, General John J. "Black Jack" Pershing—so dubbed not for any resemblance to a mugger's weapon but for his championing of African Americans in a segregated army—had been instrumental in his career fast-track into a position that would soon become a historic post. Marshall, who as chief of operations for the First Infantry Division had helped plan the first U.S. campaigns in France, had served as Pershing's senior aide from 1919 to 1924. From 1924 to 1927 he was executive officer of the 15th Infantry Regiment in Tientsin, China. As chief of instruction at the Infantry School, Fort Benning, Georgia, from 1927 to 1932, he trained many who later became key officers in World War II. Pershing had mentioned his young protégé to presidential advisor Harry Hopkins, recommending him for promotion.

As Roosevelt and his close circle of cabinet advisors, including Henry Stimson and Harry Hopkins, cast about behind the scenes for ways to improve the U.S. defense preparedness, they needed a mover and shaker in the post of army chief. At the moment the upper tiers of the U.S. defense establishment were populated by soldiers who had been born in the final two decades of the nineteenth century; many had been in their twenties during World War I. These men were now in their fifties and sixties. They were yesterday's tigers, not tomorrow's warriors.

Roosevelt recognized the need for young blood at the controls of America's military machine, mainly because while the U.S. military and political leadership was then still mentally back in the trenches of the Western Front, it was young bloods who had wrested control of Germany's political and military juggernaut. Hitler was to Hindenburg all that a savage young delinquent was to the measured inertia of a moribund authority with flab in the gut.

The Nazis had blown the doors off. They would stop at nothing to dominate first Europe and then the rest of the world. Democracy's arsenal needed leaders who were lean and mean to the bone. The Nazi movement had begun with wolf packs of street thugs whose twisted ecstasies of brutality and conquest had now become the atavistic dark ethic that propelled the German military juggernaut from conquest to conquest.

This was one factor in the selection of Marshall, who, then thirty-seven years old, had made a reputation for himself as a doer of deeds and a cutter of costs. An example from early in his career is illustrative: When Marshall had become deputy chief under Craig he made a study of the public relief program as it affected the army, discovering that two New Deal pillars, the Works Progress Administration (WPA) and the Public Works Administration (PWA) had between them squandered $250 million on War Department projects. Although a mere drop in the bucket today in GNP terms, it represented a vast sum in the late 1930s. In fact, the sum was roughly equivalent to the total annual expenditures for the War Department for the preceding fifteen years.

Marshall's investigation had exposed the fact that the aging generals who ran things had fought shy of obtaining the funds for the War Department out of fear of incurring congressional criticism should they become involved with New Dealers, whom most considered radicals or worse. Marshall had no such qualms. Via Pershing, Marshall became part of the White House backchannel operation to jump-start national rearmament in the late 1930s in the face of the mighty isolationist and appeasement bastions in Congress.

In the fall of 1938, shortly after his accession to the post of Craig's deputy chief, Marshall went to the White House to work with Hopkins in yet another of FDR's behind-the-scenes money shuffling maneuvers intended to circumvent the mandates of a hostile Congress. As a result, millions of Works Progress Administration dollars were now being surreptitiously diverted to fashion machine tools for producing small arms ammunition. Some of this clandestine industrial output was also secretly being diverted for purchase by France and Britain at bargain-basement prices.

In fact, it would not be much of an oversimplification to say that Roosevelt's multifaceted operations, which included arms-for-dollars schemes and money laundering strategies, was the direct forerunner—

indeed the modern precedent—for what were later exposed as the elements underlying the Iran-Contra scandal of the 1980s.

The differences in context are what set these two widely separated activities apart. Funds were then not being diverted to buy arms that were to be traded for hostages held by a regime inimical to the United States but to rearm the nation and help its allies, and the onset of World War II made the entire issue moot in the long run. Nevertheless, the Roosevelt White House was contravening legal acts of Congress with the active involvement of the War Department.

Be that as it may, Marshall would never lose a chance to take advantage of opportunity, no matter from what quarter it originated. For the next six years, Marshall was to direct the raising of new armored and infantry divisions, the training of troops for wartime deployment, the development of new weapons and equipment, and the selection of top commanders.

When he entered office, the United States forces consisted of fewer than 200,000 officers and men. Under his continuing direction these forces expanded in less than four years to a well-trained and well-equipped host of 8,300,000 troops. Marshall raised and equipped the largest ground and air force in the history of the United States, a feat that earned him the appellation of "the organizer of victory" from the wartime British prime minister, Winston Churchill. His was a stop-at-nothing attitude that he looked for in recommending others—such as Brehon Somervell, who built the Pentagon—for advancement when their turns came.

All this to the contrary, and barring any developments that were to follow, one thing was sure on the first of September 1939 when the retiring Malin Craig's young successor took office at the War Department: George Marshall had his work neatly cut out for him.

* * *

While Marshall's name looms large in connection with the history of the Pentagon, as it does in connection with the postwar reconstruction of a despoiled Europe via the Marshall Plan, and beyond this, in connection with Marshall as statesman during the Truman administration, other names stand out in the history of the War Department during this period. Nor should it be forgotten that despite Marshall's role as *primus inter pares*, the army chief of staff was but one of the three service chiefs who together made up the Joint Chiefs of Staff before and throughout World War II. It was not Marshall but a specially appointed chief of staff who was the principal liaison between the Roosevelt Oval Office and the War and Navy departments and served in a capacity that was identical in most respects to the postwar office of the chairman of the Joint Chiefs of Staff.

In addition to Marshall as chief of the army, Roosevelt had made the appointments of Admiral Ernest King to head the navy and General Henry "Hap" Arnold to head the U.S. Army Air Force (USAAF). Although Arnold was technically under Marshall's command (the U.S. Air Force became a separate service branch after the restructuring spurred by the 1947 National Security Act), the realities of air warfare during World War II, including coordination of bombing missions with the Royal Air Force (RAF), made the USAAF largely autonomous from the army and gave Arnold, in his own right, the full status and powers of a service chief. According to Grace Tully's memoirs, "the Boss" (as she called FDR) had regarded the triumvirate he'd appointed to head the U.S. military "as the top men on the military side . . . three men who really liked to fight and had the daring and capacity to do the tremendous jobs ahead of them," even after his "bitterness" following the attack on Pearl Harbor and disappointment with "the failures" of military commanders to warn of its approach.[5]

King, according to Tully, "was the type of sea dog whom the President really liked and understood. He loved the stories of King's toughness," and after learning the admiral had been given a souvenir blowtorch by a New Jersey senator, "wrote King a note saying he understood the Admiral was so tough he cut his toenails with a torpedo net-cutter." As to Arnold, Tully wrote that "the thing he liked most about Arnold was the General's passionate devotion to air power." White House Chief of

5. Roosevelt's bitterness may have been based in part on now declassified secret memoranda, such as one signed by Marshall less than a week after Pearl Harbor, concerning Japanese warships off the West Coast of the United States and warning of the possibility of a second attack.

Staff Harry Hopkins was also "a great admirer of Arnold and it gave the Air General a powerful friend at court." Marshall, however, was "a great favorite among the working staff at the White House," and apparently with secretaries Tully and Dorothy Brady who were "open admirers" and ribbed by Hopkins, once in front of an embarrassed Marshall, about "being unfaithful" to the Boss.

It was Admiral William D. Leahy, however, who had the closest working relationship with Roosevelt among the leaders of the nation's military forces. He was the officially appointed ombudsman between the Joint Chiefs of Staff and the White House. Like another close Roosevelt confidant, Bernard M. Baruch, Leahy's friendship with FDR dated back to World War I and, like Harry Hopkins, he was, according to Tully, "a valued troubleshooter for the Boss." Leahy "was a man who minced no words in presenting his point of view, and whether he was right or wrong, the Boss knew that 'Bill' had no personal axe to grind and meant only to serve the national interest." Nevertheless, as U.S. ambassador to Vichy, the capital of "unoccupied France," Leahy had drawn fire from some who considered him a pro-Vichy apologist.

The ambassadorship was one of several posts (including being governor of Puerto Rico, whose residents dubbed him *Almirante Lija*, "Admiral Sandpaper," which was only partly a play on his surname) that Leahy had served in following his retirement as chief of naval operations in 1939, on which occasion Roosevelt told him, "Bill, if we have a war, you're going to be right back here helping me run it."

Due to the Vichy controversy Leahy was recalled in May 1942. True to his word, Roosevelt requested that the old admiral return to national military service in the newly created billet of chief of staff. The flap over his stint as ambassador had not lowered Leahy's estimation at the White House at all. In fact, Leahy had been sent to Vichy to attempt to secretly work out some form of modus vivendi between the governments of Great Britain and the United States and Germany's Third Reich. With the tacit approval of both Whitehall and Washington, his mission was in effect to try to catalyze a political solution that might have kept the United States out of the war in Europe, albeit with Nazi Germany remaining in control of the continent. Furthermore, prior to his actual recall Leahy himself had asked to be recalled "as a means of signifying American disgust with the proceedings there" only to be urged by Roosevelt to stay on awhile longer.

It wasn't only at the White House where approval of Leahy ran high, but at the War Department too. Indeed, Leahy's recall from France was to a greater or lesser degree necessitated by his being the only choice acceptable to the three service chiefs to fill the newly created post of chief of staff. Marshall, for one, had bridled at the proposed creation of a new billet for a senior military officer who would be the president's personal advisor and liaison between War Department and White House, and Leahy's appointment took place only at the suggestion of Marshall, who deemed him the only suitable candidate to fill the post. As a result, Leahy was sworn in with the official title of chief of staff to the commander in chief, U.S. Army and Navy, the president of the United States, on July 6, 1942. As will be told later in this narrative, Leahy was to serve in the capacity of de facto chairman of the Joint Chiefs of Staff, enjoying the confidence of Harry S. Truman as he did that of Roosevelt, until his resignation and final retirement in 1949, whereupon General Omar Bradley succeeded him as the first officially appointed chairman.

Leahy's name, like that of General Leslie Groves, is often associated with the atomic bombing of Hiroshima and Nagasaki, Japan, which effectively brought World War II to a close. Groves, who was the Pentagon's head of the Manhattan Project, is discussed elsewhere. Leahy, appointed the first U.S. fleet admiral on December 15, 1944, was one of the military commanders consulted concerning using the bomb against Japan.

In his memoirs, Leahy said nuclear weapons were "of no material assistance in our war against Japan," and extant memoranda from planning sessions for the final stages of the war in the Pacific from the Truman Library reveal that, faced with U.S. casualty estimates approaching the million mark, Leahy also "urged . . . strongly on the Joint Chiefs that no major invasion of the Japanese mainland was necessary to win the war." Plans for the invasion were drafted, however, but never finalized in the wake of the Joint Chiefs' advisory and President Truman's executive decision as commander-in-chief to deploy the atomic bomb against Japan on August 6 and 9, 1945.

CHAPTER FOUR

THE BLOOD-DIMMED TIDE

I n spring 1941, Roosevelt was completing the first ninety days of
his unprecedented third presidential administration; there were no
legal term limits yet, two terms being the traditional, but otherwise
surpassable, ceiling.

The president's victory was significant, proving that New Deal
politics still had traction with the American public, but there remained
the downside of a hostile, isolationist-oriented Congress backed by
powerful special interests with which to contend. The president had won
reelection, but he still faced his old nemesis, a Medusa with a hundred
heads and as many agendas inimical to his plans.

As if to make it clear to FDR that he and his blueprint for America
were anathema to these special interests—even in the face of such clear
signs that war in Europe threatened global security and U.S. interests—the
House Appropriations Committee had further cut an already watered-
down military budget on April 3, 1940, enfeebling it to the point of near-
irrelevance. On the domestic front the Roosevelt administration was
hard-pressed by a plethora of anti–New Deal criticism and legislation,
not the least of which concerned the "Roosevelt Recession" that had as
yet not yielded to attempts by the president's chief economic advisors to
turn the ship of state around into less fiscally troubled waters.

In a roughly six-month period between the close of 1939 and the
first months of the new year, following the conquest of Poland, a period
of relative calm had settled over the western front. Germany, like a lion

digesting a fat wildebeest, was sated and dormant. This was the period some called "the phony war." Others dubbed it "sitzkrieg."

Whatever its title, the respite from battle added momentum to those interests that accused Roosevelt of "warmongering," pushing the United States into a European conflict that would work itself out in due course on its own. Nothing was happening, after all. This might be the end of hostilities. So why place American lives and national treasure in harm's way? What was the point of rearmament, after all? Such questions seemed easy to ask and answer to many Americans during this period of deceptive calm.

But the pendulum of history had nevertheless arced by now to its antipodal cusp and had begun its inevitable rebound. As spring 1940 burgeoned into summer, the Nazi war machine was once again on the move. This time the German blitz was directed at a new target: France.

On June 5, 140 German divisions attacked across a ten-mile front through the densely wooded Ardennes forest—a strategic battleground for European powers dating back to Imperial Rome's battles with barbarian tribes. Panzer tank thrusts smashed key bastions of the supposedly impregnable series of French defensive fortifications collectively called the Maginot Line, already weakened by attacks in May. Armored spearheads using mobile Panzer divisions as their cutting edge ripped through the 65 French divisions that stood in the Wehrmacht's (the German army's) path. Four days later, forces under Field Marshal Fedor von Bock had reached the river Seine while other mechanized formations under Walter von Reichenau drove down the river Oise.

As the French Tenth Army shattered like the porcelain shell of a Faberge egg, British and Polish expeditionary forces that had supported the French hastily withdrew toward the Channel coast—technically it was a katabasis, the opposite of the ancient military term *anabasis*, which meant a march to the interior. Both terms had of old served as euphemisms for a less glorious term, *withdrawal*, but a withdrawal by any other name still tasted rankly of defeat. On June 14 the Germans took Paris, with Dijon and Cherbourg following days later. The French formally surrendered on June 22, and the nation became known, from that day until it was liberated by Allied troops in 1944, as "occupied France."

This was not the only grim event of this new season of war. In the midst of the blitz on France the German Luftwaffe staged a series of attacks on England that was to become known as the Battle of Britain, sometimes prefixed by the word *first* to distinguish it from a second series of attacks, largely by V-1 and V-2 missile "vengeance weapons," later on in the war. To those Britons in the thick of it, though, and for many ever after, the chain of events is simply known as "the blitz."

By whatever name, the airborne attacks, using waves of twin- and single-engine fighters, medium bombers, and dive bombers, were intended to pound the British into submission or weaken their defensive forces to the extent that they, too, would easily be crushed by a planned cross-Channel invasion. Code-named Sea Lion by the German general staff, this invasion was scheduled to take place early the following fall.

The British knew it was coming. They marked the signs of preparation on the French coast. Moreover, they had secret information from top-secret intercepts—code-named Ultra—of high-level German military message traffic encrypted using the Enigma cipher machine— thought inviolably secure by the Germans—that made the totality and scope of Hitler's war plans clear to them.

Churchill, newly elected as prime minister, knew that England's fate depended on the RAF beating back the Luftwaffe. When the German attacks began on July 10 with one hundred German bombers and fighters attacking convoys anchored off the English coast, and then switching tactics to assault ports, airfields, industrial targets, and cities, the British met them to commence a series of air battles that were conducted on a scale never before witnessed and which grasped the world's attention for months until the Luftwaffe withdrew, beaten, by the end of October.

Third, and finally, there was the spectacle of the British evacuation from Dunkirk over five nights between May 29 and June 3, during which almost 225,000 British and more than 112,000 Belgian soldiers stranded at the port of Dunkirk were evacuated by a makeshift fleet of 997 British vessels of all types hastily assembled from whatever was available.

The British barely made it back across the Channel with their forces intact. They had lost thirty thousand men and twenty-nine aircraft, seven destroyers, a minesweeper, and twenty smaller ships in the four-day campaign that culminated on May 28 when the Belgian army surrendered in the face of the same type of blitzkrieg assault that had broken the Polish and would soon shatter the French defensive ranks.

The Wehrmacht commander, Gerd von Rundstedt, later commented that Hitler had ordered him not to use his Panzer divisions against the evacuating British and insisted that he not send German troops closer than ten kilometers from Dunkirk. Though Rundstedt was engaging in myth-making (extensive tank obstacles in the vicinity of the port made a ten-kilometer cordon sanitaire a prudent tactical measure, and no record of Hitler's supposed order exists) this withdrawal was no anabasis—it was clearly a rout and it was all too apparent that the British army had escaped mass destruction by a comparative hair.

Newsreel footage drives home the tenacity of the enemy and the threat it posed. On June 28, Hitler landed at Orly Airport just outside of Paris for a look at the city that many, including Der Führer himself, considered the epitome of Western art and culture. Images from Hitler's visit showed a city nearly deserted of civilians and civilian automobile traffic, its broad but untenanted boulevards and spacious if unpeopled plazas evocative of the desolate ruins of an abandoned Aztec city.

Across this wasteland Hitler and his retinue of Wehrmacht and SS officers, whose regalia included field gray greatcoats, black leather boots, and the insignia of a human skull set in peaked caps where Buddhists long before placed a third, mystic eye, strode as new Visigoths before a prostrate Gaul.

The führer visited the Eiffel Tower and the Paris Opera House, among other cultural stops. He left that same day, never to return, having spent little more than a scant three hours touring the city he had longed since his youth to visit, but the modern mass communications and visual media—already advanced to the stage where millions could view quickly assembled newsreel footage in movie theaters in the United States and Britain, where newspapers and magazines could be printed and distributed with far greater speed than during the previous war, and where radio (and even the recent invention, television, to an admittedly negligible extent) were bringing the voices of on-the-scene reporters like William Shirer into millions of homes daily—impressed on even the staunchest isolationist that there was no cutting deals with the regime in Berlin. By July 1940, Congress by a wide margin reversed its defense cutbacks of the previous spring.

It was not the end of the battle for the president against his opponents by any means—Congress later flip-flopped further on defense and New Deal legislation as FDR's third term went forward—but it could be said, to use the words of Winston Churchill to describe another series of events, to have been "the end of the beginning" for those in the United States who saw clearly that America would have to fight, sooner or later.

* * *

The Building was to be a symbol of determined might and national strength in time of war; it was to offer a vast and imposing facade of stark and massive walls that would loom large upon the skyline of the U.S. capital. Yet it reflected the characteristic American traits of plain-dealing and plain-speaking that were being transformed, by the machinery of politics and war, into a new mega-bureaucracy and super-government when compared to what had preceded World War II. To put it plainly, the Pentagon's persona was "all business."

If the Building was a shrine to anything it was to the spirits of practicality and the smooth and efficient application of power and technological advancement. Later, one of its own would brand that power a malign development, but Ike's farewell speech warning of the "military-industrial complex" was still decades away in the late interwar period, as the United States faced the prospect of World War II.While some would gripe about its aesthetics—or lack there of—the Pentagon had to exist and so needed to be invented. Enter Brehon Somervell.

* * *

Lieutenant General Eugene Reybold rapped the edge of the notes he'd stacked against the polished tabletop. The man in the same forest green army A-uniform sitting beside him, albeit several pay grades below him in rank, quickly glanced at his own notes on the tabletop. He was scheduled to speak next, and he was readying himself mentally.

Both soldiers wore patches emblazoned with the shield of the U.S. Army Corps of Engineers' Quartermaster Corps Construction Division. They were not only the army's builders but represented an organization that had undertaken numerous important municipal building programs across the country. Brehon Burke Somervell, familiarly called "Bill," who was waiting to address the committee, was the construction division's chief. Somervell's last big job had been supervising the building of La Guardia Airport in New York City; this pending project on the lowlands of Arlington promised to make it look picayune by comparison.

Currently a light colonel, a rank he'd attained in 1935 just prior to taking on the four-year airport project in New York, Somervell would soon be jumped from lieutenant colonel to temporary brigadier rank by Roosevelt in order to give him the leverage necessary to get things done in a hurry. Since his appointment to head the construction division in 1940, Somervell's main occupation had been to rapidly put up training camps for waves of new draftees inundating the army, a program whose timetable called for completion by April 1941.

Reybold had been fielding questions from the group of civilians seated behind the raised tribunal dais of the Senate chamber. On this hot summer day of July 22, 1940, the Congressional Deficiency Subcommittee had convened to find solutions to what by now had become increasingly clear was the United States' lack of defense preparedness in the face of a Europe torn by war. The presence of two senior officers from the Army Corps of Engineers on this first day was significant. The day's main order of business concerned plans for a new headquarters for the massive staff needed to run an army at war, should it come to that for the United States, as conflict across the Atlantic deepened.

The Public Buildings Administration, one of the many new departments created by the Roosevelt Administration, had proposed a constellation of buildings in and around the District of Columbia. The PBA's plan was based on the fact that the War Department's activities, albeit centered around the Munitions–Main Navy Building complex, were already scattered across the nation's capital in the sometimes motley assortment of buildings referred to in the previous chapter.

The army's plan, backed by its new chief of staff, George C. Marshall, who himself had the president's strong backing, was to construct a single large building with a gross interior office space of roughly five million square feet on a large tract of government land located at the foot of Arlington Cemetery, known as Arlington Farms.

"The cost of construction," Reybold had explained, "will be roughly $7 per square foot or," he looked down at the notes in front of him for only a second, "$35 million."

There was the sound of chairs creaking and a few murmurs. Had they heard him right? Thirty-five million dollars in 1940 was equivalent to billions in today's currency.

Reybold went on, "plus another million for construction of a parking area sufficient for the projected project."

"Specifics, please," asked the committee's chairman, Clifton A. Woodrum.

"I believe Colonel Somervell is better prepared to answer your questions, gentlemen." He nodded at the man seated in the front rows beside him. "Colonel . . ."

Bill Somervell nodded his acknowledgment and prepared to speak. Still a relatively young man at forty-seven years of age, Somervell looked considerably older than he actually was. His hair had already turned gray and age lines seamed his face, though it was a face that was still lean and strong in profile. In many ways the colonel was an old soldier. As a combat veteran of World War I he had lived through some tough campaigning.

Somervell knew Woodrum. In fact they'd already met more than once to discuss this. The president was pushing for the plan, but that didn't make it a shoe-in by any means, not even with Woodrum engaging in some old-fashioned pork barrel politics—building the new War Department headquarters in his home district would be good for business. It would bring in thousands of new jobs practically overnight, and what was good for business was also good for Woodrum's political career.

There were powerful opposition forces though, and they included a Roosevelt among their number. The president's uncle and chairman of the National Capital Park and Planning Commission, Frederic A. Delano, was firmly in the same camp with Gilmore D. Clarke, president of the Washington Commission on Fine Arts, who believed that a building the size of the one contemplated by the War Department would obstruct the view from Arlington across the old Hoover Airport and the Potomac into the heart of the nation's capital. It was a fine view, one of the best in the country, and they wanted to preserve it. An enormous building blocking that view was the last thing they wanted.

What's more, the position held by Clarke was not by any means a minority viewpoint. "Imagine," one Washingtonian man-on-the-street remarked, reflecting a building consensus among the denizens of the District and Arlington, "a building with thirty-five acres of roof and they say it won't spoil the view. Hell, you could put a line of garbage pails in front of a house and it wouldn't 'spoil' the view, but by God it wouldn't be very pleasant!"

Delano held to the position that the project would, as he put it, "Damage the dignity and character" of the area around Arlington Cemetery and the Lincoln Memorial. Delano had in fact brought his case before his nephew personally. Here was an opponent with a lot of clout—even if FDR was well known as a stubborn cuss who listened to everything but did exactly what he wanted, Delano was a force to be reckoned with.

There were also protests against the planned structure from many other quarters. Among these were the prestigious D.C. Chapter of the American Institute of Architects and the National Association of Building Owners and Managers. In addition to his testimony, Clarke suggested that the site of the proposed government building be moved south by about a mile, to the construction site where the Army Corps of Engineers Quartermaster Depot was already in the preliminary stages of development.

Somervell, speaking on behalf of the project's proponents, outlined the reasons the War Department needed the enormous new office building.

"The new building will increase the efficiency of the War Department. Employees won't have to waste valuable time traveling between buildings to consult each other. It will also represent a savings estimated at about three million annually in rent."

It would also free up other public buildings currently in use by the War Department, he added, and release apartments now being used to conduct staff work for residential use again. All in all the new building promised to streamline the efficiency of the War Department.

Deliberations following Somervell's summation were brief and decisive. After a few more perfunctory questions, and with the bang of Woodrum's gavel, the meeting was over. The subcommittee had voiced its approval of the plan.

The proposal would now go before the House Committee on Appropriations, and it would be at the top of the committee's agenda. Events were on a fast train. A final decision would be made within a relatively short time.

* * *

The House Committee on Appropriations met two days later on July 24. Its members in the meantime had studied the proposal for the construction of the new building. So had a sister committee, the House Committee on Public Buildings and Grounds, which also had jurisdiction over the planned new construction project. When the appropriations committee convened it approved the project that Somervell had outlined at the earlier meeting, voting in favor of the $35 million to pay for the construction in the first supplemental to the fiscal year 1941 defense budget.

This was a sizable sum for 1940. In 2004, by comparison, President George W. Bush asked for and got a $75 million supplemental to help pay for the war in Iraq. Nevertheless, the full House had to vote on the Appropriations Committee's recommendations before those funds were signed into law, and there was a lengthy debate on the House floor concerning the fitness of such a massive undertaking.

Was it really necessary? asked critics, who continued to press for an alternative plan and another site. Some even asked whether a building of such a tremendous size and such an astronomical cost was actually necessary at all (a charge, it might be noted in passing, that has echoed down through the corridors of time and warfare to the present day). The new War Department Building, they argued, would consume labor and materials already in short supply and create traffic problems whose implications for transit in and around the district hadn't even been studied. Another question concerned what would happen to the building after the war was over—assuming the United States would even enter the European conflict in the first place. What would the country do with this enormous structure after it had served its purpose and was no longer necessary?

The controversy—whipped to a frenzy by the newspapers—wasn't resolved until the end of August, when Roosevelt decided to take matters personally in hand and settle the issue once and for all. And so it was that on this unseasonably mild day the president was lifted by two Secret Service agents from his wheelchair into the back seat of his waiting open-air touring car for a cross-Potomac jaunt into the Virginia countryside. Fala, the presidential dog, was the next party to enter the car, jumping in ahead of Somervell and his arch-foe, Gilmore Clarke. As the car moved off the three occupants made an unlikely group. Clarke and Somervell avoided looking at one another while FDR, ivory cigarette holder clamped between his teeth as was his wont, declaimed on the beauty of the day while Fala barked.

"Don't worry. Everything will be settled today," Roosevelt airily avouched as the car left the White House. "We'll just go over to the Virginia side, have a look around, and pick a new site."

Clarke was cheerful too. Somervell, annoyed with the dog and with having to put up with Clarke, was anything but cheerful.

As the car passed the site where the new Jefferson Memorial was under construction, Somervell seized the moment and spoke up. He told Roosevelt that moving the new War Department building from its original planned site between Arlington Cemetery, in Virginia, and the Lincoln Memorial, straight across the Potomac in D.C., was a rotten idea. The new site they were headed for, considerably to the south of Somervell's cherished building site, was basically just a lot of dismal swamp. Putting the building there would mean additional construction and expense that would delay the project for months.

Clarke was gleeful, but he kept this to himself. He could see FDR's cheerful mood begin to evaporate as the irascible Somervell kept hammering at him. All Clarke had to do was sit tight and let Somervell dig his own grave. Even Marshall didn't like the Somervell plan. In fact, Marshall, like many others, didn't care very much for Somervell personally. Few people liked Somervell, in fact. He was just too damn pushy. He got on peoples' nerves. He wasn't a team player. He was a loner. Give him enough rope, Clarke thought, and he'd hang himself eventually.

Finally Roosevelt cut things short.

"My dear general," he bluntly told Somervell. "I'm still commander in chief of the army."

FDR had just ended the argument. The president would be the one to make the final decision, not Somervell.

As it turned out, the site that Clarke had pushed for was even worse than a mere swamp. It was, more precisely, a swampy garbage dump in whose malodorous precincts was a section the locals called "Hell's Bottom." Shacks, refuse dumps, stockyards used by the railroads to warehouse and repair their rolling stock, and a miscellany of rambling buildings that might have been saloons, pawnshops, houses of ill-repute, or a combination of all three dotted the landscape. Now and then seedy-looking types stood and gawked at the unexpected intrusion of the presidential motorcade into their tawdry realm.

Somervell was quick to seize the opportunity for revenge. Silent since his rebuke by FDR, he now told the president as diplomatically as possible, "I think the War Department is worthy of a little better place, don't you?"

"Nonsense," FDR answered with an avuncular cheerfulness that might, or might not, have been feigned. "I like it just fine."

The president told the driver to pull up at a high point overlooking the Quartermaster Depot site.

"Gilmore," said FDR to Clarke, pointing with his cigarette holder down into the swamp of Hell's Bottom, "we're going to put the building over there, aren't we?"

"Yes, Mr. President," Clarke replied with a smile made all the broader by Somervell's sullen silence. "Indeed we will."

Clarke was in ecstasy. Somervell had tripped over his two left feet. Predictably, as it were. Well, Clarke thought sardonically, it couldn't have happened to a nicer guy.

* * *

On the party's return to the White House, FDR held a final meeting with Somervell and other principals of the plan, including George Bergstrom, one of the architects, and Harold Smith, director of the Bureau of the Budget.

FDR approved of the overall plan but had some reservations of his own. But the president earnestly wanted the plan to materialize: He wanted the building to go up in one form or another, and he wanted work on it to commence as soon as possible. He had done his share. His personal intervention had broken the impasse that had deadlocked Congress, Clarke's committee, and the Army Corps of Engineers for months. Now the building was destined to become a reality.

Later that day, FDR held a press conference. He announced that the new building would be moved south from its originally planned site at Arlington Farms to the site of the unfinished Quartermaster Depot.

It would be half as large as originally planned, designed to house about twenty thousand employees—roughly the same number as the twenty-four thousand War Department employees that were now spread out across the D.C. area—instead of the forty thousand originally contemplated. As to the depot, it was to be transferred to another government-owned plot in nearby Cameron, Virginia. Other than the reduction in size and the new location, the plan for the new War Department Building would remain essentially unchanged.

As to what Somervell had to say, when reporters stopped him outside the White House for a comment he dourly snapped at them, "Why talk to me about it? I'm just a bricklayer."

Little did the president suspect that Brehon Somervell had other ideas. Somervell had no choice but to move the building site south as the president wished it. As to reducing its size, however, Somervell had privately decided that this was an issue he might well be able to finesse.

The president's decision to cut the building's capacity roughly in half wouldn't work. It was just plain dumb to go to all this trouble and leave no room to grow. In a year's time they'd need to do the job all over again, Somervell rightly reasoned.

Somervell had little patience with politicians. The soldier and builder had decided, on his own hook, to make sure that the new War Department headquarters would be spacious enough to meet the demands it would need to satisfy. And those called for at least forty thousand occupants on any given business day, nothing less.

If he moved fast enough, Somervell figured he might be able to lay the foundations and put up enough of the new building so that if and when any objections were raised it would be too late to change it back again. But he had to move fast. Very fast. Fast enough for Somervell to get the job done under the noses of Congress and the president both. It would be tricky, but Somervell, a West Pointer and holder of the Distinguished Service Cross for frontline action in World War I, among other medals, and an individual known to dismiss his critics and detractors with the terse statement, "They can all go to hell," knew he could do it.

Instrumental to Somervell's success were two other army engineers, Generals Hugh John "Pat" Casey and Leslie Richard Groves. The story is often told of how Somervell called both together on Thursday, July 17, 1941, and gave them until the following Monday to rough out the initial design for the Pentagon. It was the Brooklyn-born Casey—who after the Pentagon was built became chief combat engineer in the Pacific by request of General Douglas MacArthur and would later become chairman of the New York City Transit Authority from 1953 to 1955— that ultimately was to oversee the actual day-to-day building schedule and in effect had direct managerial control over the construction project, subject to Somervell's overall approval.

Groundbreaking began the following month: on September 11, 1941. It would pick up speed and shift into high gear after the Japanese attacked Pearl Harbor a few months later. In the end, the site was to grow instead of shrink. This included a massive landscaping development with an additional 146 acres from adjoining Hoover Airport and 57 acres from the southern corner of Arlington Farms. Some 160 parcels of land—including many of which were privately held by families living in the vicinity of Columbia Pike from which they came and who were evicted by the government despite court battles—would be used for roads and other infrastructure servicing the gigantic new structure.

"It may easily stand out as one of the worst blunders of the war period," the *Washington Post* editorialized about a month before the bombing at Pearl Harbor, as the building began to rise from the swamp of Hell's Bottom. *Time* derided it as, "the butt of Washington's quipsters." Residents of Arlington, faced with displacement and an invasion of construction personnel, had even unkinder and (for the era) unprintable things to say. Indeed, by this time most, if not all, had stopped referring to the soon-to-be-built structure as the War Department Building. Instead they had begun calling it "Somervell's Folly."

CHAPTER FIVE

THE BUILDING GOES UP

In July 1941, as Congress reversed the longstanding cuts on rearmament spending made by the House Appropriations Committee in the spring of 1940, and as debate in the United States continued over the proposal for a new War Department building, a directive from the leader of a foreign government ordered a secret conference to be convened; it would later take place at a picturesque lakeside suburb only a few miles from central Berlin. The name of the town was Wannsee; the address of the stately, white mansion with a porticoed entrance in which the talks would be held was Am Grossen 56–58. The subject was genocide. Attended by some of Hitler's most trusted intimates, such as SS Chief Heinrich Himmler and his protégé, Reinhard Heydrich, the conference had been called to set the ground rules for what its participants called the Final Solution.

Hitler, his Luftwaffe repulsed by the RAF in the 1940 Battle of Britain, had called off plans to invade the British Isles, but a major eastward push was in the offing. The Nazis had begun World War II with the invasion of Poland early the previous fall. This time the target would be Russia. For months, Allied intelligence—informed by Ultra intercepts of Enigma-coded Oberkommando Wehrmacht cable traffic—had been attempting to warn the Russians concerning Berlin's plans to break the Nazi-Soviet nonaggression pact of August 23, 1939, and stage a surprise invasion of the Russian heartland. Stalin could not be convinced, however, and the need to protect the Allied source of the closely held intelligence kept the warnings too tentative to convince the Soviet dictator.

Meanwhile, the formidable Nazi war machine geared up to deliver its hardest punch of the war so far. At 8 a.m. on a June weekend at Chartwell, Churchill's personal estate outside of London, the prime minister awakened to news that Hitler had attacked the Soviets on a 1,500-mile front stretching from Finland to the Black Sea. The first confirmed reports had arrived four hours earlier, but Churchill's admonition to his staff that he was never to be awakened "for anything less than the invasion of England" was taken literally and the news kept from him while he slept.

September found Europe convulsed in spasms of armed conflict that were quickly climaxing toward some of the worst fighting the world had ever witnessed. The German assault on Russia's second largest city, Leningrad, had commenced as the Wehrmacht sought to consolidate the sweeping gains it had made in its blitzkrieg on Russia before the onset of cold weather forced it to halt.

Britain continued to stand alone. The blitz, as the British termed the attacks from planes dropping bombs and, later on, by V-1 and V-2 missiles, was still on and would continue on and off until near the end of the war. At the height of the "blitz days" in spring 1941, when German aerial attacks moved from London to the provinces, FDR sent a fact-finding mission headed by special envoy Averell Harriman to join U.S. Ambassador John G. Winant to tour some of Britain's hardest-hit areas.

Winston Churchill, recently back in power as prime minister, personally conducted this "blitz tour." At one point in the tour, after a walk-through of the bomb-ravaged Swansea docks, the party moved on to Bristol by rail. Before they reached the city the train was halted: The worst air raid of the war was taking place as wave after wave of Luftwaffe bombers droned overhead and the sound of bomb explosions mingled with the thunder of British flak guns. The party had to wait it out until the all-clear sounded.

The United States, by comparison, still largely clung to the belief that the country might yet escape involvement in the clash of weapons and political ideologies that had engulfed Europe, little knowing that in Japan plans were already well underway to stage a cross-Pacific surprise

attack intended to cripple U.S. naval power and buy critical time for
Japan to consolidate its own military gains. In August, Congress had
almost failed to pass legislation for a compulsory draft, in fact.

The Selective Service Act, passed by Congress by a wide margin
in 1940, and spurred by war fears following the fall of France and the
Battle of Britain, splashed across every newsreel screen and newspaper
front page, was now about to expire. In the summer of 1941, despite
the German blitzkrieg against Russia, the war seemed again remote
from U.S. shores; the British had held against the blitz, and the Nazis
had turned their fury eastward to Asia, not in the direction of Atlantic
shores. It was now again possible to believe that the nation would be
spared involvement in a second Great War after all.

Army chief General George C. Marshall had testified before
Congress that, with no conscription law to bring in replacements and
a large number of recent inductees scheduled for discharge, his service,
he asserted, would face disintegration. Congress, however, was as
complacent as was the public at large, who were now responding to
renewed warmongering charges against FDR in the news media, just
as they had responded to news of cross-Atlantic fighting only a few
months previous.

Congressman Sam Rayburn, virtually alone among congressional
leaders, was convinced otherwise and lobbied for a renewal of the
Selective Service Act. Rayburn's line, "I need your vote," echoed through
the halls of Congress throughout the months of summer. In the end the
draft law passed by the narrow margin of a single congressman's vote;
the final tally was 203 aye, 202 nay—victory by a hair.

With the Selective Service Act still in place, the War Department
could be assured that even if it hadn't yet accumulated the material and
strategic resources to wage large-scale war, it would meanwhile have the
manpower to call on when and if the time ever came to fully engage
the United States in battle. Few at the moment suspected how close
that time actually was, or how rapidly, and with what grave finality,
onrushing war was approaching the shores of the American homeland.

* * *

71

On September 11, 1941, the staccato pummeling of compressed air hammers, the incessant groaning of large, heavily laden trucks, and the lugubrious rumbling of construction equipment combined with the excited shouts, songs, and curses of a thousand day laborers across the swampy waste ground of Hell's Bottom. This day marked the groundbreaking for construction of the new War Department headquarters on the cross-Potomac lowlands of Arlington.

Earlier that morning a formal groundbreaking ceremony had been held at the building site. Officials and local dignitaries, whose ranks included National Capital Park and Planning Commission Chairman Frederic A. Delano, FDR's uncle, and Gilmore D. Clarke, president of the Washington Commission on Fine Arts, gave the project their blessings, if, in the case of Delano and Clarke, somewhat belated ones.

Delano, on behalf of both the White House and his organization, cut the red ribbon cordoning off the site from a small army of construction laborers who waited beside the ranks of political worthies and important local functionaries. Once they had left the scene whistles blew, workers' shouts rent the air, and all hell seemed to break loose under a clear, almost cloudless September sky as the men descended on the site like ravenous locusts onto a field of new summer wheat.

And ravenous they were: In the weeks prior to the start of construction, word had gone out at local union halls, such as the D.C. chapter of the International Brotherhood of Carpenters and Joiners Union, which supplied many workers, that a big new government project was to provide steady work with high wages. In an America which, thanks to the New Deal, was on its way to economic recovery but still shaky on its feet, such an announcement was like the promise of manna raining from the skies. Here was serious money, the kind that could stake you to something better, the kind that you could use for a down payment on a home or a car. Many of the men, still young, and having suffered through the Depression, had never seen this kind of opportunity before. It was, for many, the chance of a lifetime.

Workers, of all ages backgrounds, some highly skilled, others without experience but eager to work and learn, poured in from all over the region. Many came from the environs of Washington, D.C. Others hailed from rural communities in nearby Maryland and West Virginia, from hard-pressed coal mining sections of southern Pennsylvania and Virginia, and even farther south from North Carolina. Here was a gathering of the tribes to erect a mighty works that would not have been unfamiliar to those who, ages before, had built the Great Pyramid of Cheops or the enigmatic Sphinx.

On August 11, the three "time and material" prime contracts for the construction project had been awarded to bid-winning construction firms, and on September 3, the second working day after the long Labor Day weekend, the mechanical engineering contract had also been awarded. When work on the huge new building—it would cover the vast expanse of thirty-five acres—reached its apogee in the winter of 1941–1942, up to thirteen thousand men could be seen working day and night, around the clock, in fair weather and foul.

On this first day of construction, although the number of laborers was still a fraction of what it would soon swell to become, it seemed as though a ragtag army had descended on a battlefield smack in the middle of nowhere to wage a Quixotic crusade against the earth itself.

Management was ready to coordinate the start of construction. Planning groups at the War Department and the contractors, which included the Raymond Concrete Pile Company of Pennsylvania, the chief architects Bergstrom and Witmer, and other groups and individuals, had been working around the clock for months. During this time hundreds of interoffice meetings had been held to draw initial construction plans, to write specifications, and to prepare rough construction cost estimates.

In addition to these planning activities meetings had been convened to work out the sizes and locations of below-ground infrastructure, such as sewer lines, and to precisely and exactly determine where each of the thousands of massive, concrete-filled steel caissons that would anchor the building's foundation securely into the marshy ground of Hell's Bottom would be driven. All of this had need to be worked out in advance of the first spadeful of earth being turned.

On the groundbreaking day of September 11, some three thousand carpenters and thousands of other workers—including surveyors, drilling rig operators, bricklayers, iron workers, cement finishers, stonemasons, plasterers, painters, roofers, and various technical specialists such as electricians, plumbers, and steamfitters—were sent to work based on a carefully coordinated plan. Labor was divided into five construction crews that put up each of the five sides of the huge building, one side at a time.

The crews erected each side or "wedge," a term still used to describe the sections of the Pentagon today and which denoted the basic segments of renovation still in progress at this writing. The sides were put up in a clockwise direction. As each wedge was completed, beginning with Wedge 1 and continuing through Wedge 5, War Department staff began to move in and get to work.

The wedges, labeled 1 through 5—corresponding to the five massive rings that intersect the Pentagon's corridors—were constructed of reinforced concrete, with pale limestone facing available only from quarries in Indiana, added later on. These limestone quarries are the same ones that supplied the facing slabs that cover the Empire State Building and the Chicago Tribune Building and filled forty-six truckloads of replacement facing material after the September 11 attacks that set the western side of the building aflame sixty years later. The façade of the Pentagon that was struck by the hijacked plane in 2001 was, in fact, the first of the five sections to be started, originally called Section A by the work gangs that built it.

A brief description of how the work actually proceeded will help paint a picture of the start of the vast enterprise. Carpenter crews, for example, worked at five separate "mills" on an assembly line system. Each mill was centrally located near each of the five massive sections. The mills prepared all of the construction infrastructure that needed to be specially made on-site. Carpenters were essential to the process at this early stage, since the building was made almost entirely of concrete—a measure deliberately taken to save critical war materials—and the concrete was shaped into beams, slabs, columns, walls, and other construction elements by means of being poured into modular wooden forms.

Day in, day out, the mills churned out the basic building blocks of the pentagonal building arising from the quagmire of Hell's Bottom. It was almost like something being built on another planet, self-contained and using the raw materials under the workers' feet to bring it into being. An example again: Most of the sand used to make the more than 350,000 cubic yards of concrete necessary to build the huge edifice was dredged from the bed of the nearby Potomac.

This was an era before plywood and drywall; all the wooden forms were fashioned from three-quarter-inch, one-by-six and one-by-eight, tongue-and-groove boards that were assembled at the mills to make the forms, and then secured with battens—flexible wooden strips used in place of nails—to hold them in place and shape the forms to the proportions of the various final building elements. The grain-like impressions made on the hardened concrete by those same wooden forms are still visible today, giving the walls of the Pentagon a characteristic wood-grain appearance when viewed up close.

After the concrete hardened—say for a section of interior wall—the boards that made up the form were quickly separated from the building element by removing the battens; then they were reused. This, by today's construction standards, was an extremely labor-intensive process: It was the same then, too, but with the enormous manpower that could be drawn upon and the massive financing that was ready to be poured into the project, it was a feasible and time-critical arrangement.

The concrete was mixed at special "batch plants" separate from the mills and delivered to the pour sites by a fleet of ready-mix trucks, with colossal pours almost every Friday. These pours often lasted well into the deepening fall evenings. They were intended to allow the concrete to cure undisturbed over the weekend until work resumed on the following Monday. The mixing and pouring of all concrete was tightly controlled by government inspectors who monitored every phase of it. Somervell had no intention of the building washing away; he intended it to last.

Concrete also gave ballast to the steel caissons that anchored the vast building into the earth of the former swampland. These caissons were pounded down deep by steam hammers in clusters of three to twelve piles each, depending on the loads calculated by engineers on the building's columns. The caissons were first driven into the ground, to a depth where their tops projected roughly a foot above grade, and then poured full of concrete. After that, two-man carpenter crews assembled four-foot-high, prefabricated wood forms around each cluster, and steel reinforcing grids were installed. More concrete pours were made to make the foundation on which the building columns were anchored.

Big industrial drill rigs, operated by Raymond Concrete Pile, were in constant operation from almost the first few minutes of construction and worked round-the-clock, seven days a week for the duration of the project. They bored into the earth to excavate the pits into which the steel caissons were to be pounded down by the monster steam hammers.

At the end of the project, Raymond Concrete Pile—which had applied for and been granted a patent on those same caissons—had driven more than fifty thousand of them fifty feet into the clay substratum that underlay the marshy ground. The combination of the mammoth drills and Promethean steam hammers gave the sound of a strange, chugging, clanking, hissing, whooshing cadence that was audible for miles around, day and night. Hell's Bottom was not to give up its title quite yet; for the moment it looked, smelled, and sounded every inch a hell's little acre.

Overseeing the labor force was an upper, supervisory tier that was composed of experienced senior engineers and job foremen. This management body not only oversaw the day-to-day job activities of the work force putting up the building but was responsible for more than manpower issues. Their responsibilities included procurement, delivery, and placement of the enormous amounts of building materials and supplies, from steel pipe casings to the green slate tiles that covered the rooftop, that had to be available at the site each day and ready to be fed into the project's ravenous maw.

From that first day when ground was broken for the Pentagon until almost literally the last minute, work proceeded at a furious pace. Section D, completed on April 28, 1942, after eight months of nonstop effort by shifts of work crews, affords an example. At 8:30 on that April morning, crews that had labored through the night, pushing almost continuously for the preceding twenty-four hours to complete the section, were told by their foreman to quickly pick up their tools and go home.

As they left the building site, the first occupants of what was to become the Pentagon's River Entrance went to work. They were members of War Secretary Stimson's staff who had been assembled outside since the early dawn hours. With their appearance at what was then referred to as the "War Department's new pentagonal building," another milestone had been reached and an era ended. Henry Stimson's vision of the big new headquarters building, one that befitted the vastness of the growing U.S. military, had finally prevailed. This meant that the days of the Munitions Building as the nucleus of the army's extensive staff activities were in effect finally over. Those members of Stimson's team who went to work that morning had left their old offices at the sprawling Army-Navy headquarters, the mini-Pentagon on Constitution Avenue across the Potomac, and had begun a migration to "Somervell's Folly" in Arlington that was to usher in a new era for the entire defense community of the United States.

Gilmore Clarke, too, and his supporters in various Washington committees opposed to the building of the Pentagon, would also find themselves vindicated. Although the navy high command would remain at its old headquarters, the Main Navy Building that was part of the old complex on Constitution Avenue, for the duration of World War II, the army's great migration to the Pentagon marked the start of a process that would culminate, albeit decades distant from that moment, in the inevitable demolition of the Munitions–Main Navy Buildings and the reversion of the site on which they'd been built to municipal park land, a bucolic transmutation that persists to the present time.

* * *

Beyond this Herculean labor, there were other projects ancillary to the construction of the new War Department headquarters. Among their various outcomes would be to more than double the $35 million cost estimate for the construction project, by the mid-1940s, to the then truly astronomical price tag of about $85 million.

There were to be two major additional development projects to the building of the Pentagon itself, and the impact of both would be extensive. One was a massive landscaping project that would change the shape of and terrain features of the countryside near the new War Department building. The other was a network of highways and superhighways whose strategic as well as municipal functions would, in the end, make major changes on the American landscape, especially on the East Coast.

The Pentagon landscaping program that graded and resurfaced a rough, three-mile equilateral triangle surrounding the Building a little more than a mile on each side, added an additional $4 million to the total cost overrun. Both the landscaping and highway rebuilding and rerouting programs began in earnest when the five sides of the Pentagon had finally been put up. In the early weeks of 1943, residents of Arlington, who had like other Americans suffered through the national trauma of Pearl Harbor, but had also lived through the local shock and awe of an invasion of chugging, groaning, grinding machinery and unwashed armies of loud and often swaggering rubes from the surrounding boonies and 'burbs, awoke to the new consternation of fresh construction efforts.

The landscaping project was no secret: It had officially commenced in September 1942, but its sudden appearance, in full swing, with hundreds of pick-and-shovel-wielding work crews supported by what contemporary accounts describe as "upwards of one thousand" bulldozers and heavy trucks, moving tons of earth and stone, and lugging still more tons of grass seed between the Pentagon and the Potomac, came as a distinct and rude shock. What the locals soon discovered was that the pre–New Deal Hoover Airport, built in 1926 and officially known as Hoover Field, which had, by 1943, been incorporated into the greater limits of nearby Washington Airport, was being flooded to create a lagoon whose sole purpose was to enhance the vista from the Pentagon's River Entrance or, to use the War Department's words, "to beautify the land around the Pentagon."

But there was little that beleaguered Arlingtonians found beautiful in this new invasion of the landscape. Moreover, the architect of this fresh outrage was well known to the media; the name was as familiar to the good people of Arlington by now, and nearly as hated, as that of Hitler or Tojo: The fiendish Brehon Somervell had struck again. While it was true that Hoover Airport was normally inundated by flooding after heavy rains, the lagoon, which would before long be officially called the Pentagon Marina, meant additional torment in the form of noise, troublesome outsiders, and blocked local roads. Today, few, if any, who have left their cars on the Pentagon's sprawling North Parking Lot are aware that the marina at their backs was once part of Washington's only major airport complex and that it had been deliberately placed underwater to beautify and dignify the view from the outer E-Ring offices of the Pentagon's chief officials. No one, to be sure, would ever now liken the new War Department headquarters to "a provincial opera house."

Perhaps more important to the broader picture was the extensive reconstruction, renovation, and extension of the road infrastructure surrounding the massive new structure. Somervell's plans for the massive new five-sided building called for an additional twenty miles of new highway to be constructed around it at an additional cost overrun of approximately $21 million.

The intended purpose of the highway system—and the system was to include new and renovated bridges as well—was to relieve the congestion that a massive amount of new road traffic (including an envisioned commuter bus line) anticipated by the erection of the world's largest government office building would ineluctably cause. Like the humungous, walloping, whale of a building that it would support, this whopping new highway system was of a decidedly futuristic design and suitably expansive in its intended purpose and contemplated scale. The highway system would incorporate a unique cloverleaf arrangement with overpasses and underpasses, more than twenty of them on completion. This feature alone would distinguish it from anything like it built so far.

This radical new design was, among other things, intended to eliminate the bane of traffic stoplights, a feature of all the local highways in the vicinity. It was supposed to streamline and greatly accelerate the overall flow of vehicle traffic of all kinds. Today, highway cloverleaves are commonplace on interstate and local routes alike, but Somervell's plans marked the first time such a form of highway construction was ever attempted, in the United States or anywhere else in the world. The highway's construction was almost as great a feat as that of the War Department headquarters building—and almost as expensive. Contractors moved more than five million cubic yards of dirt to make room for it, and somewhere between one and a half and two million man-hours were necessary to build it.

The highway project cost an additional $28 million and, along with landscaping and other cost overruns, raised the building's price tag to about $85 million on the overall project's completion in 1943. We'll shortly come to a closer look at the strategic importance of the new highways that still has bearing on our daily lives in the form of the interstate system.

CHAPTER SIX

ON THE BRINK OF WAR

As lofty an undertaking as the erection of the Pentagon might have been, it was merely a portion of a massive reorganization of both the military establishment and the federal government that took place at around the same time. The pace, extent, and magnitude of rearmament and the restructuring of the national military power structure were unprecedented. Moreover, the dual processes of extensive reorganization and expansive growth seemed destined to accelerate despite persistent and concerted efforts to block them by political opponents in Congress and their counterparts, constituents, intellectual collaborators, and allies in the commercial sector.

The national experience with Wilsonian measures had by this time led to a widespread national resentment toward and backlash against any plans or initiatives smacking of Wilsonism in any way, shape, or form. When Americans in the 1930s heard the name of the president who had preceded Roosevelt, albeit some twelve years and three presidential administrations removed, and traversing the preceding terms of Harding, Coolidge, and Hoover, they reflexively thought about utopian measures that had gone badly awry and grandiose visions of a world government that had climaxed in the bitterest experience with warfare on foreign soil ever suffered by America's sons.

By the time FDR took office, the isolationist sentiment was strong; it had become deeply rooted in the American grain. Roosevelt was popularly viewed as intent on dragging the United States into yet another Herculean death struggle to be fought in Europe. To millions of the president's countrymen it was axiomatic that to get involved with the military affairs of Europeans was suicidal. Indeed, most felt it was worse than merely suicidal, given the hardships of the Great Depression. It was also insane.

Congress, mirroring the popular will, had consistently blocked or waffled on the passage of legislation throughout the interwar period that would have led to a heightening of U.S. war preparedness. Even when national lawmakers did finally enact new and stronger national defense measures, the bills inevitably came off the House floor as compromise legislation that had, to all intents, been whittled down to largely impuissant skeletal vestiges of more robust lawmaking.

By means of neutrality legislation to impede White House initiatives to aid U.S. European allies in the fight against Hitler, by feeding public suspicion that FDR secretly intended to maneuver the country into yet another pointless and wasteful European conflict, by blocking U.S. membership in international organizations that were opposed to Axis hegemony of Europe and the war aims of the dictators, and by many other efforts and stratagems great and small, Congress—and not the White House—effectively ran foreign policy during the interwar years.

Nevertheless, and in spite of these turns of national events and obstacles of public opinion, the trend for both the U.S. political government and the country's defense establishment was to inevitably spread out and become larger and larger. It was almost manifest destiny that drove this trend, represented by the kind of traumatic event that, much later, had similar effects on and in the aftermath of September 11, 2001.

A scant three months after the rudimentary groundwork on the Pentagon was first laid down, the Japanese attacked Pearl Harbor, changing the course of world events, turning doves into hawks overnight by the millions, and dooming, in consequence, the Nipponese program for military conquest to inevitable defeat as surely as the final domino in a snaking line will fall once the first is toppled.

Practically overnight, the country was galvanized into action, the isolationist policies that Congress had enacted for years with popular backing were discredited, and in the mind of the public the lawmakers on Capitol Hill were no longer seen as competent to set defense policy for the country but were viewed with a scorn befitting pusillanimous

Milquetoasts, craven cowards, and worse. In a complete about-face of public sentiment it was now the president in the person of FDR, and the institution of the presidency, that was again perceived to be the proper seat of leadership for the nation.

As well as being a complete turnaround that lionized the president and toppled his once unassailable opponents in Congress, and in finance and industry, from their catbird seats, the winds of war and change acted like a powerful booster shot for Roosevelt, allowing the White House to have more power to direct foreign policy than ever a modern president had wielded before. Once it became clear that America was at war, and irrevocably committed to fight, Congress reversed course and granted the president sweeping powers to prosecute that war.

In short, after Pearl Harbor the White House possessed what was tantamount to a rubber stamp—on virtually everything to which it saw fit to apply its imprimatur.

Yet while Pearl Harbor was a powerful catalyst to change, and one that precipitated American firmness in the face of danger, much like a shock wave causes crystalline matter to magically materialize from out of clear solution, it wasn't magic, or fate or emotion, or sudden anger at a dastardly sneak attack that caused the change—a hammer blow had pounded the American psyche into place like a nail in a hole, but the point of the nail had been in the hole for some time; it had just needed to be driven all the way in.

Behind the scenes, impetus against isolationism had been slowly, almost invisibly, building. In truth, it had been there all along. With the attack on Pearl Harbor it had simply reached a point of psychological critical mass. Although the forces hostile to development and change were powerful and far-flung, there were also forces sympathetic and receptive to change. Their voices had been few, and faint, but they had been there all along, on the fringes of national perception.

Even as a powerfully isolationist Congress, reflecting popular sentiment and the will of influential business alliances, curbed defense and reigned in the war-making powers of the presidency, the landscape of Washington, D.C., was changing, developing, and growing, and a wave of building projects was transforming the nation's capital from what it had been before the Great War into something much more closely resembling the bustling center of government that it is today.

Throughout the country new military bases were going up, including stepped-up construction of new naval installations originally proposed by the navy's Hepburn Board in 1938, along with a vast infrastructure of major national highways and secondary roads. The onset of World War II acted as the primary stimulus for the passage of congressional legislation for a forty-one thousand mile national network of limited-access highways, known then as the National System of Interstate and Defense Highways.

Today, long after their original defensive purpose has been forgotten, they're simply called the Interstate Highway System. Collectively constituting, in many respects, an undertaking even more ambitious than the construction of the Building itself, the interstate system, begun in 1942, was scheduled for completion in the then far-flung future year of 1972! The plan, once begun, was carried out almost exactly as its planners originally envisioned. And, while the highway program was national in scope, the manifestations of its local origins in the vicinity of the War Department's colossal new Arlington headquarters were highly visible in 1942. The intricate network of cloverleaves and strange, snaking blacktop whorls, corollas, and curlicues that twisted, wound, and curved around the immense five-sided fortress in an approximate twenty-eight-mile circumference would cost taxpayers in the vicinity of $20 million. The futuristic new highway complex, its like never seen before on the American landscape, looked every bit as expensive as indeed it was. Nevertheless, it was to be only the beginning of a far greater highway system that would, in due course, link East Coast with West in a sprawling interstate system nationally underwritten but built by state contractors.

While each state was responsible for the construction of sections of the interstate in its respective territory, the states had to build according to federal guidelines that incorporated requirements set forth by the Department of Defense, with Washington contributing 90 percent of the total cost, including overruns, of which there were many that cropped up over the years it took to build the network. A similar state of affairs governed the construction of the so-called "primary system" of secondary or intracity highways and parkways, with the federal government and states each shouldering 50 percent of the overall construction costs.

These new highway systems also differed from preceding road networks in the United States in that they were intended to fulfill dual peacetime and wartime roles. On the one hand they were seen as necessary to accommodate the growing vehicular traffic foreseen as the nation grew in population and expanded in domestic and foreign commercial sectors, but the interlocking network of national, state, and local roads was all along intended to serve another purpose—one defensive in nature. As World War II brought the threat of war with the Japanese to the nation's Pacific coastal reaches and boded conflict with the Axis powers in Europe eastward from America's founding shores, the military sought both to reduce the vulnerability of the nation to the consequences of further surprise attack and to speed the movement of troops and war materiel to coastal port facilities.

The new highways were intended to serve as the key to both objectives. The entire complex network of main highways and secondary roads, as well as the bridges that served them, was designed to enable military vehicles and troop and supply convoys to bypass major urban centers, such as New York City, whose road network was likely to become clogged with civilian traffic in time of major attack. Instrumental to this design was the final major bridge in the decades-long national construction plan, one that was fully completed only in 1964: the Verrazano-Narrows Bridge that spans the Hudson River Narrows between New York City's boroughs of Brooklyn and Staten Island.

Moreover, toward achieving the grand design of the dual-use, civilian- and military-capable highway network, all sections of the highway system that were earmarked to serve as military routes were specially reinforced to allow them to safely accommodate heavy military trucks, armored vehicles, tank-carriers, and similar vehicles and equipment.

Not only do these routes remain designated with their original dual functions on military maps of NORTHCOM (the Pentagon's command echelon for the continental United States) to the present day, but the entire interstate system—such as Interstate Route 87, which runs from

New York City to Albany and Buffalo and is familiar to millions as the New York State Thruway—continues to bear the military shield emblem bestowed on it as a mark of its defensive nature long ago.

Ironically, the very bridges and tunnels that were once key components of this defensive road network conceived and begun during the dark days of World War II as bulwarks against surprise enemy attacks are now themselves primary targets for terrorists, guarded day and night by police vehicles, scanned at entrance and exit points by nuclear detection devices, and watched over by police and military helicopters around the clock.

* * *

Reorganization of national infrastructure on the brink of World War II was fueled not only by the flames of rekindled nationalism in the wake of the kamikaze attack on Pearl Harbor—another shock to the nation underlay the profound restructuring as surely as it underlay isolationism: the Great Depression itself.

While defense initiatives such as the Rearmament Act of 1938 or the War Recovery Bill of 1940 were stalled in Congress, Roosevelt's New Deal—a colloquial term with a nativist ring that had been in use probably as early as the 1840s and that the FDR White House picked up and made its own—enjoyed popular support, and it did manage to secure consistent, if at times reluctant, funding from congressional legislators. The New Deal, in turn, sparked numerous programs of public works on a grand scale, for these were both the only kinds of government-sponsored employment legislation that could put large numbers of citizens to work on short notice and the only kinds that could mobilize industry to higher levels of production at Washington's behest and in the face of stark economic conditions.

Given these facts, it was almost inevitable that, in the teeth of worsening conditions in Europe and the Nazi invasion of Poland in 1939, more and more of the growing industrial output of the United States would be turned toward the production of the armaments of modern warfare.

In this light the construction of the Pentagon can itself be viewed as an organic development of New Deal economics. An isolationist Congress might curtail the production of bombs, bullets, warplanes, and battleships, but the construction of an office building—even the largest one in the world and the home of the U.S. War Department—that was another matter entirely.

If the New Deal made anything palatable to America, it was building. Ayn Rand's novels of swashbuckling entrepreneurism, written during this same era, seem to encapsulate the trend toward a burgeoning industrial might and a giantism in construction projects that had gripped the American psyche, even if most people didn't realize it at the time. Hank Reardon, inventor of the super-powerful "Reardon Metal," the hero of Rand's novel *Atlas Shrugged*, seems in many ways to be the physical embodiment of the pervasive lines of force gravitating the nation toward the buildup of the American urban landscape that began taking place with growing power throughout the interwar years and which was stimulated to even greater prodigies of output as the economic stimulus of New Deal legislation began finally kicking in.

Could Rand have even been thinking of people like Brehon Somervell, or even his nemesis Gilmore Clarke, when she wrote the *Fountainhead* or the later *Atlas Shrugged*? The prospect is tantalizing. Like Reardon, Somervell's grand building project was considered a "folly." Its champion, also like Reardon, was an iconoclast who defied conventional yet hidebound authority, as represented by a decidedly Clarkesque protagonist, and who almost single-handedly went his own way to see that his vision was finally set in stone, steel, and poured concrete.

Also, like the buildings described in Rand's blockbuster paeans to the builder and his works, the Pentagon was a huge, streamlined mammoth of a construction project. Like its fictitious counterparts it was viewed with distaste by fussy, stodgy, and outmoded proponents of an already vanished era of construction and aesthetics, much like the real-life opponents of the Pentagon, as represented by Gilmore D. Clarke of the Washington Fine Arts Committee. The Pentagon was a monolithic, streamlined colossus that was the antithesis of all that Clarke held dear, although Clarke was in reality a visionary in his own right. With his bias toward architectural forms that conform to existing buildings and landscape and incorporate green spaces in their plans, he was in many regards a far more modern and futuristic thinker than Somervell.

Like Ayn Rand's novels, the Pentagon was the 1940s vision of futurity that flew in the face of conventional aesthetics—witness the furor raised by its real or imagined impact on the West Virginia suburban spaces it was to occupy. Both Clarke and the president's uncle, Frederic A. Delano, charged that the Pentagon would disrupt the view of the capital as one looked across the expanse of the old Hoover Airport and the adjacent Potomac River.

Numerous others, again including FDR's uncle, defamed the proposed headquarters of the War Department as a troublesome eyesore. Only after years of existence had made the Pentagon a familiar sight on the landscape did the Building seem anything but an overgrown monstrosity that the White House had dumped into the lap of decent suburbanites trying to live their lives without having to look at this huge cement blob dropped haphazardly in their midst. It could be that what the protectors of all things beautiful and serene in Virginia and Washington, D.C., were really rebelling against was something else entirely.

Like the ruthlessly driven builders of the Ayn Rand novels, the Pentagon was form wedded to function in a totally uncompromising way. It represented a future that was hurtling toward the present, a Trojan asteroid that was destined to obliterate and destroy all vestiges of a slower, less contentious, and less machine-driven past.

And there was something else, something that had to be lingering at the edges of peoples' consciousness: The Pentagon was a building dedicated to global, industrialized warfare. Its construction said eloquently what most Americans didn't want to hear; indeed it satanically whispered the very last thing that most of them wanted to hear. The Pentagon's existence declared that war was coming, and it was going to be a very big and very nasty war, dumped into the laps of formerly isolationist Americans the same way Washington had done with the giant War Department headquarters, and there was no way to avoid it. The three million-pound gorilla was now a fact on the landscape.

The Pentagon, in short, was the embodiment of war parked in the midst of a sleeping America. It was a wake-up call to defense that most good citizens, only lately having emerged from the Great Depression and still beset with woes of their own, were only too eager to ignore.

And who could blame them? Wake-up calls are unpleasant things. But they're often necessary just the same. The Japanese attack on Pearl Harbor only months after the Building began going up served only to demonstrate the need for the eyesore on Arlington's lowlands that so many had wished would go somewhere else.

* * *

The late interwar period, was an era that owed its character to a few determined individuals, a handful who made things happen, even if they had to sometimes break the rules in order to do it. Brehon Somervell was one of them. Franklin Roosevelt was another. A third was George Marshall, a name associated with the Pentagon from its inception.

Marshall, as mentioned earlier, was, since 1937 when he was groomed to succeed General Malin Craig as army chief of staff, a key force behind the Building's establishment. The native Kentuckian had been hand-picked by Roosevelt.

In those days, prior to the establishment of the modern-day Joint Chiefs of Staff, the land battle was the main object of study for military strategists. (Clausewitz had, after all, based his famous treatise of warfare, *On War*, solely on the land battle. Despite Great Britain's historical mastery of the sea, the laurels of war had been won by commanders mostly in field engagements since the Napoleonic and later wars of the nineteenth and early twentieth centuries.) It is, of course, true that naval warfare had historically made or broken national hegemons and that Alfred Thayer Mahan's *On Sea Power* was a treatise on strategy of equal import to that of Clausewitz. However, the fact incontrovertibly remains that it was the billet of chief of the army that was the zenith of career accomplishment in the U.S. military establishment during the post–World War I years.

Marshall went to work immediately, shaking things up toward meeting his brief of reorganizing the U.S. military from top to bottom.

Marshall, who had been the army's chief planner and organizer in the days before a world war again snared America in its web, remained its principal director in all theaters from the conflict's dismal beginnings down to its triumphant and victorious conclusion.

Never has one commander, through his own well-forged chain of command, possessed such a broad-ranging responsibility for the army's size, organization, equipment, training procedures, doctrine, order of battle, and overarching strategy that determined how its forces coordinated with all other American and allied military arms—indeed, for the very timing of its actions, defensive and offensive alike, tactical, strategic, and logistical in scope.

Marshall was abetted by a relative handful of aides and advisors that formed a tightly knit circle around him. The motivations and actions of many if not most of the decisions made by this close-knit group, which had the utmost impact on the prosecution of World War II and the Cold War that followed, were largely kept verbal. Little or no consistent record exists. Nevertheless, Marshall's six-year chieftainship, coupled with the generally harmonious relations with the president and Congress and Marshall's popular approval throughout his term, was a prime factor in the welding together of U.S. and Allied fighting forces during World War II to form a military machine that, once going, could not be stopped.

CHAPTER SEVEN

THE NATION GOES TO WAR

"Where were you born?"
"Brooklyn."
"Any other defects?"
—Army doctor to recruit in G.I. picture, 1945

W hen Japanese kamikaze pilots flying Zeros staged an attack on the U.S. Naval base at Pearl Harbor on December 7, 1941, the need for a reorganization of the U.S. defense capabilities became obvious to everyone. The construction of the Pentagon was then only in its first stages; it would be completed almost a year and a half later, at around the same time that Allied efforts to turn the battle tide were beginning to show their first signs of success in North Africa and just before the third, and critically decisive, Soviet offensive against the German invasion of the Russian heartland the previous summer had begun.

These developments were still some time away, though. As, wedge by concrete wedge, the Pentagon began to rise from Hell's Bottom, the United States was still grappling with domestic problems and was not yet ready to face, let alone commit itself to, the prospect of fighting a second great war. Still, while it might have been in a state of mass denial about the impending war, the nation was nevertheless in a state of slow but steady transition. Reorganization was proceeding, but it moved along at a snail's pace.

Since September 11, 1941, when the first excavations for its foundation were made, the Pentagon had been going up rapidly. The day-to-day business activities of the U.S. War Department were still being largely conducted amid the widely scattered offices that were situated in and around the nation's capital—a state of affairs not to be seen again for sixty years, when Pentagon offices were again relocated following the attacks of 9/11. During these first few months of the Building's existence, the nation, too, began to gather fortitude, like a giant rousing itself from a long slumber, awakened by sounds of onrushing discord that it could no longer ignore.

The quick fall of France to the German army in 1940 came as a blow to even the most devout isolationists in Congress and an element representing what historian Samuel B. Huntington had once dubbed "business pacifism" in the private sector, as well as in the American public. Suddenly France lay in the hands of the Third Reich and Great Britain stood alone between Hitler's Nazi minions and the United States.

As much as isolationist feeling was still central, the mood of the country had already begun to shift to the right, and this rightward shift was steadily picking up speed and momentum. The Neutrality Act of 1937, which had mandated America's keeping its nose out of Europe's business, at least as far as war went, was now being talked about as needing repeal. The Hatch Act of August 1939, which made membership in any organization advocating the overthrow of the government a bar to federal employment, was a step in the opposite direction.

America was in transition, and while by the middle of 1941 it was not yet ready to resign itself to the inevitable, it was still poles apart from Wilsonian dogma of the kind that had gripped it since the end of the Great War. There was a sense in the streets, in the bars, and in the minds of the Anglo-American populace that war was close at hand. George Orwell had given voice to premonitions of approaching turmoil for the British in his premonitory novel, *Coming up for Air*, published in 1937. The book's protagonist, a householder of the British middle class, is plagued by persistent visions of a new, titanic struggle against a Fascist, totalitarian enemy whose aftermath leads to an adumbration of the dystopia that he later created in his postwar novel, *1984*.

In the United States, Sinclair Lewis and others of the so-called Ashcan School also sniffed the wind and knew that something rank was on its way, and that it would arrive quickly and overstay its welcome. There were some who, like Ernest Hemingway, did seem in their writings to welcome the miasmic winds of conflict, who reveled in the dark, sweet ecstasies of the mass death wish for total war that throbbed in the repressed depths of the human psyche.

Ezra Pound, another contemporary literary figure, whose mawkish adoration of Mussolini and idealization of Italian fascism eventually led him to make a notorious sojourn in a mental institution, called poets, and by extension creative artists of any discipline, the "antennae of the race." By the late 1930s these antennae were distinctly quivering with forebodings of many sorts. Clearly something was in the air, and it was getting closer and closer to home.

THE NATION GOES TO WAR

The Pentagon was completed during the initial years of World War II. The headquarters of the War Department had begun to house its first occupants almost immediately, and as each new wedge of the five-sided building was completed, more staff took occupancy. Day-to-day operations began to take place from the start, continuing throughout the war as work on the Building proceeded toward its eventual completion.

Officially, the first occupants moved in by April 29, 1942, almost a year and a half since the Japanese raid on Pearl Harbor and about nine months before the official completion of Pentagon construction on January 15, 1943. Unofficially, the date of first occupancy came somewhat sooner. Working groups of mixed military staff and civilian personnel, spread across the capital and in as remote and ignoble reaches of the Washington exurbs as a bathroom-sized office in back of somebody's brother-in-law's service station in Fredericksburg, were understandably more than eager to move to better workplaces.

All except the navy, which by and large cherished its spacious and by then tradition-rich headquarters on Constitution Avenue, and whose leadership was in no great hurry to leave. The collective memory of the Puzzle Palace still recalls how War Secretary Stimson, given to pithy statements and well aware of the navy's lack of enthusiasm for what might be justly termed the House the Army Built, remarked, round about November 1943, that "the lion and the lamb are preparing to lie down together."

93

Wisecracks about the navy moving across the Potomac to what the era's media bluntly characterized as "the army's sprawling, 42-acre Pentagon building" were rife. The wisecracks turned to practical jokes as the impending move to Arlington from the navy's cherished fortress in Washington neared. In one case, a bogus memorandum, on official U.S. Fleet stationery, appeared on the desks of navy personnel. Among other things, it advised recipients that "Personnel are cautioned not to become panic-stricken by the great expanses of corridor (of which the Pentagon has 8 miles). Rumors concerning lost safaris in the Pentagon are hereby discounted, inasmuch as all but one of these safaris have been located and rescued. . . . Trained search parties will be on duty, and all corridor intersections will be patrolled at least once every two days."

Although naval intelligence was summoned to root out the culprit or culprits responsible for the memo, Pentagon lore has it that they were never found. As to the admirals and the navy's higher echelons, they all found ways and means to circumvent or entirely avoid the move to the army's house for the duration of the war.

In an over-networked era in which most important decisions in every sector of American life seem to be made by committee, such rivalries and turf-consciousness seem as ludicrous in hindsight as the opposition of a single individual, no matter how powerful, to moving the War Department into a brand new building that had only recently been completed and to demand that an entirely new one be built. Ludicrous, perhaps, but also true. Secretary of War Henry L. Stimson's single-minded determination that no member of his War Department staff occupy the low-rise, modernist building that Stimson despised had consigned the key personnel that made the gears of the United States' war machine turn to remain at the now-infamous "seventeen buildings" far longer than anticipated, no matter that the not unpleasing Munitions Building was the main hub of all the others.[6]

6. Stimson's 1929 quip, while Hoover's secretary of state, that "Gentlemen do not read each others' mail," was one of his more notorious remarks and demonstrates Stimson's penchant for strong biases that, from his position of power, often led (like his opposition to the War Department Building) to unprecedented and controversial outcomes. Stimson's 1929 pronouncement was meant to show his displeasure with a nascent U.S. spy capability, in this particular case that of cryptologist Herbert O. Yardley's so-called Black Chamber, an early intelligence analysis office set up to break secret foreign military and diplomatic ciphers. During World War II, as an article in the April 2007 *Cryptologia* magazine claims, Stimson demanded that libraries across the country pull all material on explosives, secret inks, and ciphers from circulation and report the names of anyone requesting said materials to the FBI.

In an age in which the word *Pentagon* evokes, among other things, inevitable images of cutting-edge technology in the service of fighting war—precision guided munitions, stealth aircraft, nuclear submarines, and banks of enormous screens showing multiple views of a terrorist in the Hindu Kush or an insurgent in Iraq's hostile enclaves blown to smithereens by a Reaper UCAV—the impressions made by the Pentagon's humble beginnings seem preposterous by contrast, occasionally even laughable.

Yet there was nothing even remotely laughable about the global events that had the lights burning late into the night inside those scattered workplaces. Well before the aptly named Day of Infamy of December 7, 1941, the Four Horsemen of the Apocalypse were galloping through most of the world at a breakneck pace.

A relatively short time after the first cornerstone of the Pentagon was laid down in the boggy ground of Hell's Bottom, five divisions with two hundred tanks crossed the Egyptian frontier into Sollum, forcing the British Western Desert force, consisting of the Seventh Armored and Fourth Indian Division, to withdraw. The British had been routed in France at Dunkirk in late May and early June of the previous year; they'd witnessed the swift surrender of their French allies, were pummeled by successive blitz attacks, and were facing the imminent threat of Hitler's well-publicized Operation Sea Lion, the Nazi invasion of the British Isles using airborne blitz tactics and a massive armada. In the fall of 1941 Germany also invaded Russia; the Siege of Leningrad began some three days before the founding of the Pentagon. In the Pacific and Asia, the armies of Japan already held considerable territory under the guns of the conqueror and were planning their secret masterstroke against the United States to fall before the end of the year.

This is just a snapshot, of course, but it more than serves to illustrate the seriousness of events that the War and Navy departments needed to take into account on a daily basis in their preparations for U.S. defense reorganization in the late interwar period. Consolidating the War Department's staff under one roof was, under the circumstances, a vital necessity, especially in a pre-cybernetic age in which no computer networks existed and in which there were only rudimentary technological means available for rapidly sharing information between adjacent offices, let alone from opposite corners of the nation's capital.

As the shock waves from Pearl Harbor widened like Yeats had predicted in his revelatory poem, and the blitzkrieg worsened in Europe and spread eastward into Russia, as a remilitarized Japan made fresh conquests in the Philippines, the military reawakening of the United States quickened.

Immediately following Pearl Harbor, Congress amended the U.S. Selective Service Act, lengthening the term of military service from one year to the war's duration, plus six additional months. The new draft legislation applied principally to all males between the ages of eighteen and forty-five who were judged medically fit for duty in the armed forces. This age group would be the first to be inducted, but all males between the ages of eighteen and sixty-five had to register with their local draft boards.

By the end of 1942, the army's functional strength stood at approximately 5.4 million. The figure included better than seven hundred thousand African Americans, most of whom served in segregated support units, despite an executive order of June 25, 1941, expressly forbidding discrimination based on race, creed, color, or national origin in the federal government and by federal contractors. African Americans were also among the laborers who built the Pentagon. The construction was under federal jurisdiction, the site having been acquired from the state of Virginia. Nevertheless, while the Army Corps of Engineers largely observed federal desegregation regulations, it followed the dictates of Virginia law in at least one odd respect: Though work gangs were models of integration, lavatories still remained segregated. On an inspection trip to the Pentagon site, Roosevelt was astonished to find four huge washrooms placed along each floor of the five axes that connected the Building's E to A Rings. Some of these washrooms were reserved for the use of white workers, others for those who were black.

All in all, a massive force of Americans was being assembled to fight this new and turbulent kind of mechanized, maniacally kinetic war against barbaric enemies who were fleet, devious, cruel, murderous, merciless, and bent on taking over as lords of the earth. The thousands of uniformed military and civilian staff who were already roughing it in makeshift work environments in the widely scattered offices of the War Department had their work cut out for them; they needed all the space they could get.

CHAPTER EIGHT

THE U.S. WAR MACHINE
IN WORLD WAR II

The U.S. Army under Marshall was faced with a formidable task. America was at war. It had declared war on the Axis powers—Germany, Japan, and Italy—a day after the Japanese attack in Hawaii. After Pearl Harbor, Congress gave increasing power to the president to direct both foreign policy and military mobilization.

Sweeping changes in public attitudes as a result of that kamikaze raid on a U.S. naval base reflected the new direction the nation had taken. Gasoline was rationed and everything from old clothes to scrap metal was recycled. Women began replacing men in factories that had either been rapidly built as war plants or had been retooled from their original production of commercial goods to turn out planes, tanks, and the bombs and munitions they either dropped or fired. Victory gardens were planted to supplement rationed food, and war bonds were issued and sold to finance government defense spending.

The War Department had a new headquarters, the draft legislation narrowly renewed and soon after fortified by congressional legislation provided the chiefs of staff with a vast pool of manpower to fight the war that Roosevelt had just declared, and, by comparison with the early interwar years, Congress had turned on the money faucet full throttle, pouring the first of almost limitless funds into the coffers of the U.S. armed services. The winds of change had blown full circle by now, but though the War Department found itself replete with fresh opportunities, it also found itself confronted by unaccustomed problems, faced with arduous tasks, and challenged by perplexing Gordian knots.

Marshall, officially appointed as army chief of staff in September 1939 and installed in his predecessor General Malin Craig's suite of offices in the Munitions Building (close enough to War Secretary Stimson's own offices to be reached by the secretary via what contemporary usage terms "sneakernet" for direct consultation) was now a full four-star general (he'd been acting chief since July of that year) with full authority of command. He'd been charged with expanding the army and its air force, and preparing them for full-scale, global war, but there was a catch: the recommendations of the Harbord Board. This panel had been convened by Congress in 1929 to draw up a blueprint for military reorganization in the event of another large-scale war. The blueprint had already set the pattern for reorganization by the time Marshall was appointed as chief of staff.

Marshall regarded the recommendations of the Harbord Board with skepticism, even scorn. The board's findings, based on a study of military preparedness made under the direction of Stimson's predecessor, the soon-to-be-removed isolationist War Secretary Harold H. Woodring, was a little more than a love song to the status quo. Having looked at the naked emperor, it had reported him clothed in customary raiment. The next war, the board had decreed, would be little different from that of World War I and very little in the way of the U.S. military order of battle needed changing. This included the organization of the structure of the army's general staff.

By the time Congress declared war on the Axis powers after Pearl Harbor, Marshall, who'd seen the board's recommendations as the native Kentuckian he was sees what's on the floor of a horse stable, was determined to sweep the existing structure aside and adopt an entirely new organizational approach to the many problems the United States faced in preparing to fight. The next war would pose problems and risks of an infinitely complex nature as compared with the previous war, and the existing blueprint for change was far behind the curve. Among the challenges to the chief of staff was the problem child that needed to be quickly weaned off its pabulum and raised to manhood—the U.S. Army. By the time Congress declared war on the Axis, the armed forces were a pale shadow of their former strength in World War I.

Following Pearl Harbor, millions of men were both either drafted into the U.S. military or volunteered for service. The assembled manpower reserve was large and growing larger, but numbers didn't count much in an age of what would come to be called industrial warfare, and the shavetail troops needed considerable training. The Germans were convinced that Americans didn't know how to fight, that the American G.I. couldn't stand up against the Wehrmacht soldier. The British tended to agree, wondering if the Yanks had the right stuff. The Americans had plenty of bluster and bravado, surely they had this, but could they cut the mustard when it came to a real fight?

Training this enormous army of green troops, and setting up the monumental logistics chains necessary to support it on the sea, in the air, and on foreign soil; manufacturing, stockpiling, and convoying armaments, spare parts, and ammunition to the far-flung corners of the earth; liaising with and coordinating war plans with our allies, chief among which were the often thorny British represented by a bulldog in a burgandy-colored velvet siren suit—all of these tasks and more like them faced the American military on the eve of World War II.

The U.S. Navy was also confronted by a unique set of challenges as the country geared up for war, although these were different from those faced by the army, nor were they in most regards as thorny as those that the army had to confront in the late 1930s. For one thing, the navy was not faced with the same time pressure as was the army, which, in pursuit of the Germany First Doctrine espoused by Stimson and Roosevelt, would, with troops, tanks, and aircraft, be the main fighting arm that would be poured into the European fray when and if war came. The set of contingency war plans, collectively known as the Rainbow Plans, which were by the end of the interwar period distilled and redrafted by the War and Navy departments into a set of recommendations code-named Rainbow Five, also presumed that the first and greatest danger to the United States would come from the Axis powers in Europe, not from Japan. The navy's organizational setup, doctrine, shipbuilding programs, and the rest, were also not in the same kind of trouble as were the corresponding functions and structures of the interwar army, nor was the navy faced with the same perceived need to consolidate its staff echelons under a single large, pentagonal roof as the army was, being well sited in the Main Navy Building.

In contemporary terms, the interwar army was "broken," while the navy was not. The Mahan Doctrine, the accepted blueprint for war on the high seas, remained unchallenged, and the Hepburn Board, established in 1938 as a successor to the Harbord Board and chaired by Admiral Arthur Japy Hepburn, made far more reasonable and realistic assessments of the navy's requirements for any impending wartime challenges, including recommending a nationwide construction of new naval bases, which began soon afterward, and the expansion of the U.S. Marine Corps, which went into full swing immediately after the war's outbreak.

Even following the damage done to the U.S. battle line after the attack on Pearl Harbor in 1941, the navy had little cause to challenge the fundamental tactical and strategic basis for its wartime role, for these remained as sound after the attack as they had been previously. Indeed, in the first six months after U.S. entry into World War II, and as the navy began to recover from the damage done to the fleet at Pearl Harbor, its operations were doctrinally consistent with prewar plans, including those of the Hepburn Board. These included the patrol and protection of U.S. territorial waters and escorting cross-Atlantic convoys in partnership with the Royal Navy. The operations in support of the landings in North Africa in 1942, the Battle of the Coral Sea in the Pacific against the Japanese fleet of that same year, the massive D-day armada of 1944, and the pivotal sea battles against Japan in the Pacific theater, demonstrated that the navy did not have the same pressing need to reinvent itself as did the army in the face of the Axis threat.

Indeed, it was the navy that began playing an active role even as army forces struggled to reorganize, regroup, and rearm against the Axis. While the army would see battle across the Atlantic, one of the navy's most important roles would be to defend the territorial shores of the United States against the threat of German U-boats attacking maritime shipping and Europe-bound troop convoys or attempting to land saboteurs and spies along the coasts. It's also true that the intelligence and operational planning staff for the bulk of these operations were run out of a secret office complex throughout most of World War II near New York City's Battery that was listed on the navy's table of organization as the nonexistent "Tenth Fleet," a fact only made public some fifteen years after the war's end.

An exhaustive account of the myriad activities of the Pentagon during World War II, as they connected to the battles of that war, is beyond the scope of this book, for it would take an entire book to document them. What's more, the story of the Pentagon is eclipsed by the story of World War II itself, which is the story of battles, and this story has already been told in countless forms, while the Pentagon's story has remained largely in shadow.

Emblematic of the role played by the Pentagon in World War II, as it was emblematic of the Pentagon's role throughout the Cold War and as it remains today, is its function as the organizational hub of the armed forces of the United States, one that's not only responsible for developing military doctrine but also for making sure all the right wheels turn in the right places in which the far-flung forces of the United States find themselves at any given moment. Perhaps at no other time in history was the Pentagon as committed to that role as it was in the months preceding and following D-day, the invasion of Fortress Europe via the French coast of Normandy in June 1944.

Commanding the army's effort from the "War Department's pentagon headquarters" in the spring of 1944 was a newly appointed chief of the Army Service Forces, which was the branch of the army in charge of supplying U.S. forces overseas. The new chief had just been ordered to procure, package, ship, and disperse more than one hundred thousand items needed for the army's pre-invasion stockpile, from boxcars to bazookas, from shoelaces to hand grenades.

He happened to be the same "lank, dandified," Brehon Somervell who had built the Pentagon, "a grim man with a bad cold and a hell of a job ahead," according to one of Washington's daily newspapers, who had returned from the Cairo Conference in Egypt the previous fall (at which the date for D-day had been set) with a new assignment, from Marshall, of getting it all done fast. By the middle of May 1944, the stockpiles of prepositioned materiel, at a price tag of close to $24 million, was complete, sitting in well-guarded supply dumps and warehouses on Britain's Channel coast and elsewhere on the island, ready to be loaded onto the warships of the great Anglo-American armada being assembled for the Overlord invasion of continental Europe in June 1944.

Somervell's secret weapon was the Walter Mitty–like staff officer he had chosen to direct most of the organizational work, Major General LeRoy Lutes, described by one reporter of the day as "a pale little staff officer . . . who speaks with a soft voice and is a demon for getting things done," but which official army photographs depict as having a brow so egg-like, and a pate so bald, as to make him a prototype and great-granddaddy of all nerds, geeks, wonks, and propeller-heads at the Pentagon and elsewhere that have followed ever since. Possibly as a practical joke, Somervell had given Lutes the sumptuous office at the Pentagon that had originally been intended for naval chief of operations Admiral King, who had, along with most other navy brass, steadfastly refused to move from the Main Navy Building across the Potomac into the new five-sided monstrosity in Arlington, until they were compelled to do so by a mixture of convention and legislation following the war's end.

"I didn't want the damn thing," Lutes complained in his mumbling voice to one visitor upon moving into the spacious Pentagon billet. "They built it for Admiral King and when the navy decided not to move into the Pentagon Building I fell heir to it." Like it or not, the Mark-I Egghead of the Pentagon had been installed in an office fit for a Caesar—or even a MacArthur.

Yet though unassuming in appearance and speech, and as if intended by nature to polish a chair with the seat of his pants, Lutes was one of the most formidable and fiendishly clever logistical planners ever to tread the rings and corridors of the Pentagon. Lutes had virtually singlehandedly planned the South Atlantic and Pacific supply routes that had maintained the critical logistics tails for the cutting "teeth" of fighting forces in both theaters of war. By all accounts Lutes was so good at his job that had CENTCOM had him in 1990, the stockpiles of Desert Shield would have been secreted in Baghdad disguised as camel dung, instead of sitting in Saudi Arabia. Somervell had brought Lutes along to Cairo so his deceptively mousy aide could get to work as soon as possible on the logistical end of the invasion, which it would be the Army Service Forces' job to tackle.

There was "treacherous weather" in Cairo during the late fall of 1943, weather that could unpredictably change from burning heat to chilling cold, according to one observer on the scene. It had temporarily felled even the otherwise redoubtable Winston Churchill with his third wartime case of pneumonia, and but for the timely appearance of the equally redoubtable Clemmie Churchill, his wife, might have even killed him.

Nevertheless, the indefatigable Lutes, locked away in a disheveled hotel room amid the stifling heat that alternated with freezing cold, surrounded by discarded tea cups, pastry crumbs, and army documents stamped "Top Secret," was hard at work drafting the supply plans for D-day as soon as the invasion had been agreed on. Somervell had given Lutes the order to proceed. Germs might have stopped Churchill, but nothing could stop Lutes.

After Cairo, and the plan's initial draft, Lutes embarked on a fact-finding expedition that took him through North Africa, India, China, and across the Pacific, stopping in England in between to scout locations for the big dumps to hold the supplies. At each stop in his whirlwind mission, Lutes "had to assemble the combat staffs' meticulous descriptions of all objectives to be attacked, translate them into orders for the correct types of pontoons, structural metal, fabricated units, ammunition, thousands of other items of supply."

Returning to Washington when he was through, Lutes presented the finished plan to Somervell, who then presented it to Supreme Allied Commander General Dwight D. Eisenhower. He told Somervell to send Lutes back to England for a final check before the June 1944 invasion proceeded. On the eve of the invasion, Lutes returned to the Pentagon and informed Somervell that everything was ready to go. The story of how Eisenhower's last-minute decision to launch the D-day invasion on the basis of a revised weather forecast is well-known. That of the role played by Pentagon staff officer Leroy Lutes toward the same end has been largely forgotten. Nevertheless, Lutes, who is today buried in Arlington Cemetery behind the large building in which he occupied an office that was only superficially too big for the "little man" who sat in it, played a critical role in that epochal military undertaking; it was a role representative of what the Pentagon was built to do.

BOOK TWO

MILLIONS FOR DEFENSE

The Pentagon and Its Postwar Role

The only way to win World War III is to prevent it.
—President Dwight D. Eisenhower, radio and TV address,
September 19, 1956

*Since I do not foresee that atomic energy is to be a great boon for
a long time, I have to say that for the present it is a menace.
Perhaps it is well that it should be. It may intimidate the human
race into bringing order into its international affairs, which,
without the pressure of fear, it would not do.*

—Albert Einstein on the atomic bomb,
Atlantic Monthly, November 1945

*We exist to protect these citizen stockholders, for without
their support we would be out of business.*

—*DOD 101* (Department of Defense publication)

CHAPTER NINE

THE BIRTH OF THE COLD WAR

"The ancients are the ancients, and we are the men of today."

—Moliere

By 1945, much of war-torn Europe was demolished. Yet the ferocious conflict had bestowed on the United States an unforeseen prosperity. For America the war had not only rolled back the impoverishment and privation of the Great Depression, but far outstripped the productivity and affluence that some Americans had experienced prior to the stock market crash of 1929.

The reactor that powered this economic machinery was the war itself and the U.S. defense industry that produced the ships, tanks, planes, artillery tubes, shells, rifles, bullets, bayonets, and spare parts, without which no modern army could long wage war.

As the war progressed it became not only a contest between the champions of freedom versus those of oppression, but of the peculiar materialistic and managerial culture of the Americans versus the atavistic dynamism of the Third Reich led by a self-styled visionary with a monomaniacal belief in a fate that would carry him through to ultimate victory. Hitler's conception of fate was almost the same as the "star" that Napoleon believed guided him. Both dictators were destined to fall before the material might of their adversaries. Yet time and again the history of warfare has proved that the will to win alone can't prevail over advantages of military technology and superiority in armament coupled with sound military strategy and tactics.

During the June 1944 Allied invasion of Normandy, time-on-target shelling of the beachheads—sometimes fifteen solid minutes of continued barrage—astonished the Germans who hunkered behind the concrete pillboxes, tank barriers, gun embrasures, barbed wire, and other fortifications of the Atlantic Wall built under the direction of Field Marshal Irwin Rommel at Hitler's orders.

The Wehrmacht, whose blitzkrieg warfare had punched through, then demolished the Maginot Line in 1940 and then slashed across Europe, and that had, by the 1944 D-day invasion, driven across the endless miles of Russian steppes to the gates of Moscow and Stalingrad—they had never seen anything like it before. The Americans' British allies were equally impressed, even shocked by the display of raw firepower. The manufacturing output of war materiel from the United States boggled their scales of measurement.

The difference in scale can be seen even today, as I saw it in late October 2005, after some typically American discourtesy, rudeness, and pounding on a steel-plate door meant to keep out fragments from exploding V-2 rockets got me inside the cabinet war rooms, a concrete-fortified underground command post near Buckingham Palace in London that had been the main headquarters of the British war effort throughout World War II. It was past closing time when I arrived, but I would leave London early the next day and was determined to see it before my departure.

There had, of course, been numerous bases on the city's outskirts, but to all intents and purposes the cabinet war rooms were the British equivalent of the Pentagon in the United States. Among a visitor's first impressions was that it was, like the Führer Bunker in Berlin, a warren of fortified underground connecting tunnels and contiguous rooms. A second impression was that, while in the United States Franklin Roosevelt quietly built "Shangri-la"—a secret tunnel system leading from the basement of the White House to a protected bunker a mile distant to which the president could be spirited in case of attack on Washington—there had been no major bunker building in the United States until the advent of the Cold War.

Accounts differ as to the actual location of "Shangri-la." Some place it beneath Camp David, though another credible location for it was beneath the House of Representatives. Presidential secretary Grace Tully states that Shangri-la was a "Catoctin Mountain retreat," at which she was present on several occasions in the fall of 1942, including just before the Allied invasion of North Africa. Curiously, Roosevelt often used "Shangri-la" to evade questions. For example, once asked where a bomber run had originated, he replied, "Shangri-la."

Although existing below-ground areas that could serve as air raid shelters—like the New York City subways—had been pressed into service, the country engaged in no large-scale national construction of underground facilities throughout the global conflict, and one characterized by the large-scale bombing of civilian populations in Europe and Japan to an extent that dwarfed anything seen in World War I.

While much of London had been demolished during the Blitz Years, and while Allied heavy bombers had, by war's end, filled the streets of Berlin with what one historian estimated at some ten billion tons of rubble from some 150,000 destroyed buildings, while repeated firebombing of Japanese cities had resulted in a hecatomb of civilian casualties even before the atomic bombing of Hiroshima and Nagasaki, America paid little intention to the threat of overt attack.

On the contrary, the national frenzy of building was directed toward a vast national highway system, an extensive new industrial plant, a plethora of military bases including POW camps, and the erection of modern federal and local government buildings of all kinds, of which the Pentagon was the biggest. To the public at large and officialdom at the highest levels, and despite Pearl Harbor, it appeared axiomatic that the United States was protected from foreign attack by vast oceans and skies too broad to be crossed by hostile planes.

The Pentagon had been built to mirror a fortress, but it was not actually a fortress. True fortresses, like the Palazzo Medici in Florence, were massive in substance as well as in form. A visitor to the castle of the Medicis of Florence today can immediately tell the difference between the two types of structures. It would be hard to imagine that a passenger jet crashed into that enormous heap of stones that faces a broad Florentine piazza would cause much damage even today. But the Pentagon's imposing walls collapsed within thirty minutes of being struck by a passenger jet on 9/11, just like any modern building subjected to a powerful blast—the Murrah Building in Oklahoma City or the World Trade Center come to mind—despite recent renovations that included a web of new steel reinforcements, two-inch-thick, blast-resistant windows, and walls lined with bulletproof Kevlar fabric. The Pentagon was fortress-like in appearance and not function because America, unlike Europe, was itself a fortress. The threat of attack had never entered the minds of the planners or builders, even in the wake of the Japanese attack on Pearl Harbor. It was a very different mindset than that of the Europeans.

The outlook of most Americans during the concluding years of the war reflected largely positive expectations. For most of them the war's most visible consequence on the home front was the return of a long-missed material prosperity. The gross national product had more than doubled between the onset of war in 1939 and its conclusion in 1945. The unemployment rate had plummeted from more than nine million to about one million during those same years, and the size of the civilian labor force held steady as the government created some twelve million new jobs in the defense sector, with millions more created as a byproduct of the immense stimulation of war production on the U.S. economy.

Then and today, most economists argue that if it had not been for the war, and despite the New Deal economics from the FDR administration, the United States would have likely entered a second depression after 1937. Contemporary public perception held the same views. In addition to tens of thousands of "Rosie the Riveters," there were legions who found new employment amid the booming U.S. wartime economy where, for the first time in almost a decade, jobs were plentiful, the pay was decent, and despite wartime rationing, there was more cash on hand to purchase commodities that, though not rationed, would have been viewed as luxuries during the Depression.

Even today, the Pentagon's self-image is that of a large corporation; significantly its paradigm is that of business entity, not military

THE BIRTH OF THE COLD WAR

organization, its business is management, not warfare. There is a fine distinction here but not an invalid one; it's the age-old distinction between staff and field, between trainer and prizefighter. Armies fight wars, but the DOD, which runs the Pentagon, manages the war fighters the way a manager, though often in the ring, never throws a punch in anger.

The Defense Department fact sheet, "Pentagon 101," calls the Pentagon, "America's oldest, largest, busiest and most successful company." It goes on to explain that, "With our military units tracing their roots to pre-Revolutionary times, you might say that we are America's oldest company. And if you look at us in business terms, many would say we are not only America's largest company, but its busiest and most successful."

The corporate comparison was there from the outset. From its earliest days the Pentagon was planned to be the world's largest government office building, which it still holds the distinction of being. Also from the outset, the Pentagon's purpose was largely one of management of the sprawling military infrastructure that already existed in the era of the "Seventeen Buildings" and was expected to grow exponentially as America first prepared, and then entered, the war in Europe and the Pacific. Presiding over the War Department was an able manager, General George Marshall, who when given the opportunity to command Allied forces in Europe chose to remain at his post as plenipotentiary of the Combined Chiefs of Staff and instead send his protégé, Dwight D. Eisenhower, to command Allied forces in the field.

The managerial style is ingrained in the American psyche. You ride down any Main Street or Broadway in any town in the United States even today, and you'll likely still find its telltale signs, despite the certitude of the nearness of both a strip mall and a mammoth Wal-Mart. Wal-Mart, in fact, may be the twenty-first century's answer to that same small-town mentality—the Pentagon's own press materials liken it to Wal-Mart in size, annual revenue, and employment roll! The psychology is so uniquely American and so deep-seated that Americans themselves don't quite grasp its pervasive presence. It's the thing other nationalities seem to find vulgar or callow in American culture. It's that justification of everything by how it performs in the marketplace.

113

The idea itself, the vision, can never be a justification in itself. A product has to sell. In the fierce marketplace of war, the competing vision of the Axis powers was the opposite. It addressed enterprises in terms of national will, of destiny, of blood, and of honor.

As America emerged from World War II as the successor to the European Great Powers of the nineteenth and early twentieth centuries and the Western superpower of a bipolar world, this vision would come to predominate the postwar world with often astonishing consequences.

* * *

It may or may not be paradoxical that the weapon that ended World War II was the same one, by virtue of its very existence, that began the Cold War. It might also be an oversimplification, though probably not a large one, to state that the existence of massive and ever-growing and improving nuclear arsenals by the superpowers, and the proliferation of nuclear arms into the Third World, was the key development that turned the gears of history for the next five decades.

Nuclear weapons, and the threat of an East–West ballistic exchange that would result in a doomsday scenario for humankind, quickly became the ultimate yardstick against which every movement in the sphere of international power politics was measured throughout the Cold War years.

Many, if not most, of the major events and organizations that came into being during the Cold War were influenced by this single fact. The establishment of NATO and the Strategic Air Command (SAC), the surveillance overflights of the USSR during the Truman and Eisenhower years, the Cuban Missile Crisis of 1962, even the war in Vietnam, were all closely linked to the realities made manifest by the bomb.

The existence of nuclear arsenals, and the downward proliferation of nuclear weapons technology from the big powers into the arsenals of lesser nations, rogue states, and terrorist groups, held a talismanic power over the calculations of defense and political establishments around the world. The fires that had consumed Hiroshima and, three days later, Nagasaki had given all humanity a glimpse into the ovens of hell. Here was a look into the abyss from which there was no way back.

President Harry S. Truman, acting with the approval of cosignatories to the 1943 Quebec Agreement—the agreement gave the British and Canadians an effective veto against U.S. unilateral use of the A-bomb against a third party—had been responsible for ordering the wartime use of the two atomic bombs in the U.S. arsenal on Japan. Although the bombs had been dropped on two separate missions, they had all along been considered elements of a single integrated operation; both were to be detonated over Japanese targets. Orders from General Groves, who headed the Manhattan Project, which developed both nuclear weapons, called for the use of both weapons. The president's instructions were to drop one bomb, and then the other as soon as feasible. At no time had the plans considered anything else.

Nor were suggestions from some of the physicists themselves to stage a warning drop, as one contained in the Franck Report that reached Groves' desk about a month before the Hiroshima raid, taken seriously. Since the development of the long-range B-29 bomber whose range, from newly captured Japanese outer islands such as Iwo Jima or Guam, allowed U.S. bombers to stage round-the-clock missions, Japan had been subjected to a punishing series of bombings.

Sixty-six Japanese cities and towns had been hit in a total of ninety-nine major air raids between 1943 and 1945 that, using napalm and high-explosives, had turned them into charred wastelands by the time the A-bomb was ready for use. This fact, and official estimates of an approximate million U.S. battle deaths that might be saved by Japan's early surrender, were powerful incentives to go the distance.

There was another consideration, too: The two A-bombs dropped on Japan were considerably different from one another from technological standpoints. Each bomb, with a combined cost of billions in present-day dollars, had been built using a different approach to weapons manufacture, and each was a prototype for new nuclear weapons designs that were accepted by all concerned to inevitably follow. This proved to be the case, especially in the wake of the disturbing discovery in 1946 that the Soviet Union was also in possession of a functional nuclear weapon. With World War II now over, a U.S.–Soviet nuclear arms race began that was to transcend all other considerations of the War and Navy departments and the Department of Defense that succeeded them a year later under the National Security Act of 1947.

Nuclear policy, including nuclear war fighting, became the predominant force that shaped defense acquisitions, motivated defense expenditures, and drove the restructuring of the U.S. defense establishment.

Nuclear weapons on the battlefield not only forced a thorough reassessment of combat doctrine—army field manuals, such as the 1962 FM 7-15 in the author's collection, were rewritten from the standpoint of combat operations expected to take place on a nuclear battlefield—they led to the development of entirely new weapon systems, such as nuclear-powered submarines, as well as entirely new systems of command and control, such as ARPANET, a novel scheme for ensuring the integrity of battlefield communications under nuclear attack that, repackaged for civilian use, became the Internet.

Hardly had the Hiroshima and Nagasaki bombs—frequently referred to by the code name "Tube Alloys"—exploded, than the military, with presidential approval, began the development of even more ambitious nuclear weaponry. It also led to tensions between the United States and its principal wartime allies, since the Quebec Agreement, and a secret 1944 codicil to it arranged between Roosevelt and Churchill, afforded the British "full collaboration . . . in developing Tube Alloys for military and commercial purposes . . . after the defeat of Japan." The agreement had been reaffirmed by their successors, Harry Truman and British Prime Ministers Clement Attlee and, later, Mackenzie King, who had in November 1945 reaffirmed "full and effective cooperation" in the development of nuclear weapons between the two countries.

Nevertheless, Congress, ignorant of the secret Quebec protocols, had, in 1946, passed the Atomic Energy Act, a provision of which forbade the sharing of information on the design and manufacture of nuclear weapons with foreign governments. This act of Congress effectively made the prior international agreements illegal under U.S. law.

Another bone of contention lay in the availability of uranium ore that could be turned into fissionable, bomb-grade plutonium in U.S.

nuclear reactors, such as the one at Hanford, Washington. The British had co-financed the wartime acquisition of prime-grade ore from the Belgian Congo and were not happy about a shift in U.S. cooperation.

Nevertheless, by the time of the declaration of the Truman Doctrine in a presidential address on March 12, 1947, recognized by historians as the official start of the Cold War, the nuclear stockpile of the United States would have been of little use in a war against the Soviet Union.

The dearth of raw materials out of which to refine bomb-grade nuclear explosives was one of the main reasons for this. The British, not yet in possession of a working nuke but engaged in a secret crash program to develop one of their own, were hoarding the large reserves of precious high-grade ore against the time when it would be needed.

At the same time, the exposure by red-baiting Senator Joe McCarthy of secret protocols for bilateral use of nuclear weaponry caused an uproar of protest in the Senate and House.

Against this backdrop were sobering intelligence reports that the Soviets, far overestimating the ability of the United States to stage a nuclear first-strike on the USSR, and not yet possessing the weapons or delivery systems to retaliate in kind, were rebuilding their conventional forces at an alarming rate. From an immediate postwar strength of three million troops in 1945, the Soviets began a gradual increase to more than five million by mid-1947.

The Marshall Plan was seized upon as a means of resolving the crises in nuclear arms in favor of the United States. The British, cash-poor after six years of total war and having almost exhausted a $7.5 billion U.S. loan under the plan, were pressed by Marshall on behalf of the U.S. defense establishment to trade a significant portion of their vital fissionable ore stockpile in return for a financial shot in the arm.

A deal was finally hammered out in which the United States would effectively be released from its wartime pledge of joint action in the use of nuclear weapons under the Quebec Agreement protocols and have access to both British stockpiles and colonial sources of fresh high-grade raw materials. The British got a pledge for the sharing of technical information concerning nuclear energy development, including nuclear weapons engineering.

Also complicating U.S. plans to grow its nuclear arsenal against the perceived threat from a militarily resurgent and bellicose Soviet Union was the chaos in the War Department caused by restructuring of the U.S. defense establishment after Truman's signing of the July 26, 1947, National Security Act.

The act placed the War and Navy departments under the Department of Defense, established the Joint Chiefs of Staff to head the military and a secretary of defense to preside over the Pentagon, separated the air force from the control of the army and established it as a separate combat arm, and created the Central Intelligence Agency (CIA) as well as the National Security Council (NSC). It had been the subject of months of bitter infighting among the military service branches, postwar intelligence services (primarily the Office of Strategic Services, or OSS), and their congressional supporters and antagonists.

When the dust finally settled, World War II had been over for some two years but the United States had no clear or concerted nuclear weapons policy. Despite its head start in the arms race and—so far— being the sole possessor of Tube Alloys, the United States still had few nuclear arms.

At the Pentagon, one of the first orders of business for the new Joint Chiefs of Staff (JCS) was to come up with a Cold War nuclear strategy for the United States. After weighing the pros and cons, the chiefs came to the decision that the U.S. required no more than 150 "Nagasaki-type" bombs. The JCS figure was based on a Pentagon study that envisioned, according to its wording, "attacks on approximately one hundred different urban locations" in the USSR.

"The efficient utilization of atomic bombs," the JCS study continued, "will dictate the use of one bomb only in any one attack on an objective area. Therefore, the maximum which would be dispatched in any one attack under present conditions is unlikely to exceed one hundred."

For all its authoritative-sounding language, the estimate of one hundred nukes, calculated against the megatonnage that could be delivered by any single nuclear weapon in 1947, worked out to a blast yield of a mere three megatons—total! In short, the official pronouncement of the Joint Chiefs was that three megatons was sufficient nuclear war–fighting capability to both defend the United States from attack and strike a blow against the USSR sufficient to destroy its military forces and defeat it.

Naive though this first attempt by the Pentagon to develop a credible nuclear war plan might have been, it was at least the first time since the end of World War II that the U.S. military leadership had addressed the question. From this point on the assessments would grow exponentially, as blast yields and delivery capability on both sides of the Iron Curtain became more sophisticated and nuclear command and control more survivable—within a few short years a single hydrogen bomb (H-Bomb) would, with a four-megaton warhead, pack more nuclear firepower than the chiefs' first estimate for the entire U.S. nuclear arsenal.

One thing, if nothing else, was now certain: With less than a million and a half men under arms in 1947, against at least a five million–strong army that could be fielded by the Soviets, the Pentagon had made the only choice that seemed possible. It had declared that the nuclear bomb was to be the first line of defense against the Red Menace for the United States.

* * *

Many in the upper echelons of U.S. political and defense leadership had played Lot's wife to the devastation wrought by the atom bomb, petrified as much by its sheer power as by the comparative ease by which it could be used—a single plane carrying a single bomb had unleashed the equivalent of 350 boxcars of TNT, doing more damage in a matter of seconds than round-the-clock bomber sorties dropping conventional bombs might have done in a month.

Still, the predominant view of nuclear weapons among the Joint Chiefs of Staff was that while many orders of magnitude more powerful than conventional weapons, atomic weapons presented nothing more than bigger and better defensive armaments.

Better still was the fact that in the eight postwar years between 1945 and 1953—when the Soviet Union sent its first nuclear mushroom cloud boiling up into the skies over Siberia—the U.S.A. was the only country that had the bomb. Throughout this period the word *deterrence* was used in the lexicon of warfare by its dictionary meaning only.

Deterrence, in the Strangelovian sense it later took on as the Cold War escalated, was a neologism that did not yet exist for either the American military or the White House. We had the Bomb—they didn't. The U.S. had emerged from the war garlanded with a victor's laurels. It was intact and prosperous; moreover, the USSR and the Communist system that ran it were evil while we were good, or if not good, the next best thing to it this side of heaven.

Churchill's 1946 speech, titled the "Sinews of Peace" (a play on Cato the Elder's remark that "money is the sinews of war")—popularly known as the "Iron Curtain Speech"—was the first of a handful of declarations by Western leaders that framed the basic tenets of the Cold War and the emergent postwar order.

Newly ousted as prime minister in favor of the more dovish Heath, Churchill delivered the speech in Harry Truman's home state of Missouri. The occasion was an honorary degree. Standing beside him was the president, who had invited him to speak at Westminster College in the small university town of Fulton and who had traveled there with him on the presidential train.

It was not the first time the phrase "Iron Curtain" had been used, but it was the first time the phrase became a household word, an icon representing the Manichean gap between the Western democracies and the Soviet Union. The curtain Churchill referred to was the political walling off of Eastern Europe and the USSR into a police state with militaristic ambitions.

His ultimate solution was the newly established United Nations coupled with a robust defense capability for the Atlantic alliance. If the alliance was unsuccessful, then the world would, in Churchill's phrase, "learn again for a third time in a school of war." He warned that World War III, if and when it came, would dwarf even the bloodbath of World War II.

Though Churchill never referred directly to nuclear weapons in his speech, the looming threat they posed was clear by implication, as was the fact that the Soviet Union was well along on the road to nuclear weapons development.

The Gehlen Organization, a private spy organization headed by the former chief of the German Abwehr, Reinhard Gehlen, and controlled by the War Department in the early postwar years, had been among the intelligence sources warning of the furious efforts by the Soviets to rival and outpace the West in the development of nuclear arms.

Gehlen's network had been quietly debriefing the thousands of returning former Wehrmacht and SS war prisoners who had been held in Soviet work camps. The take from the debriefings had proven to be an intelligence bonanza. Among the discoveries of 1947 were descriptions by war prisoners being made to wear heavy protective apparel, including gloves, while working certain Siberian mines.

One former POW had brought back a sample of the ore that was mined: It turned out to be uranium. Within two years following the end of World War II it had become clear that the USSR had the determination, if not yet the actual means, to become a rival nuclear power.

*　*　*

Yet, what to do? The United States had emerged from the war with a defense infrastructure that quickly began to appear obsolete in peacetime. It was like driving a battered Jeep along a badly rutted road to suddenly emerge onto a four-lane highway with passenger traffic and interstate trucking whizzing and rolling past. Where did you go from there? The defense and intelligence infrastructure of the United States seemed woefully out of step with the fast-changing times.

On September 20, 1945, less than six months after the war's end, Truman effectively abolished the OSS with the stroke of a pen, ignoring pleas from veteran spymasters such as Allen Dulles, to establish a new peacetime intelligence organization with sweeping powers.

The president fulminated against the creation of anything that might be, in the words of a newspaper editorial of the era, "a peacetime Gestapo," and only later agreed to the creation of a Central Intelligence Group (CIG) with limited powers.

But there had been pressure from many quarters, including Congress, to reorganize the U.S. defense and intelligence establishments, and in 1947 Truman, who supported defense reorganization, signed the National Security Act, an act that radically reshaped the U.S. military and intelligence landscape into its present form and one whose essential characteristics remain the same even after the extensive post-9/11 restructurings under the Homeland Security Act.

To the military establishment, the National Security Act represented a dramatic shakeup. The service chiefs had jockeyed for position, hammering out a new working relationship in the face of extensive change after months of ferocious infighting between the army and navy, both of which stood to gain and lose a great deal, depending on the final results of defense restructuring.

Perhaps the most vocal—and effective—opponent of the manifold changes proposed under the National Security Act was Secretary of the Navy James Forrestal, whose dogged opposition to the sweeping changes proposed for the Department of the Navy succeeded in doing away with some of them as well as weakening the authority of the newly created office of secretary of defense. Ironically, it was Forrestal himself who was appointed to be the Defense Department's first secretary by President Truman, who, it is claimed by some, appointed the pugnacious critic of reorganization in order to prevent him from creating more headaches for the new Department of Defense.

The above notwithstanding, the military departments and the joint chiefs had anticipated many of the coming changes. In fact, the War Department had long before implemented some of the most fundamental changes during the Marshall reorganization period of the early 1940s.

In July 1942, some six months after their first formal meeting that winter and a few months after the attacks on Pearl Harbor, President Roosevelt created the new office of Chief of Staff to the Commander in Chief of the Army and Navy, and named Admiral William D. Leahy to the post. No such office had originally been planned, but it had developed as an outgrowth of military realities; Pearl Harbor was one, but not the only, precipitating factor. Leahy, as chief of staff, would be the joint chiefs' senior officer, preside over their activities, and maintain daily contact with the president.

The admiral had been provided an office in the White House to maximize availability to Truman. Beyond this, Leahy and Truman had a working relationship that dated back to the early days of the Roosevelt administration. Since the admiral also meshed well with the chiefs, it was a good match all around. Leahy was to remain in that position for the next seven years, until his retirement in 1949, when Congress voted in a new set of amendments to the National Security Act of 1947 that created the new post of chairman of the Joint Chiefs of Staff (CJCS).

The army saw change as imminent, if not ordained; immediately after the war, General Carl A. "Tooey" Spaatz, who had replaced General Henry H. "Hap" Arnold as Army Air Force chief of staff in February 1946, weighed in with Eisenhower in arguing for the need for unity of command before Congress and in talks with the president.

Truman himself was a proponent of far-reaching overhaul of the system. "One of the strongest convictions . . . I brought to the presidency," he once told a journalist, "was that the antiquated defense setup . . . had to be reorganized quickly as a step toward ensuring our future safety and preserving world peace." The president added that the Pearl Harbor calamity had been "as much the result of the inadequate military system, which provided for no unified command, either in the field or in Washington, as it was any personal failure of army or navy commanders."

Congress was also looking into postwar defense restructuring; it had been since the spring of 1944, when the Woodrum Committee, named for Virginia Democratic Representative Clifton A. Woodrum—the same Woodrum who had been one of the most vocal critics of the building of the Pentagon back when it had still been called "Somervell's Folly"— took up the question of unified command and created the Joint Chiefs of Staff Special Committee for Reorganization of National Defense.

The committee, headed by Admiral James O. Richardson, recommended in 1945 that a single Department of National Defense be established. The committee upheld Richardson's view, with one important difference: It supported the creation of an air force separate from either the army or navy. Richardson, disinclined to see the navy lose its air arm, cast the lone dissenting vote. In December 1945, Truman recommended to Congress a single Department of National Defense to be headed by a civilian and complemented by an Office of the Chief of Staff of the military.

More fact-finding committees and policy-making boards appointed by the War and Navy departments and Congress continued the debate for another two years. Among their reports and recommendations were the War Department's Collins Plan and Norstad-Radford initiatives and the Department of the Navy's Eberstadt Report. Elements of all of these went into the much broader Department of Common Defense plan drawn up by the Senate Military Affairs subcommittee that drafted an April 1946 bill calling for a single Department of Common Defense, three coequal military service branches, and a chief of staff of common defense who would serve as military advisor to the president.

The battles—and some of them were pitched—were largely over turf. There were going to be winners and losers once the fight was over, and neither the army nor navy, nor the proponents of a separate air force such as Tooey Spaatz, Hap Arnold, or Curtis LeMay, wanted to be on the losing side. While the military departments had a tradition of looking necessity in the eyes and adapting to it, there were also powerful forces committed to preserving the status quo, at least as far as certain aspects of the art of war went.

One curious, but illustrative, example was the horse cavalry, which had continued to exist in the U.S. order of battle long after World War II was over, despite the advent of technological marvels like the nuclear bomb and strategic missiles, and which was formally replaced by mechanized armor only with the Army Organization Act of 1950. The tank had been first used in combat in World War I and proved so effective on the battlefield that a Tank Corps was created.

Nevertheless, Congress, acting on General John J. Pershing's staunch opposition to anything that might replace the army horse, had deprived it of its status as a separate combat arm and made it part of the U.S. Cavalry. The horse was deemed essential to field artillery and Major General Robert M. Danford, chief of field artillery, gave voice to the obstinate objections of the chiefs of this combat arm who regarded armored forces advocates as "betrayers of the horse" when he protested, in writing, that "horses could feed off the land, while motor trucks could not."

During the period of defense reorganization between the wars, the roles and missions of armored forces in both the United States and Europe became the subject of acrimonious debate in the War Department. As late as 1938, Chief of Cavalry Major General John K. Herr went on record as a pro-horse, anti-armor man when he stated to a congressional fact-finding committee, "We must not be misled to our own detriment to assume that the untried machine can displace the proved and tried horse." While not as well-known as Stimson's infamous quip about gentlemen not reading each other's mail, it deserves to go down in history right alongside it as one of the prewar era's most notorious gaffes.

As already mentioned, Secretary of the Navy James V. Forrestal, with the backing of the navy brass, doggedly refused to support the establishment of an Office of the Secretary of Common Defense; Forrestal and his navy constituency were even more opposed to initiatives, such as Spaatz's, to establish an independent air force. The naval chiefs had plans for maritime aviation in the postwar world, and the establishment of an air force was perceived as a significant threat. This view, and the turf battles between the navy and the newly established air force, continued into the Cold War and far beyond into the post–Cold War era.

At any rate, the president, convinced change was overdue, began to bridle at the squabbles among the services; in May 1946, he ordered Navy Secretary Forrestal and War Secretary Robert P. Patterson to resolve the differences between their departments over the implementation of the congressional Department of Common Defense plan. Chastened by Truman, the two sides got down to brass tacks but reached agreement on only eight points of the congressional plan: there was still no accord on major issues, including the establishment of a separate air force, the future of land-based aviation, the affiliations and roles conceived for the Marine Corps, and the responsibilities of the office of the secretary of defense.

Learning of the continued deadlock over critical issues, Truman called Patterson, Forrestal, Norstad, and Radford on the White House carpet, directing them to establish a Department of National Defense to be headed by a civilian appointee. Truman ordered that the navy would keep the marines, and could continue to conduct air operations, but that a separate U.S. Air Force must come into being. He further decreed that "the services should perform their separate functions under the unifying direction, authority and control of the secretary of national defense."

The president had spoken. Truman had given the last word on postwar defense reorganization. He had made it clear to all concerned that he would not tolerate any further squabbling and stalling. He had, as one of the principals to the dispute noted soon after the president laid down the law, "removed the impasse between the services." The Department of Defense was now a fact on the ground.

CHAPTER TEN

AN ARMED TRUCE

The Eisenhower years made a panoply of changes manifest on the American scene and around the world. The restructuring of the U.S. defense establishment and the controversies and growing pains that assailed the Pentagon in the immediate years since the 1947 National Security Act were to continue and, in some cases, intensify. All this to the contrary, the National Security Act, known informally in defense and political circles as the "unification law," and its subsequent amendments were in the main having their intended effect.

The Defense Department was on a trajectory toward a new organizational model that would meet the challenges of the Cold War.

Those challenges seemed to be everywhere and spreading. President Truman had left office in 1953 amid the shifting winds of political change that saw the United States and the Soviet Union squaring off against one another across increasing ideological, economic, and technological gaps like two heavyweights in a ring. Behind them were growing stockpiles of nuclear weapons and, far more important to the prospects of world peace and global security, growing availability and sophistication of the delivery systems necessary to put those weapons accurately on target across strategic distances.

Like conventional munitions, nuclear explosives in themselves are of little use unless they can be fired at, dropped on, or in some other way made to accurately strike or explode close to their intended targets.

This basic law of combat held as true for atomic and H-bombs as it did for everything else in the military arsenal, from bullets to artillery shells and everything in between. While the pace of technological change later in the Cold War—especially in the miniaturization of electronics and the refinements in bomb design that enabled more and more megatonnage to be shoehorned into smaller and smaller warheads—would eventually result in miracles of lethality such as MIRVing, cold launch–capable silos, and nuclear howitzers, the long-range, strategic bomber was, as the halfway mark of the twentieth century was reached, the only game in town if you wanted to go to nuclear war.

Rocketry was, of course, well advanced by then, but the weight of nuclear bombs was such that no rocket or missile then in existence could launch one. Beyond this, the A- and H-bombs were so heavy and so large that a one-plane, one-bomb rule continued to apply well into the 1950s.

And the Russians were still years away from strategic parity with the United States. The upshot was that as the 1940s ended, the United States could still count itself as the sole nation on earth, and the only one of the two existent global superpowers, that could launch a nuclear attack without fear of retaliation in kind.

Such a colossal advantage, while it lasted, was the sort that could and did bring on titanic delusions of grandeur. Such was the policy of brinkmanship in 1954 as articulated by Eisenhower Secretary of State John Foster Dulles, a corollary to the strategy of massive retaliation. Both arose from the heady realization that not since the heyday of the Roman Empire had a single nation wielded such an overwhelming military advantage over its adversaries coupled with the deeply held conviction that the Soviet Union was not only an empire of evil but one that was bent on a strategy of world domination by whatever means available to it. The conviction, in the United States, that the USSR would not hesitate to use its nuclear arsenal against the West if it could strike a first blow and expect a reasonable chance of surviving intact was as great as Soviet fears that the Americans were getting ready to do exactly the same to Russia.

As announced by Dulles in January 1954, massive retaliation's main tenet held that the United States was prepared to launch an all-

Henry L. Stimson was first appointed to be secretary of war in 1911 as part of the Taft administration. He served as secretary of state from 1929 to 1933 and was brought back by Franklin Roosevelt to head the War Department in 1940. *Library of Congress*

Secretary of War Stimson discussing military plans with
U.S. Army Chief of Staff General George C. Marshall during
World War II. *Author's Collection*

What is now known as the Harry S Truman Building is
headquarters of the State Department. It was originally
proposed to replace the Main Navy and Munitions Buildings
(facing page) but was so despised by Secretary Stimson that
he likened it to "a provincial opera house" and vowed that he
would never move his office into it. *State Department*

The Main Navy and Munitions Buildings as they appeared in 1918–1919 together formed a headquarters complex for the U.S. military. Their resemblance to the later War Department headquarters (as seen in an early Pentagon photograph below) is uncanny. The sprawling, four-sided Army-Navy complex was clearly a prototype of the even vaster five-sided War Department headquarters that would be built decades later in Arlington. Today nothing remains of the old Army-Navy complex. *Author's Collection*

The Dwight D. Eisenhower Executive Office Building (EEOB) was originally called the State, War and Navy Building and is still frequently called by its former title, the Old Executive Office Building (OEOB). It was the pre–World War I headquarters of the War Department. Partly due to the periodic renaming of Washington, D.C., government buildings, it has been confused with the War Department Building (completed in 1939) that's now known as the Harry S Truman Building. Construction (above) and unveiling (below) of the EEOB as State, War and Navy Building. It was built over a seventeen-year period (1871–1888). *Author's Collection*

Print showing draftsmen at work at the Navy Department, Washington, D.C., 1893. *Library of Congress*

Secretary of War W.W. Belknap appearing before the Committee on Expenditures the Committee room of the War Department in the Capitol in 1876. *Library of Congress*

The Dwight D. Eisenhower Executive Office Building (EEOB) as it appeared circa 1990. *Author's Collection*

Some of Hell's Bottom's soggiest swampland still survives as a wedge of the Pentagon rises behind it. *Author's Collection*

The Pentagon's vast rooftop is under construction (note workers perched atop superstructure at left). *Author's Collection*

The Pentagon goes up!

Heavy cranes and construction towers flank a four-story superstructure, until, ultimately, a fifth story is ordered to be constructed. *Author's Collection*

As construction continues, water still stands in the low spots of the former swampland. *Author's Collection*

Although the Pentagon would not be officially completed until early 1943, War Department personnel starting moving in during the late spring of the year before. This 1942 photo shows a full parking lot, likely a mixture of War Department staff and construction workers, thousands of whom remained on the job. *Thomas D. Mcavoy/Time Life Pictures/Getty Images*

President Franklin Delano Roosevelt (shown here signing the 1941 U.S. declaration of war against Germany) said he "liked the idea" of a pentagon-shaped building. *Author's Collection*

General Brehon Somervell, shown here (on right) being greeted by Air Transport Command head Brig. Gen. Earl Hoag, arriving at Gatow Airport in Berlin on July 15, 1945, for the Potsdam Conference. General Somervell was an important champion for the construction of the Pentagon. It fell on the shoulders of Brooklyn-born Hugh J. Casey (inset) to translate Somervell's concepts into reinforced concrete as the Corps of Engineers' project manager. *Author's Collection*

Major General Eugene Reybold, as head of the U.S. Army Corps of Engineers, was Somervell's boss before World War II and helped push the project through Congress. *Myron Davis/Time Life Pictures/ Getty Images*

The Pentagon was in most ways "the house the Army built," and as such was shunned by the navy chiefs throughout World War II. General Malin Craig (above) was army chief of staff through the late interwar period, but Roosevelt thought his views antiquated. Malin's protégé and assistant, George C. Marshall (below), had FDR's backing in restructuring and expanding the U.S. military. *Author's Collection*

Admiral William D. Leahy played a critical role throughout World War II and into the early Cold War as representative of the Joint Chiefs of Staff, giving him the distinction of being the JCS's first chairman. *Author's Collection*

The unassuming Lieutenant General LeRoy Lutes was the uncomfortable recipient of a spacious Pentagon office suite intended for Chief of Naval Operations Ernest King, who preferred Main Navy. Later Lutes played a hero's role in the D-Day invasion of Europe. *Author's Collection*

The Pentagon burns on September 11, 2001, after a jumbo jet piloted by suicidal terrorists slammed into it. *Corporal Jason Ingersoll, USMC, DefenseImagery.Mil*

Looking east across the Potomac toward the Capital in 2004, a view that shows the Pentagon has recovered gracefully. Note the boat basin in the background, which is the flooded site of the old Hoover Airport, as well as the lush trees that line the atrium at the central convergence of the Pentagon's five interior walls. *Author's Collection*

out nuclear attack in response to any major Soviet aggression, anywhere in the world. It was specifically intended to warn the Soviets that any attempt by the USSR—which, it must be recalled, had built a massive post–World War II army while Western troop levels shrank—to invade the NATO nations of Western Europe or principal Asian allies would be dealt with by the only credible means the United States had to halt a major Soviet advance. This means was, of course, nuclear attack.

Dulles and the advocates of brinkmanship saw using nuclear superiority like a gargantuan club wielded by a giant. Whenever and wherever the Soviets showed themselves as spoiling for a fight, the United States and its nuclear-equipped allies would use their decisive edge in nuclear weaponry to "push the Soviets to the brink." Faced with the draconian choice of being bombed back to the stone age or retreating to lick its wounds, the Russian bear would inevitably back down, ending the conflict.

Strategic defense became the centerpiece of U.S. nuclear strategy until the late 1950s, when the United States' long lead in nuclear weapons began to erode and the Soviets began to challenge the West for primacy in the nuclear arms race. By the early 1960s the Soviets had already reached parity with the West, and massive retaliation was replaced with new policies of flexible response and, in the mid-1960s, mutually assured destruction (MAD), which would serve as the cornerstone of U.S. nuclear policy for the next two decades. For almost the next half century, until the Berlin Wall came down and the Soviet Union broke into pieces, the prime responsibility of the Pentagon was to develop weapons, strategies, doctrines, and policies, indeed the entire order of battle, necessary to wage conventional war and deter nuclear Armageddon in the new era of a nuclear arms race between the superpowers.

No longer could classic armies be trained to wage classic warfare. No longer could the size of an army or the will to win or the mastery of the battlefield or any of the innumerable calculations made by military commanders since time immemorial be counted on to prevail in the new kind of warfare with which the world found itself faced.

No Alexander, no Caesar, no Napoleon—or for that matter no Patton or Montgomery or Rommel fighting along the lines of the last world war—could hope to prevail in the face of the new realities of nuclear conflict. The bomb rendered these recent battle tactics as irrelevant as the sparring of red and white ant armies on a dunghill beneath the hovering sole of a combat boot. The Damocletian sword of nuclear war hung over every decision that the Pentagon would have to make for decades to come.

In this atmosphere the rivalries between the advocates of sea power versus those of air power became a dominant preoccupation in the reshaping of U.S. defense priorities. Which approach was the best way to ensure the security of the United States and the NATO alliance by deterring Soviet nuclear aggression while at the same time equipping the West with a credible means of offensive warfare in the event that deterrence failed?

Behind which of the two doors was the lady? Behind which waited the tiger? The resources in money and time that needed to be devoted to solving the problem were staggering. Weapons systems never existed in a vacuum—they were linked to other systems, while those systems were keyed into strategic defense policy in a complex interlocking mesh of money, ideas, hardware, and human lives that would all be affected by the direction of the new defense posture. Careers were also on the line, and tradition—that same powerful factor that kept the horse marines in the U.S. order of battles well into the nuclear age, much like the time-honored tradition of the aerial dogfight—powerfully influenced the Pentagon's choice for the advanced tactical fighter plane in the 1990s, when stealthy missiles would kill an unfriendly plane before his threat radars even warned him of death's presence. Tradition was there, too, a hoary presence that stood behind the epaulet-decorated shoulders of military men as they convened to grapple with a set of unprecedented new developments and problems on the strategic level.

Each side had sweeping plans to meet the pressing demands of the deepening Cold War. Each side was convinced that it was right. The so-called "big bomber" advocates, led by General Curtis "Bombs Away" LeMay, preached the gospel of the heavy bomber, the strategic bomber, as the new war chariot of the American colossus. The development of the B-29 Superfortress, late in the war, had not only made possible the bombing of Japan using what was then described as incendiaries of "petroleum jelly" that had set its major cities ablaze in 1944, but had also enabled the U.S. to drop the Hiroshima and Nagasaki bombs in August 1945.

The B-29, larger, more powerful and carrying far more fuel than the B-17s that had preceded it, equipped with better bomb sighting and able to carry heavier payloads—*bomb loads* in air warfare terms—had mandated the taking of the outer Japanese islands and surrounding Pacific atolls in order to be effective. Their range was great, but not that great. LeMay was now proposing an entirely new class of super heavy bomber to be called the B-36.

It was to be a behemoth of a plane, powered by six of the largest piston engines ever built, and it was to be a true strategic bomber as well, with an operational range that would enable it to reach Moscow from airfields in the continental United States (CONUS) and deliver multiple nuclear payloads on strategic targets. The B-36, in LeMay's vision, would form the nucleus of a new Strategic Air Command: SAC, the aerial centurions of the U.S. offensive nuclear force.

Beyond this, air power advocates were convinced that aircraft were the only viable means of surveillance and reconnaissance at the strategic level.

The Soviets were hard at work developing their nuclear forces. In order to be prepared to defend against them we had to know where their bases were located, and what was to be found on those bases; we also had to be prepared to deal with whatever forms of antiaircraft defenses the Soviets might have in place to shoot down the nuclear bombers if and when they were sent on the nuclear bombing mission that would heat up the Cold War into World War III.

The U.S. Navy and advocates of sea power held an opposing view that pinned hopes of successful nuclear strategic policy on an entirely new class of supercarrier for surface warfare and on nuclear submarines that could remain submerged for months on end without needing to surface, and which would be able to cruise undetected through the world's vast oceans. Both of these naval systems would be able to pack a formidable nuclear punch rivaling—indeed exceeding—anything that LeMay's strategic bombers could deliver.

Fleets of swift planes, each equipped with nuclear missiles, and each capable of conducting surveillance deep into the enemy's heartland, could be launched from the decks of supercarriers. Nuclear submarines could be lethal, stealthy weapons. A single nuclear submarine might be built to carry more nuclear missiles than an entire sortie of nuclear strategic bombers could deliver on a single mission. A fleet of nuclear submarines could level enough atomic firepower at the Soviets to bomb them to rubble.

The hopes of the sea power advocates had been bolstered by the appointment, by Truman, of former Secretary of the Navy James Forrestal as secretary of defense. Under Forrestal's stewardship of the Defense Department, the navy had forged ahead with development of the first supercarrier, the USS *United States*. But in spring 1949 Forrestal lost his mind and wound up jumping out of a window of his room at Bethesda Hospital. Truman's replacement for Forrestal was Louis Johnson, and Johnson was a dyed-in-the wool big bomber man. Soon after his appointment in April, following Forrestal's resignation, one of Johnson's first acts as the new defense secretary was to cancel development of the carrier—an act that produced a level of consternation among the ranks of navy brass that would only be equaled by the ire among army chiefs provoked by Donald Rumsfeld's cancellation of the Crusader super howitzer soon after his investiture to office in 2001, a half century later.

The Johnson cancellation provoked a fusillade of criticism from sea power advocates that was unprecedented in U.S. military history. Its vehemence was such that *Time* magazine coined the phrase "Revolt of the Admirals" to give name to it. Whereas compromises had been the expected result of internecine bureaucratic infighting between the armed forces in World War II, the game had changed and new rules prevailed: There were almost certain to be big winners and big losers.

The reason was money, or lack of it. The defense pie, plush with four-and-twenty blackbirds in 1945 had now shrunk drastically. The U.S. military budget that had crested to $83 billion by the war's end had dropped to less than $14 billion during the Truman years, representing just under 5 percent of the gross national product. There was simply not enough money to fund both navy and air force programs—it was a case of one against the other.

In the end, though, big bomber advocates had scored a major touchdown. LeMay's B-36 program went forward full steam ahead while the supercarrier program remained only a drawing board effort of mockups and vision statements while SAC assumed the predominance in the U.S. defense effort that LeMay and his supporters had projected for it all along.

Nevertheless, events were to prove that both strategic bombers and strategic naval forces would be needed, and the age of the supercarrier, though delayed, would become a reality well before the decade was out, thanks in part to the explosion of the first Soviet bomb and the unanticipated quagmire of the Korean War, both of which turned on the congressional money spigot for the second time since Pearl Harbor.

* * *

When Truman was reelected in 1948 he presided over the completion of the continuing defense reorganization that he had begun at the end of the war.

Among the multiple developments was the assumption to the chairmanship of Omar Bradley as the first of the next seventeen chairmen of the Joint Chiefs of Staff and the North Atlantic Treaty Organization's, or NATO's, implementation of the Marshall Plan. The United States, as well, played a major hand in the 1948 partitioning of Korea that resulted in separate republics in north and south, one Communist, one West-aligned, with Pyongyang and Seoul as their respective capitals that would see America once again embroiled in war in June 1950.

In some ways more important than all the other developments, at least to the story of the Defense Department in the Cold War, the Truman administration also found itself presiding over the end product of a presidential finding based on NSC-68, a National Security Council policy paper that Truman had directed be prepared in the spring of 1950 by the group, composed of cabinet-level representatives, responsible for drafting national security policy under the 1947 National Security Act.

NSC-68 had been drafted largely in response to an event that had been code-named JOE 1 by the Pentagon. Named for Soviet leader Josef Stalin, JOE 1 signified the test explosion of the first Soviet atomic bomb in August 1949.

The test detonation of the Soviet nuclear weapon was an event that had shocked the world because it demonstrated beyond doubt that the USSR had advanced much further, and much faster, than anyone, including the newly minted CIA, had believed possible.

This, in turn, meant that the United States was no longer the sole atomic knight on the battlefield; moreover, the Soviet bomb test took place against the backdrop of an especially stormy year for postwar face-offs between East and West marked by two major crises: the War Scare of March 1948 and the Berlin Blockade, and the somewhat less discomfiting one, to most Americans, of the February 1948 Communist coup in Czechoslovakia that toppled the democratic Benes regime and installed a ruthless Communist government in its place. Finally, the detonation of JOE 1 coincided with the 1949 takeover of China by a Communist government under the leadership of Mao Ze Dong.

What became known as the Spring Crisis (alternatively known as the War Scare) originated in a postwar atmosphere of mounting tension in the wake of these and other world crises, such as a radical increase of Soviet sabotage in north German ports through which the Allies shipped supplies into Germany and heavy movements of Soviet troops and armor into Czechoslovakia after the Iron Curtain dropped between it and the West.

The state of panic was widespread. There was a building sense that the Soviets were on the move everywhere, a creeping sense of menace that the Iron Curtain would fall elsewhere, moving ever westward; would they soon be in Europe? Czechoslovakia had been the second casualty of World War II, falling to the Germans in 1939. Would it be the first casualty of World War III? There was an uncomfortable sneaking certainty that it might.

That sense of foreboding, that premonition of doom, was not limited to the masses. The flames of panic, fanned by biased intelligence reports that originated by a joint CIA–Army intelligence gathering project code-named Wringer, were shared by the commander-in-chief of European Command, General Lucius D. Clay. Wringer's objective was to compile a picture of what the Soviets were planning based on debriefings of thousands of former POWs repatriated from the Soviet Union.

The Gehlen Organization, a private intelligence network headed by former Nazi intelligence chief Reinhard Gehlen (whose services had been recruited by Allen Dulles) and which purported to have reliable contacts inside the USSR, was the source for much of the flawed data given to Clay. Reading the Gehlen report on the imminence of Soviet attack, ignoring a more sober analysis of the situation by the CIA attached to the report, hearing the roar of Soviet nuclear bombers overhead and the cadence of troops marching in lockstep, Clay—so a congressional investigation later concluded—hit the panic button.

"War may come with dramatic suddenness," reported Clay in an urgent cable to the director of intelligence, Army General Staff Lieutenant General Stephen J. Chamberlain, who immediately reacted by hitting his own panic buttons at the Department of Defense. Clay added: "I am unable to submit any official report in the absence of supporting data but my feeling is real."

The result was a combat alert to U.S. military forces around the world, while the U.K., France, and Italy were warned to take immediate measures to prepare for imminent Soviet attack. In the end, the attack never materialized, and while the Soviets might well have been flexing their muscles, later analysis which found flaws in the Gehlen Organization's report showed that they were nowhere near ready to start a war with the United States and its European allies.

A congressional investigation that followed the crisis stated, "In March 1948, near hysteria gripped the U.S. Government with the so-called 'war scare.'" The investigation placed the blame on General Clay, whose cable had "precipitated" the global alert, and on the U.S. Army in Germany, which had badly misinterpreted Gehlen's intelligence data. But Clay's view, if tinged by Cold War paranoia, was shared by many at the time.

As early as December 1947, the commander of U.S. Air Forces in the Far East wrote General Carl A. "Tooey" Spaatz, newly appointed from Army Air Force chief of staff to head the recently established U.S. Air Force, "I want to emphasize that I feel that there is grave danger of war with USSR within a few months. The world situation continues to deteriorate. . . . USSR has moved so far along the aggression road that she must continue to move along the same way. American public opinion will eventually demand that USSR be halted. . . ."

Indeed, early in the same month as Clay's worried dispatch, the president himself had written to his daughter Margaret, saying, "We are faced with exactly the same situation with which Britain and France were faced in 1938-9 with Hitler. Things look black. A decision will have to be made. I am going to make it."

That same year's Soviet blockade of East Berlin, however, was no mere scare. In 1948, following the unilateral merger of Allied zones in occupied postwar Germany into a single economic unit, the Soviet Union withdrew from the Allied Control Council, which administered the four postwar occupation zones into which Germany had been divided by its conquerors, following which the Soviets blockaded Berlin's rail, highway, and water links to the West.

For the duration of the crisis, which lasted about eleven months from 1948 to 1949, the U.S. and U.K. flew some two hundred thousand flights into West Berlin, supplying nearly two million tons of coal, food, and industrial goods. The Soviets finally gave up and lifted the blockade. The West had won a round, but there was the gnawing worry that the Soviets would start a second round, and this time might not back down so easily, if they backed down at all.

The byproducts of these shock waves were manifold; among them was the Truman military buildup of 1950 under the NSC-68 plan. As surprised and fearful at the Soviet bomb as were millions of other Americans, and in response to the 1949 Chinese Communist revolution, the president remarked, "This means we have no time left."

The rearmament, the largest since the end of World War II up to that point, ratcheted defense spending up to 20 percent of real GNP and declared a policy, thereafter called the Truman Doctrine, that warned potential adversaries that the United States would not limit itself to the defense against military incursions by foreign powers in the Western

Hemisphere alone, but would fight any Communist threat, anywhere in the world.

The Truman Doctrine was oddly prescient; scarcely two months after the president had articulated it, North Korea attacked the south across the Demilitarized Zone. This began the Korean War. Though later described as a "police action" by Truman, it was a war in every sense of the word that was to last until an uneasy ceasefire under United Nations oversight was declared three years later on July 27, 1953. The war in Korea not only became a test of the Truman Doctrine, but as it rapidly escalated, also became a test of postwar U.S. defense production capacity and the effectiveness and celerity of Cold War defense mobilization. The U.S. defense establishment responded to the challenges posed by the conflict by ramping up both manpower and industrial war production. Nevertheless, the Defense Department, particularly the Joint Chiefs of Staff, was reluctant to commit the large forces necessary to roll back the Communist North Koreans. U.S. manpower levels had fallen drastically through massive demobilization following World War II. In June 1950 total armed strength of the U.S. Army was 593,167, with the Marine Corps mustering an additional 75,370, while North Korea alone could mobilize on the order of some two hundred thousand combat troops.

Despite the Pentagon's reservations, President Truman and Secretary of State Dean Acheson pushed to commit U.S. troops to Korea under a mandate by the United Nations Security Council, which had voted to repel the invasion of South Korea (The Republic of Korea, ROK) by the North—Truman never asked Congress for a formal declaration of war—placing General Douglas MacArthur in command. An ambitious amphibious marine landing at the port city of Inchon under the command of Admiral Arthur Dewey Struble, an expert in land-and-stay operations of this type, proved the starting point for a successful campaign that recaptured the ROK capital, Seoul, with U.N. troops later crossing the 38th parallel to capture Pyongyang, the capital of North Korea, and thus moving only about ninety miles south of the Red Chinese border.

This action sparked a massive Communist Chinese counterattack that eventually rolled back U.S. forces, wiping out earlier gains.

Moreover, the shock of massive retaliation opened the door to the use of nuclear weapons. MacArthur asked for a "D-Day atomic capability" in the form of resources to launch a massive nuclear assault on the Chinese and Soviets. Truman gave it to him. By early April, 1951, the Joint Chiefs of Staff had ordered immediate nuclear retaliation against Soviet and Chinese bases in Manchuria should large new troop contingents enter the conflict. Atomic bombs more powerful than those which had been dropped on Hiroshima and Nagasaki soon awaited final arming at U.S. bases in Okinawa. In the end, partly because he became unsure that MacArthur would carry out Washington's instructions in the use of tactical nukes, Truman ordered the Chiefs to relieve MacArthur. Soon after this, the war began to lock into a brutal stalemate, which in turn led to the troubled armistice and uneasy truce that followed.

Hardly had the ink dried on the truce agreement than the Soviet Union, on August 12, 1953, detonated JOE 4—the first USSR thermonuclear weapon explosion, harnessing the same type of chain reaction as that which takes place at the center of the sun, and more powerful and destructive than the JOE 1 atomic bomb by many orders of magnitude.

The results of JOE 4 were to prove invaluable to the Soviets in the manufacture of the first functional thermonuclear weapon in 1955. Originally called the "superbomb" but soon commonly known as the H-bomb, thermonuclear armaments were true city-busters. A single medium-sized H-bomb could destroy a city the size of New York, yet the mechanics of bomb construction made possible the creation of far lighter and far more compact warheads than the huge bombs that had leveled Hiroshima and Nagasaki in 1945.

The United States had exploded a fifteen-megaton H-bomb on March 1, 1954, at Bikini Atoll in the Pacific, one almost twenty times as powerful as the Hiroshima bomb and light and compact enough to be delivered by air in conveyances other than the heaviest bombers in the U.S. inventory. Moreover, these new warheads were small enough to be fitted on missiles. The new Truman defense budget under NSC-68 had opened the floodgates of congressional spending for defense; the lean postwar budget years were a thing of the past.

Within weeks of the Bikini Atoll tests the secretary of the air force could guarantee "the maximum effort possible with no limitation as to funding" for a Pentagon program to develop ballistic missiles capable of delivering nuclear payloads to targets thousands of miles away. The age of ballistic missiles had arrived, and unlike the case of a few years before, the navy found that there was now plenty of funding for development of its own nuclear war fighting plans.

With an emphasis on missiles as nuclear delivery systems, the large "supercarriers" envisioned by the navy during the Forrestal era were no longer deemed unnecessary or impractical. Ballistic nuclear submarines equipped with scores of nuclear ballistic missiles, as championed by Admiral Hyman Rickover, offering the navy unparalleled access to the world's oceans, were also commissioned, with the USS *Nautilus* in the van.

But the Soviets, too, were ready to spend on defense programs of their own. Investing tremendous amounts of capital, manpower, and industrial plants to develop carriers, submarines, and ballistic missiles capable of rivaling Western development programs, the USSR produced the world's first operational strategic missiles. The largest of them, the R-7 Semyorka (known in the West by the NATO code name SS-6 Sapwood), developed to loft the Sputnik III satellite into orbit, were hundreds of times larger and more powerful than those developed by the Americans.

In 1957 and 1959, the Soviet Union trumped the West with those missiles, launching the first satellites—Sputniks—into orbit. While recognized as a scientific achievement in its own right, there was no doubt that those same missiles could also loft nuclear payloads high into the stratosphere, from which they could reach targets in the United States within a matter of minutes. The Soviets had just upped the arms race ante, and the United States was not about to fold and quit the game.

* * *

The questions over how to rebuild the "arsenal of democracy" in the face of what was beginning to look to like a mounting prelude to a shooting war between the United States and the USSR continued to be debated even as the new Department of Defense reorganized after 1947 and Cold War tensions waxed steadily.

Despite the truce between Robert Patterson and James Forrestal that had been declared at the Pentagon at the height of the debate over postwar defense unification, the bureaucratic shoving match between air power and sea power advocates over which side would get the lion's share of the budget continued for well over six months.

It had been Truman who had read the riot act to the military's contentious leadership, but though the commander in chief had quelled the infighting, even the president couldn't stop it completely. There was far too much at stake—careers hung on the line as well as a budget to fund military programs. This was not a crisis that could be stopped that easily. Truman had poured cold water on the flames but had not put out the fire.

The Spring Crisis of 1948, which had actually begun with an imminent Communist coup in Czechoslovakia in the late winter of 1947, marked a turning point, but the Clay memorandum that had precipitated the crisis might have been considerably more than a panic attack by a worried regional CINC (commander in chief) in response to perceived rumors of war. In hindsight the memo could have also been part of a deliberate effort to tilt the budgetary horn of plenty in the direction of air power—the initial net result of the war scare. Not only the president but Congress had weighed in on the vital question of military unification and the defense appropriations that would fund it. Several congressional committees had already issued reports, such as the Eberstadt Report, that had proved as partisan as the disputatious cabals at the Pentagon.

As the Revolt of the Admirals continued, however, Truman, acceding to the recommendations of Congress, authorized the creation of what became generically called the Finletter Commission. Officially established in July 1947, and officially called the President's Air Policy Commission, the five-member Finletter Commission, chaired by attorney Thomas Finletter, was convened to formulate an integrated national military aviation strategy. It held more than two hundred meetings and heard testimony from more than 150 witnesses before making its report, "Survival in the Air Age," on January 1, 1948. The Finletter report, much publicized in the press, recommended, as the Pentagon's first order of business, an increase in defense spending.

America's "gravest danger," the commission declared, was a failure "to carry the financial burden" of Cold War defense restructuring. "Our national security must be redefined in relation to the facts of modern war," it asserted. "Not being able to count on the creation, within the future for which it now has to prepare, of a world settlement which would give it absolute security under the law, it must seek the next best thing—that is, relative security under the protection of its own arms."

On the other hand, the Finletter report strongly came out in favor of an expanded role for air power over naval power, of the advocates of the big bomber camp over those of the supercarrier. Not only was the commission's findings a shot in the arm for big bomber advocates, it was also a boon to the postwar aviation industry, which had seen its orders dwindle to a pale shadow of wartime output after the war was won. The Finletter report called for a unified defense establishment that was to be "built around the air arm" and "based on air power."

The commission also called for a "degree of preparedness—new in American life" to provide security in the face of the perceived alarming growth of Soviet military power and the USSR's expansionist tendencies. The nation, it felt, had no choice but to beef up allocations to the Defense Department, increase readiness, and by extension, expand the defense sector to peacetime levels that were far greater than anything in the past, including the interwar period between 1918 and 1939.

"The creation of a strong Military Establishment capable of defending the country will put a disproportionate share of the power of the Government in the hands of the military, and at the same time will place new and heavy burdens on the civilian agencies of Government in matters contributing to the national security," it anticipated, adding, "Our policy of relative security will compel us to maintain a force in being in peacetime greater than any self-governing state has ever kept."

Members of the Defense Department testifying before Congress bolstered the Finletter Commission's views. Air Force Chief of Staff General Carl "Tooey" Spaatz warned the commission that, "If Russia does strike the U.S., as she will if her present frame of mind continues, only a powerful air force in being can strike back fast enough, and hard enough to prevent the utter destruction of our nation." Civilian policy makers, too, such as Averell Harriman weighed in on the side of air power. Harriman testified that the only credible means of the United States attacking the Soviet Union lay in air power. "Based upon my observations and discussions with the important leaders in the Soviet Union . . . it has been quite obvious to me—that there is only one thing which the leaders of the Soviet Union fear, and that is the American air force," Harriman stated.

As the Spring Crisis unfolded the Finletter Commission's recommendations were given added emphasis. In hindsight they were almost prescient. Here was a blueprint for Cold War defense restructuring waiting to be implemented from plans to realities. The crisis gave the commission's recommendations the momentum of a powerful push from the world of international events. In this charged atmosphere the cable sent by General Clay had the effect of a hot spark on a powder keg; it was one of those catalyzing events in history that caused a chain reaction—something like the Cold War's answer to the Zimmerman Telegram of World War I.

"Clay's cable, sent directly to Chamberlain, and not through normal command channels, was to be used as Chamberlain saw fit," wrote Clay's biographer. "Its primary purpose was to assist the military chiefs in their congressional testimony; it was not, in Clay's opinion, related to any change in Soviet strategy." General Chamberlain, after a visit to occupied postwar Berlin in February 1948, alarmed at what he considered the poor state of readiness of U.S. global forces, had warned Clay that major military appropriations might not win congressional approval. Chamberlain told Clay that public opinion needed to be galvanized to support new defense budgeting.

Whether there were hidden motives behind the Clay memorandum or not, the alarm it raised not only underscored the findings of the Finletter Commission and solidified the standing of air power advocates, it also infected the country with a war fever so contagious that it spread like wildfire. Neither the public nor the Defense Department nor even the White House were immune. On March 6, General George Marshall, now retired as army chief of staff and serving as Truman's personal envoy to China, counseled a president with war jitters to remain calm and not take action that might provoke the Soviets. That same day Secretary of the Army Kenneth Claiborne Royall asked the chairman of the Atomic Energy Commission how much time would be needed to move "eggs" (meaning nukes) to the Mediterranean, while the chief of naval operations a few days later revealed the Pentagon's plan "to prepare the American people for war."

War fever continued to spread as the Soviets consolidated their hold on Czechoslovakia; in early March the suicide of Czech Foreign Minister Jan Masaryk by defenestration had to many the same ring as Captain Reynaud's remarks, in the movie *Casablanca*, concerning a decision about whether another dead man had hung himself or been shot while trying to escape. The Masaryk death, recalled by Undersecretary of State George Kennan, "dramatized as few other things could have, the significance of what had just occurred" in Eastern Europe.

A few days later emergency plans for what were tantamount to the commencement of World War III were unsealed by top U.S. military commanders at foreign posts, while the Joint Chiefs of Staff presented Secretary of Defense James Forrestal with a high-level war plan intended to counter an anticipated Soviet invasion of Western Europe and the Middle East.

As a result of these developments the Office of the Secretary of Defense and the JCS also sought a resumption, and a package of enhancements, to the Selective Service Act. The chiefs would also ask the president for a defense budget supplemental to meet the emergency and for custody of nuclear weapons by the Pentagon. Heretofore, the U.S. nuclear arsenal had been the bailiwick of the Atomic Energy Commission, with warheads and delivery systems separately maintained as a security precaution against accidental or too-hasty use in time of national crisis.

On the eve of a planned "get tough" speech by Truman in mid-March, a CIA national intelligence estimate (NIE) declared that the agency believed that war with the Soviets was not probable only for another sixty days; beyond this all bets, including the CIA's, were off. "The country is sunk," said Truman at the day's staff conference following his morning perusal of the NIE. Morosely, the president told those present that Marshall had warned him that he might "pull the trigger" with his planned tough address, but Truman believed there was no alternative to warning the nation about the threat of impending East-West military confrontation.

When Truman went before a joint session of Congress on March 17, he told his audience that "The situation in the world today is not primarily the result of natural difficulties which follow a great war. It is chiefly due to the fact that one nation has not only refused to cooperate in the establishment of a just and honorable peace, but—even worse—has actively sought to prevent it." He concluded, "There are times in world history when it is far wiser to act than to hesitate. There is some risk involved in action—there always is. But there is far more risk in failure to act."

Toward that goal Truman advocated three proposals: passage of the Marshall Plan, enactment of universal military training, and the restoration of Selective Service. Truman had not mentioned another important end-result of the Spring Crisis—the establishment of the North Atlantic Treaty Organization (NATO) although earlier that same day the first step toward NATO's creation, the signing of the Brussels Pact, had taken place.

The Spring Crisis was not to last. It was not to be a war, nor even a dress rehearsal for a war, but a shock wave that rippled across the increasingly darkening landscape of the Cold War like a clap of summer thunder betokening a yet-distant storm. The crisis was to be quickly forgotten a few months later with an event that both overshadowed it and was itself an outgrowth of it—the Berlin Airlift.

As recounted earlier, the airlift poured immense resources into beleaguered Berlin. Mobilizing relief efforts on a massive scale, it was an explosion of activity that catalyzed the impulse to fight back against Stalin's pricking the West with what Khrushchev later called "the point of the Soviet bayonet" that had frustrated the United States throughout the Spring Crisis. To all intents and purposes Stalin was determined to force a showdown over Berlin as Clay, George Marshall (now secretary of state), and other members of the Truman Administration's "Berlin Mafia" were convinced was the case.

Operationally, the airlift, spearheaded by General Clay, was a demonstration that despite the postwar downsizing of U.S. forces vis-à-vis the Soviet military ramp-up, the Pentagon's warplanners were not afraid to act. Clay had only sixty-five hundred troops in Berlin and the Americans only sixty thousand men in the whole of Europe, whereas Stalin had three hundred divisions numbering over four hundred thousand troops within striking distance of Berlin. The Soviets had also encircled Berlin with no less than ten thousand officers from the border police, units which had been specially trained by the Soviets for this purpose.

Yet Clay firmly believed the Soviets were bluffing. He stated on April 10, "We have lost Czechoslovakia. . . . If we mean that we are to hold Europe against Communism, we must not budge. . . . I believe the future of democracy requires us to stay here until forced out." Clay, with the backing of Truman, Marshall, and the Pentagon, as well as the British military and political establishment, was determined to defend Berlin, despite the threat of war. The re-supply operation, codenamed Operation Vittles in the U.S. and Operation Plain Fare in the U.K., began on Saturday, June 26, with the arrival of the first planeload of relief supplies at Tempelhof Airport. The deployment of B-29 Superfortresses to U.S. airbases in Europe was also intended to impress Stalin. The bombers were nuclear-capable, and Stalin well knew that the U.S. outstripped the Soviet Union in this area.

Stalin still didn't back down, though, and the resupply effort stalled. It was saved by the intervention of General William H. Tunner, a USAF transportation expert who took over the resupply operation on July 27. Disparaging it as "a real cowboy operation" with "confusion everywhere," Tunner turned everything around, imposing control over the complex logistics of what was to become the largest airlift in history with a top-to-bottom reshuffling of resources and priorities.

In 1945, when the Americans arrived in Berlin, Tempelhof's lone runway was sodded and had been used only for small aircraft and fighters during the latter stages of the war. It was beautifully equipped with hangars and a large terminal building but unfortunately was surrounded by high apartment buildings. Before the airlift the grass runway had been covered with a 12-foot-thick rubber base overlaid with pierced-steel landing mats, which, though adequate for pre-airlift traffic, proved unequal to the round-the-clock pounding of the heavily-laden aircraft landing gear. Soon a force of 225 men was kept busy working on the runway between plane landings to keep the field operational. In early July construction had begun on a second runway, with a third started toward the end of the year.

In addition to "breaking" the blockade, Tunner's operation laid the foundation for the postwar system of international civilian air traffic control that exists to the present day. The airlift was an epochal turning point, clearly marking the boundary line between the uneasy postwar peace and the advent of the Cold War.

Yet, even more than the Berlin Blockade and Airlift, the Spring Crisis ranks as one of the most important events, if not the pivotal event, of the early Cold War years if for nothing else than the many institutions that came about as its result. Among these was the ascendance of air power as the principal method of the United States' projecting military force around the world, and the establishment of the Strategic Air Command as, throughout the next decade, the main nuclear war–fighting task force. Other short-term offshoots of these developments included the nascent development of stealth technology, orbital surveillance satellites, and an overarching system for fighting nuclear war known as the Single Integrated Operational Plan, or SIOP.

Also established in the aftermath of the crisis was the peacetime draft, a dramatic increase in defense expenditures, and the revitalization of the U.S. aviation industry. Finally, there was the creation of the Atlantic alliance to serve as a bulwark against the Soviet bloc.

After this event, the shape of very many familiar elements of the Cold War face-off between East and West began to make itself manifest. The Cold War had not turned into the much-feared shooting war many had dreaded, but the chill factor had drastically increased as the superpowers squared off against one another like two contentious giants, and the nuclear arms race shifted into an entirely new phase.

* * *

The buildup, development, and hegemony of postwar air power had enormous impact on the rest of the development of the Cold War. Its impact continues to be felt today, as it will be felt into the next three or four decades of the twenty-first century. Even though the navy won its case for the supercarrier—as well as a more ambitious plan, in many regards, in the form of a fleet of ballistic nuclear submarines that could range undetected amid the depths of the ocean without needing to surface for months on end—even the naval plan depended on aircraft and missilery to project its military power into land-based conflicts and onto land-based targets in any meaningful way.

Even in battles between ships at sea it would be aircraft that carried the fight between opposing naval forces. The age of the battleship had to all intents and purposes already come to a close, and naval air power had been a critical factor in all the major battles at sea in the Pacific Theater of World War II. As to nuclear submarines, their role in undersea combat would revolve around the sea-launched ballistic missile. Not only would missiles be the main weapon that would launch nuclear warheads on trajectories that would detonate them over targets far inland, but even in confrontations with enemy submarines or attacks on carrier battle groups, the object would be to prevent the other side from deploying its missiles against friendly targets.

Air power also became critical to the SIOP and the Worldwide Military Command and Control System, or WMCCS, more commonly known as WIMEX by the way the acronym was pronounced. The WIMEX, established in 1962, and which would grow to encompass all the manifold physical infrastructure for tracking, launching, and maintaining communications with nuclear forces—later including ARPANET, the Internet's forerunner—would, among other things, relay the president's instructions to nuclear forces from airborne command posts codenamed Looking Glass and Kneecap in the event of nuclear war.

But in the late 1940s and early 1950s, as the gap widened between those nations on either side of the Iron Curtain, the advent of air power meant two things in the main. The first of these was strategic military power projection. The age of the ICBM had not yet dawned, and while nuclear weapons had grown in sophistication and power, the means of reliably hitting a bull's-eye, or at least exploding them close enough to their targets for them to do their awesomely destructive work, was limited to heavy bombers in a one-bomb, one-plane payload. It would be close to another decade before fieldable nuclear weaponry was compact enough to be carried by medium bombers. Only heavy bombers could be built to loft nuclear payloads to distant targets with a reasonable chance of getting through and destroying their targets.

The second use of aircraft—and in the near term these were the same strategic bombers that were to be used to drop the bombs in the event of war—was for the purpose of aerial reconnaissance and targeting surveillance. The Soviets were engaging in testing nuclear weapons and new, long-range missiles. Their bases were located deep within their heartland, and the only way to find out what they were up to was to covertly fly planes equipped with cameras into the airspace of the USSR and bring back photographic evidence of their military programs. At this time only the long-range, strategic bombers had the "legs" to make such deep penetration overflights.

A developing corollary of this second use of strategic aircraft was to pick out and designate targets in the Soviet Union for American long-range bombers to strike with nuclear weapons if war broke out, which the growing consensus was that it would, sooner or later. Orbital surveillance satellite programs were secretly being put into action as early as 1948, but their end products would not be ready for useful deployment for at least another decade. Until these new technological developments were ready for military use, it was the proven method of the long-range bomber—the same method that had worked so well in Europe and the Pacific in World War II—that would be the keystone of the U.S. nuclear fighting force in the early Cold War years.

* * *

"Chiefs buy all this?"

"Yes, sir. We're very anxious to start on this program right away. We realize the seriousness of it, but we feel this is the only way we're gonna get this information."

"Uh-huh."

Harry Truman wasn't smiling, in fact he looked like he was playing tough-guy this morning. The visitor wasn't sure if he should say anything else. He decided to wait until the commander in chief directed a remark to him that was other than a sentence fragment or a series of grunts.

The president looked back down at the papers and maps he'd been handed fifteen minutes before by the air force two-star who sat across from him in one of the visitors' chairs facing Truman's desk in the White House Oval Office. The visitor, General Nathan Twining, the air force vice chief of staff, used the time to reflect on his orders from the JCS, trying to anticipate what the president might say and how he could best reply.

It was the fall of 1950, and Twining had only a few days before attended a meeting of the Joint Chiefs at the Pentagon. The meeting had been held in the Tank, a conference room on the Building's second floor at which the chiefs convened three times a week and conferred each Monday with the Secretary and Deputy Secretary of Defense. Chairing the meeting had been the Pentagon's newest high-profile appointee, General Omar Bradley—the first of the seventeen chairmen of the Joint Chiefs of Staff who have served between then and now.

Bradley had been appointed chairman only a few months before, on August 16, 1949, and had replaced Admiral Leahy, who had served unofficially as chief of staff to the commander in chief— the Pentagon's link with the White House—by a gentleman's agreement between the chiefs and the Oval Office. Its origins had been in the Chiefs of Staff Committee, a body made up of the heads of British land, sea, and air forces in World War II, and which had been in existence since 1923.

The United States had nothing comparable to this British coordinating agency. Roosevelt, who admired it, wanted something similar in the American armed forces. He then created an eponymous U.S. Joint Chiefs of Staff to represent the armed service branches. Leahy, tapped by FDR to serve as the informal liaison between the army and navy chiefs and the White House, now found the title of chief of staff to the commander in chief of the army and the navy conferred upon him by the president. This ad hoc arrangement, which continued throughout the war, brought the Joint Chiefs of Staff into being as an organization.

Between the ailing Leahy's retirement at the end of March and the week of Bradley's appointment in August, there had been no recognized link between the Pentagon and White House, or for that matter with the congressionally mandated civilian leadership of the Pentagon represented by the office of the secretary of defense. Congress, in the interim, had held hearings on a bill that was to be part of the amendment package to NSC-68 and was intended to define the duties and responsibilities of the chairman. Flouting a proposed ban by the Hoover Commission on appointing a service chief to be chairman (which never became law) Truman's nomination of Bradley cleared the Senate quickly; Ike's former chief of staff soon assumed the chairmanship.

At the Tank meeting attended by Twining, who had filled in that day for his boss, General Hoyt Vandenberg, the discussion had turned to secret programs that had been conducted by the Pentagon, and in tandem with the CIA and British MI-6, since the start of the Cold War. The programs, first using human intelligence assets—secret agents—such as Project Wringer to penetrate behind the veil of Iron Curtain secrecy and bring back useable intelligence on the Soviet order of battle, were unreliable. This was not surprising, considering that Wringer relied heavily on the Gehlen Organization's East Bloc spy network, which had been penetrated by the KGB and was feeding back disinformation to Western spymasters.

By the time of the Spring Crisis it had become apparent to U.S. war planners that the only reliable means of gathering intelligence about Soviet military programs was through photo-intelligence collection overflights of Soviet airspace. Seeing was, after all, believing, and when photos taken over a period of time were studied end-to-end, they provided a motion picture of Soviet developments which, checked against Wringer-derived intelligence, gave analysts as accurate a picture as could be gotten.

The covert photoreconnaissance program used the fastest and highest-flying plane available at the time—the F-86 Sabre, which would launch from B-29 bombers acting as motherships that would carry the fighters to predetermined points along the Soviet frontier. The Sabres, devoid of military markings and specially augmented with cameras and electronic sensors to record, among other things, launch telemetry from

Soviet missile test firings, would skirt the borders of the USSR then dart back to safety at U.S. bases such as those in Turkey.

Occasionally the reconnaissance planes would deviate from border flights and make incursions into Soviet airspace, but as a rule they kept to the borders. B-29s and other heavier, slower aircraft were also used to make parachute drops of spy teams equipped with radios, cameras, and other devices into Soviet territory using techniques perfected by the OSS back in the war days. One such team, made up of Ukrainians trained in what to look for, had been paradropped into the Soviet Union in September 1949, following the detonation of the first Soviet atomic test explosion; the spy team brought back confirmation that the Soviets had built a working bomb far sooner than the West had expected.

Balloons had also been used to float cameras high above Soviet territory to photograph items of interest to intelligence, harking back to airborne spying in the eighteenth and nineteenth centuries. An estimated one hundred high-altitude balloons per year were launched from bases in Western Europe in a joint USAF–USN program that began in the late 1940s.

The plan called for the prevailing winds to carry the balloons across the USSR until they reached the friendly skies over Japan, photographing the Soviet hinterland as they drifted along. Once in Japanese airspace a ground radio signal was to jettison the onboard instrumentation packages, which would parachute into the arms of waiting CIA agents.

Unfortunately the balloons had not turned out to be the greatest idea, one of the major drawbacks being that the Soviets could easily shoot them down, and gleefully ridiculed the official Pentagon cover stories explaining them as "weather balloons" by displaying captured spy cameras and military radio transmitters. At one press event in Moscow, Soviet officials showed off captured spy equipment to hundreds of journalists.

Obviously another approach needed to be taken, and that approach was to make deeper incursions into Soviet airspace than anything tried before using existing planes and bring back better photographic evidence of Soviet military projects. At the Tank meeting Bradley had informed Twining that Twining had been "volunteered" to broach the subject of the escalation of the spy plane missions to the president at the White House.

Armed with maps and papers supplied by the JCS explaining the new plan, Twining embarked on his mission. He now sat nervously awaiting the president's decision as Truman studied the documents.

To Twining's surprise, Truman neatly stacked the paperwork, picked up a pen, and signed the authorization form at the top. As the president handed back the stack, he said, "Listen, when you get back there, you tell General Vandenberg from me: Why the devil hasn't he been doing this before?" The Pentagon now had the go-ahead for an airborne reconnaissance program that was to lead to radical new spy plane designs, hair-raising missions, and stealth.

* * *

In 1953, General Omar Bradley, now, by special act of Congress, wearing five stars on his shoulders—the first and only chairman ever to achieve such rank—could look back at a distinguished career of national service. Bradley was nearing the end of his second, congressionally fixed, two-year term as the Pentagon's first chairman of the Joint Chiefs of Staff.

Between the departure of Leahy and Bradley's accession, Congress had set specific conditions on the creation of the new office of CJCS in finalizing the 1949 amendments package to the 1947 National Security Act; one of these was to fix the chairman's term to two years, with a provision for reappointment for a second two-year term—except in wartime, when no fixed limits on reappointments were in force. Bradley, who had been appointed by Truman, continued as chairman into the first year of the Eisenhower administration, a legacy appointee from the previous president.

The Pentagon had by now grown to encompass not only the building itself; the Defense Department also had stewardship of a defense establishment that stretched around the Beltway. In many respects Somervell's vision of a central headquarters building for the U.S. defense establishment had always been a step or two short of full realization.

Although the Building, since its official completion in 1943, had certainly become the central headquarters of the U.S. military, it had never completely fulfilled its intended function—to serve as the sole headquarters of the U.S. military, the immense office building within whose sprawling perimeter the staff of the defense sector—both military and civilian—would be housed.

As the Cold War reversed gears after the initial postwar drawdown of military forces and shifted back into drive, space again became a premium. Ironically, even Stimson's hated War Department building had become pressed into service to provide office space to facilitate the Pentagon's daily business. Indeed the Pentagon's official historian, the late Alfred Goldberg, surprised an interviewer during a radio broadcast following the 2001 al-Qaeda attack who suggested that the Pentagon might again spread out across Arlington as a security measure.

"Given today's modern communication technology, would it in some ways be wiser to once again spread out operations?" the talk radio host asked the historian.

"Well, in fact they are, you know. Only a part of the defense establishment here in Washington is in the Pentagon." He went on, "There are more people working for defense outside of the Pentagon than in the Pentagon. They're scattered all the way over—all over northern Virginia, Washington, and Maryland."

Bradley's tenure as chairman of the Joint Chiefs of Staff, the Department of Defense, and thus the Pentagon, not only held custody over a growing number of specialized facilities in and surrounding the capital, such as the offices of technical departments tending an ever-growing array of electronic and photographic intelligence gathering facilities, but also nominal, if not actual, stewardship of other scattered and far-flung demesnes of the burgeoning U.S. national security superstructure formed in the wake of the National Security Act.

Perhaps the largest and most secret of these was the building complex built on and around Fort Meade, Maryland, that was to form the nucleus of the National Security Agency. Other facilities under the control of the Pentagon were also either complete by this point or in the initial stages of construction.

These included the headquarters of the Strategic Air Command, located in a protected underground bunker complex beneath the rolling plains of northern Nebraska where, aboveground, Offutt Air Force Base was being equipped with runway facilities for round-the-clock takeoffs and landings of the nuclear-armed bombers on twenty-four–hour air patrol. Like SAC, the headquarters of NORAD, the joint U.S.–Canadian North American Air Defense command, would be established within the protection of the blasted-out granitic core of Cheyenne Mountain in Colorado.

There were to be numerous other underground facilities as well, as appropriations for the preservation of what came to be known as the National Command Authority during, in the midst of, and in the aftermath of Soviet nuclear attack were established—complete with living quarters and emergency command centers—in and around the nation's capital, to be expanded and enlarged as the Cold War years continued to see escalation of the East-West arms race.

Based on the principle of Roosevelt's "Shangri-la"—which had originally been a tunnel complex linking the White House with a nearby bunker but by the middle of the Truman administration referred to an underground command post beneath Camp David—and anticipating the inevitable day when Soviet bombers, missiles, or both reigned atomic destruction on the United States, facilities designed to be hardened against nuclear attack, and generally located underground, had been constructed or were already in progress.

All of these were under the control and jurisdiction of the Pentagon—as many of the surviving facilities continue to be to the present day.

* * *

Bradley, whose military career spanned two world wars and two terms as chairman of the Joint Chiefs, also presided over the unification battles that rocked the Pentagon in the shakeups caused by the 1947 National Security Act.

In part Bradley had been brought on board by Truman not only to serve in the chairman's official capacity as liaison between Pentagon and Oval Office—carrying on in the unofficial capacity assumed by Leahy during and after World War II—but also because Bradley, with a reputation for impartiality and plain dealing, was thought to be the right man at the Pentagon to take the concept of defense unification from political rhetoric to reality.

Not only did Bradley enjoy a well-earned reputation as a crack staff officer—he'd served as Eisenhower's chief of staff in the war and as army chief of staff at the Pentagon following Marshall's retirement—but he'd commanded an army in the field in the war's final months. Beyond even this, Bradley had more-or-less successfully reigned in the excesses of zeal that characterized the army's—perhaps the entire war's—most unruly commanding general, the unpredictable and sometimes ungovernable General George S. Patton, as the Allied armies slugged their way from the Normandy beachheads to Paris, Rome, and then, finally, Berlin (albeit halting just short of it for political reasons).

Bradley, the formidable general in war, proved a capable administrator in an uneasy peace, developing a reputation, among the warring defense chiefs, for what General Maxwell Taylor, Bradley's deputy chief of staff during Bradley's tenure as army chief, once dubbed "meticulous neutrality." Bradley not only fulfilled his mandate, but developed a growing reputation as an honest broker, not only with the Department of Defense and Joint Chiefs establishments, but also with the White House, and with Truman personally. The relationship between the president and the JCS chairman was forged during the drawn-out crisis of the Korean War, during which Bradley not only acted in the capacity of his position as Pentagon–White House ombudsman but also took on the unprecedented role as Truman's trusted military advisor.

Throughout the tumultuous early days of the conflict, Truman was briefed on the developing military situation every morning by Bradley at the White House, presenting to the president the recommendations of the Joint Chiefs. Then, as the crisis waned and the threat of American combat troops being forced to retreat from the Korean peninsula subsided, Bradley met with the president on Mondays, Wednesdays, and Fridays. The informal relationship between chairman and chief executive began the continuing practice of the president and the secretary of defense turning to the chairman as spokesman for the Joint Chiefs of Staff, a role that became official in later decades as new legislation further defined and enhanced the role and powers of the chairman.

As the president's trusted advocate, Bradley was also in a position to recommend, and sometimes even ramrod, ambitious, and even risky, Pentagon programs and initiatives that sometimes had lasting consequences in postwar superpower politics, and in at least one case resulted in one major snafu in already strained U.S.–Soviet Cold War relations. Such was a combination of aerial reconnaissance and surveillance initiatives, primarily of the Soviet Union, but also of Communist China, that culminated in what was dubbed Operation Overflight. This initiative, jointly administered by the CIA and the Pentagon, was under the operational control of SAC, whose commander in chief, General Curtis LeMay, held wide latitude in how far to take spy plane missions.

Overflight was ultimately to conduct hundreds of high-altitude airborne incursions into Soviet airspace, usually under extremely high-risk conditions. Jet aircraft, outfitted with cameras, had been used effectively high over the battlefields of Korea to photograph changing combat conditions and to make bomb damage assessments (BDAs) and quickly bring the intelligence back to analysts. The chiefs thought a larger operation, on a broader scale, would work effectively in spying out Soviet military ambitions. Overflight's purpose was twofold. First, surveillance missions were organized with the intent of bringing back pictorial data that would cast light on the developing nuclear weapons program of the Soviet Union.

From the Oval Office down, there was an obsessive need to know what the Soviets were up to, driven by a relentless fear of nuclear attack and a deep-seated conviction that any form of negotiation conducted by the USSR was merely a feint and a diversion to cloak their preparations for war with the United States. Thus the airborne missions were mounted in an emphatic effort to see behind the veil of deception about true Soviet intentions and learn the truth—or at least verify a truth that most Americans believed in wholeheartedly.

The second motive for Overflight flowed from the first. Should the Soviets be secretly preparing for a nuclear attack on the United States—and, again, during and after the Spring Crisis this seemed to be exactly what they were up to—the United States would not shrink from retaliation in kind. But where would the targets be located?

In the early 1950s the nuclear arsenal of the United States comprised roughly one thousand nuclear bombs, while the Soviets, slow to get started, already outnumbered the U.S. three-to-one by 1955 in operational nuclear explosives. Beyond this, the main available means of delivery was the strategic bomber aircraft, one bomb to one plane. Each bomb, therefore, had to be made to count. Not only that, the nuclear bombing missions needed to be made part of the order of battle, tied to war strategy. In short, there had to be a master plan, and targeting America's nukes was to be a part of that plan.

The plan also needed to take other things into account, such as the overall strategy of nuclear warfare—what types of targets were to be selected for attack? What level of damage did we want to inflict? Were we out to wage a controlled nuclear strike on the Soviets, one that might give them a chance to surrender? Or did we intend to bomb the Soviets to rubble? Throughout the Cold War and beyond, plans were made, and remade again to suit changing objectives and scenarios.

The Emergency War Plan proposed by SAC and approved by the Joint Chiefs of Staff on October 22, 1951, remained in force between 1951 and 1955 and was the United States' sole blueprint for waging nuclear war against the Soviets throughout this period. The plan, according to a summery in Volume IV of the *History of the Joint Chiefs of Staff*, went as follows:

> The initial strike would be launched on approximately D +6 days [the sixth day following the commencement of hostilities]. Heavy bombers flying from Maine would drop twenty bombs in the Moscow-Gorky area and return to the United Kingdom. Simultaneously, medium bombers from Labrador would attack the Leningrad area with twelve weapons

and reassemble at British bases. Meanwhile, medium bombers based in the British Isles would approach the U.S.S.R. along the edge of the Mediterranean Sea and deliver fifty-two bombs in the industrial regions of the Volga and Donets Basin; they would return through Libyan and Egyptian airfields. More medium bombers flying from the Azores would drop fifteen weapons in the Caucasus area and then stage through Dahran, Saudi Arabia. Concurrently, medium bombers from Guam would bring fifteen bombs against Vladivostock and Irkutsk.

This was the general plan, but in its nuts-and-bolts aspects the SAC Emergency War Plan encompassed a variety of smaller missions within the overall scope of the plan, and also drew on separate plans with less broad-ranging intentions that had been produced under JCS authority since the start of the nuclear era.

Plan Broiler, for example, developed by the USAF late in 1947, called for 34 H-bombs to be air-dropped on 24 cities in the Soviet Union. Plan Trojan, developed a year later in 1948, called for dropping 133 H-bombs on 70 cities in the Soviet Union, while Offtackle, a plan drafted in 1949, proposed that 220 nuclear bombs be dropped on 104 cities, with 72 nuclear weapons held in reserve.

Reaction to intelligence of known Soviet nuclear tests and analysis of the study of reconnaissance intelligence data led to further refinements in the types of targets selected to be bombed. Soviet airfields became priority targets of nuclear bombing missions with the intention of preventing Soviet air forces from launching strategic bombing missions against the U.S. and Europe. Industrial targeting categories were also added and refined; the classification "atomic energy industries," for example, was added to the JCS target set in 1949 with the intention of checking the Soviet nuclear weapons development projects in the event of conflict.

Ultimately, the various types of targeting criteria developed under the Emergency War Plan would be culled down to three main target categories in pursuit of three mission categories—Bravo, Delta, and Romeo. Bravo targets were targets selected with the intent of blunting the Soviets' capability to deliver an offensive nuclear strike against the United States and its allies. Delta targets—named for disrupting the Soviet ability to wage nuclear and conventional warfare—were intended to inflict a lower level of damage to enemy forces. Finally, Romeo targets were those selected because hitting them would retard the ability of Soviet military forces to advance into the territory of American allies in Western Europe.

By the middle of Eisenhower's first presidential term the stockpile of nuclear arms grew, aerial spy plane missions revealed increased activity, and nuclear air tasking orders became more complex due to the presence of new Soviet antiaircraft installations and faster Soviet fighter planes. The Defense Department continued to study and refine the Strategic Air Command's mission. One such study, a 1955 Defense Department document, now declassified, was prepared by the Weapons Systems Evaluation Group (WSEG) commissioned by the Pentagon to evaluate SAC capabilities in a real-world scenario in which the United States struck back at the USSR with strategic nuclear bomber missions.

The group's report, number twelve in a series of evaluations, was called WSEG-12. The Pentagon evaluation studied a scenario where the U.S. struck a large number of Soviet targets with an approximately two-thousand-bomb arsenal, including 645 airfields and 118 cities. WSEG-12 evaluated the Delta mission as the one most likely to succeed, though it would not, in the study's opinion, be enough to bring the Soviets to their knees.

The report rated the Bravo mission negatively because SAC didn't have enough nuclear weapons at the time to effect a staggering disruption of the Soviet war-waging capability. It predicted a high level of "leakage," or Soviet bombers that survived to rally and launch retaliatory nuclear missions against the United States. WSEG-12 estimated that the combined nuclear offensive would result in a total of 77 million "immediate casualties" within the Soviet bloc and leave 60 million dead.

"In support of the neutralization objective, 645 Soviet bloc airfields are attacked," it stated at one point. "Even so, this attack does not encompass all known airfields pertinent to the Soviet operational and dispersal capabilities. Some 320 Soviet emergency airfields remain unstruck [sic]. Of this total, about 25 percent might be temporarily unusable even for dispersal purposes as a result of radioactive fall-out [sic]. Thus, during and immediately after, the U.S. offensive at least 240 unstruck [sic] and uncontaminated emergency airfields would be available to the Soviets for the dispersal of their inventory of aircraft capable of delivering atomic weapons."

The DOD study predicted that most of the skilled personnel living in the 118 Soviet cities that were struck would perish and most military and civilian command posts would be destroyed. According to WSEG-12, the best chance of the U.S. prevailing under contemplated battle conditions was to launch a preemptive nuclear strike. "The Soviets are estimated to have 284 atomic weapons . . . hence it can be seen that the Soviets need to save only a small fraction of their aircraft inventory to recuperate only a few of their operating and staging bases in order to be physically capable of undertaking some level of atomic operations after our attack."

Since the Soviets only needed to save a small fraction of their operational aircraft and recuperate only a few of their command posts and staging bases, the report continued, "even under the improbable assumption that only five percent of the [Soviet] aircraft survived, seventy-five weapons could still be lifted against the U.S., and 85 percent of the remainder of the stockpile could be lifted against the U.S. overseas bases and Allies in a single strike as soon as a few bases are recuperated."

Thus, the report advocated, the United States had to allocate "more weapons . . . to the mission to insure . . . that all the important Soviet operational and staging bases are destroyed in the first strike," and that still more nukes should be allocated "for subsequent attacks designed to complete the destruction of the Soviet aircraft inventory, and to prevent the Soviets from recuperating airfields and regrouping and launching their surviving bombers."

The Pentagon white paper warned that because "the Soviets can, in a single strike against the United States, launch more than sufficient one-way sorties to lift all their atomic weapons," that, "if the Soviets launch such a strike before our offensive is begun or before our bombs fall on targets, the U.S. offensive may not materially reduce the Soviet atomic capabilities. Therefore, a factor of timing is of vital importance." WSEG-12 concluded, however, that even with twice the number of nuclear weapons currently allocated to the U.S. bomber fleet, the chances of completely preventing the Soviets from launching a retaliatory strike were slim. Unless, stated WSEG-12, "we hit first."

Nuclear war plans were developed and enhanced with new bomb aim points being added to SAC target lists. By 1956 almost three thousand potential targets had been identified, a figure which climbed to twenty thousand by 1960. With U-2 spy plane missions bringing back an ever-increasing take of targeting intelligence the Joint Chiefs of Staff cast about for a way to consolidate the U.S. plan for waging nuclear war into a comprehensive whole.

It was decided that the thousands of warheads now in the U.S. nuclear arsenal would be keyed to specific primary and secondary targets, that the disposition of U.S. and British nuclear order of battle (the U.K. being the only other Western nation then to possess the bomb) would be configured around a central operational plan. It would include plans for the use of the entire U.S. nuclear arsenal; missiles deployed in the United States as well as those on submarines and in Europe.

Indeed, the plan would take into account all the individual U.S. strategies for waging war in specific areas, such as in the Far East, Europe, and the Middle East, as well as cope with the destruction of targets in the United States and attempt to ensure that the battlefield communications network of friendly military and civil defense forces for coordinating a nuclear war and its aftermath continue to function under all conceivable conditions. The task of interpreting this set of instructions from the chiefs and creating a plan based on it fell to an interagency group working under the Joint Strategic Target Planning Staff (JSTPS), under the direction of SAC.

In 1960 the JSTPS convened at SAC headquarters at Offutt Air Force Base in Omaha, Nebraska, to begin the drafting of the plan. The group, whose members included civilian academics and active members of the military, were nonetheless unwelcome at the inner sanctum of the Strategic Air Command and especially provoked the ire of its commander, General Curtis LeMay, who did not take well to interlopers in the guts of the organization he ran in a very hands-on fashion and didn't want any outsiders to tell him where to target his nukes.

Nevertheless, the JSTPS, using early computer analysis to attach point values to specific targets, completed its plan in December 1960. It was known as the Single Integrated Operational Plan, or SIOP, first of several such SIOPs that have served as the Pentagon's blueprint for waging nuclear war from that point to the present day. Revised by successive Defense Department administrations, and incorporating changing force dispositions and orders of battle, nuclear stockpile levels, and developing weapons technology, the options available under the SIOP continue to undergo change.

Beyond the SIOP, the establishment of the JSTPS ushered in other profound changes in both nuclear and conventional Pentagon strategic planning. LeMay's antipathy to outsiders, especially civilian outsiders, tinkering with SAC's total control over nuclear war planning and war fighting was prescient in a way, for the advent of the interagency group ushered in a new age in which nuclear weapons policy making was removed from the total control of the generals and largely placed into the hands of a new breed of civilian nuclear strategists who were to leave their mark on succeeding decades.

The days in which Truman would turn to General Leslie Groves for expert guidance in determining the U.S. approach to nuclear deterrence and nuclear offensive, or left these details to the gung-ho LeMay, were soon to draw to a close. This new breed would be typified by civilian consultants to the Pentagon, the White House, and Congress such as Robert McNamara, and think tanks, such as RAND that would be the prime movers in determining America's stance toward forecasting and fighting wars throughout the rest of the Cold War and beyond into Vietnam, the Gulf War, peacekeeping in the Balkans, and the Iraq War.

Meanwhile, spy plane overflights of the Soviet Union continued to be made and bring back a growing database of intelligence on Soviet military development. While conventional military aircraft, such as F-86 Sabre fighters and B-29 and the later B-50 bombers, had been pressed hastily into service in the immediate postwar years to cobble together a workable if crude capability to mount aerial surveillance and reconnaissance missions over the heads of the Soviets, by the early 1950s they were already showing their weaknesses.

Not only were these aircraft originally all intended to fly combat and not surveillance missions, and so not ideally integrated with carrying the increasingly sensitive and sophisticated photographic and electronic equipment payloads, but they were beginning to become fair game for increasingly sophisticated Soviet countermeasures aimed at blasting American spy aircraft from the Motherland's skies. These included faster and more accurate surface-to-air missile (SAM) systems and deadlier, higher-flying aircraft like the Mikoyah-Gurevich (MiG) fighters, equipped with machine guns and air-to-air missiles. According to Soviet historian Roy Medvedev, Soviet Premier Joseph Stalin was so irate over repeated and systematic American incursions into Soviet airspace that he set in motion a crash program to develop SAMs specifically designed to knock U.S. bandits out of the skies.

Consequently, before the first half of the 1950s was over the first wave of spy planes was as obsolete as the balloons they themselves had replaced at the start of the decade, and the Pentagon was casting about for a new and better alternative. This alternative was found amid the languishing aircraft industry whose recovery, despite congressional assistance under the Finletter Commission's recommendations, had yet to bounce back to anything approaching its full wartime strength.

The event that triggered the realization of this obsolescence was an incident over the Soviet missile installation at Kapustin Yar in the autumn of 1953. Defense intelligence and the CIA had received reports of extensive Soviet missile tests being carried out at this base, about seventy-five miles east of Stalingrad. What was happening here was important; according to secret reports the Soviets were testing, for the first time, new missile systems that were prototypes of missiles that might have strategic capabilities. "We just can't ignore it," said Robert Amory, chief of the CIA's Intelligence Directorate at the time. "This is going to be a major new thing, this whole missile development, and we've got to get on top of it in the beginning and judge it."

This the United States did, but the effort ended in near disaster when a camera-loaded British B-57 Night Intruder, flown by the Royal Air Force and acting jointly with the U.S. Overflight program, flew the mission over Russia and returned to its clandestine base in West Germany on a wing and a prayer, its fuselage peppered with holes from Soviet MiGs and missile warhead shrapnel. Whether this near disaster happened, as some believe, as a result of a secret tip-off from the Soviet mole, Kim Philby, in British MI-6—Philby sang like a canary before his defection, compromising numerous missions—and despite the fact that the incident was hushed up and never made the papers, it was a case, as the British later told the Americans, of "Never, never, never again."

And so it was that a backchannel approach by the CIA was made to Lockheed Aircraft's Kelly Johnson who had designed the Lockheed F-104, the first U.S. tactical jet fighter plane, and taken it from drawing board to field trials in 141 days. Johnson said he had just the thing. "I'll take the F-104 and I'd give it wings like a tent." Johnson added, "It's a cinch."

Thus was born the U-2 spy plane that, armed with an array of sophisticated cameras and electronic snooping devices, and able to fly at eighty thousand feet or better altitudes that would stall the air-breathing engines of pursuing Soviet MiGs, successfully took over the Overflight spy missions for the remainder of the decade and into the early 1960s and beyond. Other spy aircraft, especially the SR-71 Blackbird, would be developed later on, and satellites would be placed in orbit after the 1962 shoot-down of U-2 pilot Francis Gary Powers over Swerdlovsk exposed the existence of the secret program.

The Pentagon's need to gather intelligence on Soviet programs increased with each new technological development that brought back better and clearer evidence that the Soviets were not only developing strategic nuclear missile technology, but that they were far ahead of the U.S. in many respects. More alarming than even the rapid pace of Soviet missile development was the size of the missiles—the Soviets were building mammoths compared to American rocketry. By the late 1950s the Soviets had constructed and successfully launched the gargantuan Sputnik III satellite, which weighed a hundred times more than the thirty-pound packages that the United States had struggled to place in earth orbit.

The enormous Soviet rockets raised the frightening specter of Soviet missiles reigning down a deluge of nuclear warheads on the United States and blasting the nation to radioactive rubble.

"We will bury you," Stalin's successor, Soviet Premier Nikita Khrushchev, had said later on. The existence of the Soviet Union's behemoth missiles struck a new chord of fear in the national psyche.

The United States was eventually—and after a series of glaring failures—to close this "missile gap" with the USSR, pulling ahead with smaller missiles that could be produced faster than those in the Soviet arsenal, and in far greater numbers, and able to loft lighter and more accurate warheads across intercontinental distances. Nevertheless, this fact in itself was destined to bring the world to the brink of nuclear war, for when, by 1962, the United States had hastened to a clear lead in the East-West arms race, the Soviet leader saw only one way to counter it—Khrushchev would give the USSR's large medium-range missiles the same striking power as those smaller and more numerous ones the Americans had by a single master stroke of nuclear brinkmanship. Khrushchev would place Soviet missiles in America's backyard.

He would place them on the island of Cuba, and then the Soviet Union would watch the Americans squirm as they again held the upper hand.

CHAPTER ELEVEN

CREDIBLE DETERRENTS

"Vile Casca, what does this mean?"

—Caesar to first assassin

History, as life, has its turning points. In the biography of the Pentagon there have been several, some of which, such as the Japanese airborne raid on the Pearl Harbor naval base and the Spring Crisis of 1948, we've already encountered. Others, such as the September 11 al-Qaeda attacks on the Pentagon itself, have yet to be touched on. Another turning point now appears before us in the story of the Building; the final years of the first two decades following the end of World War II, and fledgling years of the Kennedy presidential administration, mark its approach. The development that illuminates the turning point is the Cuban Missile Crisis of August through October 1962.

John F. Kennedy's 1960 presidential victory marked a division in American life that still seems in hindsight to have drawn a line between the era of the old guard in American political, cultural, and military sectors and a very different era that began to make itself manifest shortly thereafter. It was to quickly become a world obsessed by technological development, a world characterized by the compulsion to build a future technocracy so aptly represented by the New York World's Fair of 1964–1965. The symbol of the international exposition that opened at Flushing Meadow Park in the borough of Queens that spring was the Unisphere, an enormous steel globe fashioned from a grid of curved radial lines.

The globe bore huge plate steel cutouts of the five continents and was surrounded by two inclined orbital planes that might have been the tracks of satellites or might have otherwise represented the orbits of electron or quanta about the nucleus of a huge atom. Alternatively, those great, twin steel hoops might also have been the post–boost phase trajectories of nuclear missile warheads entering a final trajectory to strike enemy missile silos on the earth below.

The linkage of the Unisphere—officially representing the oneness of mankind on the face of the planet—with the less benign specters of nuclear war, space-based weapons, or orbital surveillance satellites, might have been unconscious. But in hindsight, the resemblance of the Unisphere, especially when lit by a ring of ground-based spotlights at night, to a wire grid map or diagram in a computer-generated simulation seems eerily prescient. The 1964 World's Fair seemed to raise as its icon a powerful symbol of technological change driven with lightning rapidity, of globe-spanning communications and globe-shrinking weaponry, of a streamlined futurism that went round and round and never stopped, an infinity machine racing to a computerized tomorrow of robotic weaponry and stealth warfare. As such, the architectural message connects with the message of prewar building projects offering a similar theme, preeminently the Pentagon.

The connotations and associations didn't stop at the Unisphere. The fair's exhibits only underscored the subliminal message of the Unisphere: The future is here in embryo, beautiful, proud, even majestic, but also terrifying and potentially apocalyptic. In the General Motors Futurama exhibit, in a building whose shape prefigured the starship *Enterprise*, a giant conveyor belt looped visitors seated in stereo speaker–equipped chairs around a series of dioramas depicting next-century cities linked by monorail, strange undersea bases, bases on the moon and mars, and in frozen Antarctic wastes, and other wonders of a futurity that were as sterile as a test tube cleansed of its last microbe. Similar wonders, including picture phones and flying automobiles, were to be seen at the Ford and General Electric exhibits, and at the Chrysler and SKF industries or the Hall of Science, sponsored by New York State.

As futuristic architecture, the Pentagon was itself a radical departure from the Belle Epoch architecture of the War Department Building so despised by Henry Stimson. Its message, in concrete that had been molded in wooden mason's forms into immense white slabs, was that the world that had existed before and after World War I was extinct and that a new reality, marked by streamlining and industrialization, had taken its place.

The four decades to follow were to witness the realization, if not in fact then in essence, of the vision of futurity cast upon the present by what observers in the early 1960s began calling "the new breed" of technocrats and social planners. Much was missed. The skyways and monorails whisking traffic across stark urban landscapes devoid of traffic envisioned by New York City's Robert Moses never came about, nor did even the most gifted theorists of the future envision the personal computer revolution, the Internet, or even the fact that the portable device that would incorporate television, vast libraries of information, and other wonders would be the cell phone in everyone's pocket.

Be that as it may, the essential set of expectations about the future of the twentieth century was there if one looked for it. It was a zeitgeist that tenanted every undertaking, including those pertaining to the Pentagon. Moreover, it was brought up in Eisenhower's televised farewell address on departing the White House in January 1961, in which the outgoing president warned of the growth of a military-industrial complex—he had originally intended to dub it a "military-industrial-congressional complex"—that the former supreme allied commander saw as a force that threatened to collectively cause profound, and on the whole, negative changes in the American way of life with consequences to the world and its community of nations. The future, everything—call it the zeitgeist—seemed to announce, was complex, strange, often unpredictable despite the best intelligence available. Even what future theorists the Tofflers dubbed "war-forms" would defy expectations based on past experiential norms to a far greater degree than the emerging face of World War II denied the expectations proposed in the Hoover Commission's war readiness plans of the interwar period in the approximate two decades between 1918 and 1939.

The dynamic that shaped these expectations was manifold, though driven by only a few prime movers. Chief among them were the realities of the Cold War arms race between the superpowers. The Soviet Union had first matched, then outstripped the United States in the development of nuclear warheads and the missile systems to deliver them to distant targets. Yet, according to most observers, the missile technology to which they'd committed themselves was obsolete, and by 1962 the United States, fielding smaller but more numerous missiles and lighter yet deadlier and more accurate warheads, had again pulled ahead in the nuclear arms race. While others, including former Secretary of State and NATO commander Alexander Haig, dispute this (Haig has stated, "The leaders of the Defense Department convinced themselves, while overruling more experienced men, that the Soviets were developing these clumsy systems because of technological backwardness. That was a mistake."), there is little disagreement that the existence of mighty nuclear superpower arsenals redefined the balancing game of global power projection and the political realities attendant on it.

In the late 1940s and early 1950s the Korean War could be fought in the manner of set-piece battles in the same way and using the same order of battle as the battles of World War II that had preceded it. By the time of America's involvement in Vietnam, however, an entirely new set of circumstances came into being, stemming, in part, from the threat of one or more parties to the conflict opting to escalate to the use of tactical nuclear weapons, which would then harbinger a larger and more destructive strategic exchange.

It was the Soviet Union, throughout the Vietnam War, that had been, in the view of the Joint Chiefs of Staff and the Office of the Secretary of Defense, behind the Communist regime in Hanoi, and it was the Soviet Union that might retaliate in something like the same manner that the Communist Chinese had done in North Korea, should the United States mount a conventional attack on, and occupation of, North Vietnam.

Should Soviet troops intervene, the nuclear-armed superpowers might begin the ascent of the nuclear escalation ladder. There was justification for this concern in light of past events. The Soviets had backed down and removed their missiles from Cuba in 1962, but the crisis had ended short of nuclear war by a mere hair. Were the USSR provoked into a military face-off against the United States in Vietnam its leaders might not shy away a second time.

The existence of nuclear stockpiles that were growing in accuracy and lethality was one of the factors that led to U.S. military doctrines geared to fighting limited wars in which low intensity conflict was the norm rather than total, global warfare with clearly defined stakes. Since a nuclear exchange could very well end human society as the world knew it, and would almost certainly have had a profoundly harmful effect on both East and West, it was axiomatic that there would be no victors in total war of the kind that had characterized the last two world wars.

The war in Vietnam was also the first true test of the ability of the United States to project global military power to the far-flung corners of the earth after the debacle in Korea. It was a laboratory for the tactics and style of surrogate warfare that followed Vietnam. Vietnam was also a proving ground for a groundbreaking analysis toward reshaping U.S. policy toward the Soviets contained in a book by a thirty-four-year-old associate director of Harvard University's Center for International Affairs and former policy consultant to the Joint Chiefs of Staff named Henry A. Kissinger. The book, published in 1957 and titled *Nuclear Weapons and Foreign Policy*, had in many ways been a roadmap for what was to come. Kissinger's book emphasized preparedness for regional warfare, rapid long-range power projection, and the adoption of a policy of flexible response to global military threats. Along with George Kennan's proposals for deterrence and containment and the Dulles doctrine of retaliation "by means and places of our choosing," it formed one of the cornerstones of Cold War era policy.

Strategically, however, the war in Southeast Asia was fought in the shadow of a contest of technological rivalry that pitted Soviet and American intercontinental ballistic missiles against each other. The issue of whether or not tactical nukes might be used in Vietnam was secondary to the larger concerns about East-West nuclear arms control. Simultaneous with peace talks between representatives of Washington and Hanoi were the first U.S.–Soviet meetings to discuss SALT (Strategic Arms Limitation Treaty) in June 1968. By May 1971, some eighteen months later, the two sides had been to the negotiation tables in Helsinki and Vienna sixty-eight times. President Richard Nixon was later to disparage Vietnam as "a side show" to broader strategic imperatives, including ICBM proliferation. Both superpowers were building new and more lethal long-range mass destruction capabilities.

In 1969, at the height of the war, Defense Secretary Melvin Laird, fresh from a four-day trip to Vietnam, made a twofold announcement: one, that no reduction in U.S. troops was then foreseeable; two, that the Nixon Administration's proposed anti–ballistic missile system was necessary in the face of Soviet advances in offensive nuclear weaponry. A third statement, corollary to the first two followed: Laird was opposed to more than a $500 million slash in the current defense budget, despite Nixon's hope to cut $2.5 billion from the Johnson Administration's $81.4 billion estimate. In the midst of the throes of Vietnam, the realities of policing a post–WWII Pax Americana began to take on new and often terrifying complexities that not even the Korean War had brought to light.

It would not be the last time the United States and the Pentagon would grapple with the consequences of such realities in succeeding decades.

Following the end of the Vietnam War, technological advances were coupled with doctrines of limited war to de-emphasize large standing armies and bring to the fore an array of precision-guided, "smart," then "brilliant" weapons systems that were being developed to take the place of the soldier in the loop. A defense build-down began to take place in the early 1970s in which national defense spending plunged to a Carter-era low, by the end of the decade, of 4.7 percent of gross national product, with real U.S. defense spending having shrunk by 22 percent from postwar levels. During that same period, the Soviet Union began deploying an entirely new generation of land-based strategic missiles, the SS-20, a mobile system capable of lifting three MIRV nuclear warheads and, with a range of about three thousand miles, was capable of striking any city in Western Europe, the Middle East, or North Africa from bases on either side of the Ural Mountains. The USSR had also developed new types of nuclear submarines capable of carrying long-range, sea-launched nuclear missiles and had test-flown a new strategic bomber with intercontinental range.

Conversely, the megatonnage of American nuclear weapons was halved during the same period of time. The United States did not deploy any new ICBMs, ballistic missile submarines, or bombers. The army was reduced by three divisions and the number of navy ships nearly cut in half. Even during the Vietnam conflict, substantial percentages of the Defense Department's budget went to pay the operating expenses of the war, rather than to improve the fighting capabilities of fielded U.S. military forces. By the advent of the Reagan era in the early 1980s, Department of Defense statistics show that three-quarters of nuclear warheads in the U.S. stockpile were carried on launchers fifteen years old or older, while some three-fourths of Soviet warheads were sitting on launchers no more than five years old.

Nevertheless, after 1973 the United States had abolished the draft and fielded an all-volunteer army made up of an increasing number of high school graduates who had chosen military service as a career rather than suffered being drafted into the military with reluctance. By the early 1980s, the Reagan administration began to reverse the course of the Vietnam-era build-down by instituting the largest defense buildup since World War II as well as new changes in combat doctrine that emphasized combined arms, jointness, and what came to be called the Air-Land Battle. The hand of the chairman of the Joint Chiefs was also strengthened by the Defense Reorganization Act of 1986, which among other things gave the CJCS new freedom to set priorities and to say no to individual service chiefs.

Then, in 1991, the spectacular performances of Air-Land Battle doctrine, stealth technology, and precision-guided munitions (PGMs) in Operation Desert Storm, leading to a victory of the world's fourth largest army in only one hundred days, stunned the community of nations. Congress, in its April 1992 Conduct of the Persian Gulf War Report (the COW Report), spoke with apparent awe of "a victory [that] was a triumph of Coalition strategy, of international cooperation, of technology, and of people" that would "affect the American military and American security interests in the Middle East and beyond for years to come." The war's developments and outcome shocked the Defense Department as well, leading to doctrinal formulations that were a radical new departure from accepted standards of war-waging.

The Pentagon called these collectively the RMA, which stood for Revolution in Military Affairs, and the Defense Department embarked on a program to transform U.S. military forces into what it dubbed a third generation fighting force, one that would use stealth, high-mobility maneuver, and precision-guided weapons to strike with devastating speed and accuracy. Transformation would also encompass a doctrine of global strike, in which the force could be rapid-deployed to any trouble spot on earth within a time frame consistent with strategic success. Yet, despite its far-reaching power, the Pentagon would itself become a target of global terrorism on September 11, 2001.

In March 2003, following the Bush administration's unprecedented defense buildup that dwarfed even that of the Reagan era, the program of transformation that had begun with the RMA, the Iraq War commenced with a Shock and Awe campaign that stunned the world as well as many observers in the region, such as this author, then attending an arms exhibition in the United Arab Emirates (UAE). War clouds, of course, had loomed on the horizon for some time, and the actual opening of the war was not the real surprise. For me, it was the sudden realization that a policy of containment that had been the cornerstone of U.S. diplomacy—and by extension, had figured in Pentagon war planning as well—for almost sixty years since 1945 had just been cast aside in favor of a return to something resembling the military doctrine of the Hoover Plan.

In many ways that realization, more than the flashing lights on the northern horizon, as JDAMs struck their targets and antiaircraft fire opened up in the direction of Baghdad, was an overwhelming shock. It was another turning point in the story of the Pentagon that had been announced with staggering power. In some ways, it connected up with earlier turning points, such as the Bay of Pigs invasion.

A PARALLAX VIEW

An embarrassing military fiasco had begun the Kennedy administration. On April 17, 1961, less than ninety days since JFK had taken office, a brigade of some fourteen hundred Cuban exiles trained by the CIA and equipped by the Pentagon launched an invasion on the island republic ruled by a Communist dictatorship under Fidel Castro that had cast them out. The place they landed gave a lasting name to the incident. It was called the Bay of Pigs. It was to be an incident that would continue to have consequences for the remainder of the short-lived Kennedy presidency as well as for the nation.

As former Secretary of Defense Robert McNamara tells it in his memoirs, the Bay of Pigs incident was a kind of brick wall that the new administration, rushing pall mall toward a defense restructuring that was one of its first stated tasks, had struck head-on, and which it reeled back from as if stunned. Kennedy had played his famous "missile gap" card in his election race against Republican opponent Richard Nixon and had ordered McNamara's Defense Department to tackle it as its first order of business. Team Kennedy was specifically charged with reinventing the wheel as far as U.S. nuclear war plans went.

"We immediately tackled a most urgent task—reexamining and redefining our nuclear strategy," McNamara said years later.

This was an understatement. The Defense Department's brief was extensive. It had set itself the task of dismantling the Eisenhower administration's nuclear SIOP—drafted into official Pentagon policy only the previous year—and building a new one almost from the ground up. The extensive repair work on the SIOP was deemed necessary because the Kennedy men saw it as irreparably flawed. This was largely because it had been based on a dog's breakfast of ad hoc efforts to cope with the unprecedented postwar developments in the Cold War and the perceived nuclear menace posed by the Soviet Union. These had been made first by the Truman administration and then by the Eisenhower White House. In the fifteen years since 1945 the United States' entire defense policy had been based on a kind of tropism of reaction to Soviet moves without any clear long-range planning.

Among these was the successful orbiting of the Russian satellite Sputnik on October 4, 1957, an accomplishment that shocked the West in a manner few today can easily comprehend. Sputnik's advent caused profound fear because it signified one thing in particular: If the Soviet Union could orbit a satellite today, then tomorrow it might orbit a nuclear bomb. Correspondingly, at this time the United States had nothing that matched this capability. The nation felt vulnerable, profoundly so. Americans thought the Russians might hit us anytime they chose from space, and we had no defenses, no way to retaliate in kind. The U.S. strategic bomber fleet, even if successful in wiping out the enemy, would fly home to a nuclear wasteland.

The U.S. space program had begun as a military venture under USAF control to catch up with and exceed the Soviets in missilery and space warfare, a role that continued with the establishment of the National Aeronautics and Space Administration (NASA) in 1958, though it placed the space program under civilian management. Development of missiles that could carry nuclear payloads to the Soviet Union over transcontinental distances had obsessed the Department of Defense throughout this period, in part because these were viewed as the best possible deterrent to a Communist superstate bent on global domination and unafraid to risk another world war to achieve its aim.

Readying a defense roadmap for the Pentagon in the aftermath of the "Sputnik Crisis" was the preoccupation of Defense Secretary Neil McElroy, an Eisenhower appointee who served at the Pentagon between 1957 and 1959, succeeding Charles Wilson. Sworn in only a few days after the Sputnik launch, on October 9, 1957, as the sixth secretary of defense, McElroy's tenure at the DOD was linked from the start with U.S. reaction to the Soviet technological coup and its putatively dire implications for U.S. defense policy.

It was McElroy who originally coined the phrase "missile gap," and pushed for the establishment of the Defense Advanced Research Projects Agency (DARPA), which was created under the Defense Reorganization Act of 1958 and over which he presided. DARPA's mission today tracks back to the circumstances that led to its establishment. The agency's mission statement today states: "DARPA's original mission, established in 1958, was to prevent technological surprise like the launch of Sputnik, which signaled that the Soviets had beaten the U.S. into space. The mission statement has evolved over time. Today, DARPA's mission is still to prevent technological surprise to the US, but also to create technological surprise for our enemies."

Secretary McElroy's stewardship at the Building was a successful one. In some ways it presaged that of JFK appointee Robert McNamara which began some two years later. Both men came from corporate managerial backgrounds and were adroit spin doctors when the need arose, as it often did in broaching Defense Department policies to Congress and the American public.

Nevertheless, the fundamental theme of United States defense strategy remained reactive rather than proactive in the early Cold War years, nor was it solidly anchored to the framework of a unified strategic policy that would comprehensively address the Soviet threat, a fact later underscored by the U-2 spy plane incident that took place during the term of McElroy's former deputy and successor, Thomas Gates Jr.[7] The espionage trial of U.S. pilot Francis Gary Powers in the Soviet Union pilloried the United States as a strategic blunderer and embarrassed President Eisenhower, who had directly ordered the surveillance overflights.

Beyond this, and worse yet in the view of the new arrivals at the Pentagon, was the perception that basic assumptions about how to shape U.S. defense needs, especially nuclear defense, were fundamentally—dangerously—wrong. Both Truman and Eisenhower had been bamboozled by an old-boy network of generals, statesmen, and cabinet advisors into rolling nuclear dice with the Soviet Union.

General Leslie Groves, who, as Brehon Somervell's assistant, had helped preside over the conception and birth of the Pentagon, had commanded the Manhattan Project throughout most of the war years. Unfortunately, he proved woefully misinformed concerning the speed by which the Soviets could build a working A-bomb. Groves—whose declassified memos to War Secretary Stimson show he had waxed exultant after witnessing successful tests of the A-bomb at Alamogordo, New Mexico, in July, 1945—had assured Truman that it would take them twenty years. They'd succeeded in less than two.[8]

Secretary of State John Foster Dulles had pushed through his notions of nuclear deterrence by a doctrine of massive retaliation to Truman,

7. McElroy accepted appointment to the Pentagon on condition he serve no more than two years. His designated successor, Deputy Secretary of Defense Donald A. Quarles, died unexpectedly in May, 1959, whereupon Gates, then Secretary of the Navy, replaced him as McElroy's deputy and then stepped up to the top spot at Defense on McElroy's departure on December 1, 1959.

8. "At 0530, 16 July 1945, in a remote section of the Alamogordo Air Base, New Mexico, the first full scale test was made of the implosion type atomic fission bomb," Groves wrote Stimson. "For the first time in history there was a nuclear explosion. And what an explosion!"

while General Curtis LeMay, commander of SAC, had put teeth into the doctrine by molding the Strategic Air Command into an almost privately owned sole proprietorship, and who, on more than one occasion had expressed his desire to deliver a first-strike nuclear punch to the Soviets. Not for nothing had LeMay been satirized in Stanley Kubrick's 1962 black comedy *Doctor Strangelove* as the gung-ho General Buck Turgidson (ably played by actor George C. Scott), who stalked through the movie uttering such buffooneries as, "We're gonna blast you godless Russians back to the stone age," and "Knock off the fighting—this is a war room, godammit!"

At the same time, it was charged, Truman and Eisenhower had brushed aside the views of younger but still senior military leaders if it contradicted that of the old boy network. Army Chief of Staff Maxwell Taylor had, for example, argued that the U.S. plan to counter the massive yet inaccurate and relatively few Soviet nuclear ICBMs by developing many small yet highly accurate American missiles was mistaken. The Soviets would eventually learn to build better and more numerous missiles, he stated. In time, they would have a lot of big, powerful nukes while we would have a lot of small, wimpy nukes.

This is precisely what eventually did happen. Yet the views of Taylor and others like him were peremptorily dismissed by old hands in the White House and the Pentagon. They had fought the good fight in World War II and won, and they were not about to let some wet-behind-the-ears shave tail tell them how to run the nuclear show.

The incoming leadership of the Department of Defense questioned the wisdom of basing the credibility of U.S. nuclear defense on a policy that, in essence, hinged on a state of realities that was already obsolete. Dulles' doctrine of massive retaliation only made sense if the United States had a considerable lead in nuclear weapons over the Soviet Union, but by the start of 1960, this was debatable. Moreover, even if the U.S. did enjoy nuclear superiority, the mere possession of a larger nuclear arsenal was no guarantee that the Soviets would not do something rash. In McNamara's words, "This reliance on nuclear weapons gave us no way to respond to large non-nuclear attacks without committing suicide." Kennedy stated it this way: By adopting Dulles' strategy "we had put ourselves in the position of having to choose in a crisis between 'inglorious retreat or unlimited retaliation.'" A year after the Bay of Pigs, Soviet Premier Nikita Khrushchev would make these dire predictions almost come true when he reacted to perceived U.S. nuclear superiority by initiating the Cuban Missile Crisis.

It was the Bay of Pigs incident that not only underscored to Kennedy and McNamara the mistakes of the last two administrations but served as a prelude to the far more dangerous nuclear crisis that also hinged on Cuba the following year. The clandestine invasion plan had been hatched by the Eisenhower CIA in the final year of his presidency. Having seized power in a 1959 revolutionary coup d'état, and originally pledging political nonalignment, Fidel Castro now appeared to be openly defying the Truman Doctrine by playing cozy with the Soviets in America's backyard. Ike had approved the CIA plan to do something about Castro's rash actions. The Joint Chiefs of Staff had backed the plan, as well as National Security Advisor McGeorge Bundy and the members of the National Security Council; and the CIA continued to endorse the mission.

Nevertheless, it fast proved, in the words of one historian, "a perfect failure" as Castro's forces responded more quickly and in greater numbers than had been anticipated. It was almost as if they'd been waiting. In fact, they had been. The supposedly secret brigade of Cuban exiles had been thoroughly infiltrated by Castro's agents; indeed, as it later turned out, the Cuban people, whom the Defense Department had predicted would rally in support of the invasion, instead opposed it.

The tactical blunders—which were legion—included an escape route into the mountains that lay across eighty miles of impassable swamp. In the outcome, the U.S. became the butt of international ridicule and a chastened President Kennedy became even more suspicious of the national defense and intelligence establishments than he'd been before. It had another result as well: Nikita Khrushchev, having already received secret intelligence about JFK's womanizing, and already considering him a weakling, conceived in his crafty peasant's mind the notion that Kennedy was less of a man than he and could be made to play the fool. Cuba, thought Khrushchev, though not Waterloo, would be an ideal place to test the resolve of the new president and the nation he led.

* * *

When the Soviet freighters bound for Cuba bearing missiles under protective coverings (such as those discovered by the U.S. Coast Guard ship *Vesole* during a mid-crisis inspection in the Florida Straits of the Soviet freighter *Polzunov*) began to offload their deadly cargo, the Defense Department was headed by one of Kennedy's "new breed," Robert McNamara, but the Joint Chiefs of Staff were still made up of members of the old guard. The chairman was General Lyman Lemnitzer, who had been appointed by Eisenhower in late 1960 on the retirement of General Nathan Twining; Lemnitzer had been chairman for less than four months when Kennedy became president. Lemnitzer, a protégé of General George S. Patton, was a staunch anti-Communist who had played a major role in the de-Nazification of postwar West Germany, after the German General Staff was dissolved by the Allies on May 22, 1945, effectively taking military control away from the Third Reich and placing it in Allied hands.

The program, however, fell considerably short of abolishing the participation of former Nazis in the postwar Germany military, or, for that matter, in the political or commercial sectors. On the contrary, the ranks of the newly constituted German army, formerly the Wehrmacht, now the *Bundeswher*, was chockablock with former Nazis, and Bonn's military representatives at NATO were of the same stripe. Indeed, de-Nazification was a concept often honored more in the breech than in the act, especially after the Spring Crisis of 1948 fostered the belief that the Communist menace was on the march in Europe.

Lemnitzer had been in the thick of it all; Kennedy viewed him as part of the same old boy network that had backed the Dulles massive retaliation strategy; he would keep him on for the moment pending a review of the entire Joint Chiefs of Staff system. Having accepted Lemnitzer's assurance as chairman of the JCS that the Cuban invasion would succeed, Kennedy was determined to proceed at speed in reorganizing the Pentagon in the wake of the debacle.

To begin the process, Kennedy issued National Security Action Memorandum (NSAM) 55 to the chairman on June 28, 1961. NSAM-55 set out what the new president wanted and expected of the Joint Chiefs, among which was that he regarded the JCS as his "principal military advisor," responsible for giving military advice and acting on presidential proposals for military action. Kennedy asked that the JCS furnish him with defense estimates that were "direct and unfiltered" and presented to the Oval Office "without reserve or hesitation." The president also expected the chiefs to be "more than military men" in the older sense in which the chiefs had functioned during the previous two presidential administrations.

Kennedy also took an unprecedented step: In a move harking back to Admiral Leahy's unofficial status as presidential military advisor to Harry Truman, Kennedy recalled former army chief of staff, General Maxwell Taylor, to active duty at the White House in much the same capacity. The move was unprecedented because in Leahy's day there had been no official chairman; whereas, since 1950 the chairmanship had been legally established by Congress to act as the liaison between the JCS and the White House.

In effect, Kennedy, though making it clear to the chiefs that Taylor was not being interposed between the Oval Office and the Pentagon, was creating something resembling a second chairmanship. As might have been expected, the new arrangement did not win favor amid JCS enclaves. NSAM-55 hit the Pentagon like a bombshell, and from the Office of the Joint Chiefs it looked like the new president meant to tear apart the fabric of Defense Department unification, whose arrival had come only after more than a decade of painful internecine conflict after the issuance of the 1947 National Security Act.

Moreover, the chiefs had tacitly deemed Kennedy "soft" on Castro, believing that the White House had failed to order in fighter air cover that might have saved the landing. Possibly intent on showing that the Pentagon could succeed where the CIA had failed, the JCS plan, under the newly established chairman's Special Studies Group, called for a full-scale military invasion of Cuba. The overall plan was code-named Mongoose. A subsidiary operation, code-named Northwood, provided for the contingency of creating deliberate provocations to marshal public sentiment for the invasion. A proposal, declassified under the Assassination Records Review Board and released through the National Archives, called for "a series of well-coordinated incidents" that were to take place in the vicinity of the U.S. naval base at Guantanamo Bay, Cuba. These were to include having friendly Cubans dress in Cuban military uniforms to start riots, blow up ammunition, and burn aircraft on the base, as well as sabotage and sink a ship near the harbor entrance.

Years later, McNamara told the *Baltimore Sun* that he'd never heard of the plan, nor could he believe that the chiefs "were talking about or engaged in what I would call CIA-type operations." Be that as it may, and whether or not McNamara, as defense secretary, ever received the memo from the chiefs that outlined the plan and which was addressed to him, General Lemnitzer's days at the Pentagon were to come to an end soon afterward.

In the fall of 1962, Kennedy appointed Lemnitzer to be the Supreme Allied Commander, Europe, and named Maxwell Taylor to replace him as the chairman of the Joint Chiefs of Staff. Nor may it be entirely without coincidence that a movie version of the 1962 novel by Fletcher Knebel and Charles W. Bailey II, *Seven Days in May*, which began production mere weeks before JFK's assassination, portrayed a military junta, based on a secret cabal within the Joint Chiefs of Staff, that attempts to seize the government of the United States by means of setting up a series of phony provocations indicating a terrorist threat to the nation. Curiously, the name of the fictional president in both novel and movie is "Jordan Lyman."

In his farewell address before leaving for Europe, Lemnitzer ended with a plea to the president not to change the JCS system. The fact that the chiefs did not always agree, he said, "was not a weakness to be avoided but a strength that provided reasoned alternatives on complex military issues for decision by the civilian authorities."

A little over a month later, photos from U-2 spy planes flying high-altitude envelopes launched from Shaw Air Force Base in Florida, and low-flying, camera-bristling RF-101C Voodoos—reconnaissance and surveillance aircraft retrofitted from McDonnell-Douglas F-101 airframes and the world's first supersonic spy planes—began to bring back incontrovertible evidence that Soviet nuclear missile launchers, SS-20 missile stockpiles, and dumps for the fuel to thrust them into flight were being set up in Cuba.

* * *

The close relationship between Taylor and Kennedy became one of the critical factors in handling the Cuban Missile Crisis that followed on the heels of Lemnitzer's departure from the Pentagon. The crisis itself had been a potential outcome of Cold War nuclear brinkmanship and bilateral miscalculations of tough-guy superpower statesmanship for almost two decades, for it had been developing embryonically even as the Allies convened at Potsdam to decide the fate of the postwar world.

Closer in time to the event was the meeting between Soviet Premier Nikita Khrushchev and President John F. Kennedy in Vienna in 1961, shortly after the Bay of Pigs episode, in which Khrushchev had visibly, and with apparent deliberateness, sought to intimidate the young American president during the summit. In July 1955, Khrushchev had been Party First secretary at the first Big Four summit meeting in Geneva since the war, but Vienna was six years later, and by now Khrushchev had consolidated his personal power to rule with an iron fist.

Yet the May 1960 U-2 affair, in which shrapnel from an exploding SAM SA-2 missile warhead had damaged the spy plane flown by pilot Francis Gary Powers sufficiently to cause it to crash in Soviet territory, had resulted in damaging Khrushchev's standing in the party, even if it had handed the Soviets a powerful propaganda victory over the West. A year later, during the 1961 Berlin Crisis, when East German tanks controlled by Soviet commanders had squared off against U.S. troops across striped vehicle barriers at Checkpoint Charlie, Khrushchev claimed victory, but the Soviets still hadn't chased the Americans from Berlin.

The blacksmith's son, who had risen from the mud floor of a peasant hut in the village of Kalinovka, in the *oblast* of Kursk, to the pinnacle of power in the Soviet Union, had made a career of sizing up adversaries for strengths and weaknesses, and either outmaneuvering or outfacing them in his ascent. Khrushchev had outwitted, and then destroyed,

Stalin himself along the way. He had no qualms about using the same tactics with his Western adversaries.

At Geneva, he had remarked to intimates how "that cur Dulles was snapping at Eisenhower." Khrushchev had met Eisenhower before and had not been impressed. "He was a good man, but he wasn't very tough," he wrote about Ike in his biography, *Khrushchev Remembers*. "There was something soft about his character." The son of Kalinovka's blacksmith, seeing softness, would pound at it on the anvil of global power confrontation until it broke beneath the Soviet hammer. Khrushchev had done this again and again. Although Khrushchev apparently held Kennedy in higher regard than he had Eisenhower, he nevertheless thought the young president as soft as his predecessor.

Another factor was the perceived provocation of the Pentagon's nuclear SIOP and the posture of the Strategic Air Command toward preemptive nuclear war and the Dulles policy of massive retaliation. Although Eisenhower had rejected calls for nuclear preemption against the Soviets, such as that in a 1954 JCS study suggesting "deliberately precipitating war with the USSR in the near future" before the Soviet H-bomb became a "real menace," issuing an updated Basic National Security Policy statement that "the United States and its allies must reject the concept of preventive war or acts intended to provoke war," the Soviets weren't convinced. The USSR's GRU, the approximate equivalent of the U.S. Joint Chiefs of Staff, besides, had drafted nuclear war–fighting policies of its own that matched, if not exceeded, the American concepts of preemption and massive retaliation. Soviet doctrine held as its first precept that in a war against the United States, nuclear escalation was "inevitable" and would feature "maximum" use of such weapons from the very beginning.

By 1961, Robert McNamara's Defense Department, at Kennedy's behest, had redrafted the first SIOP of 1960 to conform to Team Kennedy's repudiation of massive retaliation and reflect a new doctrine called "flexible response."

The 1961 redraft was designed to afford the president multiple options in place of a single, all-or-nothing salvo of nuclear weapons. It also conformed to a revision of the Basic National Security Policy that made not targeting Soviet cities official U.S. policy. Even Moscow was removed from the SIOP's primary target list. Henceforth, the United States would target strategic retaliatory forces, such as missile sites and bomber bases, Soviet air defenses located away from cities, and defense-related industrial plants.

Another redraft of the SIOP by the Defense Department in 1962 was even more comprehensive, resulting in option-dense SIOP 62. Nevertheless, the concept enshrined in the buzzword "mutually assured destruction," or MAD, that came out of a 1964 speech by McNamara had been in the matrix all along.

In the face of the massive destructive power that Moscow was putting into its nuclear arsenal, against the backdrop of the confrontations that the Soviet Union had provoked against the West since the Iron Curtain's fall, against the surveillance imagery showing continuous development of new and better Soviet nuclear weapons, deterrence still meant having enough nuclear weapons available to pulverize Russia to dust, no matter how finely tuned the options for deploying it.

All of these factors no doubt went into Khrushchev's calculations; the exact reasons are still sketchy, but Khrushchev, in his memoirs, gave some, if not many of them. Khrushchev, who'd joked with JFK at the Vienna summit the previous year that the Soviets had been responsible for "casting the deciding vote" in the 1960 elections "over that son of a bitch Richard Nixon" by deliberately delaying the release of captured U-2 pilot Francis Gary Powers until after the elections, so depriving Nixon of a triumph, nevertheless believed that the USSR "had to confront America."

Despite being "very glad Kennedy won the election and . . . generally pleased with [their] meeting in Vienna" as well as convinced that Kennedy "was interested in finding a peaceful solution to world problems," Kennedy proved unwilling to do so on Soviet terms. Prior to the Bay of Pigs, the United States had instituted an oil embargo against Castro's regime.

The Soviets had responded by attempting a seaborne resupply of Black Sea crude to Cuba using a tanker fleet supplied by Italy, which had backed down in the face of U.S. pressure. A vast assortment of Soviet military gear, from small arms to tanks and artillery tubes, were shipped to Cuba in 1961, and the Bay of Pigs fiasco did nothing to stop Castro's Soviet-supplied arms buildup.

Khrushchev, who was on a state visit to Bulgaria at the time later wrote, "One thought kept hammering away at my brain: what will happen if we lose Cuba? . . . We had to think up some way of confronting America with more than words. But what exactly?" Khrushchev concluded ominously: "The logical answer was missiles."

His next thought was, "I had the idea of installing missiles with nuclear warheads in Cuba without letting the United States find out until it was too late to do anything about them. I knew that first we'd have to talk to Castro and explain our strategy to get the agreement of the Cuban government. My thinking went like this: if we installed the missiles secretly and then if the United States discovered the missiles were there, after they were fixed and ready to strike, the Americans would think twice before trying to liquidate our installations by military means. . . . If a quarter or even a tenth of our missiles survived—even if only one or two big ones were left—we could still hit New York, and an awful lot of people would be wiped out. I don't know how many; that's a matter for our scientists and military personnel to work out. . . . The main thing was that the installation of our missiles in Cuba would restrain the United States from precipitous military action."

Such was the thinking that led to the installation of intermediate-range SS-20 missiles, mobile and fixed launchers, and Ilyushin-28 strategic bombers capable of striking targets in the continental United States with nuclear bomb loads.

"Soon after we began shipping our missiles, the Americans became suspicious," Khrushchev went on. "It was not long before they concluded on the basis of reconnaissance photographs that we were installing missiles."

The outcome is well-known: Sometime in the middle of 1962, medium-range Soviet missiles had been shipped to Cuba, along with a Soviet expeditionary force consisting of technicians and military personnel. The commander of this force had theater nuclear weapons at his disposal, and he had the authority to launch them against the United States.

By late October 1962, the extent of the Soviet nuclear presence in Cuba was well known to U.S. leadership. "The Americans became frightened, and we stepped up our shipments," reminisced Khrushchev. "We had delivered almost everything by the time the crisis reached the boiling point." Yet another crisis in a succession from the Spring Crisis of 1948, each one steadily escalating in its implications for World War III, was again upon the world: The Cuban Missile Crisis, once begun, threatened global doom.

After delivering an ultimatum to the Soviets to withdraw their weapons, Kennedy convened a select group of presidential advisors culled from the ranks of the National Security Council. It was dubbed the executive committee, better known by the acronym EXCOMM. The group was to meet daily with the president and Bobby Kennedy, whom JFK had delegated as his personal representative, at the White House throughout the crisis. Among EXCOMM's members was another close personal advisor to the president: General Maxwell Taylor. Kennedy had appointed Taylor as JCS chairman prior to Lemnitzer's departure, and a warm friendship had developed between the two men during daily briefings. Indeed, the relationship between Kennedy and Taylor echoed that between Leahy and Truman of the previous decade.

This special relationship was to figure decisively throughout the missile crisis, where Taylor sat next to the secretary of defense at the daily EXCOMM meetings and took part in often long and tense debates on U.S. actions. Taylor, presenting the JCS views, argued for preemptive air strikes against Cuban installations. Kennedy vetoed these, stating, "It isn't the first step that concerns me, but both sides escalating to the fourth and fifth step—and we don't go to the sixth because there is no one around to do so."

Nevertheless, the chiefs' view gradually began to prevail. "By Saturday, October 27, 1962—the height of the crisis—the majority of the president's military and civilian advisers were prepared to recommend that if Khrushchev did not remove the Soviet missiles from Cuba . . . the United States should attack the island," McNamara wrote in his memoirs. He went on to state: "Unbeknownst to us at the time, and quite contrary to CIA estimates, the Soviets then had approximately 160 nuclear warheads in Cuba, including scores of tactical nuclear weapons. A U.S. attack would almost surely have led to a nuclear exchange with devastating consequences."

The Soviets backed down the following day and began pulling the missiles out of Cuba to Castro's consternation and America's relief. What was known to only a handful of key officials at the time was that even as Kennedy held out for a negotiated settlement of the crisis, he had sanctioned the Pentagon's emergency war plans both for an attack on Cuba and for the nuclear war that was expected to inevitably follow.

In an article in the December 17 issue of *Life* replete with black-and-white photos of the invasion armada secretly assembled in Florida, an armada that included LSTs disgorging Patton tanks of the First Armored Division at exercises at Fort Pierce, navy aircraft carriers berthed at Mayport Naval Station and marines hitting a beachhead in rubber Zodiacs in a mockup of a dawn raid, and First Armored Division infantry massed for presidential inspection at Fort Stewart, Georgia, the extent of U.S. readiness was revealed in graphic detail.

"Now it can be seen," began the *Life* article titled "The Might We Aimed at Cuba." "Khrushchev retreated from Cuba under the very gun sights of the greatest array of military striking power ever massed on the American continent.

"If he had balked, five U.S. Army paratroop, infantry, and tank divisions and parts of two Marine Corps divisions, with 1,000 planes of the Tactical Air Command and 183 ships of the U.S. Navy, stood at hair-trigger readiness to sweep Cuba clean of his offensive missiles—and his puppet Fidel Castro. *Moreover, an undisclosed number of intercontinental ballistic missiles were fully operational and set to hit Russia had any attempt at retaliation come from that quarter*" [italics mine].

Ground forces, the report trumpeted, "were concentrated in the southeastern part of the United States and at the American base at Guantanamo Bay, Cuba. The extent of the power—kept tightly secret through the crisis—was revealed after President Kennedy went down to Florida and Georgia last week to thank the troops and call any aggressor's attention to what the U.S. was ready to use [*sic*]."

A sidebar went on to interviews with military personnel about how the invasion would have shaped up in the offing.

"What would the next climactic step have been like?" asked the author. An interviewee identified as "a navy officer" was quoted as saying, "Number One, we would not have made any mistakes. We could not let it look like we couldn't beat the Russians if we had to. We would have subjected Cuba to intensive bombardment." Another "navy man" added, "First you knock out the targets that can't hurt you." A "marine flyer" conjectured, "We'd sterilize the island." The interviews concluded with: "'Neutralize 'em,' said the army. 'De-sanitize them,' said the air force." The text of the sidebar ended with a remark made by the president as the post-crisis troop drawdown commenced: "Regardless of how persistent our diplomacy may be in activities stretching all around the world, in the final analysis it rests upon the power of the United States. . . ."

In the euphoria of the moment, the article, as countless others like it, had left out the sobering certainty that Kennedy had known that using that power against Cuba would have meant unleashing the apocalypse of a global nuclear war.

CHAPTER TWELVE

A NEW ERA BEGINS

S
omething new, certainly unique, and possibly uncanny, had begun happening with the Pentagon in the midst of U.S. military involvement in Indochina that some had already begun to call "McNamara's War" by around 1965. For the first time the Pentagon was becoming more than a noun that described a large, five-sided building on the west bank of the Potomac, or even a word that referred to the headquarters of the Defense Department and Joint Chiefs of Staff.

In the mid-1960s the word *Pentagon* began to take on a much broader set of connotations: The word started to become an icon, a symbol, a piece of mental shorthand, that stood for the entire military defense establishment of the United States.

Journalists began routinely using the word *Pentagon* as a convenient abbreviation for a complex of things and concepts and organizations that included the JCS, the Office of the Secretary of Defense, and even, in some cases, the order of battle—planes, tanks, guns, and hardware, and of course, troops—itself.

Other related terms and acronyms, such as "U.N." or "NATO," or even "White House," "Washington," or "Oval Office," had never taken on the panoramic connotations that the word *Pentagon* managed to quickly accumulate. Somehow, the Pentagon had entered the public imagination— not just in America but around the world—in an entirely new way.

Moreover, and somewhat curiously when compared to other similar terms, *Pentagon* became charged with an emotional magnetic field of either positive or negative polarity, depending on who happened to use the word and in what context. To some it was tantamount to pronouncing *anathema*, a word that had roughly the same connotation as *antichrist*; indeed the Yippies of the New Left of the 1960s in their 1967 March on the Pentagon conducted an "exorcism" of the Pentagon in which "spirits of evil" were urged to depart the building as though it were a haunted house. Portions of this chanted litany can still be heard, if one has the patience to search through musty stacks of old long-playing records at weekend yard sales, on an album by the aptly named Fugs, in which a recorded segment of this Pentagon exorcism opens the collection of admittedly strange songs. (The Pentagon was also the subject of levitation efforts by means of chants and, ostensibly, the application of psychic powers; some claimed it actually did rise—if only a little). The polarizing effects and connotations surrounding the building might have had something to do with popular culture and, above all, with the new mass media, especially television, that had become commonplace on the American landscape.

Developed in the 1920s, and in commercial production by the beginning of World War II, the onset of television as a mass medium had been halted temporarily by the war but was in full swing again as U.S. consumerism grew by leaps and bounds after 1945. By the end of the 1960s, miniaturization of cameras and the development of commercial communications satellite networks meant that television news reporters could file stories from even the most remote corners of the earth.

One such distant corner encompassed the embattled rice paddies, jungle highlands, rural villages, and old French colonial cities of Vietnam, in which the United States became embroiled in a savage and controversial regional war. Daily televised news reports with graphic footage from Vietnam throughout the conflict certainly had the effect of raising public consciousness about the U.S. military establishment in a way that the radio programs, newsreels, and newspaper and magazine accounts from war correspondents of earlier eras, however eloquent, could never come close to equaling.

Then, too, the tensions of the Cold War had also gripped the popular imagination and given rise to novels and popular films based on Cold War themes. Two such movies, *Seven Days in May* and *Doctor Strangelove*, have already been discussed, but there were several others that had strong impacts on the nation long after their release. Another such motion picture was *On the Beach*, a 1959 film whose plot revolved around the destruction of the world in a nuclear war and the flight, by nuclear submarine, of American survivors to sanctuary in an Australia that had escaped the ravages of nuclear holocaust; it was based on a novel by Neville Shute. Another grim Cold War film that involved the Strategic Air Command was the movie *Failsafe*, whose storyline centered around the White House and Joint Chiefs of Staff grappling with terrible decisions in the face of an escalation to nuclear war with the Soviet Union.

Television and the Pentagon again converged when, beginning a little more than a decade later, a number of news specials on the Pentagon appeared on the "Big Three" television networks. One of these, "The Selling of the Pentagon," was a *CBS News* documentary that first aired on prime time network television in 1971, during the Nixon presidency.

The subject of "The Selling of the Pentagon" was described by contemporary promotional material as the Defense Department's "public relations excesses." Seen again today, three and a half decades later, the documentary appears tame by comparison to similar contemporary news features.

The contentious aftermath of this early Pentagon documentary, however, is interesting, for it provoked a kind of shooting war in the media and in the halls of Congress, to say nothing of on street corners across the country. For the first time, though not the last, television had turned its not always impartial camera eye on the building, and the result, as might have been expected, was something like a war.

The hour-long documentary provoked an immediate storm of protest that built to a crescendo as first Assistant Secretary of Defense Daniel Z. Henkin, then Vice President Spiro T. Agnew, and next the House Armed Services Committee (whose chairman called the show "a professional hatchet job") and the House Investigations Subcommittee by way of its chairman Representative Harley O. Staggers weighed in with protests. It was charged that answers to different questions put to

Henkin by reporter Roger Mudd had been edited together to simulate a single continuous reply. Henkin cried foul when the program aired. The committee demanded that CBS produce out-takes from the program—sections of film edited from the final cut—of interviews it had conducted with members of DOD. CBS President Frank Stanton refused; the committee recommended that he be cited for contempt of Congress, a motion that was only narrowly defeated by a vote in the House.

In response, the network re-aired the original documentary a month later; the new broadcast included a twenty-minute postscript giving equal time to critics, including Agnew and Secretary of Defense Melvin Laird. It concluded with *CBS News* President Richard S. Salant going on camera to defend the broadcast as "a vital contribution to the people's right to know."

Rather than quench the flames of controversy, the rebroadcast only served to fan them hotter. In another month, as more criticism and charges of unfairness were leveled against *CBS News*, the network aired an hour-long special in a panel format in which critics and defenders of the broadcast faced off against one another.

Members of the panel included Senator J. William Fullbright—who had written a book on Pentagon public relations and defended the program—Brigadier General S. L. A. Marshall (Ret.), and a former public-information chief at the Pentagon. The controversy began to fade following the panel's hour-long debate—possibly because viewers began to fall asleep from boredom—but it was not by any means to be the last word in the media's coverage of the building nor of controversy in its wake.

Another, and far larger, eruption in the media resulted that same year from a former Pentagon employee's leak to the *New York Times* of classified DOD documents that the *Times* published as a serial beginning on Sunday, June 13, 1971, in daily installments over a period of weeks. It was halted after the Justice Department obtained a temporary restraining order against further publication, contending that "the national defense interests of the United States and the nation's security will suffer immediate and irreparable harm" should publication continue. Publication resumed following a Supreme Court decision on June 30, in favor of the *Times*.

These documents became known as the Pentagon Papers.

Collectively they compose a top-secret study of the history of the United States' involvement in Indochina that had been commissioned in 1967 by Defense Secretary Robert S. McNamara.

The forty-seven-volume study, which took a year and a half to complete, resulted in some three thousand pages of narrative history and more than four thousand pages of appended documents, making for an estimated total of 2.5 million words. The history covered America's role in Indochina from World War II through May 1968, the month that peace talks began in Paris after President Lyndon B. Johnson had set a limit on further military commitments and had told the nation, in a nationally televised speech, that he would not seek reelection for a second term. Among the historical details publicly revealed for the first time in the Pentagon Papers:

- The Truman administration decided to give France military aid in its colonial war against the Communist-led Vietminh, which, stated the Papers, "directly involved" the United States in Vietnam and "set" the course of American policy.
- The Eisenhower White House continued to provide aid to South Vietnam and engaged in clandestine efforts to undermine the Communist regime in the North.
- The Kennedy administration transformed the Eisenhower "limited-risk gamble" into a "broad commitment" in Vietnam.
- President Lyndon Johnson was left with the choice of unilateral withdrawal or broadening and escalating U.S. involvement.

The Pentagon Papers also documented growing programs of clandestine military pressure and expanded bombing of North Vietnam that, the report stated, were in conflict with the intelligence community's assessment of their effectiveness against the Communist government in Hanoi.

The leaker, former Defense Department analyst Dr. Daniel Ellsberg, stated in a magazine interview in 1971 that, "In the early sixties, before I ever got on the subject of Vietnam, I was granted interagency access at a very high level to study the decision-making process in crises like the Cuban Missile Crisis, Suez, Skybolt, U-2 and so forth. In fact, the arrangements for that study were set up by Walt Rostow, who was then head of the Policy Planning Council of the State Department."

In the same interview, Ellsberg talked about his growing dissatisfaction with the U.S. role in Vietnam; a view he claimed was shared by others at the Pentagon. "Most people felt that by this time," he stated, "most people in the government who had any experience with Vietnam had by late '67 come to feel that the official optimism that was coming out of the top, from Rusk, from Westmoreland, was quite unjustified."

Ellsberg went on to say that he had first begun delivering parts of the study to the Senate Foreign Relations Committee. "It was a decision for which I expected to go to prison for the rest of my life," he commented. It turned out to be the first step in a process of making the study public that ultimately did, in fact, wind up with Ellsberg facing a prison term.

Like the controversial *CBS News* special, the revelations contained in the Pentagon Papers now fail to evoke more than mild interest; the almost seven hundred pages of closely set type in the paperback edition taken down from my bookshelf does not make for the most riveting reading. We live in a different and, it must be said, a far more cynical era, one that seems gorged with controversy and in which very little remains secret for very long, and in which new secrets, freshly exposed to view, are quickly driven away by even newer and more scandalous ones. We envy earlier eras their comparative innocence.

The Pentagon Papers did, however, unleash a plethora of repercussions, and one of these was a building skepticism about and distrust of government authorities. The Watergate scandal, which followed, replete with G. Gordon Liddy's infamous Plumbers working out of a room tucked away in the White House subbasement, the taped conversations of Richard Nixon, and capped with the final tragedy of the president leaving office to escape almost certain impeachment, the Iran-Contra scandal of the next decade, and many others in between and afterward that include Abu Ghraib and will certainly include more in due course, have helped to turn us all into a nation of hardened skeptics.

But one more episode of the Pentagon's early appearances in the unflattering glare of the media's spotlight deserves mention. It was another *CBS News* report with newscaster Mike Wallace called "The Uncounted Enemy: A Vietnam Deception." The news hour documentary aired in 1982. Its premise, like one of Ellsberg's themes, was that the Joint Chiefs of Staff had deliberately overplayed American battlefield successes in Vietnam throughout the war and had misled the American public into believing that the United States was winning the war when it was in fact losing it.

The report implicated General William C. Westmoreland, the former commander of U.S. ground forces in Vietnam, in what it alleged was a widespread cover-up by America's military. Westmoreland, like the assistant secretary of defense of a previous *CBS News* documentary, also claimed that interviews, in which he'd appeared on camera to be uttering a continuous sequence of replies, had in fact been edited together from a series of interviews conducted over the course of several weeks. Westmoreland also claimed that key statements he had made had been left out, statements that would have changed the entire meaning of his remarks.

Although *CBS News* launched an investigation into the allegations that resulted in a fifty-nine-page in-house study, Westmoreland sued *CBS News* for $120 million but withdrew his lawsuit at the eleventh hour, after two and a half years of litigation, half a million pages of documents, thirty-six witnesses, and sixty-five days in a New York City courtroom, when his lawyer declared that the presiding judge's ruling to the jury for a verdict based on "clear and convincing evidence" rather than "a preponderance of evidence" had made the case impossible to win.

Westmoreland left the courtroom without money or even an apology from CBS but issued a statement esteeming CBS's "distinguished journalistic tradition." CBS also issued a post-trial statement, which said that it had "never intended to assert and does not believe, that General Westmoreland was unpatriotic or disloyal in performing his duties as he saw them."

The remark, qualified as it was, seemed to some as a slap in the old warrior's face. Admiral Thomas H. Moorer, former chairman of the

Joint Chiefs of Staff and a supporter of Westmoreland, later opined, "You could have said that about Hitler." The late historian Alistair Cooke wrote what he dubbed a "Letter from America" expressing similar thoughts.

It was Westmoreland, though, who had the final word on the subject. "If they had thrown in the word *apology* I certainly wouldn't have objected to it," the old soldier told news anchor Ted Koppel on ABC's *Nightline* sometime later.

* * *

It should be kept in mind that the Pentagon was always the center of controversy, contention, and debate. Before it was even called the Pentagon, before its foundation was laid down, back in 1941 it had been scorned as "Somervell's Folly." Its conception had not been an easy one, and far from immaculate. It had not even been intended to endure beyond the war. Nor had it even had a name, other than the War Department Building. Indeed, it had never had a single purpose that could be agreed upon by more than a handful of individuals at any one given time.

If it was an office building, albeit the world's largest one, then why did it play host to covert intelligence agencies? If its role was mainly to draft plans and budgets for a myriad of defense acquisitions, and if it played host to an army of civilians on a daily basis that dwarfed its uniformed military occupants, then what was the Pentagon doing with a command center bristling with links to the vast array of U.S. global might that could even launch nuclear missiles on warning? If it had been intended by Roosevelt to be converted into a records warehouse after World War II, then what was it doing on television long after the war was over?

Today's popular view of the Pentagon is a far cry from the largely negative, certainly critical, mass perception of the Pentagon in an era as recent as the mid-1980s, after the show "A Vietnam Deception" aired, to the most recent of portrayals of the Pentagon as media star.

In stark, even striking, contrast stands the television series *E-Ring* that not long ago aired weekly on cable networks. The show portrayed the Pentagon as a bastion of high-technology warfare, its corridors tenanted by men and women whose lives revolve around the nucleus of military and political power like electrons at the heart of an atom. The show's sets were slick, the dialog sharp, and the action hard-hitting. In short, by the end of the twenty-first century's first decade, the Pentagon had finally become, in media terms, "sexy."

What alchemy turned the Pentagon from the biggest office building on the planet to the biggest five-sided sex symbol in the world? Was it something to do with what Gulf War explainer and clarifier Anthony Cordesman—a straight-arrow version of Saddam's information minister of the Iraq War—dubbed, as he stood before digital map displays armed with pointer and enough military jargon to make Tom Clancy blush, "America's new military consciousness"?

Was it the fact that, like the World Trade towers on that grim, siren-filled, and smoke-clouded Tuesday in September 2001, the Pentagon also "took a hit for America"? Or does the transformation predate both events, originating in the midst of tense, and often acrimonious, congressional investigation into a covert arms-for-hostages deal between Washington and Tehran, led by a photogenic marine in a uniform he'd never worn while on White House duty during the period in question?

Was the prototype for one of *E-Ring*'s tough but bright and undeniably beautiful women the marine colonel's young and far more photogenic secretary? Perceptions have a way, it seems, of developing slowly and over time, like successive readings of terrain that collectively, and sometimes only much later, combine to form the lines on a map.

CHAPTER THIRTEEN

BEFORE, DURING, AND AFTER THE GULF WAR

I n the Building's biography, the Gulf War marks a sort of commencement ceremony. The Building, typecast as playing the heavy for decades, now got to play, during the first—and so far the last—war to gain lasting and unanimous popular favor with the American public since World War II, a leading role. The Gulf War marked several firsts in many areas. These included the first "smart" weaponry deployed routinely in theater combat, the first operational theater deployment of the F-117A Stealth Fighter, the first use of Tomahawk Land Attack Missiles (TLAMs) with upgraded guidance packages and warheads, in combat, and the first battlefield explosions of giant BLU-82B "Daisy Cutter" bombs—then the largest non-nuclear (conventional) explosives in anybody's arsenal—since Vietnam.

Desert Storm also marked the first appearance of the first African-American chairman of the Joint Chiefs, as well as the first time a chairman became an overnight media superstar. The Gulf War also marked at least one prominent last to its many firsts—the last sailing into harm's way of the battleship *Wisconsin* and the last time the boom of her mammoth sixteen-inch gunnery would be heard near enemy shores. Finally, the Gulf War marked several largest and biggest, such as the night tank battles that matched U.S. Abrams M1A1 main battle tanks (MBTs) against Soviet T-72 MBTs and proved U.S. mechanized armor second to none.

The Gulf War also marked a media first. It was the first televised war—indeed the first media war—in the history of the world. It's certainly true that the Vietnam War was a nightly staple of evening television news hours for about a decade between the mid-1960s and 1970s, and that ABC's *Nightline* was originally created to cover the Iran Hostage Crisis of 1979; it's also true that embedded media personnel exposed reporters to the hazards of combat and gave viewers vivid coverage of the war in Iraq. Nevertheless, the Gulf War, with its glitzy logos, elaborate sets, location coverage, and expert commentary, set the standards for what was to follow, including, in the opinion of some, the high-gloss backdrops of televised CENTCOM briefings during the Iraq War.

* * *

To really understand the impact of the Gulf War on the biography of the Pentagon, indeed on the "new military consciousness" of America as framed by Cordesman, we have to go back to the previous decade, to the middle years of the Reagan administration and beyond.

The Reagan defense budget of fiscal year 1985 marked the largest postwar military budget in U.S. history. It was second only to the fiscal year 2002 defense budget, totaling almost $400 billion, which marked the largest single increase in national defense spending since the landmark Reagan-era budget of 1985. The FY 2003 budget, which succeeded it, was even higher. On February 4, 2008, the White House submitted a $515.4 billion defense budget for FY 2009 to Congress, a $35.9 billion increase over the Bush administration's FY 2008 budget. Like other budgets since the commencement of the Iraq War (FY 2003), this budget continues to seek funding for force sizing increases for the U.S. Army and Marine Corps, asking $15.5 billion for the army increase and $5 billion for the marines in FY 2009.

The massive Reagan defense spending was intended to roll back the defense drawdowns of previous presidential administrations that had reduced U.S. military strength since the end of the Vietnam War. Between FY 1968 and then, the military's purchasing power, in real dollars, had sharply dropped. By 1974 it had fallen by 37 percent, to plunge even lower by 1979 as the Soviet Union continued to pump up its military machine to steroidal levels.

"Because of Vietnam and Watergate," wrote Alexander Haig, "the U.S. had, for some time before Carter took office, been too distracted to act like a superpower." Haig went on, "The consequences were devastating. The whole balance of the world was disturbed. Our enemy, the Soviet Union, had been seduced by the weakness of the American will and extended itself far beyond the natural limits of its own apparent interests and influence."

The Brezhnev Doctrine, Haig avowed, had been formulated to spread Soviet hegemony around the world. "We were witnessing the conjunction of Soviet ambition and a maturing Soviet global reach." The sharp increase in Reagan-era defense spending was aimed at nothing less than stopping the Soviets before they overwhelmed the Western democracies through both surrogate wars marked by low-intensity conflict in Central and South America, even Mexico, and through a possible full-scale conventional attack on Western Europe across the plains of Germany and through what strategists termed "The Fulda Gap" into the heart of Middle Europe. Reagan believed that the world was on a collision course with nuclear Armageddon. He felt his mission was to prevent doomsday from happening. Reagan's instinctive solution to the crisis was one that harked back to Truman—build up U.S. armed forces to reach parity with, and then exceed, the Soviets. Outface them and force them to retreat. Roll the Soviets back from their postwar encroachments into former Western bastions around the world.

Under Defense Secretaries Caspar Weinberger and Frank Carlucci, and the Joint Chiefs chaired by General David C. Jones, then General John W. Vessey Jr., and finally by Admiral William Crowe, the Reagan Defense Department undertook a policy of military force transformation that was without precedent. The Pentagon's principal manual of doctrine, *FM 100-5*, was thoroughly revised in 1982 to reflect a new emphasis on combined arms and Air-Land Battle strategies and tactics instead of defensive battle that had marked previous doctrine.

The emphasis would now be on the offensive, using rapid maneuver, precision firepower, and strategic depth, where forces would be trained and equipped to strike simultaneously across what might be hundreds of square miles, and do so from air, land, and sea. Other elements of the new Defense Department order of battle included the controversial concept of fighting "winnable" nuclear war.

The most visible expression of the Reagan buildup, and the ones that caught the most fire with the popular imagination, were the exotic weapons systems that were developed by the Pentagon throughout this period. These included the already-mentioned Stealth Fighter but also many others, such as the B-2 Stealth Bomber, the B-1B Lancer Strategic Bomber, and the "Buck Rogers" weaponry that was intended to form the backbone of the Strategic Defense Initiative's (SDI) defensive shield against Soviet strategic nuclear attack, better known by its nickname "Star Wars."

The Reaganauts were intent on—some might even say obsessed with—arming the U.S. and its European allies to fight and prevail in nuclear war fighting against the Soviets on all fronts. Virtually every item of new weaponry—especially the revolutionary stealth aircraft and Star Wars missile shield—was intended to play a part in the offensive and defensive sides of waging nuclear war. Stealth aircraft, for example, were actually, and in effect, conceived as a means by which U.S. nuclear weapons could be accurately and survivably delivered to high-priority targets inside the Soviet Union.

The planes were designed to be able to evade Soviet early warning and SAM radars, drop nuclear bombs or launch nuclear-tipped ALCMS (air-launched cruise missiles), and then return to their staging areas, often across strategic distances between continents, for rearming, refueling, and retasking. Star Wars, or SDI, was intended to create a multilayered defensive shell of space-based weapons (in contravention of the U.S.–Soviet nuclear SALT treaty then in effect between the superpowers) that would—at least in theory—destroy incoming ICBMs and their MIRVed warheads before they could strike their designated targets in the United States.

New classes of nuclear ballistic submarines (SSBNs) were also developed, especially to counter advanced Soviet submarine designs, as well as new surface ships, such as the Ticonderoga-class AEGIS cruisers whose computer-linked SPY-1 radars were designed to track as many as a hundred targets simultaneously and respond to each.

Among these new types of weapons were "smart" and even "brilliant" weaponry, such as the Tomahawk missile that could fly around corners to detonate its warhead on a target hundreds of miles away from the launch point and reached by a tortuous flight path across mountains, down the length of valleys, and even across a maze of streets and avenues. These missiles carry warheads that might be conventional, nuclear, or something exotic, such as the Spin-1 warhead enhancement that draped carbon-metal filaments around the Iraqi power grid's high-tension lines in 1991 to short out portions of its electrical system.

As the Soviet Union broke up, partly due to internal pressures and partly due to the pressures from outside the Iron Curtain resulting from the Reagan arms buildup, there was a euphoria in the nation that was in many ways the direct antithesis of the Cold War's grim premonitions of nuclear doom.

Reagan, it seemed, had averted Armageddon. The world would be saved. Moreover, America would arise as the unchallenged superpower after some fifty years of bipolar brinkmanship. Movies and novels reflected this new turn of mind. One such movie, *War Games*, released in 1984, told the story of a teenage computer buff who accidentally connects with the computer of the North American Aerospace Defense Command (NORAD), only believing that he's networked into a mere computer game.

In fact, the young computer geek is connected to a computer named WOPR, which stands for War Operations Plan Response, with which he plays a game called Global Thermonuclear War. WOPR mistakes the game for the real thing and proceeds to launch a preemptive nuclear strike on the Soviets. Fortunately the scientist who built WOPR comes to the teen's aid—and the world's—and sets up a game of tic-tac-toe, which WOPR hasn't been programmed to win.

Losing at tic-tac-toe WOPR decides that nuclear war is also unwinnable and cancels the nuclear mission. With its lavish high-tech sets, featuring large flat-panel display screens in authentic-looking military command centers (although NORAD complained about supposed inaccuracies), the movie was an instant hit with gadget-loving Americans who, already excited by Star Wars and stealth, began to see the Pentagon and NORAD as immense technological fun houses—frightening enough to scare you to death sometimes, but always exhilarating to play around in.

Behind the scenes, at least as far as the public went, was new and far-reaching legislation that was to have as many or more earthshaking results as any smart weapon. This was the Goldwater-Nichols Department of Defense Reorganization Act of October 1, 1986. Goldwater-Nichols brought nothing less than a palace revolution to the rings and corridors of the Pentagon. It was, in fact, the first major reorganization of the Joint Chiefs of Staff in almost thirty years and the most significant change to the joint system since the National Security Act of 1947.

Goldwater-Nichols not only greatly enlarged and enhanced the authority of the chairman, it also for the first time established the position of vice chairman (the post of assistant defense secretary was by then long-established), and it also conferred broad new powers on the commanders in chief (CINCs) of the unified commands.

While the act was looped into the Pentagon's new military philosophy of jointness, it at the same time appointed the chairman, instead of the chiefs, as the official military advisor to the president, the National Security Council, and the Secretary of Defense. As before, the chairman would consult with the chiefs but be their official delegate to the White House; what the Pentagon called "splits" or disagreements at the JCS level were not to be routinely delivered to the White House or the defense secretary's office but worked out and brought from the Pentagon by the chairman. As one former chairman put it, the 1986 act ended the chairman's official role as "messenger boy" from the chiefs who would offer his own views unofficially in the Oval Office.

There were other new powers and responsibilities conferred on the CJCS as well. The chairman was now, according to the Joint History Office, "charged in broad terms with assistance to the president and the secretary of defense in the strategic direction of the armed forces; strategic and contingency planning; advice to the secretary of defense on military requirements, programs, and budgets; and development of the joint doctrine, training, and education of the armed forces." Perhaps most important, while the 1986 act redefined the military chain of command as running from the president to the secretary of defense to the CINCs, the president "might, however, direct that communications between himself or the secretary of defense and the CINCs be transmitted through the chairman and might designate the chairman to assist him and the secretary 'in performing their command function.'"

Among Goldwater-Nichols' (and subsequent amendments that further enhanced the chairmanship, such as Public Law 102-484 signed by President George H. W. Bush in October 1992) long-term impacts was to pave the way to the new and broad powers that gave Colin Powell wider latitude in forging military policy than chairmen representing the JCS in previous wars, such as Vietnam and Korea.

"Assuming I was confirmed," Powell wrote in his biography, *My American Journey*, "I would be the first full-term chairman to possess Goldwater-Nichols powers."

The unexpected departure of Admiral William Crowe, who had announced his intention not to serve a second term as CJCS, had paved the way for Powell's appointment. To the surprise of many in the Bush administration and at the Pentagon, Richard Cheney, then defense secretary, had chosen Powell from a short list of successors.

Bush, hearing of Cheney's choice, wondered aloud if Powell's appointment might not cause him trouble with more senior generals and admirals. If confirmed, Powell would not only be the first African-American chairman but also the youngest; as he put it later, the fourth star on his shoulders was only a few months old at the time. Powell had told Cheney he wasn't worried, the chiefs would support him; it turned out he was proven right. With Bush's recommendation, Powell's appointment sailed through Senate confirmation hearings.

Powell's tenure as the chairman of the Joint Chiefs of Staff was only a day old when a call from Joint Staff Operations woke him in the middle of the night to alert him to a building crisis in Panama. A coup there was brewing against the regime of strongman Manuel Noriega. As the crisis mounted, one American, a CIA agent, was being held hostage; later a marine would be killed by Panamanian troops. Noriega, who'd made a small fortune in selling his services to a mixed bag of hirers that included the CIA, DIA, the Soviet KGB, and Colombian drug cartels, was then under indictment in the United States on narcotics trafficking charges.

Despite reservations from advisors at a Sunday morning White House meeting, Bush decided to activate an invasion plan prepared by the chiefs, code named Blue Spoon. It was a week before Christmas, and the White House was decked out with festive gewgaws as the advisory group, including Powell, Cheney, and National Security Advisor Brent Scowcroft, arrived to brief the president.

Bush, wearing red socks, the left embroidered with "Merry" and the right with "Christmas," heard the pros and cons and then decided to invade. "Okay, let's do it," he said, gripping the arms of his chair and getting up. "The hell with it." The meeting was over. The invasion was on. Renamed Operation Just Cause (which in Powell's view had a better ring to the public ear), it marked a series of military firsts, one of which was the first forced extradition of a head of state and another the first operational use of the F-117A Stealth Fighter.

Just Cause also marked two other firsts. "Panama was the first major foreign crisis of the Bush administration," wrote Powell. "It also presented the first serious test of the chairman's new role under Goldwater-Nichols. In the past, the chiefs had voted to achieve a consensus that the chairman could carry to the secretary of defense and the president. Now, I was the principal military advisor."

In fact Powell later took every advantage of the powers conferred on the chairman by Goldwater-Nichols in expanding the perquisites of the CJCS. Early on he used the act, and despite opposition from the chiefs, Powell expanded the Atlantic Command, a key component of NATO, implementing jointness and combined arms doctrine. Powell was also instrumental in applying these concepts to the NATO force structure after the Berlin Wall came down, Checkpoint Charlie was removed from the Potsdammer Platz in Berlin, the Soviet Union disintegrated, and the Cold War officially came to an end.

The first post–Cold War era chairman advocated downsizing of the U.S. military, the closing of bases, and the creation of a transformation force tailored to fighting wars in regional, rather than global, theaters. Translated into action during the Gulf War, the 1986 JCS reorganization produced a unified and simplified chain of command during the Desert Storm Campaign of 1991, one that straight-lined down from the White House to the secretary of defense, then to the chairman, and finally to the commanders in chief in the combat theater.

As a result of these sometimes radical new developments in military technology, unification of command and refinement of combat doctrine, and in the restructuring of the Joint Chiefs of Staff resulting from Goldwater-Nichols, by 1990 the United States, on the eve of the Gulf War, was uniquely prepared to launch an offensive against the fourth largest army in the world.

The "Mother of all Battles" predicted by Saddam Hussein (and which some Western analysts believed would result in upward of thirty thousand casualties) was over in one hundred hours, with Iraq the loser and its military might destroyed, in most cases, before tanks, antiaircraft guns, SAMs, or other weapons could even aim, let alone fire, at Coalition invaders. As to the Iraqi air force, most of it had, by the conclusion of Desert Wind, the "Shock and Awe" opening phase of Desert Storm, been sent by Iraq's president-dictator to sanctuary in neighboring Iran.

The fast, decisive outcome of this short, epochal war not only shocked its friends and dismayed its enemies but surprised all hell out of the Pentagon itself. Something new, it was clear, was happening, and that something was soon dubbed a Revolution in Military Affairs, or RMA. It triggered a worldwide reassessment of military doctrine in the United States, Europe, the Soviet Union, the Middle East, and, for that matter, everywhere else.

Among the continually developing list of phrase-words and neologisms that grew out of this reassessment was that of force asymmetry—the concept was key to RMA; it stated that with the right mix of weapons, supported by the right combined arms doctrine, even a small force could have an effect on the enemy that was greatly disproportionate to its numerical strength.

The concept of asymmetric warfare was born, and it was one, through stealth technologies and through smart weaponry, that was to continue to revolutionize and streamline pre–Gulf War era "second-generation" military forces into leaner, meaner, smarter, and more lethal "third-generation" forces.

But asymmetric warfare was a double-edged sword, for its primal lesson was that Davids might again kill Goliaths by using even simple weapons and tactics, and it gave the courage of bloody deeds that might be done to the would-be freedom-fighters of a very different stripe who began to weave doctrines based on it into the warp and woof of their own secret plans.

BOOK THREE

AN AXIS OF EVIL

The First Wars of the Twenty-First Century

We're determined that before the sun sets on this terrible struggle, our flag will be recognized throughout the world as a symbol of freedom on the one hand, and of overwhelming power on the other.

—General George C. Marshall
addressing West Point's Class of 1942,
six months after Pearl Harbor

Iraq also has developed, produced, and stockpiled chemical weapons, and shown a continuing interest in developing nuclear weapons and longer-range missiles.

—Under Secretary of State for Arms Control and International Security John R. Bolton, in "Beyond the Axis of Evil,"
an address of May 6, 2002

CHAPTER FOURTEEN

A DISCORD OF PEACE

On September 11, 1991, some six months after the end of Desert Storm, hard on the heels of the U.S.–led Coalition victory in the Gulf War, amid post–Cold War euphoria and the dismantling of the last tatters of the Iron Curtain in Eastern Europe, the Pentagon celebrated its fiftieth birthday. Parallels between the world of 1941, when the Building first began going up, and the world of 1991 were striking.

When ground was broken in Hell's Bottom to begin a race against the clock to complete the Pentagon before the United States became swept into a second war in Europe, the future of the always fragile peace of the interwar years appeared bleak.

Now, with the Berlin Wall present only in pieces sold by souvenir hawkers, with the former Soviet Union now the Commonwealth of Independent States and shrunk back to the old czarist borders of 1658, with the Kremlin seeking democratic reforms modeled on Mikhail Gorbachev's principles of glasnost and perestroika, with the Carter-brokered peace treaty between Israel and Egypt still holding, with a stable, if not surging economy at home, and—amid the afterglow of victory—with U.S. citizenry united behind Desert Storm and thankful for the swift, decisive victory, the United States and most of the industrialized world was charged with a new sense of confidence and trust in the future.

It was a potent new wine and the world, or much of it, was stoned on it. The future did not hold nuclear terror, the fallout shelters—such as those dating back to 1957 and 1959 just discovered in the foundation of the Brooklyn Bridge as this book nears completion—had long been taken down, the signs in the street that pointed toward the uncertain sanctuaries of cellars and subway stations had either long been removed or rusted into artifacts of a bygone age of panic and paranoia whose meaning had by now been largely forgotten.

The Soviet Union was gone, and from its wreckage a people—the Russians—emerged who were no longer enemies, and if not exactly allies, then at least were friends. The United States, basking in the rhapsodic aftermath of success, had emerged from the Cold War stronger than ever before. The nation's old enemies were gone forever, it seemed. The United States was now the sole surviving superpower on the planet. The world was at peace, finally, after fifty years of continuous, relentless struggle and uncertainty.

The twentieth century was on its way out, and the remainder of its final decade, its *fin de siecle*, would not, like the end of the previous century, be a mere threshold to hell. The twenty-first century glowed brightly in the distance, like a comet in the skies, slowly drawing closer. The evils of a turbulent past would never be repeated. This future would be a good one. No Hitlers. No Stalins. No Auschwitzes or Cold Wars. The fact that the United States was around to roll up its sleeves and get its hands dirty to make it a good one made that future as sure as a done deal. Here was the payoff for all the sacrifices, all the money, all the blood, sweat, and tears since the first troop ships of World War I had quit U.S. shores for Europe in 1917. We'd gone through hell to get here, but by God, here we were at long last. *Finally*.

The world had been used to long, deep drafts of the grapes of wrath. It had drunk that bitter cup to the dregs. But, ah, this sweet wine—when had such wine as this been last drunk? Only at one other time in Western history had there been such a time, and only for one country. Napoleon's France had known it after the Battle of Austerlitz. They had called the euphoric postwar order the Sun of Austerlitz. But not even the Sun of Austerlitz came near to equaling the euphoria of this new age of peace, the warmth of this new solar radiance.

Historians had already given this serenity a name. It was the Pax Americana, a global peace guaranteed by the might of a benign superpower. Though its name harked back to another world peace, long ago administered by another military superpower, this peace would not require tribute to any Caesar to keep it going. The United States wanted nothing from any other country except friendship and cooperation. We're all in this together, said the United States. Just do your bit and don't dump your garbage in our backyard and we'll be okay.

At least one historian, the Japanese scholar Mishimo Tanaka, made headlines when he went so far as to declare that history itself was over. There would be no more of what made history what it was—war, famine, pestilence, turmoil. That was all done with now. So history itself was an outmoded concept. History was . . . *history.*

There were some exceptions to the general rule, though. If war was on its way into the dustbin of historical relics, if "legs," "grunts," "dogs," "G.I.'s," or any of the numerous other names for soldiers were no longer needed, thank you, in wars that would be increasingly fought by weapon-bristling robots that swept out of the night skies to mete out surgically precise destruction to the enemy, and if a twenty-first-century squad or a platoon of land warriors could fight better and move faster than a company or brigade in World War II or the Korean War, then the U.S. military could be downsized even more than it had already been prior to the Gulf War. So much for the army.

As to the navy and air force, the new dynamics of a one-superpower world changed the rules of the game almost overnight. Without the threat posed by the Soviet Union the navy's mission had imploded like a supernova turning into a white dwarf. How many carrier battle groups were necessary in a world where the Soviet navy—for a while the world's largest—was either made up of half-completed hulks rusting in dry-dock or ships in the hands of Moscow's former satellites, who, it need not be added, had no intention of giving back their newfound playthings.

How many SSBN's were needed to patrol the world's oceans and form the so-called third leg of the U.S. nuclear triad if a nuclear missile exchange with the Soviet Union was no longer in the cards? What role was a blue water navy to play in the New World Order that had arisen out of the turmoil of the Cold War with such startling rapidity and far-reaching implications for humanity?

The air force faced similar hard questions. Though its Stealth Fighter had proven itself the hero of Desert Wind and Desert Storm, an entire new array of third-generation advanced tactical fighter aircraft was already either on the drawing board or in prototype field testing during and after the Gulf War. Did the United States really need new air wings made up of replacements for the F-15 and F-16s that had served the nation so well since Vietnam and had performed so ably in the Gulf?

And what was the point of spending billions more taxpayers' dollars to produce yet another fleet of advanced B-2 Stealth Bombers, whose sole purpose was to sneak into the airspace of the USSR and light up the landscape with nuclear mushroom clouds? The same went for a strategic bomber that had never quite made the cut, the B-1B Lancer. Here was a plane that was to complement the B-2 and deliver far bigger nuclear payloads—a plane that could bust apart Moscow or St. Petersburg, smash them to rubble.

But the Lancer's terrain-following radar system—the digital eyes that would enable this nuclear heavyweight to fly so close to the ground that Soviet radars could not see it and at supersonic speeds so swift that SAMs and ground artillery could not accurately target it—this didn't work correctly. Was there any point in fixing the problems that plagued the completion of these pterodactyls of war? Or was the B-1B a living fossil, a throwback to a past age, already past any reason for existence and doomed to extinction along with the Soviet Union that it had been built to blow to smithereens in a nuclear war?

On the eve of its fiftieth anniversary, as the huge armies that it had assembled in the Middle East began their stateside withdrawals, as bases began to close in the continental United States, in remote Pacific outposts, and on the soil of a Europe that American armies had twice gone far from home to defend against tyranny and oppression, the Pentagon grappled with the implications and the consequences of the Pax Americana and the New World Order that was implicit in the concept. The Building had been built as a house of war, and if Mars himself lay broken-backed in the dust of history, already half buried in the mud of the Tigris and the sands of the Iraqi deserts, then what did the future hold in store for the Pentagon?

The intelligence agencies that had been established by the 1947 National Security Act with the fury of reaction to the belligerence of the fast-rearming Soviet Union were also reeling from the feather-light blows of the sudden outbreak of peace. What would the role of the CIA be if its arch-foe, the Soviet KGB, was now something akin to an ally?

If the director of the Central Intelligence Agency could share coffee, crullers, and bon mots in the comfort of the director's office at Langley with his former Soviet opposite number, how many field agents were necessary for the intelligence gathering on the Russians that had thus far been the CIA's main reason for existence? Were the U-2 or the SR-71 Blackbird—the latter newly if transiently revamped for post–Cold War surveillance missions following an over hasty mothballing in 1989— needed in a now fairly open Russian society, and in an age when orbiting spy satellites, even commercial ones, and unmanned aerial vehicles could bring back intelligence that was better and cheaper than the take from the planes?

The defense sector was equally perplexed. As Congress scaled back defense acquisitions to an all-time low in the nine years between the end of the Gulf War and the administration of George W. Bush, major U.S. defense contractors from McDonnell-Douglas to General Dynamics underwent significant, sometimes drastic, downsizing. American defense firms, like their former Soviet counterparts and European business partners, began turning their energies toward building better washing machines and microwave ovens instead of faster and deadlier jet fighters or stealthier attack submarines.

* * *

Amid the unaccustomed discord of peace that came like a virgin bride to a house that had trafficked only with the bawds of war, the Pentagon marked the fiftieth anniversary of its completion in 1993 with little fanfare. Celebrations were held only in 1997 and 2000, the first to commemorate the fiftieth anniversary of the Department of Defense and the second to mark the fiftieth anniversary of Armed Forces Day. While a fife and drum marching band played on the Pentagon Parade Field,

CJCS General Henry Shelton and Defense Secretary William Cohen paid tribute to "unsung" military and civilian heroes of the DOD.

Meanwhile, behind the scenes, work was already underway on a renovation program so ambitious that it rivaled even the original bold Somervell plan that had first raised the Pentagon in 1941, with workers laboring around the clock in three shifts. Time and wear-and-tear had taken an inevitable toll on the Building. Floors, walls, and ceilings were deteriorating, coming apart in some places.

Not only had Somervell needed to do a fast job of erecting the Pentagon, cutting corners along the way, he'd had to contend with repeated instructions from Roosevelt and Congress to cut back on fixtures made of construction materials with military applications, which resulted in the general's "stripteasing" the Pentagon of anything made of brass, copper, steel, or other strategic metals that could be salvaged to make bullets, artillery shells, tanks, or the hulls of capital ships. Everything from metal toilet stalls to doors were ripped out in the midst of the original construction. In the end, Somervell had stripteased the Pentagon down to the bare concrete bones.

As solid an edifice as it was—proved by the inability of the airliner that struck it on 9/11 to penetrate deeper than its two outer rings—over time the Building had begun to show its age. Deterioration had set in and basic infrastructure, from plumbing to electrical conduits, had begun to wear out and fall apart. In other cases, parts of the vast structure, like the water heating and air conditioning systems, had long gone past their expected service lives and were overdue for replacement.

In at least one case, something necessary had been left out from the outset—the Rotary Road that pedestrians approaching the River Entrance needed to cross on their way into the Building was like running a speeding gauntlet of commuter traffic. The rebuilding plan called for the construction of a pair of South Terrace pedestrian bridges and a series of bus shelters.

Other new construction was done to address a preoccupation with security in an age where terrorist attacks, or even conventional enemy assault, was for the first time a possibility that couldn't be ignored as too farfetched as it had been in the early 1940s. Back then, America had been considered invulnerable to direct enemy attack, but times had changed. New construction would include a Remote Delivery Facility (RDF) and the relocation of the Washington Metro entrance that ran beneath the Pentagon to a location outside the premises. If this author could envision the plot of a thriller where a terrorist, equipped with a small tactical nuke, could blow up the Pentagon from a Metro subway tunnel, then so conceivably might terrorists themselves.

New windows with bulletproof glass were also to be added—among the few exceptions that already existed were the chairman's office, where Powell, taking over from Crowe, had been dismayed to discover that the office windows had been blacked out with paint as a security precaution. Powell had ordered the old windows ripped out and one-way bulletproof Mylar windows installed instead. The windows gave Powell unobstructed views across the Potomac to the heart of the capital with sailboats plying the Tidal Basin visible in between. With no one at the bus stop directly below his fourth floor office able to see in, Powell later said he'd found himself "in an ideal position to watch the daily human drama, from little cabals of Pentagon officers to lovers arranging trysts."

The plan would create more usable space, too. The space of the Pentagon basement was to be doubled so that a 1.1 million-square-foot mezzanine could be added. The way office space was configured would also be changed. What the contractor's prospectus called "single-use" office space was to be renovated into modular areas that could serve multiple roles that sometimes changed from week to week and month to month. With the possibility of an administrative department staffed by civilians turning into a military war-planning headquarters practically overnight, the new interiors had to be flexible and multipurpose.

"Although there were still some offices with permanent walls from slab to slab, much of the office space is open, and modular furniture is used to define work spaces," the prospectus put it. The renovation also installed an entirely new pathway for information systems and telecommunications, without which the Pentagon would be unable to function in the twenty-first century.

Originally the Pentagon's wiring had been designed for running vacuum cleaners and connecting telephones. No one then had dreamed of an information revolution that would pile every office desk with copiers, computer terminals, and scanners and hang wide screen televisions on many walls. As a result the Pentagon had as many as thirty localized power outages every day, and sometimes more than forty during the winter months, when the Building's chilled occupants used space heaters to compensate for the obsolete heating, ventilation, and air-conditioning systems that had long since worn out.

Thousands of linear feet of high-capacity fiber optic cable for two separate networks, one carrying classified, the other unclassified data, were installed in what the plan called a "ductbank" that wound around the five sides of the Building. Connections from the ductbank feed into the building through "spine walls" to connect the main cable network to individual offices. Replacement of the Pentagon's heating and refrigeration plant (H&RP), long past its prime, was as critical to the Building's computers as it was to air condition the offices against the notoriously hot and humid summers in the region. According to DOD statistics, the Pentagon's massive computer systems would begin shutting down in as little as ninety seconds if cooling was impaired.

In 1990, as Saddam's armies overran and occupied Kuwait, the Concept Plan for the Pentagon Renovation had already been drafted. The plan was described by the Defense Department as "[entailing] the equivalent of demolishing the interiors of three buildings the size of the Empire State Building, refurbishing them from top to bottom without disturbing the occupants or disrupting their work, and completing the renovation on a strict budget of $1.2 billion."

In practical terms this meant moving out more than five thousand people per wedge with all of their equipment while keeping operations of those five thousand displaced Pentagon staffers going round the clock while renovations were being carried out. A Pentagon spokesperson likened this process to "someone coming into your house and upgrading your old black-and-white television to color without turning the set off or hampering reception for even one moment. It has demanded a staggering degree of planning and preparation."

Then, in 1991, the process moved another stage forward with the Defense Authorization Act that transferred control of the Pentagon

Reservation from the administrator of general services to the secretary of defense and also established the Pentagon Reservation Maintenance Revolving Fund to pay for the renovations (it would also for the first time give the defense secretary the power to set rent rates for non–DOD Pentagon tenants, such as shop owners on the Mezzanine).

The Pentagon Project, as the plan became generally known, was put into action in 1992, after the Building had received National Historic Landmark designation by Congress. Work on renovating Wedge 1 began that year with demolition taking place almost under the noses—or more precisely, the feet—of the Building's denizens, as work crews ripped out walls, floors, pipes, and electrical ducts, and began the six-phased program that is still going on and, with new changes implemented after 9/11, scheduled for completion in 2015.

Finally, the plan called for refacing new additions to the Pentagon—specifically the two South Bridges and RDF—with slabs of Indiana limestone hewn from the same quarry that Somervell's staff had tapped back in 1941. Unknown to the planners, more of that same limestone would be needed later on to repair damage caused on 9/11.

* * *

They flew the suicide jet in God's name, with prayers on their lips and hatred in their hearts.

They had hijacked Flight 77 at Dulles International Airport soon after its departure at 8:10 that morning, a Boeing 757 jetliner—like the other three passenger jets commandeered by terrorists that fateful September Tuesday—bound for California. Also like the other aircraft it had lifted off the runway with tanks fueled to their maximum capacity, ready for a transcontinental flight.

As the plane reached cruising altitude, a flurry of small metallic clicks rippled through the cabin as seat belts were unbuckled. Cell phones began chiming as passengers turned them back on. The terrorists' phones also went off. The news was good. Less than a half hour before, at 9:03 a.m., Flight 175, hijacked out of Boston shortly after eight o'clock, had rammed the South Tower of the World Trade Center.

Now both towers were burning, the North Tower having been struck by Flight 11, also out of Boston, at 8:45 a.m.

The jubilation that now surged through them was greater than the joy that some of them had felt, months before, at the flight school in Florida where they had trained to pilot big jets like this one, when the news reached them that the USS *Cole* had been attacked. They had embraced each other then, and blessed their leader. But with the jubilation came the sudden anger that they had held in check for so long. They wanted to embrace as comrades once more, but more than that they wanted to draw the blood of the enemy that surrounded them. They had to act quickly. Already they could hear the raised voices of passengers who, like themselves, had just learned that the World Trade Center had been hit by planes and was burning. So far the reports had nothing to do with terrorism. Then, moments later, the captain's voice came on over the public address. "Attention passengers," he began.

The captain's next words were hardly out before, belts unbuckled, they had risen from their seats, drawn the box cutters from their pockets, slid out the razors, and locked them in place.

Then they began slashing. Seized with an insane glee, they laughed maniacally as they drew first blood and watched it spurt and gush.

Passengers were now screaming, hysterical with panic. Shouting at them in broken English, the terrorists began pulling those from seats at the front of the uncrowded commuter flight and herding them to the back of the plane. Those who, like a male flight attendant, got in the way, were slashed savagely and repeatedly by the hijackers. The sight of the crewman's blood gushing out onto the seats and the carpeted aisle, splashing against the window as he collapsed across a row of empty seats, discouraged the others from putting up a fight. Threatened with those blood-tipped razors, numb with shock, those passengers who had confronted the hijackers backed slowly toward the rear and slid into vacant seats.

By now the cockpit door was open. The captain and copilot had been alerted, and the captain was already out, heading toward the commotion at the rear, from which he could already hear shouts and screams and the cacophonous sounds of dozens of cell phones blaring a devil's chorus of clashing melodies. This was bedlam, but he knew what to do. The plane was being hijacked. The captain thought back to training he'd received. In the event of a hijacking there was one rule to follow: Remain calm and cooperative. Hijackings rarely resulted in loss of life unless the hijackers were provoked.

That might have been true in the past, but this time it was different. The captain didn't get a chance to do much talking. Three men with hate-contorted faces rushed him. Two pinned him against a row of seats while the other cut his throat. His last sight was the leering visages of his executioners. The copilot suffered the same fate. His corpse was dragged to where the captain lay and dumped there.

One of the hijackers now climbed into the pilot's seat and grasped the controls. The 757's two massive turbine engines howled as the giant aircraft swung in a narrow arc in the skies over western Ohio and began to fly back in the direction from which it had originally come. The loop in the air was beginning to close, but other circuits were also closing. Circuits in the mind. Circuits of history. The hijackers were now again sullen. The euphoria of the first savage minutes of the attack was replaced with a deathly calm masking a cold, implacable fury. The symbolic import of their actions had been factored into the terrorist operation; vengeance feeds on symmetries of meaning, purpose, and action; it is a closing of loops and a retracing of circles.

The month of September had already lent its name to one terrorist group, Black September, to commemorate the bloody ousting of the Palestine Liberation Organization from Jordan in 1970 by King Hussein. Then, too, the jetliner's target was replete with symbolic meaning, not the least of which was the fact that the Pentagon had first gone up on a September morning exactly fifty years from the moment that the lightly boarded but fully fueled plane had taken off.

It's arguable whether or not the symbolism of the airport itself played any role in events. Dulles International had been named after one of the architects of Cold War policy and a personage instrumental in establishing the skein of events that was to endow the Pentagon with a central role in the global events following World War II.

Along the circuitry of revenge an electric current flows that is so powerful it ignites minds primed with hate like bundles of dynamite.

Wars have been fought to get that rush, societies have pined for it—
Germany and England both lusted for that mass high of satisfied revenge
in 1914, with the United States catching the fever soon thereafter. Like
the Germans sick with the war fever of 1914, the hijackers were about to
be dashed against the Scylla and Charybdis of folly as they followed the
mesmerizing siren's song that drew them toward their fiery deaths in the
Building's outermost rings. Like kamikaze pilots before them they would
in the end accomplish little or nothing, except to raise the anger of the
United States to the boiling point and make the nation thirst for revenge.

It was a good day for flying. The weather along the eastern seaboard
of the United States was clear. The skies were intensely blue; I can
remember how, on that same morning, I watched the immense curved
plume of gray-brown smoke from the tops of the burning World Trade
towers drift across the Hudson River against that incredibly clear blue
sky and was thinking then that it was the same sky as the one in the
painting by the elder Brueghel where Icarus, having flown too close to
the sun, his waxen angel's wings melting, began his slow, inexorable
plunge to destruction on the industriously tilled fields below.

It was a morning of Indian summer, one of those mornings that
seem suspended between what has been and what is to come, and on
this morning what was to come was a foretaste of Apocalypse. For the
hijackers, though, the weather was something to give thanks for. It was
good flying weather. They had spent months learning to fly jumbo jets
in Florida. They were still novices, but even novices with a smattering of
training could hit the broadside of a barn—or ram a plane into buildings
the size of the World Trade Center towers and the Pentagon on a crystal
clear morning such as this one.

At the controls, the hijacker pilot kept the jumbo jet on course,
re-crossing Kentucky into West Virginia and moving steadily east. The
new pilot ignored the voices from the cockpit radio, then switched it off.
The rogue plane, like the other three that had been taken that morning,
was being tracked by ground stations that included NORAD as well as
FAA flight controllers. The only sounds in the cockpit were the pings
and beeps from the flight console and the steady drone of the twin-engine
turbines that propelled Flight 77 toward its target.

Soon the aircraft had crossed back into Maryland, on a return vector a few miles south of its original flight path. In a matter of minutes the hijackers' target appeared in the distance. Through the cockpit windows the pilot saw the first outline of the large building across a rolling, tree-clad landscape that had just begun to show an autumnal riot of colors.

The morning sun shone through the Plexiglas, and wands of golden light waved across the faces of the hijackers as the pilot made a small course correction and the plane turned and dipped slightly to skim low over treetop level toward the Pentagon's northwestern side. In the last minutes and seconds of the death flight, motorists on the highway complex passing the Pentagon saw the immense aircraft's underbelly sweep overhead, almost near enough to brush the roofs of their cars.

It was 9:43 a.m., the start of another Tuesday morning workday, as the shadow of death swept over them. In the next few seconds the plane flew low enough across the highway to clip the antenna from an SUV and shear lighting stanchions that flanked the roadway. In the last half second before impact the plane was less than five hundred feet from the Building's west wall and flying nearly level to the grassy ground.

A hundred feet and a tenth of a second from impact, its right wing struck a large generator used by a construction crew, swinging the rogue plane leftward and elevating its right wing. It traveled another seventy-five feet in the next few microseconds. The plane's left engine struck the ground at nearly the same instant, breaking off, as the aircraft's nose plowed into the Pentagon's west wall.

A heartbeat later a thunderous explosion split the air as Flight 77 collided with its target. As the impact crumpled the steel airframe like paper and sheared off what was left of the wings, the fuel in its tanks ignited a fireball that engulfed the Pentagon's exterior and shot columns of flame into the interior spaces of the enormous building. The impact blew a gaping hole between Corridors Four and Five from the outermost E-Ring clear through Ring C and ate away at Ring B. Those in the cockpit died instantly, blown to pieces and vaporized by the inferno. Those at the rear of the aircraft survived a split-second longer. Forensic investigators would later determine that the plane had been vaporized before it had penetrated to a distance roughly equal to the length of the fuselage.

In the ring corridors of the Pentagon at the epicenter of the blast, those army and navy operations personnel which occupied that wedge were instantly incinerated or blown to pieces. Some escaped with nonfatal injuries. Luckier personnel, unharmed after the shock wave rocked the Pentagon to its foundations, took shelter in the center courtyard or escaped through the South, Mall, River, or Metro Concourse entrances, gasping from the acrid smoke they'd swallowed on the way out. Fires burned for more than two days, yet in the undamaged core of the Pentagon, military planners and civilian engineers were soon back at work, charting a course for rebuilding and planning military strikes against al-Qaeda bases in Afghanistan.

Since that clear-skied Tuesday that erupted into flame with such terrible suddenness, America has felt the rippling of shock waves that continue to echo down through the corridors of time.

Even as many clamored for revenge on the terrorists who had placed America under attack for the first time since Pearl Harbor, others tried to balance evil with hope. "I know that there is only the smallest measure of inspiration that can be taken from this devastation," Senate Majority Leader Tom Daschle said soon after the attacks. "But there is a passage in the Bible, from Isaiah, that I think speaks to all of us at times like this: 'The bricks have fallen down, but we will rebuild with dressed stone; the fig trees have been felled, but we will replace them with cedars.'" Even the president, who had earlier said, "The pictures of airplanes flying into buildings, fires burning, huge structures collapsing have filled us with disbelief, terrible sadness, and a quiet, unyielding anger," later added, "Terrorist attacks can shake the foundations of our biggest buildings, but they cannot shake America."

Rebuilding the Pentagon commenced as soon as the fires were out and the debris and rubble of destruction had been cleared away. As Defense Secretary Donald Rumsfeld, caught by news camera personnel near the Pentagon's South Parking as flames engulfed the Building, told reporters within hours of the attack, and as fires still burned, "The Pentagon is functioning. It will be in business."

The rebuilding of the Pentagon's outermost E Ring was completed exactly a year later, on September 11, 2002, the self-imposed deadline of construction crews. After more than 1.5 million man-hours since the 9/11 attack, the Building reopened, a survivor of a baptism by fire, a symbol of American military might and democracy's strength in the face of adversity, ready for the next page in its biography to be written. And, indeed, as Persian poet Kahlil Gibran once penned in his epic poem *The Prophet*, "The moving finger writes, and having writ, moves on: nor all your piety nor wit shall lure it back to cancel half a line. . . ."

That next page was not long in coming.

CHAPTER FIFTEEN

SHOCK AND AWE

Abu Dhabi sits on an island in the Persian Gulf littoral, occupying the approximate geographic center of the seven former British Trucial kingdoms that collectively make up the United Arab Emirates today. Abu Dhabi is the capital of the UAE, just as it had once been the principal sheikdom of the original seven oil-rich desert tribes.

From the upper stories of either of the ultramodern city's two four-star hotels, the Hilton and the Millennium, in air-conditioned luxury suites that front Abu Dhabi's gleaming white sand beaches, an American business traveler can look out across the Gulf and see the past, present, and future of the Middle East; he can also glimpse something of the future of his own nation, which is linked to the region by ties of money, politics, guns, oil, and most recently, blood.

At the end of March 2003, the Persian Gulf is a glossy sheet of slate beneath an incandescent sun that signals the start of the hottest part of the year. Only an hour before a sandstorm had blown through, but now the early morning sky is tranquil, the waters calm. In the near distance, to the immediate left, the coastline of Qatar is visible. Looming much larger on the right is the southern coastline of Iran, a Persian Goliath that dwarfs both Qatar and the UAE combined.

Far off in the distance, visible more in the imagination than to the naked eye, lies Kuwait and the spit of coastline that marks Iraq's only gateway to the Gulf. Beyond their northern reaches, and invisible to view, are Syria, Jordan, Israel, and Egypt. Behind the city rises part of the Hadramaut massif, a towering plateau with craggy escarpments and eerily wind-carved sand dunes on its flanks. It conceals the arid vastness of the rest of the Arabian Peninsula, hidden like some silent, sleeping giant, beyond the rocky highlands that rise along Jebel Dhanna at the extreme western edge of the UAE's coastal plain.

There are direct flights from Paris, Bonn, and Rome to Abu Dhabi International Airport, a sprawling ultramodern complex of spacious terminals at the end of Sheik Rashid Al Maktoum Street with jetways spoked around the circular arrival and departure lounges built by a French-German-Italian design consortium. Adventure tourism and international banking attract a globetrotting clientele to this corner of the Gulf.

In late March 2003, inbound flights would be stacked up over the island; customs and security staff would need to be expanded. The backpackers would forsake the local beaches for the arid scenic wonders of nearby Ras Al Kaimah or Sharjah. The kingdom's hotels would be booked solid, the overflow taken up by other hotels along the Emirates' coastline. The reason was this: Abu Dhabi was about to host its sixth international defense exposition, IDEX 2003. It was heralded around the world as the biggest arms fair on earth. It would turn out to be that and considerably more.

As IDEX 2003 opened on March 16, the United States and Great Britain were giving Saddam Hussein a final grace period to declare the existence and whereabouts of the weapons of mass destruction he was accused of harboring, or else flee the country. When the U.S. ultimatum ran out at midnight on March 19, it was almost a certainty that the U.S.–U.K. coalition would begin its second blitz on Iraq in twelve years.

At IDEX the show would go on. It would have to. Sheik Kalifa Bin Zayad al-Nahyan, crown prince and deputy commander in chief of the UAE, who officially opened this expo as he had done the previous ones, declared that, war or no war, IDEX would proceed as planned.

And so it did proceed, closing on the night of March 20, the final day of IDEX 2003 marking the first day of the air war phase of the coalition war on Iraq. Early that same morning Baghdad was convulsed by a high technology bombardment made up of layers of smart munitions, some dropped from planes, others vectoring in with robotic precision and lethal stealth, while electronic warfare subjected the invisible "fifth dimension" of the battle space to cybernetic attack.

Clearly, this was not an attack in the World War II mode, nothing like an incendiary raid over Berlin or Tokyo seen in grainy monochrome films. In fact, events would play out far differently than even those of the astonishing air assaults, dubbed Desert Wind, that commenced on the night of January 16, 1991, when coalition tactical air struck Baghdad the first time around.

In the spring of 1943, British Lancasters or American Flying Fortresses would make high-level runs above a target, drop their two-thousand-pound "dumb" iron bombs, and turn around, often flying through dense clouds of killer enemy flak, shadowed by Zeros or Messerschmitts that mercilessly strafed them with machine-gun fire. Such tactics no longer applied at the dawn of the twenty-first century; nor was the grace under fire of that past war's bomber pilots necessary anymore.

For one thing, the Iraqi air force had been crushed early in the Iraq War; friendly air forces now owned the skies. Most important, in the spring of 2003 air attacks on Baghdad came from all directions at once and used an often complex mixture of weapons, manned and unmanned. Cruise missiles, such as TLAMs or Tomahawk Land Attack Missiles, vectored in from miles away. F-117A Stealth Fighters—really more fighter-bombers than true fighter planes—ghosted through radar coverage and placed GPS-guided Joint Direct Attack Munitions, or JDAMs, on their targets. Workhorse planes aptly named Hercules lumbered through the night at high-altitude ceilings on missions that might soon include dropping enormous, subnuclear yeild MOAB bombs from the extended ramps of their open cargo bays.

The covert star of the show was a B-2 Stealth Bomber that launched a JDAM into the compound of Saddam Hussein's Presidential Palace in the heart of downtown Baghdad. Acting on intelligence that the Iraqi dictator had taken refuge in a bunker deep below the streets of the city center, the Stealth was used as an instrument of assassination, now declared legal under international rules of engagement. The JDAM was equipped with a specially hardened nose assembly that could penetrate deeply buried bunker complexes. It was hoped that the devastating strike would kill Saddam and as a bonus also eliminate his two sons and principal heirs to the Iraqi leadership.

From the high windows of a multistory hotel on Abu Dhabi's coast in the early morning hours of March 20, the strobing flashes that lit up Baghdad's skyline were distantly visible in the nocturnal blackness to an American visitor to IDEX. Later that same afternoon the ground phase of the war would commence with coalition incursions near the Kuwaiti border. By the time IDEX officially closed for the next two years later that same day, the highly mobile allied troops would have penetrated more than sixty miles into southern Iraq.

Although they would encounter stiffer resistance than expected during the course of the next three weeks, the new, light, mobile, and highly lethal forces that spearheaded the assault on Iraq would score rapid territorial gains. They would soon take the capital. In the end, the assault would prove a vindication of the Pentagon's vision of what the U.S. Defense Department termed military transformation.

On April 11, twenty-two days after the close of the world's biggest arms exposition, at a White House press conference, President Bush declared that the war on Iraq was won.

"The Saddam regime has ended," CENTCOM's commanding general, Tommy Franks, would next tell the assembled media, and then Press Secretary Ari Fleisher, speaking for the White House, would add, "The regime is gone."

Saddam Hussein was either dead or in hiding and the hunt for the weapons of mass destruction that he had been said to harbor would, though failing to turn up any "smoking gun," be in full swing. As the first of the planes laden with IDEX attendees heading for home began to take off from Abu Dhabi's international airport, the allies were already well on their way to winning the lightning-swift ground war and ousting Saddam Hussein from power. Dead or alive, Iraq's dictator was now irrelevant to the future of the region. Other forces would shape the country's destiny from now on.

* * *

There was more than just a geographical proximity between IDEX 2003 and the events taking place several hundred miles to the north of the exhibition site on the closing day of the arms expo. The weapons systems and the digital information systems that are critical to the operation and support, indeed the success, of modern weaponry deployed in the strikes on Iraq were first previewed at earlier IDEX expos and other defense shows like it around the world a decade before.

Those military systems, and the tactical framework in which they were to be used, nestled like mailed fists inside velvet gloves, were byproducts of the successful prosecution of the Gulf War of 1991, after which a "Revolution in Military Affairs" was proclaimed by the Pentagon. Just as the weaponry, strategies, and tactics of the Gulf War had vindicated the Vietnam-era weapon systems of the 1970s, many of whose offshoots—such as stealth and Tomahawk cruise missiles—were then used for the first time in actual combat, the Iraq War confirmed the utility of weaponry on display at IDEX 2003.

There are likewise connections between the biography of the Building before and following the September 11, 2001, attack to the end of the tenure of Defense Secretary Donald Rumsfeld, whose conclusion and immediate aftermath mark the culminating chapters of this book. Rumsfeld's appointment signified the changing of the guard at the Department of Defense and the ushering in of a new era distinguished even at the outset by unprecedented budgetary increase and growth in the defense sector on the one hand, and on the other, an obsession with the holy grail of "transformation," a term with almost magical connotations in Pentagonese. At the same time it harbingered conflict between DOD's new civilian overseers and the career military that made up the Joint Chiefs of Staff, whose core beliefs concerning defense had been hammered into shape on the brutal anvil of the Vietnam War.

The Shock and Awe phase of the Iraq War that an American visitor to the UAE watched unfolding in late March 2003 at closer range than a Tomahawk missile can fly was in part, perhaps in large part, to be a vindication of the implementation of an array of new weaponry and strategic doctrine whose development and realization had been one of the first orders of business of the incoming Bush administration. Bush and his running mate, then former Defense Secretary Richard Cheney, had harped on this one string over and over again during the campaign year of 2000.

Yet their clarion call was a note that had, to many, rung hollow then, during the close of the Clinton years, years of military drawdown in the aftermath of the Soviet collapse, years after the stunning victories of Desert Storm in which the United States had thwarted Baghdad's power grab for Kuwaiti—and later, perhaps, Saudi—petroleum and had left Iraq isolated and its military neutered, years in which even the genocide in Yugoslavia had been tidily put to a halt without the intervention of U.S. ground forces, years during which, in short, most of the world seemed to be in a relative state of peace and when, for the first time in decades, the U.S. economy ran at a surplus and not a deficit.

It had seemed almost a non sequitur for Bush to declare that America's military forces lacked the capabilities of fighting a protracted war when no war clouds loomed on the horizon. It had seemed almost ludicrous for Cheney to belabor his rival in a televised vice-presidential debate with a point-by-point assessment of U.S. defense shortcomings, much as Bush had previously done to Democratic presidential candidate Al Gore, when it seemed obvious that after Desert Storm the list of America's potential military adversaries at any time in the near future had fallen near to zero. It had seemed, in sum, that Team Bush, contending— as Bush himself was later to state with some surprise in the aftermath of victory—against prosperity and against peace had been trying to pathetically raise a straw man against a tide it had little hope of turning.

And yet, three years after the Bush victory, with a Congress stunned by the attacks of 9/11 closing ranks behind the Oval Office in voting defense allocations and supplementals at levels exceeding even the giant budgetary figures at the height of U.S.–Soviet confrontation in the Reagan 1980s, a U.S. military that was already embarked on the road to transformation launched attacks on Iraq that seemed to be hot off the pages of Pentagon position papers and vision statements by the armed service branches—like the navy's Copernicus Forward, the air force's Global Engagement, and the Joint Chiefs of Staff's Joint Vision 2010— on what a lighter, faster, and yet more lethal American military force might look like in the twenty-first century, and about the strategic and tactical goals that such a force might accomplish.

The fledgling Bush administration's fiscal year 2002 Defense Department budget, totaling almost $339 billion and representing a 33 percent increase over the fiscal year 2001 budget (the last submitted by Clinton administration Defense Secretary William Cohen), marked the largest single increase in national defense spending since the peak-year Reagan-era budget of 1985—a budget, it should be remembered, designed to fund a military buildup intended to fight the Soviets in World War III and which saw the United States spending some $30 million every hour on defense, twenty-four hours a day, seven days a week. The $364.4 billion post-9/11 fiscal year 2003 budget, which funded Iraq War operations, included a $79.5 billion emergency supplemental to cover the war and its immediate aftermath. The $368.2 billion fiscal year 2004 budget included an $87.5 billion supplemental largely earmarked for the Coalition Provisional Authority, or CPA, the administrative agency responsible for postwar Iraq. The fiscal year 2005 budget, which was a percent higher than the preceding budget, would include an additional $25 billion supplemental appropriation to cover continued operations in Iraq. The fiscal year 2006 budget included a $150 billion supplemental.

Shock and Awe was the embodiment of everything that Rumsfeld's appointment to the E-Ring had augured back in 2000. The onslaught of rapid mobile ground forces into Iraq across the Saudi and Kuwaiti borders coupled with the near simultaneous deployment of tactical air that ranged from the initial bomb-loads released by Stealth aircraft to heliborne attacks on Iraqi outposts was like a fast-forward playback of Desert Storm minus the tank battles. The rapid drive to Baghdad was more Rommel than Schwarzkopf, and it eclipsed even the blitzkrieg that the United States and its British coalition partner had unleashed in Afghanistan over the course of the previous seven months. There, in the 2001 air strikes that marked the commencement of Operation Enduring Freedom (OEF), similar lightning warfare had used new types of missiles and explosives to dismantle the stony hives excavated from the entrails of the Hindu Kush in which al-Qaeda and Taliban had sheltered from post-9/11 U.S. retribution.

Rugged mountains, rising in places to nearly twenty-five thousand feet above sea level, cover about four-fifths of Afghanistan. From the Pamir Mountains in the northeast, the giant Hindu Kush range runs southwestward across the country, cutting Afghanistan roughly in half. The name of the range literally means "Killer of Hindus." Supreme Court Justice William O. Douglas, in his 1957 travelogue *West of the Indus*, wrote that the name originated when northern raiders, like Genghis Khan in the seventh century and Ibn Batuta in the fourteenth, recrossed the Kush with large numbers of captives who, said Douglas, "died like flies crossing this cold, cruel, mountain range."

Alexander the Great also crossed the Kush into Afghanistan, as did the Russians in the nineteenth and the Soviets in the twentieth centuries who, wrote Douglas, "are drawn like a magnet" to Afghanistan. Douglas described seeing huge piles of concrete blocks that had been installed by the British "as a roadblock against [Soviet] tanks" at the western end of the Khyber Pass, which empties into the vast Afghan plain below like an enormous funnel made of rock. The concrete blocks "filled the whole canyon, with spare ones to roll across the road." Neither Douglas nor the Afghans had apparently foreseen that in the next Russian invasion mechanized armor would be airlifted in, not driven across.

U.S. airstrikes in 2001 commenced the war against the Taliban and al-Qaeda in Afghanistan during Operation Enduring Freedom, and although the USMC composed the mainstay of U.S. ground forces pursuing land operations under the banner of Operation Northern Forge (ONF), bombardments from standoff distances were the muscle behind the U.S. fist that hammered mercilessly at the strongholds buried deep in the Kush.

The primary weapons used in the "shock and awe" attacks on Afghanistan in 2001 were Tomahawk missiles with thermobaric warheads and massive, five-thousand-pound GBU-28 munitions, dubbed "cave-busters." Thermobaric weapons are essentially fuel-air explosives that use atmospheric oxygen to ignite a high-explosive charge rather than carry their own oxidizer in the warhead; they kill not only by means of blast effect but by rapidly depleting the underground bunker systems of breathable oxygen, making them effective yet brutal weapons against enemies seeking shelter and protection amid cave systems, tunnels, and buried bunker complexes.

Nevertheless, the Taliban had been allied with those who had visited barbarous deaths on thousands in New York, at the Pentagon, and in the confines of a hijacked jet bound for the capital. B-1B, B-2, and B-52 bombers (one B-52 reportedly had "NYPD—We Remember" painted on its nose) and FA/18 and FA/14 fighters launched from three carriers in the Arabian Sea (the *Enterprise* and *Kittyhawk* were positioned below the Persian Gulf and the *Vinson* between the Horn of Africa and South Yemen) saturated targets on the flat, low-lying plains, including suspected Taliban strongholds, with cluster munitions and precision-guided weapons such as JDAM, the GPS-guided gravity bomb used later in the March 2003 in air strikes on Baghdad.[9]

Moreover, the American military machine looked then like a juggernaut that no power on earth could be expected to stop. Not for nothing had the sovereign state of California elected the Terminator as its governor in the same election year that had swept George W. Bush to power. It was not warfare a la Schwarzkopf that was in play now, but a cybernetic behemoth that strode across obstacles, crushing them underfoot the way Schwarzenegger's famed robotic alter ego crushed all adversaries beneath his titanium heel. America was now the Terminator. A lone vigilante on a mission of retribution that, like a throwaway line in a scene from *Terminator III*, invited any opposition to America's right to strike where it pleased in the national interest to "talk to de hand." American go-it-aloneness had risen to unprecedented heights in its pursuit of a new policy of preemptive warfare. America's position was that it was answerable to none but itself in the wake of surprise attacks on the homeland that dwarfed even the destruction of Pearl Harbor in 1941.

Even at home, those who called for a formal declaration of war against al-Qaeda—fast identified as the organization responsible for the atrocities—had no truck with the Oval Office. Addressing the nation

---

9. The strikes on Afghanistan marked the first time the B-2 Spirit, otherwise known as the Stealth Bomber, was deployed in combat from an overseas base, Diego Garcia, a ten-square-mile coral atoll in the southern Indian Ocean and the site of a British naval base. JDAM stands for Joint Direct Attack Munition.

on September 20, 2001, scarcely more than a week from the terrorist hijackings and martyrdom mission attacks, the president vowed his resolve to "Smoke 'em out," prompting metaphors of vigilante justice and editorial cartoons of Bush as an Old West town sheriff who shot from the hip and asked questions later.

Bush's rhetoric resonated with most Americans, though. Images of the collapse of the World Trade Center towers and of the Pentagon engulfed in gouts of smoke and flame were inescapable for months after the fact. Thousands had perished in a horrifying cataclysm and a full year would pass before the remains were excavated and something like a complete roster of the dead could be known. Then a weaponized strain of anthrax—in short a biological weapon—would be disseminated to victims via the postal system. Some foreign observers had deemed America to have gone mad, but America had merely gotten mad and was determined to vent its anger and seek retribution and justice.

The U.S. would fight back and repay shock with shock and awe with awe in almost Biblical measure. Newspaper headlines seemed to show that the national mood favored retribution. No matter that by 2001 few strategic targets tractable to air strikes existed above ground: "The Soviet Union pounded [Afghanistan] year after year after year. Much of the country is rubble," said Defense Secretary Rumsfeld on October 9, 2001, the second day of joint U.S.–U.K. air raids on Taliban targets in Afghanistan. What seemed important was that the United States was finally retaliating against those who, in the view of most, had staged the atrocities of 9/11. The mass media pulled a few punches, hitting as hard in print and on the tube as any bomb payload from a B-52.

Representative was the *New York Post*'s "America Strikes Back" series coverage of OEF in late autumn 2001 where stories with headlines like "Herat's All, Folks!" and "Tali-Bam!" celebrating the war's first attacks were interspersed with pre-strike and post-strike aerial surveillance photos of Taliban airfields in Herat, Garmabak Ghar, and other locations. The media displayed a blatantly vengeful martial mood that was to be seen again during the airstrike phase that two years later opened the Iraq War. Despite wishful thinking and official reality engineering about the oft heard-of but rarely seen better angels of "unity," the post-9/11 reality was marked more by a crabs-in-the-barrel case of war nerves that saw members of an already fragmented American society lashing out in anger at anything and anybody in sight.

Now, for the first time, there was a focus for that anger, a burning-glass through which the hot plasma of national animus could be turned in a single direction. Commentary from a forty-one-year-old New York City firefighter and a twenty-seven-year-old Midtown secretary published in a daily newspaper was characteristic of the mood in the streets: "We need to find out who's responsible for all this garbage and eradicate them," said the firefighter. Said the secretary: "When this happened, I thought, 'Get those em-effers.' I was hoping we'd so something."

Yet, unnoticed and playing no part in the debate and dialog that attended U.S. war plans and war fighting after September 11, 2001, and as the U.S. prepared to invade Iraq, was this fact: For the first time since the start of the Cold War, the United States had unilaterally opted to cast aside the policy of containment that had served it so well and so long since it had been outlined in George F. Kennan's "Long Telegram" of 1946 and codified years later in the National Security Council policy statement known as NSC-68. In flouting the United Nations, in brushing aside the contumely of even its closest allies, the United States in pursuing the war in Iraq had ended sixty years of holding containment as its first principle of statecraft.

No matter that it had originally been devised as a bulwark against the Soviet Union. Containment was containment, and in stopping short of occupying Baghdad in 1991, and instead opting to isolate Iraq by sea, land, and air embargoes, containment was again the option of choice on the regional level. With Shock and Awe of 2003 the United States had crossed a Rubicon of sorts, and if George Bush made an unlikely Caesar, it was nevertheless an Imperial America that seemed to now confront the world at large: one armed with the most formidable weapons systems ever devised, miracle weapons that could strike with pinpoint accuracy and devastating force. In an even more drastic manner than it had done in the Gulf War, the U.S. seemed to have cast off the last vestiges of Cold War policy that called for a cautious appraisal of the East-West power balance, a sober weighing of options and often elaborate diplomatic maneuverings before a major military operation might be mounted.

Yet also unnoticed amid the rapid movements of light-armored infantry, as mechanized units converged on Baghdad from their cross-border staging areas, was that in the downsizing of conventional forces—including reductions in the size and changes to the composition of infantry formations—in the push to re-footprint the U.S. military, the Pentagon had created an army that might not be best equipped to prevail under new conditions that would inevitably arise once the initial objectives of the wars in Afghanistan and Iraq had been secured and the initial aims had been accomplished. Despite the E-Ring's justified preoccupation with defense transformation, the leveraging of high-technology assets could only take the coalition war machine so far. It was like sex. It might be easy to get in, but once you did you had to finish what you started or it was all for nothing.

And in land-and-stay warfare, where military occupation almost always resulted in lengthy tours by occupation troops, there had never been a substitute for boots on the ground and superiority of numbers. Perhaps the final lesson of the Gulf War that had escaped the total recall of war planners preparing for the Iraq War had been one of the main military metaphors associated with both air and ground warfare during the highballing hundred days of Desert Storm: Desert warfare more closely resembles naval warfare than it does land war and that, as MacArthur ably demonstrated in a positive way in the Pacific and in a negative way in Korea, forces could either destroy or seize objectives, or alternatively, choose to bypass and isolate them, because in such theaters of war the sustainment of operational tempo is paramount.

As long as the force was in motion, gaining ground and securing objectives, it was winning, and obstacles, once isolated, could be mopped up later. But MacArthur, master of high-mobility warfare, leapfrogger of the Japanese outer islands, had pressed his luck in Korea after a meteoric push inland from Inchon and had become mired in places like the Chosin Reservoir, where U.S. troops had stuck like flies on tarpaper, or like spinning wheels churning up mud.

More to the point, there should have been other warning signs from history. At the turn of the twentieth century America had become mired in the Philippines. The British had been in Baghdad once before, in the 1920s, and they had been in Afghanistan in the 1890s. In 1920 the British occupied Baghdad and were faced with a mass revolt of largely Shiite origins. They had tried in vain to suppress the uprising for months before finally succeeding at a high cost in treasure and lives, and had then changed their objectives and begun to withdraw, leaving Iraq in the hands of elite client caretakers—the same ones that Saddam Hussein had overthrown a generation later.

The Soviets, too, had experienced military sticker shock in Afghanistan in the 1980s, and the United States had then deliberately and successfully abetted the Afghan mujahedeen in bogging down the Soviets in a quagmire that led to the Kremlin's order to withdraw its badly mauled and demoralized forces from the region in 1989. It was around that time that President Ronald Reagan had uttered his famous one-liner regarding another favored army of insurgents, the Nicaraguan Contras. Their cause, he'd said, stood as "the moral equivalent of the founding fathers."

Perhaps that may have been so, and yet it was the Afghan mujahedeen, whose name in Arabic means "warriors of jihad," "jihadists," or "holy warriors," who not only were supplanted by the Taliban in 1990, but as what the CIA termed "the Afghan alumni" also gave rise to the core membership of al-Qaeda, including Osama bin Laden. Virtually since the first days of Operation Iraqi Freedom when Private Jessica Lynch and the 507th Maintenance Company had blundered into an ambush in a suburb of Baghdad that killed eleven members of her unit and made her a prisoner, it had become apparent that the war plan calling for a swift occupation and pluperfect regime change might be chimerical. Toto wasn't in Kansas anymore. Lynch had been a member of a logistics unit that had not been trained or equipped for engagement in firefights.

In World War II cartoonist Bill Mauldin called soldiers like Lynch "garritroopers," troops that operated behind the lines. They carried mint-condition rifles and wore polished combat boots, but they had no business in battle. (In her testimony at hearings before the House Committee on Oversight and Government Reform on April 24, 2007, Lynch paraphrased what she'd earlier told newscaster Diane Sawyer about her alleged heroism under Iraqi fire; she claimed the Pentagon had erroneously portrayed her as a "Rambo from West Virginia," when she had in fact never fired a shot during the ambush that led to her captivity. It must also be noted that Lynch had not refused the Purple Heart, Prisoner of War, and Bronze Star medals that she'd been awarded on her return to Virginia either.)

The lesson that came in the aftermath of this brief and one-sided firefight was that in Baghdad there was no rear and no front, that the United States was in the midst of a guerilla war, and that the goal of a fast stabilization of post-Saddam Iraq with only a fraction of the forces that might have otherwise been deemed necessary to do the job, followed by a handover to new democratically elected leadership was, to put it somewhat bluntly, a plan with some holes in it. In Afghanistan, too, the warlordism that had preceded and coexisted with the fanatical rule of the Taliban had never been quelled, with the result that still armed and still powerful warlords almost immediately began to fill the power vacuum left in the wake of the crushed Taliban and their al-Qaeda allies.

In the seven-odd years of the Rumsfeld stewardship of the Department of Defense, events have moved at warp speed, and they are events that have brought the Pentagon into the spotlight of American consciousness and have thrust it into the center of debate in a manner eclipsing even that of the Vietnam War.

There is an old adage: "Be careful what you wish for, you might get it." The two regional wars that the Defense Department's doctrine of transformation called for simultaneously fighting with an all-volunteer military, equipped for multidimensional, high-mobility operations, materialized in the aftermath of 9/11 like a malign genie from a brass lamp or a demon from Pandora's box. Seven years down the line, as this book nears completion, the prevailing doctrine has begun to be stood on its head by critics within and without the Pentagon and the Department of Defense as terms like "overstretch" and "Vietnam syndrome" are aired by friends and foes of defense alike. Indeed, Donald Rumsfeld had mused to *Time* reporters for a December 21, 2003, issue that, "We may need a bigger Army" (though adding that he saw no reason for change at the moment).

If the Biblical story of Genesis began with pure motives, proceeded to the bite of an apple, and ended with a withdrawal from Paradise under the omen of a flaming sword, then here, too, face to face with the first sizeable serpent of the New World Order, we must venture to the beginning of an era of relative calm, when the Garden was still serene and a new man appeared in its midst. It is to the beginning of the Rumsfeld era at the Pentagon that we will presently turn.

CHAPTER SIXTEEN

THE PENTAGON BEFORE AND AFTER

The hijacked American Airlines Flight 77 out of Washington's Dulles International Airport on its transcontinental flight to Los Angeles, a Boeing 757 loaded with flammable aviation gasoline that belly flopped into the Pentagon's River Entrance at the start of the September 11, 2001, business day and detonated like fuel-air munitions, did so in the midst of the most thorough renovation in the Building's history. Congress had designated the Pentagon a national historic landmark in 1992, following a series of political, bureaucratic, and legal shifts and turns that had resulted in a concept plan of 1990 and the Defense Authorization Act of 1991 that paved the way for renovation to commence.

By January 1999, in a kind of reversal of the Pentagon's first days in the spring of 1941, "spaces"—as rooms of any kind in the Pentagon are frequently termed by its denizens—in Wedge 1 served by Corridors 3 and 4 were vacated and staff were relocated to something along the lines of the "Seventeen Buildings" days before Somervell's Folly rose from the boggy wastes of Hell's Bottom. By 2000, renovation of Wedge 1 was largely complete and reoccupied by a sizable portion of the Building's approximately twenty-five thousand military and civilian personnel, and a similar process of exodus, relocation, demolition, renovation, and reoccupation had begun for Wedge 2.

Since Wedge 1 happened to closely correspond to the spaces in the Building occupied by the headquarters offices of both the secretary of defense and the chairman of the Joint Chiefs of Staff, the completion of renovated areas of the Pentagon was fortuitous to the incoming members of Team Bush, whose business would be conducted in surroundings that had steadily succumbed to the wear and tear of nearly six decades of use and neglect prior to the extensive renovations that had preceded their arrival. The renovated spaces, however, may also have figured in drawing the fire of terrorist enemies. In hindsight, the two hijacked passenger jets that struck the twin towers had rammed their targets at sections of the uppermost floors precisely calculated to cause maximum damage to the latticework of structural supports that bound each of the buildings together, almost like huge sheaves of wheat, and caused the collapse that soon followed.

The concept of a warrior culture hero who, in death, lays waste to the cities of the enemy, or perhaps an angel visiting divine judgment on cities of wickedness, is an ancient one, and though admittedly more Biblical than Koranic, is arguably embedded in the sinews of Middle Eastern history and thought. Osama bin Laden, scion of a Saudi Arabian family that owns and operates one of the world's premier construction firms, who had commanded the resources of that family combine to import state-of-the-art machinery to hollow out and turn the mountainous reaches of Afghanistan into formidable redoubts for himself and his minions, was also capable of determining the structural pressure points of the World Trade Center towers and to direct his martyrs to strike just those points in order to bring down, like a latter-day Samson, the towers seen by al-Qaeda as icons of the American Philistines, glass pillars of the Great Satan.

Surely also the choice of the newly reconstructed Wedge of the Pentagon which faced Washington Boulevard on the Building's southwest side was also intentional, indeed symbolic. If the twin towers stood as the temple of Baal or Moloch, then the Pentagon was the Americans' temple of Mars, from which their war gods cast down their thunderbolts and in which their high military priesthood tendered their oblations. Here was another temple to be brought low by latter-day Nazerites, who like their forebears, purified themselves with daily prayer and abstinence, even as they sojourned in the house of their enemies. The final prize would have been the White House itself, had the fourth hijacked plane not been forced down by the sacrifices of thirty-three passengers and seven crew members. (This passenger count excludes the four hijackers who also died in the crash of Flight 93.)

Yes, the Pentagon had been rocked from without, yet at the same time it was engaged in being rocked from within. A cleansing sword had been unleashed upon its entrenched cabals by a holy knight of the realm on a mission of supreme importance. That armored saint was Donald Rumsfeld, whose mission was from the outset a restructuring of the way the Pentagon was run and who conducted the military affairs of the United States of America as thoroughgoing, if not more so, as the renovation program that was alternately tearing down and rebuilding the Building floor by floor and wall by wall.

* * *

As will be recalled, the War and Navy departments of the late interwar period, between World Wars I and II, made up an organization that to all practical intents and purposes was under the direction and control of the military. When, by the mid-1930s, the Roosevelt administration saw the war clouds looming over a Europe in political and economic anarchy and an Asia convulsed in armed conflict, and recognized them for what they were, the White House sought an extensive restructuring of defense.

George Marshall, now army chief of staff, was appointed to oversee the enterprise, once Congress had finally backed the president, and Marshall, taking command in 1939, it need not be pointed out, was a soldier, not a civilian. Marshall's billet was as army chief of staff; there were as yet none of the later developments that followed the postwar legislation that established the chairman of the Joint Chiefs of Staff, nor had the office of secretary of defense been instituted with the full powers attendant on its modern chief. In 1939, when Marshall was installed at the War Department, the army analog of what is now the secretary of defense was the secretary of war, and the holder of that office was Henry Stimson. While Stimson enjoyed many of the perquisites of modern secretaries of defense, the long and the short of it was that while the civilian sector had oversight of the War Department, the uniformed military made virtually all the important operational decisions that were not linked to the spheres of political expediency and national policy.

Thus it had been throughout World War II and thus it largely continued following the new and in many ways more thoroughgoing defense reorganization that followed the allied victories. As the Cold War escalated and deepened into a standoff of nuclear-armed titans, the Pentagon's purple-suiters (military personnel wearing the differently colored uniforms of their respective armed forces are called purple-suiters when they are working in a Department of Defense office) continued to hold as their perquisite the development of operational plans while the Building's civilian leadership at DOD pursued their rightful concerns, which included the implementation of policy as established by the president, acting, primarily, on the advice and guidance of the National Security Council.

Then, a change came about. The Vietnam War brought a shift in power to the Pentagon's civilian sector. Robert McNamara, defense secretary throughout the Kennedy administration and through most of the Johnson years, brought with him a new philosophy of civilian control of the Joint Chiefs of Staff, and later, President Lyndon Johnson himself would loom over military maps and dioramas of Southeast Asia, personally selecting targets to be bombed in Vietnam. When, in 1975, the United States had withdrawn its forces from the Asian subcontinent, the U.S. military, especially the army, seemed to have become a hollow force. The view of many commanders was that the army was in trouble. That it was, in military parlance, broken.

Some, like Team Bush's appointee to the cabinet rank of secretary of state, Colin Powell, sought to fix it again. As they rose in the ranks, replacing the early Cold Warriors at the Pentagon, the Vietnam veterans became the new Pentagon elite. It was they who made up the service chiefs, and they who formulated the core doctrines that would determine the nature of America's defense posture throughout the five presidential administrations to follow from the debacle in Vietnam. Central to their thinking was that the United States must at all costs avoid sinking into the Vietnam syndrome again, to avoid, as Powell put it in his biographical memoirs, "halfhearted wars for half-baked reasons." (Powell's propositions for what constituted reasonable and prudent conditions for going to war were so often stated when he was CJCS that they were collected into what became known as the Powell Doctrine, a set of questions beginning with, "Is the vital national security interest threatened?" and "Do we have a clear attainable objective?" and ending with, "Is the action supported by the American people?" and "Do we have genuine broad international support?")

The reason for this was clear: It had been the ideologues like McNamara, warrior dilettantes like LBJ, and the hardliners in both political camps that had broken the army. And all of them had worn civilian suits. The military must, therefore, set doctrine and make operational decisions on the strategic and tactical levels. While the civilians had as their mandate and legitimate right the setting of policy, the actual implementation of that policy should—must—be left entirely up to the commanders themselves. This, the key legacy of Vietnam, had left an indelible mark on the Joint Chiefs of Staff, one of whose main proponents was Colin Powell, who as the fledgling administration of President George W. Bush took office was to become the head of the Department of State.

The legacy of Vietnam was to prove to be the foundation of new friction between the civilians and the purple-suiters at the Building.

* * *

Newly sworn in as secretary of state, Powell fast began raising questions that did not jibe with the worldview of Vice President Richard Cheney at a maiden press conference.

"Our armed forces are stretched rather thin," he had said, as Cheney looked on, visibly discomfited at what he'd just heard.

Here was a departure almost as much from holy writ as it was from the new administration's defense doctrine. For one thing, Powell was no longer chairman of the JCS, he was a civilian, and his duties at state would not have the state of U.S. military readiness as a prime concern. Cheney might then have been gobsmacked by the realization that Powell might in time wield considerable clout at the Pentagon as well as at state. If Powell's notions of waging war were different than Cheney's—and this they seemed—then Powell's appointment might well prove troublesome in heretofore unanticipated ways.

President Bush's supporters were also concerned about that much power residing in a single charismatic and respected figure.

The answer, in the view of some defense observers, was to find a new secretary of defense who was, in his own right, a Zeus to fulminate at this outspoken Apollo and keep Powell in check. During the last few months of the Clinton administration, outgoing Defense Secretary William S. Cohen had been serving since his predecessor William J. Perry's 1997 resignation, and while he was still at the Pentagon as the new administration officially took over, his days as acting secretary of defense were numbered.

Cohen, a New England Brahmin whose most prominent connection to the U.S. defense establishment had been his empanelment in the Senate's Iran-Contra hearings of the Reagan years, was a Clinton appointee who had succeeded both Perry and Les Aspin before him, making him the third defense secretary appointed during the Clinton terms. Aspin, recruited from the House Committee on Armed Services, which he then chaired, had replaced Dick Cheney as defense secretary in 1993 after the 1992 Democratic presidential win but had resigned under fire in the aftermath of the humanitarian aid mission to Somalia that had metamorphosed into an ill-fated bid to bring a democratic government to a nation that apparently preferred warlordism.

Somalia had proven Aspin's Waterloo as secretary of defense as well as an icon for the perceived reluctance of the Clinton administration to deliver troops and combat materiel to zones of conflict in which the U.S. was involved sufficient to accomplish the mission. Later it was used as a metaphor for "nation-building" that George W. Bush had reviled in the 2000 election year debates only to fall victim to himself three years later in Iraq on a scale that dwarfed that of Somalia. The mission to the Somalian capital, Mogadishu, was characteristic of the immediate post–Cold War era, which had forced Pentagon policy wonks under both

Cheney and Aspin's tenures as defense secretaries to coin new acronyms for military missions in the new world order. These included Operations Other than War (OOTW), under which heading the mission to Somalia proceeded as Operation Restore Hope in December of 1992.

U.S. involvement in Somalia had first begun in August 1992, when Operation Provide Relief commenced with the George H. W. Bush Administration's decision to support multinational relief efforts under U.N. sanction with military transports of humanitarian supplies to the war-torn republic on the Horn of Africa, a nation strategically flanking Saudi Arabia across the narrow Gulf of Aden. As the crisis worsened under Cheney's watch at DOD, the Joint Chiefs, chaired by General Colin Powell, were tasked with planning a major coalition relief effort to Somalia under U.S. leadership. U.S. Marines landed in Somalia on December 4, 1992, commencing Operation Restore Hope, and quickly began to secure key objectives. Humanitarian aid supplies began arriving as army reinforcements locked down remaining trouble spots.

The Clinton administration took over the show in January 1993 with Aspin installed as Cheney's successor at the Defense Department and with Bush administration holdover Powell still serving as CJCS. By the spring the situation in Somalia had begun to unravel, and Mogadishu, which had been torn by civil strife before the U.S. stepped in, became a battleground again. Asked by Powell to beef up U.S. military power in Mogadishu, Aspin declined. A mounting toll of U.S. casualties there which was perceived to result from the defense secretary's negative response had Aspin's critics in Congress calling for his resignation. Aspin's departure from the Pentagon occurred some eleven months later, in December, 1993, for what Bill Clinton, announcing the move, cited as "personal reasons." Aspin's berth at DOD was filled by William J. Perry in early February 1994, the same week Aspin officially left the Pentagon.

Perry, who resigned in 1997, later stating his decision was "largely due to the constant strain of sending U.S. military personnel on life-threatening missions," had been instrumental in trimming the defense budget and in introducing defense reform at DOD. Cohen, who had served on the Senate Armed Services Committee, Senate Intelligence

Committee, and Governmental Affairs Committee, was also a Republican, making his appointment to head DOD one of the rare instances where competence for the job led to the crossing of party lines.

Despite the presentation of a proposed fiscal year 1998 defense budget of $250.7 billion, which had originally been prepared by Perry and represented 3 percent of U.S. estimated gross domestic product for that fiscal year, Cohen was not only viewed as an outsider by the purple-suiters at the Pentagon but, worse yet, was considered a political Amalekite and defense neophyte by the Cold Warrior faithful who had close tie-lines not only to DOD but to many if not most of the arms contractors who made up the global defense industry as well. Indeed, to the defense sector, Cohen was tantamount to Mephistopheles, for he had presided over the streamlining of the Defense Department begun by Perry and which represented what many considered a painful restructuring of the entire military-industrial complex and the largest rollback of U.S. military installations at home and abroad since the end of the Cold War. The Clinton years, as well, had proven lean times for the defense contractors—domestic as well as foreign—who did business at the Pentagon, and Cohen, like Perry before him, was hit by the semipolitical fallout.

In the continental United States, base closings had risen to epidemic proportions, and overseas, the number of American military facilities had shrunk dramatically as troops were called home and military bases either closed entirely or, as in the Philippines, were handed off to local administrators while a nation basking in the triumph of high-tech weaponry over the fourth largest army in the world and freed from the threat of Soviet aggression continued to cut combat manpower levels to the bone. As defense secretary, Cohen had presided over the process of vertical integration of the defense industry that took place on a large scale through the 1990s as U.S. defense contractors merged into a few huge, dominant companies, particularly in the aerospace sector. The mergers, claimed spokesmen for defense contractors, had been necessitated both by Defense Department budget cuts and unprecedented cancellations and changes to weapons development and production programs.

At the same time, and not without paradox, defense cutbacks had either doomed or sharply curtailed the deployment of the very cutting edge military technology that had so handily won the Gulf War for the United States and its coalition partners. From the F-117A Stealth Fighter to the B-2 Stealth Bomber, across the board to next-generation attack submarines such as Seawolf, even to surface vessels such as Ticonderoga-class Aegis cruisers and Nimitz-class nuclear carriers, research and development programs that had developed military hardware with astonishing new capabilities had been stalled or cancelled by a Congress intent on reaping the peace dividend brought about, in large part, by America's high-technology lead over both adversaries and allies alike.

Perhaps most inauspiciously, the aging F-15 and F-16 fighter planes, air superiority fighters that had been since the close of the Vietnam War the most superb, agile, and virtually unconquerable military aircraft in their class, were nearing the end of their service lives. The Advanced Technology Fighter (ATF) program of the late 1980s and early 1990s had been instituted in order to develop, test, and field replacement aircraft for America's frontline combat aviation assets.

Successors far more agile and far stealthier than the Cold War–era mainstays of the USAF were already—as was the case with the F-22 Raptor—in the production phase or, in the case of the F-23 Joint Strike Fighter, in the prototype phase—in the final stages of design and testing. The new warplanes were needed primarily because the former Soviet Union had been modifying its own frontline fighters— the Mikoyan-Gurevich MiG-29 and Sukhoi-class SU-35 fighter planes into advanced versions (like the current MiG-35 Fulcrum-F and the SU-37 "Terminator," respectively)—to the point where freshly upgraded Russian models were reaching, or had reached, rough parity with their U.S. counterparts. And these planes were formidable combat platforms, especially in an age where the aerial dogfight had largely given way to engagement at long-range with supersonic missiles.

While the Soviets were no longer overt adversaries, they were nevertheless in need of hard currency, and they had few scruples about selling their warplanes, diesel-electric submarines, surface vessels, tanks, and small arms, as well as military expertise, to any world power with the cash to pay for them, no holds barred. This made them competitors, not enemies; but in the realm of defense sales, it made them dangerous competitors whose unchecked sales of military technology could erode the ability of the United States to prevail in armed conflict against its enemies.

While the Raptor was ready to fly and the JSF could be rapidly put into production, the will to allocate funding for these big-ticket projects was lacking in Congress. The United States now enjoyed a sizable lead over any potential adversary, went the prevailing reasoning, so why invest in weapons systems that have no pressing need today and may be irrelevant in tomorrow's wars? Such was the prevailing mindset in the Senate and House.

Cohen's perceived lack of insider's fingertip-feel familiarity with defense matters seemed to be brought home to his critics when he held up a five-pound bag of Domino sugar in a televised morning news program, warning the nation that were the white crystals in the bag the biological weapon agent anthrax instead of plain sugar he would be holding in his hand sufficient biological agent to kill millions. Military professionals who knew that without an effective delivery system—a way to spread the biological or chemical weapon agents—five pounds of anthrax would not only have nothing like Cohen's stated effect but that within a short space of time most chemical or biological weapons would lose their effectiveness entirely. The key to effective deployment of such weapons was always rapid dispersal over as wide an area as possible; it was a feat, the soldiers knew, that was extremely hard to accomplish under actual conditions of attack.

Perry, with credentials more acceptable to denizens of the Puzzle Palace, had mollified the DOD brass hats, but there had been little question of Cohen's staying onboard in the face of a Republican win in the 2000 presidential election. A central plank of the Bush election platform had also been defense reorganization and restructuring, but along different lines than Team Clinton's. Team Bush had campaigned for a revitalized military better equipped, in its view, to fight the regional post–Cold War battles the United States was expected to face as the new century wore on and the old conditions of bipolar superpower competition and conflict became a thing of the past. They had succeeded in painting Team Clinton as soft on defense, and they were vocally intent on injecting steroids into the Department of Defense, at least to pump it up in the right places. Indeed, George Bush seemed at times to be gearing up to be a war president in the immediate absence of anything close to a war the country might have to fight; the vice president was a former secretary of defense and the secretary of state a former chairman of the Joint Chiefs of Staff. National Security Advisor Condoleezza Rice was a team player and staunch defense hawk as well. Here was a White House with more than its share of defense advocates onboard.

Now, with Colin Powell as secretary of state, the former army general, seasoned Cold Warrior, and Desert Storm media star uttering statements—and public statements at that—which sounded decidedly heretical to the would-be architects of a new defense policy built around the central tenet of doing more with less, and investing in high-tech weapon systems armed with precision weapons and controlled by robotic intelligence in place of the standard military issue, Mark-1 infantry grunt, there appeared to be a lack of what might be called strategic balance at the White House cabinet level.

Powell was a heavyweight, but he was not a hawk in any conventional sense. Powell's war-fighting ideology was essentially that of a Clausewitizian pragmatist. You sought out the enemy's centers of military gravity and you either attacked at these precise focal points or you fell back and regrouped to fight another day.

Years before, at a CENTCOM briefing during the early phases of the 1991 Gulf War, Powell had told reporters, "Our strategy to go after this [the Iraqi] army is very simple: First we're gonna cut it off and then we're gonna kill it."

Powell, then chairman of the Joint Chiefs of Staff, was referring to a military strategy known as "decapitation." The phrase titillated the media, which seized on it with gusto for flurry upon flurry of sound bites. Yet Powell had only been speaking Pentagonese. The concept, by comparison with more esoteric military jargon, was merely mundane. If you could kill the enemy's infrastructure, kill the tanks, kill the communications linkages, kill the eyes, ears, brain of the enemy—in short cut off the head—then the enemy's ability to successfully resist would be neutralized and your forces could quickly, and without suffering undue casualties, prevail. [10]

Powell was a pragmatist; as a career soldier he well knew the strategic limitations of occupation, especially occupation of hostile urban areas, to say nothing of Baghdad itself, where the British had run afoul of Iraqi xenophobia and militant fundamentalism close to a century before. Moreover, this was the first commandment of the post-Vietnam and post–Cold War Pentagon: Thou shalt not become mired in counterinsurgency warfare, yea, though thou may envelop and contain, thou shalt not be caught in a quagmire. It was as if Powell had climbed down from a mountain with two stone tablets in his arms. Here was a respected, charismatic figure whose pronouncements could not be brushed aside. Powell might conceivably wind up running both state and defense.

Powell's attitudinal focus presented marked differences in thinking to that of defense ideologues like Cheney, many of whom had never seen combat, and whose perspectives, if broader in some respects due to an overarching Weltanschauung, held that political ends generally justified military means. If he was to remain as head of the State Department, there had to be a heavyweight at the helm of DOD as well. Cheney had a former administration colleague in mind. A heavyweight who was also a defense hawk: Donald H. Rumsfeld, a veteran conservative torchbearer, squarely in the same camp as Cheney and Bush in the realm of defense ideology. Bush agreed on the choice. There was to be a new chief at the Puzzle Palace.

* * *

The appointment would mark Rumsfeld's second tour of duty at DOD. Appointed at the age of forty-nine—making him the youngest secretary

10. The Defense Department was awarded the National Conference of Teachers of English annual Doublespeak Award in 1991, citing euphemisms from the Gulf War such as "servicing the target" (bombing) and "force packages" (warplanes). Chairman of the conference's Doublespeak Committee and editor of the *Quarterly Review of Doublespeak*, Professor William Lutz of Rutgers University, told the *New York Times* that, "The misuse of public language by the Department of Defense merits some form of recognition." The award prompted the Pentagon to defend its terminology. "'Force package' indicates you're going on a mission," said a DOD public information specialist. "'Warplanes' doesn't indicate you're doing anything."

of defense ever to hold office—he had served as defense secretary during the presidential administration of Gerald Ford in the 1970s. Rumsfeld had then served for some fourteen months and presided over the aftermath of the Vietnam War.

He had come to the Pentagon by way of the Nixon White House, where he was a central, if controversial, advisor who rankled Nixon by his win-or-get-out approach to the war in Southeast Asia. Nixon had planned to oust Rumsfeld after the Watergate trials, which Nixon had expected to weather, were behind him. It was Nixon instead who left the White House and Rumsfeld among those who had survived the political storms. Now, as secretary of defense under Gerald Ford, Rumsfeld brought with him a young and trusted aide named Dick Cheney, who later succeeded his boss as head of the DOD during the first Bush administration.

Rumsfeld was considered the perfect man for the post of defense honcho in 2000 because he advocated precisely those changes in military doctrine and force structure that were high on the checklists of George Bush and Dick Cheney. Yet there was a worm in the apple—the culture, among the Joint Chiefs, built on the legacy of Vietnam and shared by Rumsfeld's own colleague, the new secretary of state.

The military was of one consensus: It needed to maintain control. The main part of the military's vision was to prevent the Vietnam syndrome from reasserting itself. That meant that hard-liners, driven by ideology and not by clearly achievable military goals, were to be kept out of the decision matrix. Missions were to be clearly defined. Objectives were to be accomplishable. Military realities had to be separated from ideological fantasies. It was a doctrine that stressed a central fact that was later to become the bone of contention before the Iraq War's first year was out—having the right force structure, with enough forces to get the job done and a strategy that stressed the achievable over the politically correct or ideologically cherished. To implement the kind of changes wished for by the White House, the new defense secretary would have to overturn nearly three decades of military control of Pentagon operations and reassert control by the civilians at DOD that most of the brass hats believed had caused the disgrace and defeat of the Vietnam epoch.

A first order of business for both the White House and Rumsfeld himself was to find a strong deputy, one who liked his boss, who would evince the same heavyweight's credentials and support the secretary of defense in a new and more hard-line approach to U.S. defense policy. The unanimous choice was another defense veteran, and Foggy Bottom insider, Paul Wolfowitz, who had formerly served as an undersecretary of defense during the first Bush administration. Like Rumsfeld and his previous boss at DOD, Dick Cheney, Wolfowitz was committed to fundamental and far-reaching changes in U.S. defense policy, and also like the key players at the White House, Wolfowitz believed that the status quo in the Middle East was in need of change if the United States was to continue to occupy a secure place in the twenty-first-century world order. And like both the president and vice president, changing the Middle Eastern status quo meant, above all else, getting rid of Saddam Hussein.

Beyond this, Wolfowitz had earned a reputation as a brilliant, if controversial, military thinker in his authoring of a DOD white paper that came to be known colloquially as "The Wolfowitz Memorandum." This Pentagon study, officially published as the Regional Defense Strategy of January 1993 as Wolfowitz left the Pentagon during the first year of the Clinton administration, called for a reassessment of the order of battle that would shift defense posture from the immediate post–Cold War focus on a global war fought in two major theaters, with reserves for a third potential regional hot-spot, to one geared to fight two regional wars only. In addition, the Wolfowitz study called for U.S. forces to prepare for fighting what the study termed "preemptive warfare."

A corollary of the first two premises was that U.S. military forces would be downsized considerably—by as much as 40 percent by some estimates—in favor of the establishment of a military comprised of light, highly mobile elements that could be rapidly fielded to trouble-spots around the world and would be backed up by the formidable array of high-tech, precision-guided weaponry that could stealthily and surgically seek out and swiftly destroy enemy strongholds and forward positions far more efficiently than could be accomplished using conventional forces pursuing conventional tactics.

Translated into real-world terms, the strategy called for sending platoons instead of companies, companies instead of battalions, and battalions instead of divisions, into regional trouble spots. These relatively small-footprint forces could be shuttled from rearward areas to battle zones by combat helicopter or lightweight armored carriers, like Bradley or the proposed Future Infantry Vehicle, inserted into the battle space in small groups to conduct active reconnaissance and use sophisticated computer-networked links to direct a host of advanced weaponry to take out priority targets.

One such weapon might be a class of unmanned, missile-firing planes known collectively as UCAVs, pronounced *you-cav* and standing for "unmanned combat aerial vehicles." Other weapons might, in time, even be light and smart enough to be fielded by units themselves. A platoon might, carrying portable missile launchers, pack more firepower than a World War II–era tank brigade. The type of warfare naturally favored special forces units, like the army's Rangers or the navy's SEALS, over conventional infantry. Such forces had specialized in the types of commando operations that already used many of the techniques that would become the norm under the new proposals.

In addition, all forces would have jointness as a common objective. Jointness meant that the entire United States war machine would be far more modular and interoperable in scope than it had previously been. Not only would command, control, communications, computing, and intelligence—known by the military acronym C⁴I—be accessible to all friendly forces operating in theater, but it would be accessible to even distant command posts thousands of miles away in which CINCs could exercise command from virtual environments that would give them a bird's-eye view of the fighting from imaging platforms on land, sea, in the air, and from orbital space. Computers would aid them in their process of critical decision-making. Interoperability extended beyond the digital realm as well. Military hardware from armored vehicles to rifles and the ammunition that troops carried would also be developed to be part of the jointness doctrine whose end result would be what Pentagon war planners began to describe as "a system of systems." It was heady stuff, all right. But could it ever work?

The philosophy of preemptive warfare, with all it implied, and as espoused by the incoming secretary of defense, stood at loggerheads with most defense thinking at the Pentagon. Institutional resistance was sharp and widespread. For one thing, the new thinking enshrined a doctrine of war fighting that proposed to accomplish with advanced weaponry, precision guidance, and stealth what traditional military doctrine deemed possible only with the deployment of conventional resources—boots on the ground, massed infantry and armor, long logistics trains, and ample time to prepare for the mission.

The futuristic way of fighting at first disparaged as Nintendo warfare had paid great dividends in the Gulf in 1991, but the consensus among the Joint Chiefs of Staff was that this approach could not be applied to all, every, or indeed many military contingencies. One such contingency was the occupation, by the United States with or without coalition allies, of a Middle Eastern country, specifically Iraq—one of the centerpieces of the administration's early goals. It was one thing to crush Saddam's army in the desert and dismantle the military and political centers of control in Baghdad with coordinated Tomahawk and Stealth attacks. It was another thing entirely to invade and occupy Baghdad, with or without having won the hearts and minds of its populace.

The incoming defense secretary found himself at odds with army Chief of Staff General Eric Shinseki, whom many believed had been unfairly belabored by Rumsfeld at policy sessions where the new, take-charge secretary of defense sought to assert his dominance over the chiefs. Shinseki was a hero of the Vietnam War who had been wounded in action and who still bore the scars of battle.

The army, bridling at Shinseki's treatment, sided with him. Rumsfeld's struggle with Shinseki was a continuation of the longtime power struggle between the civilians at DOD and the purple-suiters. Many members of the Pentagon brass felt as if they had been slapped in the face.

But the lesson was this: Rumsfeld was now in charge. The civilians were in control—again—like it or not. The lesson was a bitter one for Pentagon brass in the main. Yet the incoming defense secretary and his staff were anathema to the leadership of the U.S. military. How long, after all, could he hold out against the chiefs? In the eyes of the consensus

Rumsfeld was in many ways a marked man. He was at war with his own house, and thus presided over a house divided against itself. Many in the administration laid odds that he would soon be forced to resign. For nearly the past three decades it was gospel that those civilian administrators who tried to shake up the status quo at the Puzzle Palace were doomed to failure. Donald Rumsfeld would, it was believed by many, soon take his rightful place as merely another footnote to the Building's history.

Nevertheless, it was 9/11 and its aftermath that cast Rumsfeld in a new and more favorable light at the Pentagon and gave his policies a shot in the arm. When the Pentagon's Potomac-side walls were brought down amid smoke and fire, news cameras caught Rumsfeld running toward the inferno, heedless of danger. The secretary of defense's courage scored him points with the military. It was after 9/11 that attacking Iraq, originally proposed by Rumsfeld as an option early in 2001, was now on the business agenda at the White House, a plan now deemed worthy of serious consideration. Almost alone among the cabinet chiefs Colin Powell disagreed: It was al-Qaeda that had engineered the September 11 attacks, and its power base was in Afghanistan; therefore, attacking Afghanistan and defeating the terrorist shadow-government there should be Washington's first priority and the U.S. military's primary objective. Iraq could wait.

But Iraq held attractions of its own, as a target of opportunity if nothing else. In addition to that, the undoing of the status quo in the Middle East was seen by the new administration as a central goal for the attainment of a peaceful twenty-first-century global order. Iraq had been isolated and contained since the end of the Gulf War; it had no air force that could pose a credible threat to a U.S.–led invasion, and coalition airstrikes throughout the 1990s had destroyed successive attempts by the Hussein regime to rebuild both its military communications network and re-weaponize its ground combat forces. One such airstrike, by warplanes of the U.S.–U.K. coalition, dubbed Desert Fox, had in 1998 trashed Saddam's last hope of installing a viable threat radar system that might give advance warning of a future coalition attack.

Iraq was vulnerable, a vulnerable target, its soft underbelly exposed, and if taking out Saddam might invite criticism initially, it would not provoke lasting ire, especially if wartime gains could be quickly consolidated and if regime change swiftly brought about a new, democratically elected leadership in Iraq. When intelligence evidence surfaced that seemed to implicate Saddam Hussein in the development of weapons of mass destruction as well as potential ties to al-Qaeda, it was sufficient provocation for the administration to opt for war. Against the counsel of Powell, plans of attack were finalized. Afghanistan would be the first objective, but Iraq would, before much more time had passed, be next.

The new defense secretary was further vindicated as the war in Afghanistan commenced. While the CIA had a plan that relied on covert warfare in Afghanistan, Rumsfeld pushed for special operations using small-footprint commando forces that would embody the principles of military transformation that he had been appointed to bring about. The White House drafted a plan that was, in final form, a synthesis of both the DOD and CIA programs. Scalpeled from the decision loop was General Shinseki and the army, whose emphasis on the use of large-footprint conventional forces, preceded by air strikes from heavy bombers and necessitating ample time to build up pre-positioned logistics stockpiles and place ground forces in reserve, all ran afoul of the current new thinking at the Pentagon.

CENTCOM's still extant post–Gulf War plans for a second war in the region were in many, if not most, ways the diametrical opposite of the new thinking. The army's plan called for more than a half-million troops to occupy and secure Iraq and at least seven months to build up for the offensive. This was clearly at odds with what the administration wanted done. The U.S. Marines would, in part, reap the benefits of the change in priorities. The doctrine of the corps was far closer to that of the Pentagon's new administrators than that of the other service branches. So was the history of the Marine Corps; it had shown for more than a century that "a few good men" could achieve military successes that were beyond the scope of larger combat formations.

The unconventional approach—special forces mixed with CIA covert operatives and friendly nationals used to identify targets, then smart weaponry brought to bear on hostile strong points in order to smash them, showed success in Afghanistan. Rumsfeld had seemed to have vindicated himself. When, in 2002, war plans against Iraq were firmed up, Rumsfeld advocated a similarly unconventional approach based on high-mobility operations. Iraq would be attacked. By the time the dust settled it would all be over; Saddam would be history and the United States would be in control.

On the eve of war, in February 2003, the president, in his State of the Union Address, revealed to the nation that Saddam Hussein's Iraq harbored weapons of mass destruction that might, if allowed to fall into the hands of terrorists, unleash "a day of evil unparalleled in history." The *casus bellum* needed no further elaboration. It evoked the infernos that had brought down the World Trade Center and a good part of the Pentagon and scenes of the awful struggles aboard the fourth jetliner that had mercifully been brought down before it struck the nation's capital.

"I will not wait on events while dangers gather. I will not stand by as peril draws closer and closer," the president had solemnly declared. "The United States of America will not permit the world's most dangerous regime to threaten us with the world's most destructive weapons." The stage was set for war.

* * *

Months later, in June 2003, as coalition forces rapidly consolidated their initial gains and secured Baghdad, after Saddam Hussein had vanished from sight and his sumptuous presidential palaces became the headquarters of occupation forces, after the dictator's massive statues were pulled down and honorific banners emblazoned with gigantic images of his face had been torn from Baghdad's walls, after the Taliban hideouts in the rocky vastness of the Hindu Kush had been blown to smithereens by high-explosive gravity bombs that killed the terrorists more in the manner of exterminating pests in a hole than combatants in wartime, after the protests of the Europeans and the Saudis and the antiwar contingents at home had taken on the unmistakable ring of those who paid no more than lip service to the just cause that Americans overseas were sacrificing their lives to serve, former National Security

Advisor Condoleezza Rice gave a speech at the International Institute for Strategic Studies in London.

Since the dark days of September 11, 2001, she said, ". . . the world's great powers see themselves as falling on the same side of a profound divide between the forces of chaos and order," and that the coalition led by the United States and United Kingdom has "deposed two of the cruelest regimes of this or any time" and pledged "to deny the most dangerous weapons to the world's most dangerous regimes."

Other observers had cast these first major military enterprises of the twenty-first century in almost Spenglerian terms. What was taking place, it was avowed, was nothing less than a "battle of civilizations" between the proponents of order and democracy on the one hand and the cabals of chaos and despotism on the other. One thing was certain: The invasion of Baghdad had been accomplished in a matter of weeks and with a troop strength equal to that of only a handful of divisions; it had secured a city only slightly smaller than New York City with nearly seven million inhabitants of a country with twenty-four million citizens.

General Tommy Franks, CENTCOM's commander and theater commander in chief, had been in charge of the battle plan, which had required his falling into line with the Rumsfeld Doctrine that relied on small, agile ground forces assisted in reconnaissance, surveillance, and target acquisition by fast, mobile networked linkages to UAVs, manned aircraft, and satellites, and supported by air cover that could be called in to deliver follow-on strikes using precision-guided munitions. The Rumsfeld plan had called for a comparatively tiny force of sixty thousand troops for the 2003 Iraq invasion. Franks had argued that upwards of four hundred thousand "boots" would be required, a total based not only on the Joint Chiefs' operational plan for a second Iraq war, but also on the half-million troops requested by CENTCOM for the successful 1991 Gulf War. Franks' numbers had more bearing on securing postwar Iraq, though, and the pressure was on from the White House to get the lead out and deal definitively with Saddam Hussein, whose departure from Baghdad was seen as crucial to defeating the forces behind 9/11 and preventing another recurrence, or even worse, a nuclear catastrophe using weapons of mass destruction that Saddam was believed to have produced since the Gulf War's end. Besides, Franks had been given his orders and like a good soldier, it was his to do or die, not ask the reasons why.

Yet behind the scenes at the Pentagon, as in restive enclaves of Baghdad, in outlying towns and cities such as Fallujah and Najaf, and in the Sunni strongholds in and near Ar Ramadi to Baghdad's north, developments had begun to emerge that would, in time, challenge the most significant tenets of defense transformation, throw Operation Iraqi Freedom into crisis, and again cast the long, dark shadows of Vietnam across the ring-girthed corridors of the Pentagon itself.

CHAPTER SEVENTEEN

THE WAR ON THE BUDGET

There is no doubt that the Vietnam War still holds lasting trauma for many who served there and for the American public in general. Traumatic events can take insidious hold. An acquaintance who this author frequently drives places in his car explains that he doesn't have a driver's license because, a former supply truck driver in Vietnam, he's morbidly afraid of having wartime flashbacks and losing control of a vehicle. This author's desire for fresh air on a sunny Tuesday morning in early September led to a stroll across the Brooklyn Bridge that caught him mere blocks from Ground Zero as the twin towers fell amid an avalanche of debris and clouds of toxic smoke, burying thousands beneath untold tons of rubble.

Once the germ-seed of trauma infects the psyche it may take root and become systemic. The trauma of Vietnam is still widespread and, in military circles, still a systemic contagion of the spirit. It is understandable that a U.S. Army, chastened by the experiences of the war in Southeast Asia—an army described by the epithet "broken" by many of its commanders after the United States' 1975 withdrawal—gave rise to a new leadership echelon at the Pentagon whose mindset of "no more Vietnams" echoed those of Holocaust survivors who swore oaths of "never again."

Yet truth has many facets, and the interpretation of events is never black and white. Otherwise how do you explain the clear popularity of Rumsfeld's second appointment as secretary of defense? How do you explain the apparent esprit de corps that embraced, in America's house of war, the adoption of modernization programs by all three service branches of the United States military throughout preceding presidential administrations? How to explain such military bywords as "revolution in military affairs" that, like "transformation" itself, came into the lexicon of military commanders in the euphoric course and aftermath of the 1991 Gulf War?

Or for that matter, how do you explain the actions of the Defense Department in the wake of the terror attacks of 9/11 without taking into consideration events that, if for no other reason than their brutality coupled with their immediacy, might well rank with Vietnam in branding an indelible stamp into the thinking processes of the custodians of America's defense establishment, as they did to U.S. citizens in general, and to American friends and allies around the world. In the final analysis, it may be that in times of grave crisis, when faced by an unanticipated threat from an enemy whose thought processes are, at base, incomprehensible, that there are actions and responses, but that explanations that await a calmer time are absent in the heat and grief of the moment.

If, months before September 11, 2001, Rumsfeld's oft-argued mandate was to reassert civilian control of the Department of Defense (which in real terms meant control of the Joint Chiefs of Staff, since DOD itself is headed by the civilians), then there was also a significant new leadership change at the helm of the Joint Chiefs of Staff that was in keeping with Rumsfeld's new responsibilities as secretary of defense. This was the naming of USAF General Richard Myers for the post of chairman of the Joint Chiefs in the first week of September 2001.[11] Recall, for a moment, that congressional legislation had, by the early 1990s, increased and better defined the powers of the CJCS, in effect placing the chairman in the position of leader of the chiefs, rather than as ombudsman between often conflicting factions; he was the military's advocate to the secretary of defense and the president.

---

11. Myers' appointment, delayed in part by the 9/11 attacks and in part by the legally mandated retirement on September 30 of his predecessor, officially took place on October 1, 2001. Prior to the appointment, Myers had served for nineteen months as vice-chairman of the JCS.

Myers, who was then forty-nine, was a blue-suiter with a history as an effective commander; he also had a reputation as an able staff officer whose commitment to transformational policies was a good fit with that of the White House and DOD. He replaced departing CJCS, army General Henry Shelton, a Clinton appointee who had served in a caretaker role since the end of Clinton's term of office. Myers' nomination and subsequent appointment as CJCS was then viewed by most observers as not only key to the successful implementation of military modernization programs judged essential to defense transformation, but also that Myers would be a wizard of trimming the institutional fat that had accumulated in the Pentagon's arteries and hardened them to change. In the months prior to the September 11, 2001, attacks, the hinge-pin on which transformational policy turned was viewed as making the Pentagon fiscally leaner and meaner.

A September 3, 2001, editorial in the weekly *Defense News*—viewed by many as the Stone Tablets of the Washington defense establishment— stated that, "if transformation is to truly take effect, Myers will have to adjudicate between military services long attached to their budgets and concepts of operations. He must help force less senior generals and admirals to accept change."

While 9/11 and the kamikaze attack on the Pentagon itself necessitated a speedy shift from accounting to councils of war, the vector sum of policy remained fixed. On the day of Myers' appointment, the secretary of defense unveiled the congressionally mandated Quadrennial Defense Review, or QDR. Despite 9/11, the yearlong study, virtually complete on the day of the September attacks, recommended sweeping cost-cutting and consolidation measures, stating, "The Department of Defense is committed to identifying efficiencies and reductions . . . that can be reinvested to accelerate the department's transformation efforts." Base closings and cost-saving reform initiatives to ongoing defense programs were part of the 2001 QDR's short list of recommendations.

In short, Myers was to be onboard to shake things up on the third floor at JCS as much as the new secretary of defense had been hired to do on the fourth. Nor was cost-cutting even new as a creed. On the contrary, "more bang for the buck" had been Pentagon gospel for a good many years. It was only now, however, that an incoming White House administration had sought to back up campaign promises—indeed, in some cases what sounded like campaign lectures—with actions that were to be honored in the act rather than, as previous administrations had done, in the breach. In his acceptance speech Myers had told a favorite story that seemed to sum up his intentions at the Pentagon. NASA, Myers had said, had spent vast amounts of money and time to develop a zero-gravity pen for astronauts to use in outer space. The Soviets, went the general's tag line, had merely used pencils.

The story addressed the central organizing principle of military procurement, for procurement wasn't just what modernizing and streamlining the U.S. military was all about, it was the invisible hub around which the spoked rings of the Pentagon's corridors revolved, year in and year out. Central to the policy argument for transformation was the perception that the vast array of infrastructure necessary to fight wars—indeed to come to grips with the new face of twenty-first-century combat in the wake of both the Cold and Gulf wars—was outdated and in drastic need of replenishment and modernization.

The U.S. order of battle was a vast, intricate, and incredibly complex machine built from an array of war-fighting equipment and personnel that was divided and subdivided into specialized formations that were designed to fulfill specific objectives in military operations in war as well as in peace. One army division was equipped and trained to wage war in mountainous areas, another in jungle terrain, a third in desert warfare with mechanized support from tanks and armored carriers, a fourth for vehicular transport of troops and supplies. Strategic nuclear forces under STRATCOM (Strategic Command) encompassed nuclear weaponry that would, if ever used, be delivered from land, surface, air, and undersea platforms from supersonic bombers to nuclear submarines. The navy not only administered bases around the world and an immense assortment of vessels and aircraft, but also encompassed the U.S. Marine Corps, itself a self-contained fighting force equipped to fight anywhere in the world. A full breakdown of the U.S. order of battle could easily fill a book in itself.

Immediate post–Cold War manpower figures put the U.S. military personnel total at more than two million, and even with cuts following drawdowns in the wake of the Cold and Gulf wars (such as the "Base Force" plan of the Bush administration and the "Option C" plan proposed by Clinton-era Defense Secretary Les Aspin) that sought to reduce personnel levels by at least a half-million, the overall numbers of standing U.S. military forces were such that they dwarfed all the militaries of all other nations. Canada, by contrast, had an active manpower figure of eighty-nine thousand; Germany at a little over four hundred thousand; the United Kingdom at two hundred ninety thousand. And while the former Soviet Union (now the Commonwealth of Independent States, or CIS) still topped the scales with more than two and a half million personnel, that figure was based on the total including the breakaway republics of Armenia, Kazakhstan, Turkmenistan, Tajikistan, Kirghizia, and Uzbekistan, in which Russian troops were still technically deployed. Only the People's Republic of China (PRC) military forces, with a little over three million active military personnel at the end of the Gulf War, down from about four million in 1980, dwarfed those of the United States, but China was not a superpower in the same sense as the United States. Despite its large ambitions as a great power, the PRC was a regional power only, and conflict with the United States, if it ever occurred, would be largely a war of navies, not land armies.

The U.S. defense budget was similarly monumental when compared with that of any other military in the world, including that of the CIS. The draft Russian defense budget for fiscal year 1992 was estimated at 384 billion rubles, or $226 billion, though it, like the Soviet Union itself, had not survived the breakup and was a budget that existed only on paper. The Canadian and U.K. defense budgets were about $38 billion and $10 billion in U.S. dollars, respectively; China's, while not exactly known, was estimated at somewhere between $12 and $15 billion U.S. dollars.

By comparison, the United States budget of $274.3 billion for fiscal year 1993 dwarfed those of its major global competitors and allies combined. Beyond even this, it had boomed significantly since the end of World War II; by the Reagan era it had ballooned to monumental size to overshadow that of the Vietnam War.

The figures tell the tale: From 1980 to 1986, the Pentagon's budget doubled, to $281.4 billion up from $140.7 billion. After inflation, this represented a 50 percent increase. In fact it represented the biggest peacetime expansion of the U.S. military in the nation's history. The enlargement of war-fighting forces was defended as necessary to curb Soviet expansionism and counter the worrisome Russian buildup of both its conventional and nuclear forces. Around Boston, Los Angeles, Seattle, St. Louis, Washington, and dozens of other metropolises the military buildup had catalyzed a burst of economic expansion. While the unprecedented enlargement of the defense sector might have contributed to the collapse of the Soviet empire, it had also been funded by massive governmental borrowing, which created a federal budget deficit that was to the history of American economics what the defense boom was to war. Now that the Soviets were no longer perceived as a threat, domestic concern shifted to the economy; the budget deficit was careening out of control and Congress was about to step on the brakes.

Even if procurement had not been a central issue, by the early 1990s the great disparity in the size, structure, and cost of U.S. military forces, with respect to the military undertakings that the forces were likely to engage in, would in themselves have dictated considerable change at the Pentagon, including change at the organizational level. But global force disparities were not the only issue at stake. As the Cold War ended, too little was spent to replenish aging trucks, main battle tanks, and warplanes or to commence or complete new construction projects, or to manufacture and disseminate the plethora of goods, services, and infrastructure that enable a nation to go to war. Consequently maintenance expenses for existing stocks, many approaching obsolescence, began to soar.

The Department of Defense had begun to find itself in the position of paying for the upkeep of equipment that was outmoded, obsolete, or approaching obsolescence while unable to afford their replacement with new weapons systems more in keeping with the realities of what some had disparagingly, others almost reverently, called the New World Order, and in paying the costs of training for new systems.

It appeared that the Pentagon was locked into a vicious circle. It was robbing Peter to pay Paul. It was remaining static in a dynamically changing world that might, sooner or later, produce a new threat for which the U.S. military was unprepared, or not as well-prepared as possible.

The consensus was that costs needed to be cut in order for new programs to be funded. It was not only the consensus of the military in general, it was the consensus of Congress whose mandates for military budget streamlining included the Gramm-Rudman-Hollings Balanced Budget and Emergency Deficit Control Act of 1985, and the Gramm-Rudman-Hollings Balanced Budget and Emergency Deficit Control Reaffirmation Act of 1987, both collectively known shorthand as "Gramm-Rudman." It, and the succeeding Budget Enforcement Act of 1990 that modified Gramm-Rudman, aimed at cutting what was at the time the largest budget deficit in U.S. history—and one, it must be added, that owed its girth to defense sector growth.

The big question at DOD was how to accomplish the mission. Successive cutbacks that had slimmed down Pentagon budgets in the approximate decade separating the end of the Cold War from the presidency of George W. Bush had proven an impediment to modernization.

A new, largely Republican Congress might vote more money to defense, but probably not enough. The saying in the halls and spaces of the Pentagon when the Rumsfeld team came in was that something at defense was broken, but it wasn't the U.S. military. Instead it was the U.S. military's accounting system that was thus characterized and deemed in need of an immediate fix.

CHAPTER EIGHTEEN

THE GRAVITY OF THE THREAT

To put a finer point on it, the budget war was of paramount concern at the Pentagon before the Iraq War and the war on terror crashed into it and swept it from the forefront to become a Maginot Line of Defense Department business. Yet before 9/11, winning this battle of the fiscal bulge was considered an unassailable cornerstone of defense on which the course of the post–Cold War U.S. military hung. And if bureaucrats, wonks, and bean-counters would be its front-line troops, then they would have an uphill battle against forces as entrenched and dangerous in their own right as any faced by combat troops in shooting wars.

In 2001, as the Bush administration came in, budget reform had a significantly different meaning from that of about a decade before. Back then, at the Cold War's end, it had meant giving less government money to the defense sector. Today it meant working out ways to efficiently make use of the funding that was allocated for defense—not shrinking the Pentagon, as in the old days, but toning up its muscle, exercising away the post–Cold War midriff bulge. It was to prove a difficult exercise program.

The entrenched forces, after all, held ground deemed sacred, and each adjudged their own cause as more just than the rest. The chiefs might have favored budget reforms in theory, but when it came down to the nitty-gritty, each was as turf-conscious as their predecessors had been back in the late 1940s, during a period of restructuring so chaotic it may well have driven a defense secretary (James V. Forrestal) to suicide. Such reforms meant the cancellation of programs, and the chiefs cherished their programs above all else.

Each service branch was painfully conscious that its loss, however slight, might well prove another service's gleaning. The very heart of the culture of the Pentagon was threatened with radical surgery. Not only did individual careers hinge on how the brass hats performed in front of their peers, but the brass were all well aware that the movement of a decimal point from one spreadsheet column to a neighboring cell would, in real-world terms, translate to the loss of tanks, ships, guns, ammunition, and manpower; not only this, but it might almost certainly be a loss at the expense of one service branch to another better favored by the winds of institutional fortune and the momentary exigencies of shifting geopolitics.

Yet now, in 2001, it was clear that the front-rank players were going for the money shot. Among the incoming secretary of defense's first acts was to fire off a twenty-page set of guidelines to the Joint Chiefs. Part of the Rumsfeld memo directed the chiefs to institute such arcana as performance standards, activity-based costs, and output-based metrics—wonk-talk for calculating the value of goods, services, and infrastructure, and how to pay for them. The clarion call had been sounded: The concepts of the boardroom, and not the battlefield, would be vital to defense reform programs. The wizard wonk in his fourth-floor tower sent down his white knight to make it so on the third floor—Myers would straighten out the books.

The upshot would be as new as it was old, and what would start out as figures on spreadsheets would translate into tanks, guns, and soldiers in the field. Cato the Elder had said it two thousand years before to a different Senate than the one currently in session: *Money is the sinews of war.* There was no doubt that it was as true now as it was then. But where had the bad cholesterol of fiscal adipose come from? The answer to that is connected with another ancient concept, that of hubris, which is defined as the overwhelming pride that tempts the gods to anger, and often incites them to war.

* * *

Ever since the fall of an actual wall in 1989, the one that had separated East and West Germany since the early 1960s, the Pentagon had been gripped by a kind of institutional manic-depression that had reminded one of the lyrics to a song by a former army private from Seattle turned rock musician named Jimi Hendrix: "I know what I want, but I just don't know how to go about getting it."

The Berlin Wall was one of the most powerful and enduring symbols of the Cold War, its grim facade, topped by barbed wire, surmounted by machine-gun nests, and cordoned from the East German side by a death zone of no-man's land in which many would-be escapees to the West had already perished, stood as nothing else for the polarizing geopolitical dynamics that marked the state of bipolar East-West relations throughout the Cold War.

When the wall came down, piece by piece and chunk by chunk, it marked one of those rare turning points in human history that, as few others can, stand as signposts dividing the place where past and future diverge. One such lump, festooned with graffiti, had even found its way to President George H. W. Bush's desk at Camp David. He'd told troops at a marine outpost in Saudi Arabia during the pre–Gulf War Operation Desert Shield in a November 1991 Thanksgiving Day speech that he kept it as a reminder "of our steadfast role in the worldwide explosion of freedom."

Once the wall had fallen, once Checkpoint Charlie—another potent symbol—was removed, there was a pervasive sense that nothing would be the same again. That intimation was borne out as icons of the Cold War began to crumble across Eastern Europe and the Soviet Union itself began to break up and topple like the statues of Lenin and Marx that were pulled from their pedestals by mobs in the grip of a perceived euphoric liberation from the chains of Russian Communism.

In 1991, the Cold War was judged by both the United States and the newly confederated Commonwealth of Independent States that had emerged from the wreckage of the Soviet Union, as well as by history, as finally over. More than that, a winner had been unanimously declared. The United States stood alone in the center of the ring. America was the sole remaining superpower. Its rival on the world stage for nearly a half-century now lay in ruins, the might of its military machine broken amid the wreckage of a fallen empire. The main reason for the collapse was fairly clear: The Soviet monolith had imploded under the crushing weight of its own inertia.

The stagnant Soviet economic and sclerotic political systems had been a debacle inherited by Mikhail Gorbachev when appointed premier after the death of Brezhnev; indeed, Gorbachev's appointment was in itself a signal that matters had become so grave that the *vlasti*, or oligarchy of government and industrial bosses who were the true powers behind the scenes, felt compelled to place a reformer in the Kremlin, to bestow upon Gorbachev, as the Russian saying in these matters went, the Crown of Monomakh. Events proved that it was already too late; despite and because of the reforms taken by the new regime between 1985 and 1990, the downward slide of the Soviet economy snowballed into an avalanche that tumbled the entire edifice of Russian Communism with it to the foot of the mountain.

Yet the Soviet dream had not been dashed upon the merciless shoals of economic failure alone, or, to put it otherwise, the stresses that had impacted on the economic burdens that had eaten away at the underpinnings of the Soviet system were not entirely of native origin. The Cold War had been a real war, and global in scope, so-named because it had been fought differently from the two global hot wars that had preceded it.

Like other wars, the Cold War had pitted power blocs led by rival political, economic, cultural, and military systems against the other, led by primary combatants, which in the Cold War's case were the two global superpowers, the United States and the Soviet Union. Also like other wars, there had eventually been a victor. If the United States stood above the shambles of its enemy's defeat, it did so at a price, and the final payment installment on victory had in all probability been the massive, unprecedented military buildup of the Reagan years.

The presidential campaign of Ronald Reagan was a crusade for supply-side economics and one-upping the Soviet Union, which Reagan and his top advisors—nominee Defense Secretary Caspar Weinberger, future CIA Director William Casey, and the soon-to-be secretary of state, former army general and NATO chief Alexander Haig—perceived as an "evil empire" bent on taking over the world, even if global Soviet domination meant nuclear war with the United States. The same view was held by many as a self-evident truth that needed little elaboration or validation.

Hadn't the Soviets armed themselves to the teeth? Hadn't the Soviet navy outpaced that of the United States and become the supreme naval force in the world? Hadn't the Soviets built a new class of stealthy nuclear submarines packed with sea-launchable nuclear-tipped ICBMs? Hadn't they built a land-based force of rail-mobile nuclear missiles with strategic range and MIRVed warheads capable of hitting targets in the United States? Didn't the Soviets enjoy a sizable superiority in numbers over the size and average megatonnage of the U.S. nuclear force? Didn't their published and avowed military doctrine call for a decapitating first nuclear strike against the United States that would destroy the silos of land-based nuclear missiles before the United States could retaliate? Wasn't the Kremlin poised to launch nuclear weapons at U.S. allies in Europe, specifically Germany, and pour armored divisions across the plains of the Fulda Gap, and hadn't they already invaded Afghanistan? And weren't the Soviets arming surrogates around the world, including those close to home in Latin American countries like Honduras and Nicaragua? The answer to all those questions, and others equally disturbing, seemed to be an incontrovertible "yes."

In seeking to even the score against the Soviets, the Reagan administration sought to challenge them on every level, including threatening to pull the United States out of the Strategic Arms Limitation Treaty of 1979. Better known by the acronym SALT II, the bilateral agreement between the United States and USSR had set limits and guidelines on many key aspects of the superpowers' nuclear arsenals toward the goal of establishing nuclear parity by placing numerically equal limits on their nuclear arsenals and by limiting both modernization of existing weapons systems and the number of MIRVed missiles—those equipped with more than a single warhead and whose individual warheads could strike more than one target. Faced with the serious threat of the United States scrapping the treaty, which had been the subject of congressional debate since the late 1970s and as yet unratified—and, perhaps more to the point, faced with a U.S. leadership that had openly advocated a revamping of nuclear weapons technology as well as the jettisoning the Cold

War nuclear gospel of mutually assured destruction in favor of a winnable nuclear war—the Soviets agreed to abide by the treaty.

Under the Reagan administration, the Pentagon's defense budget doubled from what it had been when the president took office. It's been exceeded now only in the costs of paying for the Iraq War. Throughout the 1980s the Department of Defense embarked on a buildup whose primary purpose was to roll back the Soviet military machine and whose secondary purpose was to undermine the foundations of the Soviets' machinery of state. The second purpose would follow as a natural corollary of the first: the USSR had overstretched its economy in order to invest a substantial portion of its gross national product, or real GNP, into pumping up the Soviet military on steroids.

In retrospect, and even when one considers the travails of the war years since autumn 2001, the sum total of the military operations, the research and development of new weapons systems, and the shaping of new battlefield doctrine by the Pentagon presents an ingenious and staggeringly prolific display of activity within a relatively short period of time, and during a period in which, despite the ongoing Cold War, it must be recalled was officially a time of peace. On the operational side, the list includes a series of largely covert battlefields on the ramparts of the Soviet empire, such as Afghanistan, and war zones in America's backyard, such as those already mentioned, that were for the Soviets' far-flung outposts of apparent colonial aspirations. Such a list must also include the conclusion of the Iran Hostage Crisis that had bedeviled and been the bane and undoing of the preceding administration of President Jimmy Carter that came about in the first months of the Reagan presidency.

On the developmental side stood the gee-whiz, Buck Rogers projects that captured the imagination of the media and quickly became powerfully emblematic of a United States that had regained the prestige of a superpower, especially to its foes, including the Iranians who had stormed its embassy in Tehran and taken its staff hostage, and the Organization of Oil Exporting Countries, or OPEC, who had held the nation hostage beneath the "oil weapon," as well as the Russian Bear that had risen up to swipe at an American Eagle whose wings it had deemed to have grown heavy in flight.

These weapons seemed at times to verge on science fiction; indeed, one of them had taken its name from a movie genre that had been dubbed "space opera." The Strategic Defense Initiative, or SDI, that popularly became known as Star Wars, was to have created what the Pentagon termed a space-based "defensive shield" around the United States that would have been impervious to incoming Soviet nuclear missiles. While the SDI orbital shield was never built, combat systems in some ways more astounding were eventually unveiled.

These were aircraft that were invisible to hostile radar, first the F-117A Stealth Fighter and then the B-2 Stealth Bomber, which had strategic range and could penetrate deep into the Russian heartland to deliver nuclear payloads against its cities and industrial plants without being detected on Soviet radar. There was also the MX missile system. A leftover defense initiative from the Carter presidency, the MX was to be a rail-mobile system of missile launchers that would lift advanced nuclear ICBMs into low orbit, from whose nose cones up to fourteen conical warheads, each the approximate size of a human being and each about seven times more powerful than the Hiroshima bomb, would scatter like the seed-pods of some deadly milk thistle to rain pinpoint-accurate devastation upon enemy targets continental distances removed from their launch points in the Southwest. Like SDI, the MX system was never completed, but like Stealth, a host of other weapons were eventually brought to fruition.

The accomplishments were impressive, but by the same token, the Reagan military buildup represented a series of astonishing boondoggles, snafus, and mismanagement at the Department of Defense that resulted, by the end of the Cold War, in popular disenchantment with the Pentagon and congressional action to cut back on defense programs already in progress—such as production of the F-117A and B-2 Stealth aircraft—and to curb funding for additional Pentagon growth.

The fat lady had sung: the Soviet threat had diminished, and if the United States emerged as the Cold War's victor, it was not without a certain tarnish on the eagle-headed escutcheon of defense.

* * *

One such blemish was the revelations concerning a secret arms-for-hostages deal that had leaked to Congress and which ultimately became known as the Iran-Contra Scandal, or, borrowing from a scandal that had rocked a previous presidential administration, Iran-gate. Another group of scandals had far-reaching implications for the future of defense, for unlike Iran-Contra it did not involve an ad-hoc and clandestine cabal of secret operators, but hit at the heart of the Pentagon itself.

"If you were going to approach the Russians with a dove of peace in one hand," Reagan had reasoned, "you had to have a sword in the other."

From the Reagan Oval Office had come a directive to Reagan's cabinet that boded heavy atmospherics at the Department of Defense. From here on out, budget restraints would not apply to defense spending as they did to other sectors of the U.S. economy. Defense was sacrosanct, and money was to be no object in the race to close and ultimately surmount the defense divide with the USSR that the Reagan White House held to be an article of faith. If George W. Bush had expressed the belief that he had been chosen by heavenly fiat to lead the nation against Terrorist International and its rogue state supporters, then Ronald Reagan had also entertained a true believer's zeal to win the Cold War by closing the military divide between the United States and the "Evil Empire" that he had called the USSR in his June 8, 1982, speech before the British House of Commons, a speech whose coinage mirrored Winston Churchill's address at Westminster College in Fulton, Missouri, in 1946 that had added "Iron Curtain" to the ideological Cold War vocabulary.

Incoming Secretary of Defense Weinberger said that the United States' goal would be to double defense spending over the next two years. In particular Weinberger sought to develop a navy that was "a lot bigger [and] stronger" than that of its post–World War II heyday during the closing years of the Vietnam War and, by extension, bigger and stronger than the Soviet navy. The Pentagon, stressed Weinberger, had to be equipped to simultaneously fight two large-scale regional conflicts, as opposed to the "one-and-a-half-war" doctrine that had been a foundation stone of U.S. military doctrine since Vietnam.

To pay for these apocalyptic defense objectives, DOD's first Reagan-era budget of 1982 was equally redoubtable; by some estimates exceeding the total profits, after taxes, recorded by U.S. corporations for any year in history. Indeed, U.S. defense spending went off the Richter scale when compared to the combined outlays requested by Congress for health, education, employment, agriculture, energy, transportation, environmental protection, natural resources, and law enforcement in the federal budget for the same fiscal year; it was some 50 percent higher than all of them put together. By 1985, the wave crest of the Reagan defense bonanza, the defense sector was expanding about three times faster than U.S. industry as a whole.

To fuel this exploding supernova, the Defense Department spent an approximate $30 million every hour, twenty-four hours a day, seven days a week. During this period the Pentagon's expenditures roughly out-scaled the revenues of General Motors by a factor of three. And this was just the beginning. Defense Department spokespeople, including the secretary of defense, testified before Congress throughout the Reagan defense buildup that before long the price tag for national defense modernization would reach figures on the order of about $50 million per hour, or roughly $1.1 billion each day, including weekends and holidays.

Whatever the geostrategic end results of this unexcelled military ramp-up, regardless of whether or not the Cold War ended with the fall of the Soviet Union and the emergence of the United States as the sole global superpower, the circumstances attendant on the new Reagan order at the Department of Defense represented an epochal event for defense contractors and Beltway defense lobbyists alike. When corporate sharks smell blood in the waters a feeding frenzy is inevitable, and to CEOs of defense corporations in the United States the savor of raw meat deal-making in the offing was unmistakable. A chain of price-gouging, back-room deals and big-time taxpayer rip-offs not only supplied ammo for the cabals of DOD critics; now even the Pentagon's unswerving congressional supporters were biting their nails. The roof was on fire, but by the mid-1980s bipartisan lawmakers were threatening to turn off the Department of Defense's money hose.

Contractors' scams ranged from the ridiculous to the sublime and back again. One defense firm had billed the government for babysitters for executives' children, another, donations to an art gallery and, in one glaring instance, a kennel's stud fees for a CEO's prize dam schnauzer.

Caught in the executive feeding frenzy, Boeing charged Uncle Sam for widgets like giveaway key fobs meted out to political supporters and the California-based aerospace company's corporate sponsorship of a paper airplane competition. Nothing was sacred, including la-di-da country club membership fees, restaurant and bar tabs, and hotel and motel stays for government officials, as long as the taxpayer footed the bill, and even though this was in direct violation of numerous federal regulations.

General Dynamics, the nation's chief defense firm and the manufacturer of Trident nuclear submarines, falsified gift vouchers for one high-ranking defense official. During one tense six-hour hearing before a House subcommittee, company officials were accused of destroying internal documents to try to throw federal auditors off the trail. In hindsight, the company's chairman reportedly remarked that there had been "some mistakes made," and that certain bills looked "very wrong to us." One member of the panel lambasted the defense company for participating in a "textbook case of fleecing the U.S. taxpayer."

Strange reports from the E-Ring began to emerge about bizarre overcharges that almost defied comprehension; hammers that cost $400, toilet seats that went for 600 bucks a pop, $9,000 wrenches, and 500 percent markups on aircraft-engine parts. In one case a 67 cent bolt cost the Pentagon $17 and change. A pair of pliers was purchased by DOD with a price tag of $2,000, and in another case an ashtray aboard a naval E-3A Hawkeye AWACS aircraft was acquired at the bargain price of $600, resulting in Navy Secretary Lehman taking disciplinary action against two officers. Government lawmakers and defense critics alike developed massive cases of institutional heartburn. Some defense-watchers alluded to the charges being covers for "black budget" line items diverted to "black world" or covert programs, but these were individuals who'd watched too many spy movies. Conspiracy theory wasn't de rigueur when greed, the obvious motive, was coupled with opportunity, which in the defense boom years existed in abundance.

Tales of abuses, offenses, and scams kept making news. A coffeemaker on a C-5A airlifter cost $7,400 because USAF specifications mandated it be tough enough to survive a crash; the commercial version cost a fraction of the price. As if all that weren't enough, billions of dollars worth of spare parts in the Pentagon's inventory were found to be obsolete or redundant. Lawmakers suddenly discovered that bashing the Puzzle Palace was a sure bet to get press attention and prove their mettle to voters. "It was an eight-year gravy train ride," commented Democratic Senator David Pryor of Arkansas after the dust had settled and a Department of Justice sting operation called Illwind had made arrests and resulted in criminal indictments. "It was the industry's finest hour—in terms of balance sheets."

Federal investigators launched the DOJ's first wave of felony prosecutions of major defense firms following the spare parts affair. By the spring of 1985, fully half of the top one hundred suppliers to the Department of Defense were under some form of criminal investigation. The number of new defense fraud investigations begun that year was four or five times higher than in average previous years. In March, General Electric was indicted and pleaded guilty to charges of defrauding the government by falsifying time cards for Minuteman ICBM maintenance personnel.

It was getting to be time for E-Ring damage control machinery to lurch into action. GE and several other large contractors were temporarily suspended from Pentagon procurement programs; some types of payments to other contractors were temporarily suspended.

Among the usually staunch friends of DOD and supporters of defense contractors who'd been soured by the events was Senator Barry Goldwater who then chaired the Senate Armed Services Committee. What had kindled the Arizona Republican's wrath was the discovery of a $4 billion slush fund of unallocated Pentagon dollars. The huge piggy bank's existence had been, according to the E-ring, discovered completely by accident by defense accountants during a regularly scheduled audit. Its disclosure to congressional legislators angered the combative Goldwater. The *Washington Post* quoted the influential senator characterizing Defense Secretary Caspar Weinberger as a "goddamned fool" for failing to maintain tighter track of the department's fiscal expenditures. "When you go home, and your wife asks, 'What about this $600 toilet seat?' and you can't explain it, you're in bad shape," fulminated Goldwater on the Senate floor.

In his defense, Weinberger responded, "I was obsessed with the idea that we might not have much time [to counter the Soviet threat] . . . not nearly as much time as we had in World War II," he said sometime later. Political leaders had to be made to understand that the United States was in "an absolutely vital catch-up position," the secretary of defense concluded. While in the face of congressional ire and the presence of ongoing federal investigations, Weinberger pledged to administer tighter audits and assured Congress there would be no more $600 toilet seats purchased by DOD. He still insisted that he had a historic mission to fulfill, however. In the same breath, he bluntly informed Senate panel members that, wrongdoings to the contrary, the defense budget must keep growing fast enough to outpace the Soviets. Weinberger further warned the Senate that blue-penciling any part of the Pentagon's spending roadmap could prove, "the most dangerous thing you could do."

Despite investigations by Congress and the Department of Justice, it was the collapse of the Soviet Union that more than any other single factor put an abrupt halt to the budget windfall years for defense contractors and the no-holds-barred defense expenditures that had marked the final acts, throughout most of the 1980s, that brought down the curtain on the Cold War. By the first year of the new decade, the magnetic poles of defense funding had turned volte-face; the Pentagon now witnessed a diametric reversal of fortune.

It was then 1990, the Berlin Wall had fallen, the two Germanys were reunited after nearly five decades of East-West military and ideological confrontation, and the steamroller of war that had once been the armed forces of the Soviet Union was now little more than a hollow shell leaking a fortifying yolk of arms and technical expertise that smaller nations, like Iran, Libya, and Pakistan, rushed to lap up like so many thirsty mice on the floor of a hen-house after the arctic fox of the Cold War had decamped.

The Pentagon, with Defense Secretary Dick Cheney at the helm in the E-Ring, now had some hard choices to face.

CHAPTER NINETEEN

A SHRINE ON THE FIELD OF MARS

T he extent of the power vacuum created by the implosion of the Soviet Union took time to sink in. The United States was like a war veteran who dove off the bed at the sound of firecrackers in the night. An apocalyptic struggle had been waged against an enemy that required constant vigilance. The battle even extended into that "wilderness of mirrors" that CIA Director of Operations James Jesus Angleton had lifted from a poem by T. S. Eliot to describe the shadow-landscape of Cold War espionage against the Soviets.

Leadership echelons reacted to the defeat in a way similar to heavyweight prizefighter Muhammad Ali, punch-drunk and staggering after having gone fourteen rounds against Smokin' Joe Frazier in the 1975 Thrilla in Manila world championship bout. Ali, exhausted, was near the point of collapse. It had been, he'd later revealed, "the closest thing to dying." The bout was over, but the realization of victory took time to penetrate the fog of inertia brought on by the titanic struggle that had preceded it. The United States, at the Cold War's end, was like the champ in Manila.

The colossal statuary of the Motherland's fallen leaders became prone specters of the recumbent colossus. It took time to sink in, but the realization eventually came. The Soviets had been checkmated. The Cold War—what had been, to all intents and purposes World War III—was over. A consensus in Congress and in the military began to build: A sprawling defense system that had evolved over the last half century mainly to thwart the Soviets was now outmoded. Changes were necessary; some said drastic changes, because the world itself had changed, and the geopolitical relationships between its nations had altered radically. The United States could not afford to fight tomorrow's warfare by yesterday's rules and with yesterday's weapons and doctrine. Change had to be implemented now.

The world, by and large, was now in a state of peace on a scale probably not seen since before World War I (the interwar years, it will be recalled, saw much of Europe and Asia torn by economic chaos, social upheaval, and the ravages of war). Some announced the age of a Pax Americana, a golden age of global peace ensured by the fact that the sole surviving cultural, economic, and military superpower in the world was also commonly acknowledged also to be the most benign in history. As ancient Rome had once spread its beneficence across the breadth of the known world, so the United States, as the inheritor of Rome's status in what the U.S. president had termed the New World Order, would do the same.

Yet there were those at the Pentagon to whom this view was anathema as the 1990s began. They were not prepared to accept the Cold War victory so quickly and responded to critics of the slowness of institutional change and restructuring at the Pentagon with skepticism.

In a 1990 interview Colin Powell, then chairman of the Joint Chiefs of Staff, said, "In Europe we want to show the Soviet Union the same picture they have seen all along—a group of nations that are willing to make a real investment in their security. And a real investment in combat forces, not quartermaster clerks." Powell didn't see the need for a radical restructuring of U.S. forces in Europe. "It's not at all clear to me that a balanced downsizing is not the right answer. I've seen no particular Soviet capability disappear; I've seen no part of the world where we have an interest go off the map."

The Soviets, in 1990, were to Powell still a threat. He had served as national security advisor to the Reagan White House from 1987 until his appointment to chairman of the JCS in 1990 by President George H. W. Bush. Powell had been appointed national security advisor on the same day that Caspar Weinberger announced his resignation after serving almost seven years as defense secretary (making him the longest-serving secretary after McNamara and Rumsfeld) and under the cloud of the recently disclosed Iran-Contra Affair (he would soon be placed under indictment by Iran-Contra Committee Independent Counsel Lawrence Walsh).

Now, in 1990, Powell (at fifty-two) served as the twelfth chairman of the Joint Chiefs of Staff. He was the youngest so far to serve in that post; he was also, along with only Eisenhower and Alexander Haig, the third general since World War II to reach four-star rank without ever having been a divisional commander. It was Powell's new civilian boss at the Pentagon who had been responsible for Powell's quantum jump in rank. This was Richard Cheney, among whose first acts as incoming secretary of defense was to promote Powell to four-star rank.

Like Powell, Cheney was not in favor of a rapid drawdown of U.S. defense priorities and global commitments. If Powell, who wrote in his autobiography, *My American Journey*, that he remained haunted by the nightmare of the Vietnam War in which he had served two tours, bore a skepticism about the enemy then Cheney brought to the E-Ring a savvy veteran politico's skepticism about not believing all that met the eye. Although Cheney was committed to the tenets of a New World Order philosophy, in which the United States would play a more dominant role militarily—and take unilateral actions that might have been unthinkable during the Cold War—he was also opposed to a shrinkage of U.S. military assets around the world.

Where Cheney most differed from the chairman of the Joint Chiefs of Staff was in his reasoning about the threats to the Pax Americana. The previous year, Cheney had orchestrated a military operation whose objective—regime change—prefigured that of the Iraq War some fourteen years later. This operation, code-named Operation Just Cause, was set in motion to remove the president of Panama from power and ultimately bring him to trial on criminal conspiracy charges (under the RICO act that had been previously used to prosecute international drug traffickers) and put him behind bars (where he remains to this day). Noriega, called "Pineapple Face" by Panamanians because of his pockmarked complexion and the grenade-like roundness of his visage, and who had received military training in the United States at the elite School of the Americas (an officer training school for Latin Americans who would later go on to prominent military and political careers in their home countries), now stood on the wrong side of the power curve of the New World Order.

The Panamanian president had not only sought to nationalize the Panama Canal but had been a brutal dictator who had oppressed his people and who had, according to federal investigators, the Defense Intelligence Agency, and Interpol, among other similar organizations, aligned himself with international organized crime and was making Panama a haven for drug and gun runners. In short, Noriega was a bad guy whose removal was not merely necessitated by America's regional self-interests, but was also required to liberate the oppressed people of Panama and install a democratic regime in the dictator's place.

President George H. W. Bush had made the War on Drugs a priority of his administration; while international terrorism was thus far a plague in Western Europe, Southwest Asia, and other distant places, the scourge of drugs was very much on the president's mind. It was time for Noriega to meet his fate. By 12:45 a.m.—H-hour on December 20, 1989—Noriega's time was up.

The invasion of Panama City that commenced in the pre-dawn darkness was not only a textbook example of transformational warfare doctrine—employing surprise, precision-guided munitions, operational depth, jointness, and rapid operation tempo—it was also, in hindsight, a startling prefiguration of both Enduring Freedom air operations in Afghanistan and the Shock and Awe campaign that commenced the Iraq War, whose distant rumors and lights were the source of one sleepless night for a mild-mannered weapons specialist sojourning in Abu Dhabi in March 2003. The strike on Panama marked many firsts, chief among which was the initial combat deployment of the F-117A Nighthawk, more commonly known as the Stealth Fighter. It also marked the use of a joint force of twenty-four thousand U.S. troops, about half of which were made up of special operations elements that included navy SEALs, army Rangers and Delta Force, with air support from Blackhawk helos and the AC-130 Spectre gunships. Here, as in Iraq, U.S. forces quickly secured the capital city and stormed the presidential headquarters, the *Commandancia*, which was soon ablaze, only to find their target, the country's maximum leader, had flown the coop. Like Saddam Hussein, Manuel Noriega was apprehended sometime later in somewhat less than presidential condition.

Operation Just Cause demonstrated a number of things to the Pentagon, whose military analysts would study it—as all military undertakings are studied—in part as a blueprint for future war plans and war games in support of planned future exercises. One thing it demonstrated was that the type of long-range force projection that Colonel Charlie Beckwith had planned, but failed to execute, in Operation Rice Bowl in 1979 had been tactically feasible if operationally flawed. (Rice Bowl is the name for the planning phase of the mission that became better known as Evening Light or Eagle Claw.) Rice Bowl had been secretly okayed by Jimmy Carter as a force option bid to rescue the hostages held by Islamic militants in Tehran.

Like Just Cause, it had employed a mixed force comprising of U.S. Army, Marine Corps, Navy, and Air Force personnel: Delta Force soldiers and Rangers on the ground, marines providing crews for the navy RH-53D Sea Stallion helos that would be used for short-range transport from "Desert One" to Tehran and back, the navy providing the USS *Nimitz* for the helos to stage from, and the air force three special operations MC-130 Hercules for long-range troop and materiel transport, three EC-130s bearing fuel reserves for the extraction phase of the mission, and two AC-130 Spectre gunships, whose job it would have been to blast the militant-controlled U.S. embassy with enough firepower to chew its walls to pieces. The main reason Eagle Claw failed was because the ambitious plan called for highly coordinated joint operations that required doctrine, hardware, and training programs that didn't exist in 1979. For that matter, the Reagan-era invasion of Grenada, code-named Urgent Fury, had also suffered from many of the same operational ailments that had plagued Jimmy Carter's abortive hostage rescue mission to Tehran.

Ostensibly fearing that modifications to a runway at a new international airport then under construction harbingered the creation of "Soviet-Cuban militarization" of the Caribbean island republic, and asserting that American students on the island were being held hostage, President Ronald Reagan ordered a military operation to seize the island and forcibly bring about regime change. The casus belli was largely a pretext. The invasion of Grenada was actually motivated by the presence there of large numbers of Cuban troops after a series of coups d'état had instituted a "revolutionary people's government," suspended the Grenadian constitution, and begun a military buildup with Cuban and Soviet aid. Reagan feared the creation of a second Cuba in the Caribbean.

Whatever the reason for the invasion, which commenced in the early morning of October 25, 1983, it represented the first large-scale military operation staged by the U.S. since the Vietnam War, with the deployment of approximately seven thousand U.S. troops, in tandem with an Eastern Caribbean Defense Force made up of some three hundred soldiers from countries comprising the Organization of Eastern Caribbean States (OECS).

The Grenada invasion quickly succumbed to a boondoggle syndrome similar to Eagle Claw's for many of the same reasons that included faulty intelligence, lack of joint inter-service communications between the elements of the attacking forces, and the absence of a feasible joint concept of operations. In the Monday morning quarterbacking that followed at the DOD, at the White House, and in the halls of Congress, recommendations to rectify the errors of planning and communications, as well as toward remedying the lack of military technology necessary to successfully conduct missions of this scope, began. These would have impacts on conflicts yet to happen. Organizationally, the events would lead to the 1987 formation of the Special Operations Command (SOCOM).

It was ten years after Eagle Claw and six years after Grenada by the time Panama became the target, and many things—including the technology of warfare and the absence of a competing world superpower—had changed. At the Pentagon, the lessons learned were legion, one of which would prove a glimpse into the future: In the post–Cold War scheme of things the reality was forces with a leaner footprint, that cost less money to field and train and which were supported by advanced technological aids, such as precision-targeting and high-resolution reconnaissance and surveillance to enable real-time decision-making at both theater and distant command centers. In other words, the age of "Nintendo Warfare" had begun in earnest, intimating the future policy and doctrinal shifts that would lead to transformational concepts like preemption.

All well and good, but Panama was a case of regional warfare against both a soft target and a hollow force. The Soviet Goliath now lying prone at David's feet presented a spectacle as startling as anything witnessed by any Lilliputian that swarmed over the bound form of Gulliver. Indeed it was a Swiftian bargain. Could the United States stake its future on replacing the catapults and siege engines of industrialized warfare that had served it so well and so long against so formidable a threat with slingshots and pebbles? Neither Cheney nor Powell was ready to make that conceptual leap just yet.

Yet the ineluctable fact was that drawdown was in the air, and its bold new jet stream blew through the halls of America's chief foreign allies at NATO headquarters in Brussels. The United States' NATO allies were also in the process of negotiating important new treaties in the aftermath of the Soviet breakup. Europe, which had been faced by the Soviet military for decades since the end of the war, was protected by overseas deployments of American troops armed with nuclear weapons.

With the two Germanys now reunified, the Europeans were eager to do several things. One was to reorganize NATO in keeping with post–Cold War realities, another was to negotiate with the CIS and its former East Bloc satellites militarily organized as the Warsaw Pact, a third was to negotiate mutual defense treaties with other European states, and a fourth was to reduce the size of U.S. forces on European soil. Furthermore, while America itself reacted with measured disbelief to the onset of the Pax America—and the Imperial role it would inherently play—the NATO countries were of a different consensus.

A 1993 essay titled "The Reluctant Empire," by defense analyst and longtime NATO observer Dr. Ezio Bonsignore writing from Bonn, Germany, seemed to have incisively summed up the view from the ramparts of NATO.

"Does the U.S. perceive that history . . . is knocking at its door?" he wrote. "Does the U.S. see the momentous occasion to change and reshape the future of mankind as a whole that is now at hand, and which will fade away forever if not grasped? Does the U.S., as the world's only true Superpower, have at least some tentative idea about how and when to use its force? Does the U.S., to sum it up, realize that it has become an Empire?" If the United States failed to exercise its historic New World Order role, Bonsignore concluded, ". . . then we will have no other choice than continue with our past and present practices—nations defined by increasingly unreasonable ethnic or geographic borders, fighting each other until a much more ruthless world master can eventually emerge to sweep them all away."

From such encomiums the path might be short indeed to the yawning jaws of Apocalypse in the approaching millennium, which was now just a decade away, if the United States did not make a swift and decisive redefinition of its global defense mission. The position of powers great and small can be transitory; the world is unpredictable. By mobilizing its entire population for war to form a conscript army, Napoleonic France had overrun Europe and become the preeminent continental power by 1805, when what was remembered in the afterglow of victory as "The Sun of Austerlitz" had seemed to shine favorably upon the French in this decisive battle against the Third Coalition.[12] French victories mounted as Imperial France struck eastward, deep into the Russian heartland, and on September 14, 1812, the emperor, leading his troops, beheld the golden domes and spires of Moscow. But the reign of empire was to prove brief and its victories Pyrrhic; the Grand Armeé entered a Moscow deliberately set aflame to thwart it, and on June 18, 1815, less than three years later, the Napoleonic empire was crushed at Waterloo. France's moment as a superpower was over in a historical instant. No nation, not even the United States, can be immune to the caprices of fortune and the riptides of fate.

But for the United States at the end of the Cold War, the roadmap was there for all to see; the precursors of what the new U.S. military posture would look like from the vantage point of the E-Ring were

12. Russia, Austria, and Sweden joined Britain in what was known as the Third Coalition. It was to no avail. Austria and Russia were defeated at Austerlitz on December 2, 1805. Napoleon crushed the Prussians at Jena on October 14, 1806, and the Russians at Friedland on June 14, 1807. His triumphs were marked by treaties (the Peace of Tilsit) in June to July 1807 that brought most of Europe to his feet.

already visible. The moment must be seized . . . or potentially lost. In May 1990, the United States and Soviets announced they were close to a pact to cut both countries' nuclear missile stockpiles by 30 percent and to agree on curbs on the development and deployment of chemical and biological weapons of mass destruction. Unilateral cuts to the U.S. defense budget had already been implemented. Deeper cuts of 25 to 50 percent of the then $300 million Pentagon budget were proposed by proponents on both sides of the political spectrum.

But seizing post–Cold War opportunities meant going beyond merely hammering swords into plowshares. The genie was out of the bottle; the chance at global hegemony was too good to pass up. In March 1992, portions of a February 18 classified Pentagon draft policy plan were leaked to the *New York Times* by an unidentified Defense Department official who, stated the *Times*, "believes this post-Cold War strategy debate should be carried out in the public domain." The excerpts from the draft of the "Defense Planning Guidance for Fiscal Years 1994–1999," would later become known as the Wolfowitz Memorandum.

The forty-six pages made available to the *Times* seemed, above all, to chart the chief post–Cold War mission of the United States to be "convincing potential competitors that they need not aspire to a greater role or pursue a more aggressive posture to protect their legitimate interests."

In short, the classified policy draft seemed to advocate as policy the prevention, by the United States, of the reemergence of superpower competitors in Western Europe, Asia, or the territory of the FSU; a policy that quickly became known as "benevolent domination." In order to achieve this objective, the plan called for the adoption of the Bush administration's Base Force proposal: the creation of a 1.6-million-member military over the next five years, at a cost of about $1.2 trillion, and the building of a global security arrangement that preempted Germany and Japan from pursuing a course of substantial rearmament in the future.

The concept of preemptive warfare was contained in the document under the heading of Defense Strategy Objectives: "While the U.S. cannot become the world's 'policeman,' by assuming responsibility for righting every wrong," it stated, "we will retain the preeminent responsibility for addressing selectively those wrongs which threaten not only our interests, but those of our allies or friends, or which could seriously unsettle international relations."

The plan was a roadmap to the future, but what sort of shadows did this futurity cast on the present? Under that same heading, the report stated: "The U.S. must show the leadership necessary to establish and protect a new order that holds the promise of convincing potential competitors that they need not aspire to a greater role or pursue a more aggressive posture to protect their legitimate interests. . . . Finally, we must maintain the mechanisms for deterring potential competitors from even aspiring to a larger regional or global role."

The leak started the damage control machinery at DOD revving in high gear in a way not seen since the Pentagon Papers had been released to the *Times* some two decades before. Here was a statement from the E-Ring that seemed to augur a radical break with the policy of collective internationalism, which the U.S. had pursued as a strategy that had evolved since the end of World War II and whose symbol was the United Nations, a body that could globally mediate disputes and police outbreaks of international violence. It also looked like a blueprint for an American empire, one that was determined to impose a Pax Americana on the rest of the world, by military force or by other means, if necessary, and become the inheritor of the grandeur and supremacy that had been achieved by classical Rome under its Caesars.

Once leaked, the draft policy statement's implications did not wear well with either a public looking forward to a promised "peace dividend" and which balked at marking the Cold War's end with a new military buildup, nor with allies and foes abroad who saw in the plan the seeds of American empire. Yet the plan, to all intents and purposes, had not been plucked from thin air. The view from the ramparts of NATO, already cited, was representative of the belief among many observers of global defense that the United States was, and rightfully should behave, as an empire, albeit a benevolent one, for it was in the global interest that America seize its responsibility to do so; in a world fragmented along the collapsed fault lines of Cold War power, in which breakaway republics had become the unanticipated caretakers of nuclear arsenals, and in which rogue states were vying for the spoils of the nuclear endgame, the alternative might well be a long Yeatsian night of apocalyptic anarchy that was the antimatter universe of a world finally at peace.

Already rump states like Ukraine, now heir to the title of the world's third largest nuclear power after the United States and Russia, which in December 1990 demanded $2.8 billion to dismantle and destroy its nuclear weapons, were playing what looked like nuclear blackmail games with the United States. Already warlords and organized crime had become the de facto government of entire swathes of former Soviet territory, and these shadow governments had even absorbed entire contingents of former Soviet military troops into their private armies; already there was no way of knowing how much nuclear material, and of what types, had slipped through porous borders. From the perspective of such developments a projected new role for the United States as global hegemon looked like manna rather than gall.

In the end, and after months of debate, the plan's most powerful and outspoken supporters, Defense Secretary Dick Cheney and Chairman Colin Powell, bowed to the winds of criticism and made an about-face. A restive presence among the sixteen NATO nations had also been signaled to the E-Ring and Oval Office—on Friday, May 22, 1992, Germany and France announced the formation of an all-European military corps called the European Defense Force, or EDF, and invited other nations to join.

The EDF would function within the NATO envelope to respond to crises where NATO member nations declared their interest, but the new security alliance would also respond independently in crises where NATO interests were not directly involved. The timing of the announcement was a pointed rebuke at any U.S. plans that might curb the formation of emerging security alliances in Europe. And while the guidance's draft version had proclaimed a "victory" over the Soviet Union, the published policy statement, now deferring to the Kremlin's sensitivities, referred to only a "great success" in the discrediting of Communism as an ideology and the collapse of the Soviet Union, and it also cited the United Nations as a tool for global security.

The final, revised draft of the policy study stated, "One of the primary tasks we face today in shaping the future is carrying longstanding alliances into the new era, and turning old enmities into new cooperative relationships." Nevertheless, the guidance (so called because it represents a "guidance" from the president and the secretary of defense to the four military services on how to prepare their budgets and mobilize their forces in the future) continued to reject calls in Congress to make deep military cuts and—citing Dick Cheney's and Colin Powell's public testimony that cuts too deep in defense spending could create a broken military and tempt bad actors like Iraq to try their luck—pressed for the Bush administration's Base Force concept of an upsized 1.6-million-soldier military with increased spending. It also reserved the right of the United States to take unilateral, preemptive action to protect its global security, committing the United States "to act independently, as necessary, to protect our critical interests" and to prevent "any hostile power from dominating a region critical to our interests." Significantly, in light of the Iraq War and Operation Iraqi Freedom, it added that such "consolidated, non-democratic control of the resources" in a region "could generate a significant threat to our security."

After all was said and done, the May draft represented a considerable softening of the original guidance, not all of which was made public with some sections still classified. The defense posture of the United States as implemented by the Pentagon would turn back to more conventional preoccupations, favoring what was described as a collective approach to post–Cold War defense issues, one favoring the promotion of regional stability through cooperative relationships and alliance-building over hegemony and the interventions of the United Nations.

The United States would continue to act as *primus inter pares*; it would continue to build coalitions among allies; and it would continue to prepare for military force readiness to meet the demands of a rapidly changing global defense environment. There was to be, after all, a Pax Americana, but a goddess bearing a cornucopia, an olive branch, and a sheaf of grain, and representing the Spirit of Peace, was, as of old, to have, as a token, a shrine on the Field of Mars.

* * *

But how to maintain readiness on such treacherous ground? Both civilian and military leadership of the Pentagon could not overlook the fact that the breakup of the Soviet empire had destabilized the global balance of power in some places while increasing stability in others. Around the fringes of the old empire were ethnic tensions ready to explode, such as those that would consume the Balkans throughout the 1990s, while the breakup also left vast stockpiles of weapons up for grabs; these conceivably included nuclear weapons.

Then there were rogue states like Iraq, Iran, North Korea, or Libya, and adversaries like China—how would they react to the power vacuum left by the Soviets? For that matter, wasn't it possible that the Soviet Union would simply reconstitute itself under a new form of dictatorial government after a period of regrouping? In a few years it was not inconceivable that a new and more formidable Soviet Union, perhaps under the leadership of a military junta that was ready to risk anything, including nuclear brinkmanship, might turn its fury against Europe and the United States. There were too many unknowns for Cheney, Powell, and the more conservative strategists at the Department of Defense.

One of the answers was provided by Iraq's invasion of Kuwait in 1990 that gave rise to the Gulf War. During its approximate one hundred hours duration, the war tested and vindicated and bore out many assumptions that could only be hypothesized about beforehand. One of those tested assumptions that directly bore on the questions that Cheney as secretary of defense had pondered the previous year under pressure from defense watchers in Congress, the private sector, and among NATO allies in Europe, was that neither Soviet weaponry nor Soviet military doctrine was any match for that of the United States. The military forces of Saddam Hussein had, before Desert Storm, composed what was arguably the fourth largest army in the world.

Numbers can be argued back and forth, but one salient factor cannot—this is the fact that it was Soviet military doctrine that provided the basis upon which the Iraqi armed forces were trained, just as Soviet military equipment provided the mainstay of Iraq's war-making capability. In each instance, the successes of U.S. operational doctrine, coupled with advanced weaponry, were on a scale totally out of proportion to what any analyst—and one has only to read the prewar predictions of the pundits to see this—could have suspected in their wildest imaginings.

Take, for example, the tactic of saturating the skies with antiaircraft fire, nicknamed triple-A. This was a battle-tested technique that had been used against the Soviets themselves in Afghanistan. It was described by most experts as having no defense. Few who watched the air war phase of the Gulf War, Desert Wind, commence with live coverage from camera crews in Baghdad in 1991 will forget the images of gun crews positioned on rooftops hurling concentrated tracer fire at the night skies. And few will forget that this concentrated triple-A failed to hit a single F-117A aircraft which instead—as ghostly gun camera video revealed— used precision-guided munitions to blow apart skyscrapers with the godlike ease of little boys lopping the heads off flowers, and returned to do it night after night.

On the ground, in a pitched night fight, U.S. Abrams main battle tanks (MBTs) squared off against T-72 tanks that were the top-line MBTs in the arsenal of Soviet mobile armor in what was called the biggest tank battle since World War II. Though this was numerically correct, here, too, the battle was unevenly one-sided, with smoke plumes from the wreckage of burnt-out T-72s rising high into the air as next day's dawn broke over the battlefield.

The world watched and was stunned. The Soviets watched and were disgraced at the beating that, by proxy, they had taken at the hands of the United States and its coalition allies. The global verdict was that something unprecedented had happened: It was a revolution in military affairs, shortened to the acronym RMA in Pentagonese. Both the Soviet Union and the United States knew what the RMA meant. As matters now stood, the Soviet Union would be utterly defeated in a conventional war with the United States and its NATO allies in Europe. It was no contest; they could not hope to prevail conventionally.

While many other factors came into final play—including the incoming administration of President-elect Bill Clinton—to shrink the overall footprint of U.S. forces domestically, to roll them back from bases in Europe and distant outposts elsewhere, to champion the use of high-tech weaponry combined with rapid-mobility tactics, and to negotiate further cuts in the East-West nuclear arsenal, it was the Gulf War that loosed the floodgates of transformation upon the many still reluctant forces at the Department of Defense and the defense sector to whom change represented the end of lifetime career paths. It was too late to turn back, though. A few years after Desert Storm, defense transformation would be mandated by law, and the Pentagon would have to follow suit. And, like it or not, the United States was now more than *primus inter pares*; it was a superpower with a capital S emblazoned on a metaphorical union suit of red, white, and blue.

CHAPTER TWENTY

PREP WITH STEEL

Prep with Steel, Lead with Lead, Count the Dead
—a tank warrior's aphorism

I n 2001, defense reform was going to be Don Rumsfeld's first order of business, simply because it would have been at the top of any incoming secretary of defense's A-list. How new reform initiatives were to be implemented were matters for the DOD and Congress to negotiate, but defense transformation per se was by no means a perquisite of the E-Ring. On the contrary, it was the law of the land. As should now be evident, a succession of enactments since the end of the Cold War that extended across three preceding White House administrations mandated many, if not most, of the initiatives that the Department of Defense began to take in 2001.

These initiatives ran the gamut from budget management to base closings to cancelling or funding specific defense programs to configuring conventional and nuclear forces. While defense reform, to a greater or lesser extent, has always been on the defense slate, it's fair to say that the end of the Cold War and the geopolitical metamorphosis that took place continuously in its aftermath, as well as the revolution in military affairs following the Gulf War, presented the Defense Department with a more radical set of challenges, opportunities, and problems than at any time since the late interwar period in the final years of the 1930s, including the year of the National Security Act of 1947 and the peak years of the middle 1980s.

If the Soviets were to be confronted with a U.S. military pumped up to a Schwarzenegger physique, the undertaking was nevertheless along familiar lines of developments. Weapons programs were initiated to develop bigger, better, faster—and in some cases, sneakier—armaments; nuclear defense was postured to a geostrategic dynamic that was an extension of World War II; the branches of the armed services were still trained, based, and deployed in much the same manner as they had been in Vietnam, which was, in itself, a war fought in a manner and under conditions similar to World War II land operations in the Pacific and Southeast Asia. The Goldwater-Nichols Act of 1986 had, in fact, charted the high-water mark for the Reagan buildup; to all intents and purposes its implementation was a matter deferred to the next administration.

It had been a different ballgame ever since the Berlin Wall came down in 1989. The challenge of dealing with the rapid pace of reform initiatives, which first Cheney and then the three Clinton-era secretaries of defense (Aspin, Perry, and Cohen) had faced, was now on Rumsfeld's plate as well. For that matter, the same pressure to change had also been the driving force behind similar initiatives among the United States' NATO partners in Western and—as the 1990s unfolded—Eastern Europe, as well as in the former Soviet Union. The major legislation that drove transformation was the Defense Restructuring Act of 1996 (DRA) and the Base Realignment and Closure Acts (BRACs), the first of which was enacted in 1990.

The DRA followed where Goldwater-Nichols had left off, bringing into being a broad range of initiatives that left an indelible impact on U.S. defense. These initiatives included the transformational policy plans of the individual service branches, such as Army after Next (preceded by Force XXI and Land Warrior 2000), From the Sea, and the USAF's Copernicus Forward, as well as Joint Vision 2010, the Joint Chiefs' war plan. It also gave rise to initiatives and task forces such as the (still ongoing) Future Years Defense Plan (FYDP), the 21st Century Security Strategy Group, and the preparation of a key Pentagon document at the direction of Defense Secretary William Cohen called "Transforming Defense." Perhaps most important, the DRA also gave rise to the Quadrennial Defense Review. The QDR, of which the third and most recent was virtually complete during the week of September 11, 2001, was designated to be undertaken by the Defense Department every four years, hence its title. According to DOD, it was to be "a blueprint to military transformation."

The QDR followed on from an embryonic study called the Bottom-up Review, or BUR, which took place under Defense Secretary Les Aspin in 1993. The BUR's purpose was, according to its preamble, "to define the strategy, force structure, modernization programs, industrial base, and infrastructure needed to meet new dangers and seize new opportunities." It was to be the first thorough appraisal of where the United States stood with regard to force readiness and power projection in the new postwar era.

Significant in connection with the defense reform initiative was the already mentioned defense policy paper, "Transforming Defense." If the QDR itself was a blueprint, then "Transforming Defense," prepared by a task force that included officials from the Defense and the Joint Chiefs of Staff that had been established under a subsection of the DRA, was a roadmap to the future of the U.S. defense posture. It addressed and made recommendations on the gamut of concerns that included the DOD's Planning, Programming, and Budgeting System (PPBS), advocated new initiatives in what the report termed "Homeland Defense," made recommendations for new global commands under a Joint Forces Command, and posited what the report outlined as six potential future global scenarios with which U.S. military forces might have to contend, termed "alternative worlds."

What is extraordinary about this roadmap for defense is that many of its major tenets were adopted by what the media termed "neoconservatives" of Team Bush as the main plank of its platform for defense reform. As was the case with Goldwater-Nichols, while the theoretical and legislative framework was developed in a preceding presidential administration, their de facto implementation fell to members of the succeeding administration.

If the September 11, 2001, attacks had an almost immediate and profound impact on those portions concerning budget reform on the one hand, they were a catalyst toward implementing a number of operational reforms during the warfare that followed the attacks on the other.

Some of the recommendations for transformation that wound up having an impact are worth noting in detail:

- The Cold War policy of containment is outmoded.
- Homeland defense is considered a priority; the Defense Department is to run it. ("Defense is but one element of the broader national strategy.")
- Adopt Army After Next concepts (mobile, small-footprint units with equivalent or greater lethality than large, heavy formations).
- Reduce or eliminate Cold War infrastructure without delay (i.e., programs like Commanche, a tank-killer helicopter originally developed to destroy Soviet armor).
- Reform the acquisition process ("Rethink the Planning, Programming, and Budgeting System.")
- Emphasize jointness, information dominance, speed and mobility, and the ability to project military power rapidly across global distances.

The roadmap to the future of U.S. defense readiness that was spelled out in "Transforming Defense" made recommendations that appear to have been much on the mind of the new secretary of defense and the new chairman of the Joint Chiefs of Staff in 2001. The preoccupation with both was initially cutting the bureaucratic red tape in the way of defense acquisitions and trimming the fat that padded the cost of most of the plethora of things that the Defense Department acquired, from Dixie cups to air superiority fighter planes, in the course of any given fiscal year. It's held to be axiomatic among domestic and foreign contractors who would like to sell to the Defense Department that while it's often far less complicated to pitch a sale to the Pentagon than it is to many foreign defense ministries, the hard part is winning the competition programs that many minor, and virtually all major, acquisitions must undergo.

The Office of the Secretary of Defense is a house deliberately divided between a policy branch and an acquisitions branch. At the top of the DOD hierarchy sits the secretary of defense; directly below is the deputy secretary of defense. Below this top level and between the two undersecretaries of defense (one for policy and one for acquisitions) is an executive secretariat that is headed by a special assistant to the secretary. The secretariat is a key element in the operation of the Pentagon and is important to the operation of both wings of the DOD hierarchy. This layer of the Pentagon power structure is especially significant since it serves the Defense Department much in the same way an operating system serves a computer.

The secretariat controls the paper flow, including cables and memoranda (much of this "paper" is digital but neither "information," "documentation," "communication," or like terms quite convey the concept as well as does the original, if antiquated, term) from the secretary, undersecretaries, and assistant secretaries to and from the rest of DOD and between DOD and other agencies, government institutions, and private sector entities that do business with the Pentagon. These include the White House, State Department, CIA, National Security Council, and U.S. outposts abroad. The secretariat is also in charge of the round-the-clock operations center at DOD, which often makes the first reactions to crises and decides which other agencies to contact first in response. It's axiomatic that no secretary of defense can run the Pentagon effectively without a loyal lieutenant in the executive secretary's billet.[13]

Below the secretariat layer are the two offices of the Undersecretaries of Defense for Policy and Acquisitions. Finally, there is the large base of the departmental pyramid that forms the largest layer, in numerical and operational senses, of the Defense Department. This layer is topped by the assistant secretaries of defense for a variety of departments that run the gamut from international security affairs, to legislative affairs, to public affairs on the policy side and from defense research and engineering, to production and logistics, to research and technology on the acquisitions side.

Here it should be mentioned that this is the primary side of the defense organizational substructure whose mission is strategically linked to the Defense Advanced Research Projects Agency, more commonly known by its acronym DARPA. The agency operates as

13. As a bit of Pentagon trivia, the famous (or infamous) card deck of Iraqi bad guys, whose Ace of Spades features a photo captioned "Saddam Husayn Al-Tikriti, President," followed by a Joker giving an interesting table of Iraqi military ranks (Jundi, for example, means "basic private," Jundi Awwal means "private," as well as "private first class," the Joker informs us). While the deck in the author's possession bears the insignia of the Defense Intelligence Agency on its face and states in three places that it's "Issued by Intelligence Agency of United States of America 2003," the cards, in actual fact, were the brainchild of Defense Department executive secretariat staff members.

the main research and development center for technology-intensive military projects for the Defense Department. One of DARPA's better-known projects was the development of the Stealth fighter and bomber; lesser known projects have been Warbreaker, tasked to develop unmanned aerial and unmanned combat aerial vehicles (UAVs/UCAVs), and the Joint Warrior Interoperability Demonstration under the army's C⁴I For the Warrior (C⁴IFTW) program, one of many initiatives to "upgrade," "aerospace," and "digitize" the dismounted infantry soldier and give him or her something like the firepower of a two-legged, MRE-fueled tank. While it is a government agency, and under the command and control of the Defense Department, DARPA is headed by a civilian appointee and its ranks are largely civilian. DARPA is also an agency that is, in actual fact, scattered throughout the country, and whose outposts range from government-funded battle labs at universities and military bases to contractee workshops in postmodern corporate buildings seen on the grassy outskirts of expressway cloverleaves across the length and breadth of the country.

Another curiosity of the Defense Department's table of organization is the fact that among those agencies that are under its control is the National Security Agency. Though established in the same 1947 National Security Act that created the Defense Department, this mammoth intelligence-gathering agency, with a budget that is as reportedly vast as it is intentionally secret and which occupies a headquarters at Fort Belvoir, Maryland, that is to all intents and purposes a small city, is, except on paper, completely autonomous from the Pentagon.

The final layer of the Defense Department comprises the deputy undersecretaries of defense, whose responsibilities on the policy and acquisitions sides echo and supplement those of the assistant level. This last level is commonly held to be the level at which much of the day-to-day work of the Pentagon and Defense Department gets done, which is one reason why this is commonly known, in Pentagonese, as the "working level" at DOD.

While the policy side of the Pentagon most commonly makes news, it's the acquisitions side that might be characterized as the workhorse of the Defense Department. Here is where, to coin a phrase, the bovine excrement really hits the whirling blades. It is also where most of the money is spent and earned, paid in and paid out. The Pentagon not only buys in overwhelming quantity, it is also the arbiter of many sales to domestic markets and all military sales to foreign countries; these sales not only include big-ticket military hardware like fighter planes, tanks, armored personnel carriers, helicopters, ships, and subsurface vehicles, but also encompass hundreds of other items of value to foreign militaries, including so-called dual-use items that could have both peacetime and wartime applications, from body armor to combat simulation and training software.

While policy matters have an abstract and theoretical component, whatever their consequences in the real world of combat, the business of acquisitions and sales—officially called procurement—at the Pentagon is a nuts-and-bolts, dollars-and-cents issue that swells the agenda of the Department of Defense. Indeed, it's held as axiomatic to many at the Pentagon that procurement drives policy and not the other way around; that the conventional and nuclear weapons systems in the inventory of the U.S. military (as well as the number and disposition of troops) determine what the policymakers can do with the armed forces at any given moment and centrally figure in the domino-like chain of extrapolations based on the changing winds of war and peace that determine defense policy for the future.

Thus, on the eve of 9/11, what Rumsfeld called the "procurement conundrum" and "budgetary change" were uppermost concerns among the newly installed DOD leadership. The financial system of the Defense Department was key to the heart of transformation and modernization, and it, and the accounting system, had not functioned smoothly in decades. New programs resulting in new missions, new weapons, upgrades to existing systems, and a raft of other initiatives all had to be funded.

As the saying on the street goes, if you want to play you've got to pay. In a peacetime international environment, where defense spending had plunged to a peacetime low during the tenure of the last three defense secretaries, where a host of legislation existed onward from Gramm-Rudman and Goldwater-Nichols designed to curb military spending, defense expenditures could not be counted on to increase by as much as the department would have liked. Such was the rationale behind the "war on waste" that Rumsfeld declared at the Pentagon on September 10, 2001.

The announcement followed the September 9 announcement of the overhaul of the Foreign Military Sales Program (FMS). With annual foreign defense sales overseen by the Pentagon valued at approximately $10 billion, FMS was a prime income generator both nationally and for the purposes of defense funding. Yet the process had been bogged down by bureaucratic red tape and a complicated paper-based bidding system called LOA, which stood for Letter of Offer and Acceptance System and which produced the export licenses and end-user certificates required by foreign purchasers of U.S. arms, spare parts, and related equipment.

Clinton administration Deputy Defense Secretary John Hamre had initiated some streamlining of FMS, but a faster track was now wanted. Hamre had begun pushing for FMS reforms following complaints from senior foreign defense officials who warned the Defense Department of an exodus by foreign customers from the FMS system to direct commercial sales, which were seen as more flexible, businesslike, and user-friendly.

Although there were limits to what foreign governments could buy from the U.S. defense sector without the approval of DOD, billions of dollars annually were spent on military equipment—like field kitchens to heavy trucks to dental machinery—that could be transferred via direct sales channels. Beyond this, other avenues existed for foreign buyers to acquire more sophisticated military weapons systems and technologies via U.S.–based middlemen and shell companies that could bypass the FMS system entirely. Streamlining FMS was therefore a necessity to keeping the Pentagon running on an even keel.

Another aspect of the war on waste at the Pentagon was which defense programs to cut and which to fund, decisions that would make their way into the QDR that was in the process of preparation. Again, cutting obsolescent programs was not a matter at the sole discretion of DOD leadership; it was a legislated responsibility of the department. There were programs that would be scaled back but would continue. Such were the F-22 Raptor and F-23 Joint Strike Fighter programs. Both fighter planes had been years in development, with the F-22 in production and the Joint Strike Fighter in the prototype stage.

The production of these new jet fighters, developed to replace the aging F-15 and F-16, respectively, was contingent on the projected military uses for them. The new planes were extremely stealthy—as stealthy as the F-117A Nighthawk—and their combat systems and avionics were orders of magnitude beyond any plane in production or development by any other global competitor. They were, in fact, too advanced for their own good. To bring the planes into full military production would be more expensive than maintaining and upgrading existing warplanes: The fighters, for all their capabilities, lacked a clear-cut mission. To date, the F-22 fighter wing is made up of a so-called silver bullet force that, at least a dozen years after the Raptor went into production, has never flown in combat.

The fate of another weapons system that had been in development for at least a decade at the cost of billions of dollars called Crusader was more somber. Crusader was developed under the AFAS/FARV plan to develop an Advanced Field Artillery System/Future Armored Resupply Vehicle for the army. The system was to be a next-generation self-propelled howitzer with a dedicated artillery resupply system, FARV, developed to replace the M-109A6 Paladin self-propelled howitzer and M-992 field artillery ammunition supply vehicle that had been in use for decades. The Crusader system would have been able to spray a mix of high-tech artillery rounds at a firing rate of between ten and twelve rounds per minute, and could fire both conventional and nuclear-tipped shells. The big gun would blast out a continuous stream of artillery fire at a rate of one round every four to five seconds, fed by a robotically controlled automatic loader with a two-hundred-round capacity that would keep feeding rounds into the artillery tube and which could automatically rearm and refuel itself.

Crusader ammunition would be precision-guided in some cases and could be fired out to ranges of fifty kilometers, which is a little more than thirty miles. Beyond its formidable capabilities, the Crusader program was a defense initiative with enormous pork-barrel popularity with congressional supporters and their constituencies back home; pieces of the program had brought jobs to the backwaters of America. The system's development had begun near the close of the Cold War, and its original purpose had been to rain artillery down on hordes of Soviet troops pouring across the Fulda Gap into Western Europe. Expensive and heavy, the Crusader was out of step with the trend for lighter, more agile ground forces and was now considered a dinosaur. The program was canceled by the Pentagon in early 2002.

The total projected cost of the Crusader program was $11 billion; more than $2 billion had already been spent at the time it was cancelled.

Another casualty was Comanche, which was axed for similar reasons, albeit two years later in 2004 and after a total development cost of approximately $38 billion and after about two decades of program development. Like Crusader, the RAH-66 Comanche had been developed as a high-technology countermeasure to the cheaper, less advanced, but numerically greater armies and armaments the Soviets were projected to send streaming across the East-West demarcation lines at the commencement of World War III.

Comanche, a two-seater helicopter, would have replaced the A-10 Thunderbolt, a redoubtable relic of the Cold War era that was originally fielded in 1975, whose sole purpose was to hunt down and kill mechanized armor. This it did exceedingly well, except that in a projected war against a peer enemy with newer tanks and mobile armor, and better anti-aircraft weapons, it was not considered effective or survivable enough. Comanche, an agile helicopter with advanced avionics, targeting, and battle-management systems, and equipped to fire an array of precision-guided missiles, was to have been the answer.

Comanche was killed as much by the Cold War's abrupt end as by developments in arms technology that had cut into the heart of its armor-busting mission. One of these developments was the perfecting of so-called top-attack munitions. These, like SADARM, fielded by the United States and the French STRIX, were brilliant mortar rounds that could be fired from a variety of platforms, including main battle tanks.

Once SADARM was airborne, sensors in its nose began tracking the ground for armor; as it fell back to Earth a small parachute deployed and small rockets corrected the falling round's downward trajectory to home it toward the most vulnerable spot in any tank—the top of the turret. SADARM was so effective against enemy armor that tank crews invading Iraq in 2003 declared it to be their round of choice. It had a low dud rate, was more effective against armor than advertized, required no training to use (it could be fired like any other tank round), and never failed to kill armor ("three rounds will kill at least one tank . . . never missed" states a DOD report, "Fires in the Close Fight," on lessons learned in Iraq, whose opening motto is used as the title of this section).[14]

Unlike these legacy systems, the V-22 Osprey convertiplane, a tilt-rotor aircraft that is a hybrid between a fixed-wing aircraft and a helicopter, wound up receiving continued funding. Although the aircraft's development was marred by several crashes that resulted in fatalities, a special panel convened by the Armed Services Committee decided the Osprey was vital to future operations of the Marine Corps, which needed the V-22 to transport rapidly combat personnel and their equipment from the decks of carrier battle groups stationed in the waters off the coast of potential regional trouble spots. The Osprey is now in production.

Such were the preoccupations of the Pentagon in the year preceding the 9/11 terrorist attacks. The attacks represented a national trauma that left behind a death toll far in excess of Pearl Harbor. In the apocalyptic moment, the United States found itself under attack, and the dynamics of war underwent a sudden power shift.

By October 1, 2001, the Defense Department requested up to $40 billion more in funding. As it had done in past crises, Congress voted the funds, and the Pentagon, now overseeing the battles in Afghanistan, was gearing up for preparations to take the fight to what was deemed another bastion of the Axis of Evil. Iraq was next.

---

14. Like Paladin, the venerable A-10 Warthog is still in service, both having outlasted their planned replacements.

CHAPTER TWENTY-ONE

DISCONTINUITIES OF GOVERNMENT

Two more years would pass before the Shock and Awe was to begin. Behind the scenes at the White House and the Pentagon, momentum for the push was building. Not only had lives been lost at the Pentagon, but the 9/11 attacks had come closest in modern memory to bringing about a disruption of the continuity of government. Not even the Japanese kamikaze attacks on Pearl Harbor had such an impact.

Although they had not been dignified as acts of war (Congress had refused to vote a formal declaration of war against al-Qaeda), the three-pronged attacks had certainly set in motion government activities consistent with a bona fide act of war; indeed, these activities had been plans made originally in the depths of the Cold War to preserve the continuity of the U.S. government against surprise nuclear attack by the Soviet Union. The result was the discreet evacuation of members of government, including the White House, congressional, and Defense Department leadership, to places referred to as "undisclosed locations," by the media.

Since the Cold War brought with it the threat of the figurative lopping-off of the heads of state by a countervailing nuclear exchange, there have been ongoing efforts to insulate government leaders from nuclear war and preserve a National Command Authority, or NCA. (The Internet was one of the byproducts of this effort, stemming from a need to create a totally failsafe way to transmit tactical information to civilian and military war planners.) It will be recalled that the Roosevelt administration built the tunnel system code-named "Shangri-la" to guard the president against a second Pearl Harbor–style bombing attack on the capital; the author's misadventures in the Cabinet War Rooms beneath London will also be remembered from an earlier chapter. Contingency plans accelerated during the Cold War and included not only deeper and more commodious underground bunkers but elaborate evacuation plans for Washington leadership.

In his 1964 film, *Dr. Strangelove*, director Stanley Kubrick satirized the dark, inhuman logic of nuclear war. The film, subtitled "How I Stopped Worrying and Learned to Love the Bomb," featured a concluding scene in which Strangelove, speaking with a German accent said to have been deliberately reminiscent of the young author of an influential study concerning nuclear weapons and foreign policy named Henry Kissinger, quells the fears of the assembled leaders by promising they'll have "ten women to every man," among other comforts, as they spend the next one hundred years underground. The movie coined the word "Strangelovian" as an adjective for end-of-the-world logic applied to unthinkable catastrophe.

Yet if the Defense Department had overseen the construction of underground bunkers in the United States during World War II, then there had been a veritable tunneling boom in the postwar years designed not only, as mentioned above, to preserve continuity of government, but also to preserve command and control of war-fighting forces before, during, and after a nuclear first strike. These became known as deep underground facilities (DUFs).

As the Cold War gave way to the Gulf War and the advent of conventional and unconventional munitions designed to penetrate bunkers, those bunkers got deeper, as well as more numerous—one CIA estimate suggested a figure of more than ten thousand deep underground bases worldwide; of these, approximately one thousand are deemed to be strategic, buried command centers and bunkers for the protection of national leaders in time of war.

Among these are the headquarters of NORAD, made up of a system of huge steel rooms supported by enormous shock absorbers inside the hollowed-out granite shell of Cheyenne Mountain, Colorado. More central to this narrative is the Pentagon's underground command bunker system, the Alternate National Military Command Center (ANMCC), commonly called Raven Rock. It's located some seventy miles from the capital in the Catoctin Mountains astride the Maryland–Pennsylvania border, within the boundaries of Fort Ritchie, Maryland. The site is built into a small mountain called Raven Rock, from which the facility takes its name (the early borings of the Truman administration, completed in 1953, are today known as Site R).

Raven Rock contains a single steel building set on massive springs; inside, along with hospital, dining, and sleeping facilities, is a command center that can duplicate every aspect of the National Military Command Center, a suite of highly secure rooms in the Pentagon that is the nation's main military command post. It was to both secure facilities that Pentagon brass and VIPs, including Defense Secretary Donald Rumsfeld, were at times shuttled in the wake of the 9/11 terrorist attacks, according to some observers.

Beneath the White House, a buried bunker complex known as the Presidential Emergency Operating Center played host to senior cabinet officials, including then National Security Advisor Condoleezza Rice, as well as Vice President Cheney, on several occasions during and since 9/11. It was here that then White House Press Secretary Ari Fleisher revealed that Cheney had "modern technology available to him" during the vice president's absences from the White House throughout the early period of the crisis.

On September 11, 2001, the president also headed for a number of undisclosed secure locations, some of which were deep underground. On October 9, 2001, the vice president was moved to what Fleischer called "an undisclosed, secure location" as a "security precaution" against reprisal attacks on the eve of U.S.–led coalition air strikes on al-Qaeda and Taliban bases in Afghanistan. "This is a time of war," added Fleischer. "It is a time to take all proper precautions."

Congressional leaders, including those among the fifteen in line of presidential succession, such as (at the time) Tom Daschle, Richard Gephardt, and Trent Lott, were hustled from the Capitol to places of safety. The departments of Justice, State, Treasury, Defense, and the CIA were evacuated—an estimated twenty thousand personnel from the Pentagon alone. Security personnel bristling with weapons patrolled the White House grounds.

By contrast, it must be added, rank-and-file White House staff members were told simply to run for cover. In an Associated Press interview, First Lady Laura Bush said the "very young women who work for me [went] to a secure location. The rest were told to run from the White House when they thought that fourth plane was going to come there." (The actual instructions from the Secret Service were, "Women, drop your heels and run," according to news media.) Among these prudent actions numerous other precautionary visits to undisclosed locations, by both Bush and Cheney, followed in subsequent months and years; Cheney was said to have been brought by Secret Service personnel to the vice-presidential quarters at the Naval Observatory during several periods of high alert.

Since even a summary account of buried military and government facilities in the United States, and their relationships to those of other nations, including the former Soviet Union, would easily fill a book in themselves, suffice it to be said that a gauge of the seriousness with which the al-Qaeda martyrdom attacks were viewed was the speed and secrecy with which wartime evacuation plans were instituted to protect not only the national leadership but also the national defense infrastructure and the machinery of command and control that is the province of the Pentagon.

However, to risk belaboring a point, it's also significant that one of the consequences of the Gulf War was to touch off a spate of bunker-building by the principal antagonists of the two succeeding regional wars. Reason: Smart weaponry coupled with stealth proved how easy it was to demolish military and political command centers housed in above-ground facilities. Consequence: Underground facilities were the only solution with anything approaching a guarantee of survivability.

Beneath the streets of Baghdad, as within the rugged mountain ranges of Afghanistan, protected bunker systems had been constructed that could, it was hoped, afford places of refuge against future attack utilizing similar weapons and tactics. Within a short time span following 9/11, nevertheless, overhead surveillance from space-based imaging platforms to high-altitude UAVs would be bringing real-time visuals to officials in command centers at the Pentagon and other command posts in the United States that showed those buried redoubts breached and demolished by precision-guided munitions like JDAM.

The first wars of the twenty-first century prosecuted by the Pentagon were to, in effect, begin in a high-tech apotheosis of warfare among the cave-dwelling troglodytes of archaic epochs. To cite from another Kubrick film, *2001*, it was as if the millennium had delivered the message that the primitive bone-cudgel that a simian warrior hurled skyward in the film's opening scenes should have transformed not into the stately white wheel-within-wheel of a space station, but the batlike specter of the Stealth bomber instead.

* * *

The motives for waging war, and the reasons for strategic blunders and success, are more cryptic than explainable and are more often than not explained after the fact. Those who seek after a coherent appraisal of the Iraq War should expect, like students of previous conflicts, to fall at least to some degree prisoner of their own conjurations. It's not within this book's scope to attempt to make a detailed description or analysis of the wars in Afghanistan or Iraq, anymore than to have done the same for the other conflicts throughout the Pentagon's history. To have attempted this would have been to have written several other books.

Yet insofar as the history of the Building encompasses the history of the wars the United States has fought since, and even before, World War II, the story of the Pentagon must touch on at least those aspects central to the narrative's objectives, designs, and overarching plan. Central to this purpose, and, I think, central to a full grasp of the nature of these regional conflicts, is their connection to two developments on the evolutionary landscape of American ideas on defense policy and the powers of the president since the end of the Cold War era. Both of these have already been touched on, albeit in other connections.

As to the first; it's been suggested earlier in this chapter that among the cornerstones of transformational defense reform have been ideas associated with the notion that the United States emerged as the sole surviving superpower (what "Transforming Defense" termed the "preeminent political, economic, and military power in the world today") and that, as global hegemon, the United States perceived itself given a new historic mission to fulfill.

This mission committed the United States to concepts like forward defense, global power projection, and formation of ad hoc "coalitions of the willing," and reserved to the United States the decision to act unilaterally in order to protect its strategic interests. Rather than an invention of "neoconservatives" of the Bush administration, the set of hypotheticals collectively making up the concept of preemptive warfare have been a part of the defense reform policy and strategic planning of the Defense Department for at least most of the last two decades.

What changed with the sense of strategic military missions of the Clinton and Bush administrations, and in large part set them apart, was in the determination of under what circumstances—when, where, how, and why—this longstanding policy framework would translate into direct intervention. Faced with the crisis in Yugoslavia that included mounting genocide, the Clinton administration shied from committing U.S. ground forces in large numbers to the conflict and reacted with an interpretation of policy consistent with coalition warfare and U.N. participation.

But that was before the shockwaves of 9/11. In their train, and faced with intelligence reports (reliable or less than reliable) of weapons of mass destruction in the hands of Saddam Hussein, the possibility of any presidential administration electing to launch a fairly extensive military operation in Iraq would have increased exponentially.

It would mainly have been a question of strategic depth of mission: How far would the United States go? How long would it plan to stay? How extensive would its objectives be? Preemption itself would not have been a substantial policy issue in any case, nor necessarily even the developments, like classification of terrorists as enemy combatants prosecutable by military tribunal and subject to internment in offshore prison facilities, that have attended the Global War on Terrorism.

All of these measures were made with the bipartisan approval of Congress and with continual congressional appropriation of supplemental defense budgets. As to "regime change," it was George Bush who had campaigned forcefully against the putative adventurism of Clinton's "nation-building" in the former Yugoslavia that had involved the United States in a foreign morass, and if regime change is not central to and enshrined within nation-building, then what is?

Second, the powers of the executive branch to wage war, as granted under Articles I, II, and III of the Constitution, have always been somewhat cryptic, and presidents, in their capacities as commanders in chief, have rarely failed to take full advantage of the theory of "inherent powers," based on past presidential actions not challenged in the courts, to turn what the Constitution called a "duty" under the commander in chief clause into constitutionally granted "powers."

Thus presidents, in ordering military actions by the issuance of executive orders and presidential findings, clear the way and broaden the scope of possible action for their successors in the Oval Office. Congress, though having rights reserved for itself, both constitutionally and by subsequent enactments, has generally closed ranks behind the president (though often not without a great deal of wrangling first). Correspondingly, despite the provision for "collective judgment" between Congress and the White House prior to taking military action under the War Powers Act, modern presidents have not hesitated to use what Gerald Ford, who ordered the bombing of Cambodia in order to secure the release of U.S. seamen held captive on the merchant vessel *Mayaguez* in May 1975, referred to as his "executive power" and "authority as commander in chief."

There may be said to be an "invisible Constitution" where the invocation of emergency presidential powers to wage undeclared war are concerned. In the Iraq War, decades of transformational policy and more than a century of presidential priorities combined behind a secretary of defense empowered with a mandate from the Oval Office to reaffirm the civilian control over the Joint Chiefs at the Pentagon in determining the scope and direction of defense reforms.

The change would emphasize a new sense of strategic mission that had begun to take form in the mind of defense strategists as the Soviet Union crumbled and fell and the Cold War ended. It would embody the reforms that Dick Cheney and Colin Powell had contemplated as defense secretary and chairman of the Joint Chiefs of Staff under the first Bush administration, reforms based on the conviction that the United States was the preeminent superpower and arbiter of the world's destiny coupled with the conviction, shared by Donald Rumsfeld, that the wave of future warfare was the fielding of light, mobile forces that could hit hard, move fast, and take more ground in a day than previous armies might in a month.

Iraq would be the test. The presence or absence of weapons of mass destruction to the contrary, the strategic implications of Saddam's continued rule in a post-9/11 world was enough of a casus bellum for the hawks that nested amid the arid precipices of executive war powers. It was perceived to be time for America to make a clean sweep of potential breeding grounds for terrorism, and the Middle East had become—with its fundamentalist armies, the endemic corruption of its power elites, and a supply of wealth with which to fund terrorist strikes on the United States as practically limitless as the supply of oil beneath the Arabian sands—the dismal swamp of foreign evils.

Besides, Great Powers, first the British and French followed after World War II by the Americans, had been playing imperialist power politics in the Middle East for decades. It had, after all, been the first two Great Powers that had largely drawn the map that gave several of those Middle Eastern countries—including Iraq—their present borders. If the existence of WMD was quickly challenged as a pretext, then so was the notion of sacrificing national blood and money to bring democracy to an Iraqi people who seemed to have done well enough without it for a very long time and had never asked for it.

No, it wasn't so much that the justification for war was ludicrous, even propagandistic—most had been that or worse, including the ones given by George Bush on Thanksgiving Day 1990 for the Gulf War in his "This Will Not Stand" address to troops in Desert Shield in Saudi Arabia, where he'd charged, among other things, that Iraqi troops had ripped Kuwaiti babies from incubators and thrown them on the floor and had pledged to "liberate" a Kuwaiti people who had always lived under a theocratic autocracy and who would continue to do so after the Gulf War was over. No, it was about something entirely different: the fact that

Americans would rally behind a president who took the nation to war in order to protect it from further disasters. That and nothing else.

"I will not wait on events while dangers gather," George W. Bush had promised the nation on the eve of war in 2003, invoking, as other presidents had done before him again, executive powers and privileges embodied in the use of a first-person pronoun. The nation would act in its own defense because it had seen that no other power on earth possessed the determination or the means to do it on its behalf.

If the plan worked, if the war was won, and if won within a reasonable time and at reasonable cost, then the nation would continue to rally behind the flag. But should the toll in lives and dollars, in blood, sweat, and tears, rise too high, or should the effort fail, then groundswells of discontent might rise to vex the hawks, as it had done to Truman because of Korea and Lyndon Johnson, and to Johnson's Secretary of Defense Robert McNamara, because of Vietnam.

* * *

In 2003, after some ten months of development, an attack plan for Iraq had been hammered out. General Tommy Franks, as commander of CENTCOM, which oversees operations in the Middle East, had been given command of invasion forces. Franks, who had served in Vietnam and had commanded the Second Infantry Division in Korea between 1995 and 1997, and later commanded Third Army Central Command in Atlanta, Georgia, had directed the war against the Taliban in Afghanistan in 2001.

He would later be appointed commander in chief of coalition forces in Operation Iraqi Freedom. Franks oversaw the development of a modified attack plan that would emphasize speed, mobility, and engagement in depth over numbers in striking at Iraq and rapid consolidation of control over the country. One hundred forty thousand troops would accomplish the job. The figure was an accommodation between DOD's working numbers, which were considerably less, and those of the Joint Chiefs of Staff, which were considerably more.

The disparity in troop strength figures pointed out a fundamental difference between the ideologists of defense transformation and the career military at the Pentagon. The suits and the uniforms were on two separate planets in some regards. Their grasp of the theoretical may be high, but of the practical often smacks of dilettantism, wishful thinking, and worse. At the core of the lessons of the debacle in Vietnam that have impressed themselves on the collective memory of the chiefs is the fact that both President Lyndon Johnson and Secretary of Defense Robert McNamara were overpowering presences whose micromanagement of the apparatus of waging the war was often in conflict with the most basic instincts of military commanders.

Here, again, was a defense secretary skilled at management yet at variance with core doctrinal creed that commanders held as articles of faith. Rumsfeld, like McNamara, had come to the Pentagon from the business sector; like McNamara, Rumsfeld had sought to introduce cost-management innovations at DOD. (Unlike McNamara, Rumsfeld had been secretary of defense once before.)

It has been alleged that Franks caved in to Rumsfeld in giving his imprimatur to a war plan with troop deployment levels of insufficient strength to secure Iraq once it was in the hands of coalition forces. The remarks of Franks' colleague, General Eric Shinseki, himself a decorated Vietnam veteran, to the Senate Armed Services Committee on February 25, 2003, four months before the end of his term as chief of staff of the army and some three weeks before the Shock and Awe phase of Operation Iraqi Freedom was to commence, gave a window into the internecine fault lines between the E-Ring and the JCS.

Pressed by panel member Senator Carl Levin (D-Michigan) to provide a ballpark manpower figure that would be necessary to stabilize postwar Iraq, Shinseki reluctantly answered that he thought an occupation force of "something on the order of several hundred thousand soldiers" as "a probable figure that might be required." Shinseki's reluctance to state a figure at odds with the modified war plan was evident. The exact colloquy went as follows:

> **Senator Levin:** General Shinseki, could you give us some idea as to the magnitude of the army's force requirement for an occupation of Iraq following a successful completion of the war?

General Shinseki: In specific numbers, I would have to rely on combatant commanders' exact requirements. But I think . . .

Senator Levin: How about a range?

General Shinseki: I would say that what's been mobilized to this point, something on the order of several hundred thousand soldiers, are probably, you know, a figure that would be required. We're talking about post-hostilities control over a piece of geography that's fairly significant, with the kinds of ethnic tensions that could lead to other problems. And so it takes a significant ground-force presence to maintain a safe and secure environment, to ensure that people are fed, that water is distributed, all the normal responsibilities that go along with administering a situation like this.

If Shinseki had voiced the convictions of military convention, he had also dashed across no-man's land and drawn hostile fire. What the Roman legionnaires of Caesar, Tiberius, and Augustus had learned in protracted warfare against the Goths, Visigoths, Gauls, and Dacians, and their later successors the Sassanid Persians, and what the British had learned against the denizens of Northern Ireland, or for that matter what the French had learned in Algeria and Vietnam, was no less true at the dawn of the new millennium.

Pentagonese acronyms like OOTW (operations other than war) or MOBA (military operations in built-up areas) might give a high digital gloss to this age-old form of warfare, but the occupation of foreign countries was a primal form of warfare whose integral dynamics remained largely unchanged from those wars of old. You needed boots on the ground in overwhelming strength in order to prevail in the mission; Baghdad alone was a city second only in size to New York. An occupier would need troops in sufficient numbers to secure it. And apart from the lessons that might be gleaned from the annals of Tacitus, Martial, or other ancient chroniclers of the wars of the Caesars, there was the supreme lesson of the Gulf War to take into consideration.

That lesson was that while the United States, leveraging its high-technology war-fighting resources, might be able to roll across a regional antagonist virtually unresisted, the question of how it would fare in the face of insurrectionist opposition was one that was yet to be decided. Historically—and history must take even the American Revolution into consideration—insurgencies have tended to be the ultimate victors. Even if the objective was to bring regime change to a nation that would to all intents be receptive to it once Saddam Hussein and the Ba'ath Party were forcibly removed, and coalition presence was to have finite limits, it might easily be a matter of years of occupation in Iraq. There was every reason to advocate numbers over infrastructure, boots on the ground over stealth in the air.

The response from DOD was predictable. Clashes between the general and the secretary of defense were well known. Shinseki, reserved and soft-spoken, had been "wire-brushed" more than once by Rumsfeld—chewed out unfairly in front of his colleagues to put him in his place—at Pentagon planning sessions. He and other senior military officers who disagreed with DOD policy had been made examples *pour encourager les autres* in a deliberate effort by the civilian leadership to exercise and consolidate positive control of the JCS.

At the crux of everything was the key concept of defense transformation: doing more with less, and, accordingly, fighting and winning wars with a fraction of pre-transformational manpower levels versus the army's almost visceral perception that it was numbers that counted. Nobody was arguing that a second Desert Storm would fail to bag Baghdad; the question was about what would happen afterward. The original DOD contingency plan in the event of a second war in Iraq, OPLAN 1003-98, contemplated troop levels of up to five hundred thousand. According to the memoirs of two generals, Rumsfeld rejected such figures as "the product of old thinking and the embodiment of everything that was wrong with the military."

The consensus among the JCS, as recorded by the generals, was that the OPLAN "reflected long-standing military principles about the force levels that were needed to defeat Iraq, control a population of more than 24 million, and secure a nation the size of California with porous borders." Rumsfeld's numbers, in contrast, seemed to be pulled out of thin air. He had dismissed one of the military's long-standing plans and suggested his own force level without any of the generals raising a cautionary flag.

Rumsfeld and Wolfowitz reacted strongly and in keeping with transformational thinking. The several-hundred-thousand troop estimate was called "far off the mark" by DOD, and Wolfowitz expressed, to the House Budget Committee on February 27, 2003, the belief that it would be "hard to believe" more troops than planned would be needed to take Iraq, force regime change, and stabilize Iraq.

Secretary of State Colin Powell had worldviews, collectively enshrined as the already mentioned "Powell Doctrine," that were often diametrically opposed to those of Dick Cheney and Don Rumsfeld. Powell, who had at the time of his appointment to the cabinet expressed the view that U.S. forces were overstretched, weighed in on the side of the army. Throughout the planning stages of the Iraq War, Powell had found himself at loggerheads not only with administration hawks, but opposed to the entire necessity of going to war against Iraq.

It had been Powell who, as chairman of the Joint Chiefs, had advocated containment of Baghdad rather than occupation in 1991. His reasoning then was about the same as it was between 2001 and 2003: The army was not built for extended operations. "We don't do jungles," a Gulf War military wag had said after Desert Storm. The same reasoning could be applied to cities.

Even with enough manpower—on the order of the half-million proposed by OPLAN 1003-98—every historical, doctrinal, and operational precedent argued that the going could turn ugly. If the game was worth the candle, then America would be good to go.

But was it? This hinged on two main questions: First, was there an al-Qaeda–Saddam link? Second, did Saddam Hussein have stockpiles of functional weapons of mass destruction—chemical, biological, or nuclear—or did he have a weapons program close to producing them?

Powell was not convinced, but in the end he hewed to the White House line and brought the U.S. case against Saddam Hussein before the United Nations. Saddam Hussein was in possession of weapons of mass destruction, Powell stated to the General Assembly on the eve of war. He had to be stopped before he used them or put them in the hands of al-Qaeda.

If Franks, like Powell, in the end came to an accommodation with those who advocated a second war in the Gulf to deal with the threat posed by Iraq, then the existence of WMD was perhaps central to the decision loop. Franks, who stated in 2005 that "No one was more surprised than I that we didn't find [WMD]" in Iraq, also made public his pre-invasion fears of the consequences of another terrorist attack on the United States using nuclear, chemical, or biological weapons. Such an attack might, he believed, "cause our population to question our own Constitution and to begin to militarize our country in order to avoid a repeat of another mass, casualty-producing event. Which in fact, then begins to unravel the fabric of our Constitution."

If there was a rush to judgment on the existence of Iraqi WMD, then it was not without precedent. It had been known for decades that Saddam Hussein wanted nuclear weapons and other weapons of mass destruction.

In June 1981, the Israeli air force struck the Iraqi nuclear reactor at the Al Tuwaitha Nuclear Research Center located some eleven miles outside of Baghdad at Osirak (alternatively, Osiraq, named for Osiris, Egyptian god of the Underworld) in order to thwart Iraqi production of enriched uranium of weapons grade. The airstrikes, using eight F-16 fighters to drop the bombs that smashed the reactor dome and six F-15s for escorts, killing ten Iraqi soldiers and one nuclear engineer supplied by the French, was code-named Operation Opera. The loss of the reactor dealt a serious blow to the Iraqi nuclear program, which might have given Saddam Hussein a working nuclear warhead by the mid-1980s if successful.

Israeli intelligence was also said to be behind the execution-style murders of Yahva El Meshad in a Paris hotel in 1980 and Canadian arms genius Gerald Bull in London in that same year. Both were thought to have been involved in clandestine weapons programs for Iraq; Bull was the inventor of a gigantic artillery cannon of Jules Vernian proportions that could have hurled a nuclear warhead clear across the

Middle East. Later on an Iraqi defector revealed that U.N. weapons inspection teams had been duped in searching for conventional facilities for manufacturing bomb-grade nuclear fuel, whereas Iraq was having success with a method called calutron separation for which the teams were not prepared to search.

Could any wiggle room be afforded, after 9/11? Could the U.S. afford to play at wait and see? Finally, there was also the pressure of transformational defense reforms. As has been shown earlier, these reforms, which mandated the use of drastically reduced troop levels combined with precision firepower and deep battle engagement that cuts off reinforcement echelons before they can reach the front—in short all the elements of the Air-Land Operations that proved so successful in Desert Storm—were by now core tenets of the protocols and codes of operational doctrine. When the DOD chiefs and their aides stated that such a lean force could do the job, they had holy writ on their side.

They also had a postwar plan—throughout 2002 a special planning group made up of Iraqi exiles and Gulf War veterans had been preparing a reconstruction plan.

"Let me run this thing, and hold me completely accountable," Rumsfeld had told Bush. DOD was to control the entire operation from start to finish.

No matter that the Iraq War and Operation Iraqi Freedom mark the first time the United States has had an all-volunteer army on extended deployment or that the new, transformationally enabled military had never been built to sustain either protracted land-and-stay operations or MOBA operations, nor, for that matter, that the debacle in Somalia was the last time such operations were attempted.

A historical moment had arrived as had the awful crisis that had in large part produced it. In hindsight, that it was seized in the end, and against all odds, is not all that terribly surprising.

* * *

As this narrative concludes the still ongoing conflicts in Iraq and Afghanistan, as well as in the Horn of Africa and elsewhere, must recede into the background as the Building again takes the fore. The aim of this book has been to chronicle the history of the Pentagon, and while these first regional conflicts of the twenty-first century are of pressing concern in their own right, they are but mile markers in the continuing saga of the Building.

Besides, the final pages of their stories are yet to be written. Eclipsed by Operation Iraqi Freedom have been developments across a broad spectrum of events, and emerging from the four corners of the earth, that will frame the issues with which the Pentagon will have to contend throughout the rest of the first millennial decade and beyond.

So, too, the guard has changed at the Defense Department, and the career history and personal attributes of Secretary of Defense Robert Gates will play a key role in determining the direction, texture, and pace of institutional and doctrinal change at the Pentagon. Some of these will decide what role the Pentagon might play in domestic security matters, others will concern the defense posture of the United States in respect to new and developing threats not only from the transnational nexus of terrorist groups but also from potential regional adversaries of the near future; there will also be new challenges to face in defense relations between the United States' NATO allies and from the former Soviet Union and China, to name but two global players.

Defense transformation, including budgetary reform, will be of central concern for the duration of Gates' term as head of the Defense Department, just as it had been for his predecessor, as it will almost surely be for Gates' successor as well. The Building itself will mark a not unimportant milestone by decade's end when the massive rebuilding operation—prolonged by the 9/11 attack—is scheduled for completion. Like the World Trade Center towers the Pentagon will continue to represent a symbol of America to would-be attackers that, as in the past, will exert an almost magnetic attraction and continue to place the Building at the top of the list of targets for future martyrdom mission–style attack plans, or even more exotic forms of annihilative assault using weapons technology that threatens to proliferate downward from the arsenals of nation-states into the hands of transnational and non-state actors.

These, like al-Qaeda, compose not so much fanatical religious or quasi-criminal groups, but a nascent form of would-be non-national power, extending across national boundaries that collectively represent the first real threat to the nation-state in history, and a direct threat to what one deputy defense secretary once referred to as a post–Cold War "zone of peace" in industrialized Western nations. Stability operations, great and small, with the nonproliferation not only of weapons of mass destruction but of conventional weapons capable of precision strike at long range, will continue to be on the short list of missions for U.S. military forces.

The Pentagon will continue to reap the achievements and contend with the shortcomings of the Rumsfeld legacy for years to come. Sworn in as secretary of defense on January 20, 2001, Rumsfeld resigned, effective December 18, 2006, as the second-longest-serving Pentagon chief, after McNamara, in the Building's history. Including his service as the thirteenth secretary of defense under Ford from 1975 to 1977, Rumsfeld's departure fell a mere nine days short of making him the longest-serving of all defense secretaries.

Rumsfeld's main accomplishments in office lie in his being the first defense chief to actively take on the challenge of fielding a transformed twenty-first-century military force into two near-simultaneous major regional conflicts, in essence taking transformational policy as outlined in defense papers like "Transforming Defense" and turning them into armor in the field, boots on the ground, and planes in the air. His main shortcoming is almost a corollary or reverse doppelganger of the preceding: in order to accomplish this aim Rumsfeld overshadowed and circumvented the Joint Chiefs of Staff to drive home his policies in a manner not seen at the Building since McNamara's tenure throughout the Vietnam War.

Lionized on his departure by longtime political collaborator Vice President Dick Cheney as "the finest secretary of defense this nation has ever had" and excoriated by former wartime guest of the infamous Hanoi Hilton, John McCain (R-Arizona), ranking senator on the Senate Armed Services Committee, who pronounced, "Donald Rumsfeld will go down as one of the worst secretaries of defense in history," the final page of Rumsfeld's impact on U.S. defense has yet to be written, and the outcome of the conflicts that are ongoing as these words are set down will have significant impact on how that page will ultimately read.

For that matter, the impact of former Defense Secretary Dick Cheney, who presided over the Pentagon in the critical period at the Cold War's end and whose evolutionary policies for defense reform link them to the Defense Department of today, cannot be overlooked in an aggregate appraisal of the Pentagon throughout the Bush years; nor that of Colin Powell, the chairman of the Joint Chiefs of Staff who served with Cheney during that period and, together with Cheney, was a principal architect of the Gulf War.

The tensions behind the scenes between Powell, who saw peril in the radical departure from the army's OPLAN 1003-98, the blueprint for a second land-and-stay Iraq operation, and the proponents of the revised battle plan, which included Cheney, then National Security Advisor Condoleezza Rice, and Rumsfeld himself, as well as Powell's conflict with Rumsfeld over the usurpation by defense of many of the ancillary functions that state would normally be expected to have played in any postwar rebuilding of Iraq, have also had profound impacts on the way the Iraq War has so far played out.[15]

For that matter, the impact of the Bush presidency itself on defense cannot be overlooked, for here was a chief executive who took his prerogatives as commander in chief more seriously than many if not most of his predecessors since Vietnam, including his father, the only other president to preside over a major regional conflict that saw a multidivisional commitment of U.S. ground forces since Richard Nixon. All in all, the proposition can safely be advanced that the last Bush administration, representing a conjunction of former Cold Warriors, veteran defense hands, and advocates of transformational defense policies—label them "neocons" or not as you like it—composes an epoch in post–World War II history that is unique in its effect on how the United States structures its defensive capabilities, fights its wars, and

15. The operational plan for the 1991 Gulf War also called for five hundred thousand U.S. troops. Therefore, plans for similar troop levels should not have been a surprise to anyone in 2003, including members of the Senate Armed Services Committee before which General Shinseki gave his estimate.

treats its global allies and enemies, and thus unique in its impact on the Pentagon.

Moreover, the restructuring of the executive branch of government under the Homeland Security and PATRIOT acts, which have collectively represented a more far-reaching set of reforms than even the postwar National Security Acts of 1947 to 1949, has had an impact on the Defense Department that might betoken new domestic roles for military forces that raise constitutional challenges and impinge on some of the nation's most cherished founding principles dating back to the Revolution.

It may be significant that it was Dick Cheney and not Don Rumsfeld who defended requests by the Defense Intelligence Agency for personal information by the issuance of "national security letters" to credit bureaus, telephone companies, and financial institutions for information on suspected targets of espionage and terrorism investigations. Within a five-year span from 2002 to 2007, the DIA issued information requests in about five hundred investigations.

Cheney defended the activity as "an authority that goes back three or four decades" and is reaffirmed in the PATRIOT Act, but the DIA's actions raised the ire of members of the House Intelligence Committee, which charged it exploited a legal gray area and convened investigatory hearings. Moreover, the committee charged that it should rightfully have been the FBI, which has national jurisdiction over such domestic investigations, and not the DOD, by which any investigative action should have been taken. The National Security Acts prohibit the Defense Department—and the National Security Agency, which is, at least on paper, a department of DOD—as well as the Central Intelligence Agency from engaging in domestic investigations, law enforcement, or counterespionage activities.

With Robert Gates in control of the Defense Department, policy questions regarding domestic activities, ranging from spying to the use of military forces in response to future domestic terrorist attacks, are on the table. As pressing an issue, if not more so, is how to fix an army that critics and proponents alike have called "broken" by the protracted warfare in Iraq. It became apparent by 2004 that the expectation of a fast transition from invasion to postwar consolidation to orderly transfer of power from the Coalition Provisional Authority set up to administer the country by the U.S.–U.K. alliance to a popularly elected Iraqi government was chimerical.

Yet the continued deployments of U.S. ground forces to deal with a growing insurgency from combative Sunni provinces, from restive corners of Baghdad itself, and from border areas with Saudi Arabia, Syria, and Iran have not only overstretched an all-volunteer U.S. Army beyond the parameters of its inbuilt elasticity, but have threatened to deplete its ability to contend with threats elsewhere in the world, now or in the near future, including those that might foreseeably involve its NATO allies.

Gates will contend with building consensus to overturn many of the fundamental tenets of both defense transformation and the Revolution in Military Affairs. These changes would almost certainly include a much larger footprint for the army, the potential for a renewal of Selective Service, and cutbacks in funding for high-technology innovations such as Stealth.

On the other hand, the military successes in the Gulf that led to the declaration of the RMA have given rise to strong counter-pressures for continued reforms to policy and combat doctrine. Swarming, sometimes called BattleSwarm, is one of these. Air-Land Operations, also called the Air-Land Battle, was a strategic and tactical doctrine that was first developed by a study group working out of TRADOC, the Pentagon agency tasked with matters of training and doctrine, between 1986 and 1987. Less than five years later, Air-Land Operations, which emphasized jointness of forces and tactics such as deep-strike and stealth operations, became the centerpiece of the Gulf War and led to the postwar Revolution in Military Affairs, whose lessons were further developed under Joint Vision 2010 and transitioned to the regional wars of the early twenty-first century.

BattleSwarm tactics, relying on network-centric battle operations, are designed around cellular combat elements, described in a RAND study for the USAF as "pods" in formations called "clusters." The USAF study calls Swarming a "seemingly amorphous, but…deliberately structured, strategic way to strike from all directions, by means of a sustainable pulsing of force and/or fire, close-in as well as from stand-off positions [deploying]…myriad, small, dispersed, networked maneuver units."

Whether, as some now charge, America finds itself in a situation closer to the end of the Vietnam War than the close of the Gulf War, and whether or not, as Colin Powell stated in December 2006, the active army is "broken," this author predicts the strategic conceptual battle at the Department of Defense between Gulliver and the Lilliputians— representing large, conventionally configured forces versus light, third-generation forces with striking power leveraged by stealth, mobility, and network-centric warfare—is far from over.

Nor, for that matter, are threats to an increasingly perilous and unstable post–Cold War world order. Of immediate concern to the Defense Department, and to Gates as secretary of defense in particular, are developments in other regional theaters that include Asia, Europe, and Russia, as well as Iran, a nation on Iraq's doorstep from which the ominous rattling of sabers has been heard to increase with the news of the mounting body count in Baghdad. A growing tone of belligerence has been heard from Moscow, too, where in his May 1, 2007, state of the nation address, President Vladimir Putin said that Russia was reemerging as a "major power" and warned foreign nations against "meddling in [Russia's] internal affairs."

Putin's address also contained a sobering revelation for allied members of U.S.–led NATO. Putin disclosed that Russia would put a freeze on CFE—the 1990 Conventional Forces in Europe Treaty between NATO and the Warsaw Pact—pending ratification and implementation of the latest renewal of the treaty. The importance of CFE to Europe is not only such as to cut to the heart of U.S.–NATO relations; the agreement also threatens to pit European security interests against those of the United States. The bone of contention is the deployment of National Missile Defense (NMD) installations in Poland and the Czech Republic that has been taking place throughout the fighting in the Persian Gulf region and in Afghanistan.

The CFE Treaty was designed to give NATO and Russian-led Warsaw Pact forces rough parity with each other. Since 1990, NATO member nations have viewed CFE as a critical guarantor of the post–Cold War peace in Western and Eastern Europe. It seems that the Kremlin's anger with ABM installation on the fringes of the CIS was not only the root of Putin's warning about foreign interference but also behind the CFE freeze. Europeans, who had seen ratification of the latest of the CFE treaties first negotiated with a prostrate CIS in 1990, frozen in 2007 by Moscow, are now faced with the U.S. plan to deploy ABM installations throughout the peripheries of the former Soviet Union, including its Eastern European border states of Poland and the Czech Republic.

There is by all accounts a growing Russian perception that the United States, now viewed as victim to an "Iraq Syndrome" comparable to the "Vietnam Syndrome," has bled its vigor onto the fields of Mars and lost its appetite to fight while, and at the same time, having drastically cut back its troop deployments in Europe, has left the NATO nations vulnerable, and that, consequently, NATO member states, perceiving their vulnerability and aware that the United States may be tied down elsewhere in the world, pose no legitimate threat to a Russia with expansionist aims backed by the military power to exercise and fulfill those aims.

At the close of the Cold War, it is pointed out by Alexander Khramchikhin, a spokesman for the analytical department of the Institute of Political and Military Analysis in Moscow, a semi-official organ of the *Stavka* or general staff of the Russian armed forces, that in 1989 there were four U.S. divisions—an army brigade in West Berlin and nine tactical air wings—stationed in Europe. There are now currently two U.S. divisions, one brigade and three air wings, in NATO countries. But those two divisions in Europe exist only on paper.

In actual fact, both are now deployed in Iraq. The perception at the "Fishbowl," the Russian cognomen for its equivalent of the Building (and headquarters of the GRU, which is similar, though by no means identical, to the organizational structure of the Joint Chiefs of Staff), is that not only will the United States blink first in any confrontation with Iran or North Korea, but that because of its overstretched army and lack of pre-positioning in Europe, it would be unable to come to NATO's aid in the event of war.

Ancillary to this viewpoint, which was expressed by General Yuri Baluyevskyi, chief of the Russian Stavka in May 2007—who also stated his conviction that CFE was "on the verge of collapse" to reporters at NATO headquarters in Brussels, Belgium, "because Russia did not want it"—is that the NATO states are ruled by pacifist weaklings who do not have the will, or for that matter, credible means, to wage defensive or offensive war against a determined enemy.

The steady enlargement of NATO, rolled up to the outer demesnes of the former Soviet Union, is viewed by both Kremlin and GRU as another provocation. This growth is backed by the Prague Summit Accords of 2002 and the NATO Freedom Consolidation Act of 2007, which won congressional approval on March 9, 2007, and which follows a continuing series of U.S. legislation adopted since 1994 strongly backing the enlargement of NATO and its embrace of former members of the WP that might opt to join its ranks. Beyond this there is growing popular sentiment on the Russian street against pro-Western policies since the so-called 2006 Orange Revolution in the Ukraine, which repudiated rule by a pro-Moscow old guard in elections that were marred by violence and bloodshed.

In April 2007, one of Robert Gates' first international visits as secretary of defense was to Moscow where he met with Vladimir Putin and Russian Defense Minister Anatoly Serdyukov in an attempt to sell the Kremlin on the U.S. missile defense shield and suggested that cooperation with the Pentagon would be in Russia's interest. The anti–ballistic missile defense installations going up in Poland and the Czech Republic are intended to protect the United States against ICBMs that might be launched in the future from Iran or North Korea, should those countries develop long-range missile launch capabilities, Gates told them.

Sergei Rogov, head of Moscow-based Institute of U.S. and Canadian Studies, believed the Gates trip showed a U.S. interest in negotiating with Moscow prior to implementing Europe-based ABM defense on its own. Since the United States and Russia signed the Strategic Offensive Relations Treaty (SORT) in May 2002, envisioning a bilateral strategic nuclear reduction upward of two thousand missiles by the end of 2012, deployment of a U.S. missile shield "would lead to a new arms race." Rogov added that, "We are on the brink of a new 'Cold War' if one looks closely at our [Russian–U.S.] present day relations."

At a news conference after Gates' meeting with Putin, Baluyevskyi rejected Gates' overtures. The Stavka chief said, "The real goal [of the deployment] is to protect [the U.S.] from the Russian and Chinese nuclear missile potential and to create exclusive conditions for the invulnerability of the United States." The general also warned his counterparts in the Department of Defense that Russia would monitor U.S. missile defense installations in Europe if they were ultimately deployed and develop "an adequate response to U.S. actions."

Baluyevskyi's linkage of Chinese nuclear capabilities with those of Russia is also telling: The former Soviets have for decades now been the principal foreign military suppliers of the People's Liberation Army (PLA), and perhaps more important to Sino–U.S. relations, to PLAN, the People's Liberation Army Navy. The Russians have armed Beijing with weapon systems that have direct potential during any confrontation between the United States and China in the South China Sea, a region that is home to two nations with which the United States has had longstanding ties and defense treaties; Taiwan and the Philippines.

Among these weapons are advanced Improved Kilo-Class diesel-electric submarines (known in Russia as Project 636 boats), which are extremely stealthy underwater to sonar detection, and Sovremenny-class destroyers (known as Project 956 Sarych "Buzzard" vessels), equipped with the Moskit antiship missile and Shtil SAM systems, which, like the Russian Backfire nuclear bombers, nicknamed "B-1-skys" because of their close patterning after the U.S. B-1B Lancer, are extremely close in design and operational capabilities to the U.S. Aegis vessels and their advanced SPY radar. Russia has also sold Kilos to the navies of Iran, Poland, Indonesia, Algeria, and India, to name a few global defense customers.

Like Aegis, Sovremenny vessels can track hundreds of simultaneous targets in the air and on the surface of the ocean and concurrently prioritize and target multiple threats with missiles and Vulcan-gun fire and launch cruise missiles far inland from the littoral seas in which they operate. Moreover, a joint series of Sino-Soviet naval exercises held in 2005, as well as Chinese military doctrinal publications, have made U.S. defense strategists increasingly concerned that in a confrontation with

China over Taiwan or over another strategic objective, PLAN might use "anti-access" strategies to interfere with U.S. ability to deploy or operate military forces overseas in defending its strategic interests and defending its regional allies.

It is not inconceivable that the United States may have blundered strategically in departing from containing Iraq to waging something close to what Colin Powell once called "halfhearted warfare for half-baked reasons." History records—has inscribed in its annals time and again—that wars, and specifically key battles fought in wars, have been the breakers of great powers, sapping their strength and that of their allies at critical historical moments and permitting that of their military and economic competitors to rise to a stage in which they may offer open challenge. Even if active war does not break out, the great power emerges diminished in prestige from the face-off, fair game for tomorrow's savaging. Even if the great power wins a limited war, or emerges victorious from a major war, even if the great power's homeland is not invaded, it will surely see the continuing rise of its competitors in global status and a further diminishment of its own power.

Then again, in an age of weaponry capable of incalculable destruction, a single grave misreckoning on the part of any combatant could conceivably begin an escalation process leading to a horrifying endgame. In the bipolar world of the Cold War, where two nuclear superpowers faced off against one another, each possessing the capability to unleash Armageddon on its antagonist, regional debacles like that of the Soviets in Afghanistan and the United States in Vietnam could be regarded as, to paraphrase Richard Nixon's phrase, strategic "side shows." In a multipolar world of shifting alliances where yesterday's staunch allies, such as the NATO nations, can become tomorrow's players in a new *Ostpolitik*, where a former Soviet Union declares itself on the path to resumption of superpower status, where transnational entities aspire to a status equal to nationhood, and where rogue states such as Iran and North Korea are governed by demagogues with nuclear fevers, the United States cannot afford to confuse, as the old Zen razor has it, the map with the territory. Yet while presidential administrations, defense policies, and ideologies of war all may change, one thing seems certain: It's to the Building that the United States will continue to turn, as long as America continues to endure, to make its battle plans and to lead its fight.

APPENDIX A
Timeline of Critical Events in This Book

There are milestones in the biography of the Building. This timeline traces key events that take place throughout the course of the narrative.

THE INTERWAR YEARS
July 1914—World War I begins.

November 11, 1918—World War I Armistice.

1919—A peace settlement for Germany is reached.

1920—The War Depreciation Act puts in place a radical reduction in U.S. defense spending.

1922–23—Hyperinflation hits Germany, Poland, Hungary, and Austria; new currencies are issued. Plans are drawn up for the development of the Northwest Rectangle in Washington, D.C.

1924—The Dawes plan is enacted. Britain returns to the gold standard.

July 1931—A banking crisis confronts Germany; controls on its economy are introduced.

September 1931—Britain leaves the gold standard.

June 1932—The Lausanne Conference signals the end of German reparations; Britain adopts general and imperial tariffs.

1933–1939—Oppression worsens in Germany.

April 1933—The United States leaves the gold standard.

June 1933—The World Economic Conference convenes.

1937—The Neutrality Act is passed; America is not to intervene in foreign conflicts.

WORLD WAR II (PRIOR TO U.S. DECLARATION OF WAR)
1934—FDR authorizes a massive rebuilding of the U.S. Navy.

1936—The Spanish Civil War begins as the left-wing Popular Front wins national elections and a right-wing coup d'état led by army Generals Emilio Mola and Francisco Franco starts a cycle of bloody fighting. Moscow publishes a new constitution that appears to set the USSR on the road to democratic government. In Venice, Italy, Hitler and Mussolini proclaim the Berlin-Rome Axis.

March 7, 1936—Hitler sends troops into the Rhineland, which had
been demilitarized by the Versailles Treaty, taking over a region
intended to serve as a buffer between France and Germany.

August 1936—The first of three major show trials begins as charges of
treason leading to jail or death are leveled at leading figures of
the Communist party and government. These include many
of the "old Bolsheviks" associated with Lenin.

1937—Construction of the battleship *North Carolina* commences per
Roosevelt's defense buildup. Development plans for Northwest
Rectangle in Washington, D.C., are advanced; groundbreaking
commences.

July 1937—Japan strikes China. Japanese troops cross Marco Polo
bridge, taking Peking within weeks. This is regarded as the
official start of World War II.

1938—Hitler uses the threat of force to incorporate Austria into the
Third Reich in a so-called *"anschluss."*

Spring 1938—Hitler begins making demands on the Sudetenland, an
area of Czechoslovakia containing a large German population;
he demands it be placed under the protection of the Reich.

September 1938—The Munich Conference takes place. Neville
Chamberlain, British prime minister, meets with Hitler,
Mussolini, and Edouard Daladier of France. German demands
for the Sudetenland are met. Chamberlain ironically declares
that the conference has achieved "peace in our time."

1939—Italians invade and take over Albania.

March 1939—Hitler gives the lie to "peace in our time" by
dismembering Czechoslovakia, with help from Hungary.
An entire nation disappeared from the world map.

May 20–21, 1939—British are routed at Dunkirk as Germans reach the
Channel coast.

Summer 1939—Hitler demands that Poland return territories that had
been part of Germany before World War I.

August 1939—The Hatch Act is passed, making membership in an
organization advocating overthrow of the government a bar to
federal employment.

August 23, 1939—Hitler and Stalin reach a secret agreement to partition Eastern Europe.

September 1, 1939—As Hitler invades Poland, General George Marshall is appointed army chief of staff.

Autumn 1939—The president signs a secret order to begin development of the atom bomb.

Winter 1939–1940—A lull in the fighting marks the period known as the "Phony War" broken by the German invasion of Denmark and Norway on April 9, 1940, and the conquest of the Netherlands, Belgium, and Luxembourg in May.

April 3, 1940—The House Appropriations Committee cuts the U.S. military budget.

June 14, 1940—The Germans enter Paris leading to French pleas for an armistice on June 17.

July 19, 1940—After German attacks, Congress reverses course on armament cutbacks.

Autumn 1940—The Luftwaffe is defeated in the air war over England that became known as the "Battle of Britain," effectively ending Hitler's plans for a seaborne invasion of the British Isles called "Operation Sea Lion."

November 1940—FDR is reelected to an unprecedented third term as U.S. president.

July 31, 1941—Reinhard Heydrich, chief of the SS death squads, receives a commission from Himmler to plan and carry out the Final Solution.

August 11, 1941—The prime contract for the Pentagon's construction is awarded after War Secretary Stimson refuses to occupy the just-completed War Department Building, built to replace the old State, War, and Navy Building.

September 3, 1941—A mechanical engineering contract is awarded to Pentagon contractors.

September 11, 1941—Construction of the Pentagon begins as Nazis assault Leningrad; Hitler orders more defense priorities to the German army and homeland defense.

December 1–15, 1941—The Soviets score their first major victories against the Wehrmacht.

WORLD WAR II

(Dating from the U.S. Declaration of War)

December 7, 1941—"A day that shall live in infamy": Japan attacks
Pearl Harbor; the United States declares war.

April 29, 1942—Construction of an initial Pentagon section is
completed as the tide of battle begins to turn in North Africa.

July 1942—The Joint Chiefs of Staff create the new office of chief of
staff to the commander in chief of the army and navy and
name Admiral William D. Leahy to the post.

Summer 1942—The third Soviet offensive begins.

January 15, 1943—Official date of Pentagon's completion. The
Pentagon's first occupants move in.

1944—A secret codicil to the Quebec Agreement affords the British
"full collaboration . . . in developing Tube Alloys [nuclear
weapons] for military and commercial purposes . . . after the
defeat of Japan."

June 1944—An Allied armada invades Europe on what comes to be
known as "D-day."

August 1945—World War II ends after Japan surrenders.

THE COLD WAR

September 20, 1945—Less than six months after the war's end, Truman
effectively abolishes the World War II intelligence agency, the
OSS (Office of Strategic Services), with the stroke of a pen,
ignoring pleas from veteran spymasters.

December 1945—Truman recommends to Congress a single
Department of National Defense, to be headed by a civilian
and complemented by an office of the chief of staff of the
military.

1946—Churchill delivers his "Sinews of Peace" speech; coining the
phrase "Iron Curtain," it becomes known as the "Iron Curtain"
speech, marking the start of Cold War.

April 1946—A Senate Military Affairs subcommittee drafts a bill
calling for a single Department of Common Defense, three
coequal military service branches, and a chief of staff of

common defense who would serve as military advisor to the
president.

May 1946—Truman orders Navy Secretary James Forrestal and War
Secretary Robert P. Patterson to resolve their departments'
differences over the implementation of the Congressional
Department of Common Defense plan.

March 12, 1947—Truman declares the "Truman Doctrine" in a
presidential address.

Mid-1947—The Soviets have by now increased their troop strength
from an initial postwar low of 1.5 million to more than 5
million.

July 26, 1947—Truman signs the National Security Act, establishing
the Department of Defense, the Joint Chiefs of Staff, the U.S.
Air Force, the CIA, and the National Security Council.

March 1948—The so-called Spring Crisis, in which the Soviets seem to
be mobilizing for war in a series of East-West face-offs, begins.

November 1948—Truman is reelected; he presides over the completion
of the continuing defense reorganization that he had begun at
the end of the war.

1949—Following Admiral Leahy's retirement, Congress votes in a new
set of amendments to the National Security Act of 1947 that
creates the new post of chairman of the Joint Chiefs of Staff.

August 1949—The Soviets detonate their first atomic bomb in a test
explosion that surprises and stuns the West.

June 1950—The Korean War begins after North Korea breaches the
postwar 1948 partition between the northern Communist and
southern democratic states.

1953—General Omar Bradley nears the end of his second,
congressionally fixed, two-year term as the Pentagon's first
chairman of the Joint Chiefs of Staff.

July 27, 1953—The Korean War ends with an uneasy ceasefire under
United Nations oversight.

January 1954—Eisenhower Secretary of State John Foster Dulles
announces the nuclear war strategy of massive retaliation.

March 1, 1954—The United States explodes a fifteen-megaton

H-bomb at Bikini Atoll in the Pacific, one almost twenty times as powerful as the Hiroshima bomb and light and compact enough to be delivered by air.

1957—The Soviet Union trumps the West by launching the first satellite, *Sputnik*, into Earth's orbit.

May 1960—Shrapnel from an exploding SAM SA-2 missile warhead damages a spy plane flown by pilot Francis Gary Powers, causing it to crash in Soviet territory. This begins the U-2 Affair.

December 1960—The Single Integrated Operational Plan, or SIOP, is adopted. It's the first of several such SIOPs that have served as the Pentagon's blueprint for waging nuclear war from that point to the present day.

April 17, 1961—Less than ninety days after JFK takes office, a brigade of some fourteen hundred Cuban exiles trained by the CIA and equipped by the Pentagon launches an invasion of Cuba at the Bay of Pigs.

1962—The Pentagon's Worldwide Military Command and Control System, or WMCCS (more commonly known as WIMEX by the way the acronym is pronounced) is established.

August 1962—The Cuban Missile Crisis takes the United States to the brink of nuclear war with Russia.

1964—The concept of Mutually Assured Destruction, or MAD, is promulgated in a speech by Defense Secretary Robert McNamara, becoming a Cold War buzzword.

1971—"The Selling of the Pentagon," a *CBS News* documentary first airs on prime time network television during the Nixon presidency. It marks the first TV news production of its kind on the Pentagon.

Sunday, June 13, 1971—The *New York Times* begins serializing the Defense Department–commissioned history of the Vietnam War known as the Pentagon Papers.

1982—The Pentagon's principal manual of doctrine, *FM 100-5*, is thoroughly revised to reflect a new emphasis on combined arms and Air-Land Battle strategies and tactics instead of defensive warfare that had marked previous doctrine.

1985—The Reagan defense budget of fiscal year 1985 marks the largest postwar military budget in U.S. history.

1986—"The Uncounted Enemy: A Vietnam Deception" airs on *CBS News*. Its premise is that the Joint Chiefs of Staff had deliberately overplayed American success in Vietnam throughout the war.

October 1, 1986—The Defense Reorganization Act (also known as Goldwater-Nichols) strengthens the hand of the chairman of the Joint Chiefs; among other things it gives the CJCS new freedom to set priorities and to say no to individual service chiefs.

Late 1990—The Concept Plan for the Pentagon Renovation is drafted. The plan is described by the Defense Department as "[entailing] the equivalent of demolishing the interiors of three buildings the size of the Empire State Building, refurbishing them from top to bottom without disturbing the occupants or disrupting their work, and completing the renovation on a strict budget of $1.2 billion."

September 11, 1991—The Pentagon celebrates its fiftieth birthday.

December 25, 1991—The Cold War abruptly ends when the hammer and sickle flag flies for the last time over the Kremlin. Serge Schmermann reports from Moscow in the *New York Times* the following day that, "The Soviet state, marked throughout its brief but tumultuous history by great achievement and terrible suffering, died today after a long and painful decline."

POST-COLD WAR ERA TO SEPTEMBER 11, 2001

February 1991—Operation Desert Storm begins, revealing the spectacular performances of Air-Land Battle doctrine, stealth technology, and precision-guided munitions (PGMs).

1992—The Pentagon Project, as the plan became generally known, is put into action after the Building receives a National Historic Landmark designation from Congress.

1997—The Department of Defense marks its fiftieth anniversary.

1999—Operation Allied Force in the Balkans concludes.

2000—The fiftieth anniversary of Armed Forces Day is celebrated, with the defense secretary and chairman of the Joint Chiefs paying tribute to the "unsung" military and civilian heroes of DOD.

September 11, 2001—The Pentagon is attacked by terrorists who crash a hijacked passenger aircraft into its northwestern facade, setting the Building ablaze. Rebuilding commences the following day.

October 7, 2001—The United States, supported by the United Kingdom, begins its attack on Afghanistan, launching bombs and cruise missiles against Taliban military and communications facilities and suspected terrorist training camps.

March 2003—The invasion of Iraq begins with a "Shock and Awe" bombing campaign on March 19, 2003 as United States forces unsuccessfully attempt to kill Saddam Hussein by destroying a hardened bunker complex in which the Iraqi leader is thought to be hiding. Attacks continue against a small number of targets until March 21, 2003, when the main coalition bombing campaign begins.

April 5, 2003—Baghdad is seized by coalition ground forces following a rapidly moving offensive that commenced the previous day.

January 26, 2005—The Senate confirms the appointment of Condoleezza Rice to fill the Cabinet post of secretary of state recently vacated by Colin Powell. Rice formerly served from 2001 to 2005 as national security advisor to the administration of President George W. Bush.

September 2006—The resignation of high-echelon U.S. military commanders in Iraq takes place, ostensibly because of dissatisfaction with U.S. policy in the Iraq War. The media dubs it "The Revolt of the Generals."

November 8, 2006—President Bush announces his intent to nominate Robert Gates to succeed the resigning Donald Rumsfeld as secretary of defense. Gates is unanimously confirmed by the United States Senate Armed Services Committee on December 5, 2006.

December 18, 2006—Defense Secretary Donald Rumsfeld's resignation
takes effect and Robert Gates is sworn in as his successor.
Rumsfeld's two terms as secretary of defense, first under
President Gerald Ford and then again under President George
W. Bush, make him the second-longest-serving defense
secretary in history, his tenure falling just nine days short of the
record set by Robert McNamara.

January 10, 2007—President Bush announces a troop "surge" in a
televised address as part of an overhaul of the administration's
Iraq strategy. Bush proposes an increase of some twenty-one
thousand U.S. troops, four thousand of which would be
marines.

December 18, 2007—In an interview with *Stars and Stripes*, Army
Chief of Staff General George Casey says "the U.S. Army is
out of balance. . . . [W]e're consuming our readiness as fast as
we're building it, and so we're not able to build depth for other
things. We're running the all-volunteer force at a pace that is
not sustainable."

December 30, 2007—899 American troops died in Iraq in 2007, making
2007 the costliest for the U.S. military since the 2003 start of
Operation Iraqi Freedom, according to *ABC News*.

January 26, 2008—A new wave of bombings in the Iraqi city of Mosul
leads to an intensification of fighting.

March 10, 2008—President Bush avows that U.S. strategy in Iraq
is working but adds that it needs more time. In all, he tells
members of veterans' organizations at the White House, the
U.S. troop surge has proven a successful strategy in Iraq.

March 27, 2008—President Bush, saying that "normalcy is returning
back to Iraq," argues that the U.S. troop surge has improved
Iraq's security and catalyzed economic progress and political
stability. As he speaks, Iraqi military forces backed by U.S.
war planes are locked in pitched battles in the southern city of
Basra against entrenched Shiite militias.

April 23, 2008—General David Petraeus, ranking U.S. commander in
Iraq, is tapped to lead Central Command (CENTCOM), the

military command overseeing all operations in the Middle East. Petraeus' second-in-command, Lieutenant General Raymond Odierno, is tapped to fill the post just vacated by his boss.

APPENDIX B
Secretaries of Defense and Chairmen of the Joint Chiefs of Staff

SECRETARIES OF DEFENSE

Term of Service	Name	Home State	Administration
1947–1949	James V. Forrestal	New York	Truman
1949–1950	Louis A. Johnson	West Virginia	Truman
1950–1951	George C. Marshall	Pennsylvania	Truman
1951–1953	Robert A. Lovett	New York	Truman
1953–1957	Charles E. Wilson	Michigan	Eisenhower
1957–1959	Neil H. McElroy	Ohio	Eisenhower
1959–1961	Thomas S. Gates Jr.	Pennsylvania	Eisenhower
1961–1963	Robert S. McNamara	Michigan	Kennedy
1963–1968	Robert S. McNamara	Michigan	Johnson
1968–1969	Clark M. Clifford	Maryland	Johnson
1969–1973	Melvin R. Laird	Wisconsin	Nixon
1973	Elliot L. Richardson	Massachusetts	Nixon
1973–1974	James R. Schlesinger	Virginia	Nixon
1974–1975	James R. Schlesinger	Virginia	Ford
1975–1977	Donald H. Rumsfeld	Illinois	Ford
1977–1981	Harold Brown	California	Carter
1981–1987	Caspar W. Weinberger	California	Reagan
1987–1989	Frank C. Carlucci	Pennsylvania	Reagan
1989–1993	Richard B. Cheney	Wyoming	G. H. W. Bush
1993–1994	Les Aspin	Wisconsin	Clinton
1994–1997	William J. Perry	William J. Perry	Clinton
1997–2001	William S. Cohen	Maine	Clinton
2001–2006	Donald H. Rumsfeld	Illinois	G. W. Bush
2006–	Robert M. Gates	Kansas	G. W. Bush

CHAIRMEN OF THE JOINT CHIEFS OF STAFF

Term of Service	Name	Service Branch	Administration
1949–1953	Omar N. Bradley	Army	Truman
1953–1957	Arthur W. Radford	Navy	Eisenhower
1957–1960	Nathan F. Twining	Air Force	Kennedy
1960–1962	Lyman L. Lemnitzer	Army	Kennedy
1962–1964	Maxwell D. Taylor	Army	Johnson
1964–1970	Earle G. Wheeler	Air Force	Johnson
1970–1974	Thomas H. Moorer	Navy	Nixon
1974–1978	George S. Brown	Air Force	Nixon
1978–1982	David C. Jones	Air Force	Ford
1982–1985	John W. Vessey, Jr.	Air Force	Carter
1985–1989	William J. Crowe	Navy	Reagan
1989–1993	Colin L. Powell	Army	G. H. W. Bush
1993–1997	John M. Shalikashvili	Army	Clinton
1997–2001	Henry H. Shelton	Army	Clinton
2001–2005	Richard B. Myers	Air Force	G. W. Bush
2005–2007	Peter Pace	Marine Corps	G. W. Bush
2007–	Michael G. Mullen	Navy	G. W. Bush

APPENDIX C
The Pentagon on the Pentagon

The Pentagon and the Department of Defense produce a variety of statistical information sheets, press releases, and news briefings about themselves, from which the following information was derived. (Original documents available on the Defense Department website, Defenselink.com.)

ABOUT THE PENTAGON

The Pentagon, headquarters of the Department of Defense, is one of the world's largest office buildings. It is twice the size of the Merchandise Mart in Chicago and has three times the floor space of the Empire State Building in New York. The National Capitol could fit into any one of the five wedge-shaped sections. There are very few people throughout the United States who do not have some knowledge of the Pentagon. Many have followed news stories emanating from the defense establishment housed in this building. However, relatively few people have had the opportunity to visit with us.

The Pentagon is virtually a city in itself. Approximately twenty-five thousand employees, both military and civilian, contribute to the planning and execution of the defense of our country. These people arrive daily from Washington, D.C. and its suburbs over approximately thirty miles of access highways, including express bus lanes and one of the newest subway systems in our country.

Over two hundred thousand telephone calls are made daily through phones connected by 100,000 miles of telephone cable. The Defense Post Office handles about 1.2 million pieces of mail monthly. Various libraries support our personnel in research and completion of their work. The Army Library alone provides three hundred thousand publications and seventeen hundred periodicals in various languages.

Stripped of its occupants, furniture, and various decorations, the building alone is an extraordinary structure. Built during the early years of World War II, it is still thought of as one of the most efficient office buildings in the world. Despite 17.5 miles of corridors it takes only seven minutes to walk between any two points in the building.

The original site was nothing more than wasteland, swamps, and dumps. Over 5.5 million cubic yards of earth and 41,492 concrete piles contributed to the foundation of the building. Additionally, 680,000 tons of sand and gravel, dredged from the nearby Potomac River, were processed into 435,000 cubic yards of concrete and molded into the Pentagon form. The building was constructed in the remarkably short time of sixteen months and completed on January 15, 1943, at an approximate cost of $83 million. It consolidated seventeen buildings of the War Department and returned its investment within seven years.

THE PENTAGON: FACTS AND FIGURES

The Pentagon—a building, institution, and symbol—was conceived at the request of Brigadier General Brehon B. Somervell, Chief of the Construction Division of the Office of the Quartermaster General, on a weekend in mid-July 1941. The purpose was to provide a temporary solution to the War Department's critical shortage of space. The groundbreaking ceremony took place on September 11, 1941. The building was dedicated on January 15, 1943, nearly 16 months to the day after the groundbreaking.

- Prime contract awarded 11 August 1941
- Mechanical engineering contract awarded 3 September 1941
- Construction begins 11 September 1941
- Grading contract awarded 24 September 1941
- First occupants move in 29 April 1942
- Construction completed 15 January 1943
- Total land area (acres) 583
- Government owned (acres) 296
- Purchased or condemned (acres) 287
- Cost $2,245,000
- Area covered by Pentagon building (acres) 29
- Area of center court (acres) 5
- Area of heating and refrigeration plant (acres) 1
- Area of sewage structures (acres) 1
- Access highways built (miles) 30

- Overpasses and bridges built 21
- Parking space (acres) 67
- Capacity (vehicles) 8,770
- Cost of building $49,600,000
- Total cost of project (including outside facilities) $83,000,000
- Gross floor area (sq. ft.) 6,636,360
- Net space for offices, concessions, and storage (sq. ft.) 3,705,793
- Cubic contents (cu. ft.) 77,015,000
- Length of each outer wall (ft.) 921
- Height of building (ft.) 77 3.5
- Number of floors, plus mezzanine and basement 5
- Total length of corridors (miles) 17.5

At the Time of Construction Number of:
- Stairways 131
- Escalators 19
- Elevators 13
- Fire hose cabinets 672
- Rest rooms 284
- Fixtures 4,900
- Drinking fountains 691
- Electric clock outlets 7,000
- Clocks installed 4,200
- Light fixtures 16,250
- Lamp replacements (daily) 250
- External windows 7,754
- Glass area (equals 7.1 acres) (sq. ft.) 309,276

DOD 101: AN INTRODUCTORY OVERVIEW OF THE DEPARTMENT OF DEFENSE

What We Do
- Warfighting
- Humanitarian Aid
- Peacekeeping
- Disaster Relief
- Homeland Security

We are warfighters first and as such have no peers.

And with the same dedication and patriotism we are proud to be performing a variety of other very important missions for the American people and our allies around the world.

Whether it's saving lives, protecting property, or keeping the peace, the U.S. military stands at the ready to keep America strong and free.

Our Most Important Resource
It's not tanks, planes, or ships, it's . . . PEOPLE.

We will never compromise on the quality of our most important resource: the people who have chosen to serve you and serve the nation.

They are your sons and daughters, brothers and sisters, husbands and wives. People of whom we are very proud.

These are the best of America.

Our Bottom Line
- To provide the military forces needed to deter war and to protect the security of the United States.
  - Everything we do supports that primary mission.
  - Nothing less is acceptable to us, or to the American people.

Our Global Infrastructure
The national security depends on our defense installations and facilities being in the right place, at the right time, with the right qualities and capacities to protect our national resources. Those resources have

never been more important as America fights terrorists who plan and carry out attacks on our facilities and our people.

The Defense Department manages an inventory of installations and facilities to keep Americans safe. The Department's physical plant is huge by any standard, consisting of more than several hundred thousand individual buildings and structures located at more than five thousand different locations or sites. When all sites are added together, the Department of Defense utilizes over 30 million acres of land.

These sites range from the very small in size such as unoccupied sites supporting a single navigational aid that sit on less than one-half acre, to the army's vast White Sands Missile Range in New Mexico with over 3.6 million acres, or the navy's large complex of installations at Norfolk, Virginia, with 78,722 employees.

Worldwide Presence

Department of Defense employees work in more than 163 countries, and 450,925 troops and civilians are overseas both afloat and ashore. We operate in every time zone and in every climate.

In Comparison ...

In terms of people and operations, we're busier than just about all of the nation's largest private sector companies.

The Department of Defense has a budget of $419.3 billion and more than 3 million employees; Wal-Mart has a budget of about $227 billion and employs about 1.3 million people; Exxon-Mobil has a budget of $200 billion and employs almost 98 thousand; the GM company budget equals $181 billion, it has a workforce of 365 thousand people; and Ford has a budget of $160 billion and employs 354.4 thousand people.

We Hire the Best

The Department of Defense mission is accomplished seeking out our nation's best and brightest. Ninety-five percent of our employees have high school diplomas versus 79 percent of the national work force; 5.6 percent of our troops have master's degrees versus 4.9 percent of the national work force.

We Instill Values

Even with top notch recruits we would not be successful if we didn't provide leadership, professional development, and technical training throughout their careers; we constantly build and reinforce core values that everyone wearing a uniform must live by: duty, integrity, ethics, honor, courage, and loyalty. Our core values are leadership, professionalism, and technical know-how.

Who We Work For

The Chief Executive Officer

Our chief executive officer is the President of the United States. Along with the secretary of defense and the National Security Council, the president determines the security needs of the nation and then takes courses of action to ensure that they are met. The president, in the constitutional role as commander-in-chief of the armed forces, is the senior military authority in the nation and as such is ultimately responsible for the protection of the United States from all enemies, foreign and domestic.

As part of the Constitution's system of checks and balances, our budget must be approved by the U.S. Congress, which acts as our board of directors. We accomplish this by working with various committees of both houses, primarily those dealing with funding, military operations, and intelligence. Their decisions affect our well being and range from setting civilian pay raises to funding major troop deployments.

The Stockholders

If the president is our CEO, and the congress is our board of directors, then our stockholders are the American people.

Our stockholders know us pretty well. Almost everyone has had a family member or friend who either works for us now, or used to.

We exist to protect these citizen stockholders, for without their support we would be out of business.

How We're Organized

Directions for military operations emanate from the National Command Authority, a term used to collectively describe the president and the secretary of defense. The president, as commander-in-chief of the armed forces, is the ultimate authority. The Office of the Secretary of Defense carries out the secretary's policies by tasking the military departments, the Chairman of the Joint Chiefs of Staff, and the unified commands.

- The military departments train and equip the military forces.
- The chairman plans and coordinates military deployments and operations.
- The unified commands conduct the military operations.

Office of the Secretary of Defense

The Office of the Secretary of Defense helps the secretary plan, advise, and carry out the nation's security policies as directed by both the secretary of defense and the president.

Four key advisers work with the secretary of defense in critical areas of policy, finance, force readiness, and purchasing.

Basically, they manage ideas, money, people, and material.

Policy

Our coordinator for ideas, formulates national security and defense policy and integrates policies and plans to achieve security objectives.

Finance

Our chief financial officer, oversees our budgetary and fiscal matters, conducts program analysis and evaluation, and oversees programs to improve general management.

Force Readiness

Our force readiness director, or "people" person, oversees personnel management; the National Guard and Reserve; health affairs; training; and personnel requirements and management, to include equal opportunity, morale, welfare, and quality of life issues.

Purchasing

The purchasing director oversees all matters relating to buying, researching, testing, producing, and moving material goods, advises on the use of new technology, protects the environment, and controls the department's use of atomic energy.

Train and Equip the Services

We train and equip the armed forces through our three military departments: the Departments of the Army, Navy, and Air Force. The U.S. Marine Corps, mainly an amphibious force, is part of the Department of the Navy. The primary job of the military departments is to train and equip their personnel to perform warfighting, peacekeeping, and humanitarian/disaster assistance tasks.

Army

The U.S. Army defends the land mass of the United States, its territories, commonwealths, and possessions; it operates in more than 50 countries.

Navy

The U.S. Navy maintains, trains, and equips combat-ready maritime forces capable of winning wars, deterring aggression, and maintaining freedom of the seas.

The U.S. Navy is America's forward deployed force and is a major deterrent to aggression around the world. Our aircraft carriers, stationed in hotspots that include the Far East, the Persian Gulf, and the Mediterranean Sea, provide a quick response to crises worldwide.

Air Force

The U.S. Air Force provides a rapid, flexible, and when necessary, a lethal air and space capability that can deliver forces anywhere in the world in less than forty-eight hours; it routinely participates in peacekeeping, humanitarian, and aeromedical evacuation missions, and actively patrols the skies above Iraq and Bosnia. U.S. Air Force crews annually fly missions into all but five nations of the world.

Marine Corps

The U.S. Marine Corps maintains ready expeditionary forces, sea-based and integrated air-ground units for contingency and combat operations, and the means to stabilize or contain international disturbance.

Coast Guard

The U.S. Coast Guard provides law and maritime safety enforcement, marine and environmental protection, and military naval support.

Prior to the terrorist attacks of September 11, 2001, the U.S. Coast Guard was part of the Department of Transportation during peacetime and part of the U.S. Navy forces in times of war. However, since the attacks, it has become part of the Department of Homeland Security. The U.S. Coast Guard provides unique, critical maritime support, patrolling our shores, performing emergency rescue operations, containing and cleaning up oil spills, and keeping billions of dollars worth of illegal drugs from flooding American communities.

Guard & Reserve

The National Guard and Reserve forces provide wartime military support. They are essential to humanitarian and peacekeeping operations, and are integral to the Homeland Security portion of our mission.

Our National Guard and Reserve forces are taking on new and more important roles, at home and abroad, as we transform our national military strategy. Their personal ties to local communities are the perfect fit for these emerging missions.

Office of the Chairman, JCS

An all-service, or "joint" service, office supports the chairman of the Joint Chiefs of Staff in his capacity as the principal military advisor to the president, the National Security Council, and the secretary of defense.

Its "board of directors" consists of the chairman, his deputy, the vice chairman, and the four-star heads of the four military services.

The chairman plans and coordinates military operations involving U.S. forces and as such is responsible for the operation of the National Military

Command Center, commonly referred to as the "war room," from where all U.S. military operations are directed. He meets regularly with the four service chiefs to resolve issues and coordinate joint service activities.

Unified Commanders

The nine unified commanders are the direct link from the military forces to the president and the secretary of defense. Five of the unified commanders have geographical responsibilities while the other four have worldwide responsibilities.

The secretary of defense exercises his authority over how the military is trained and equipped through the service secretaries but uses a totally different method to exercise his authority to deploy troops and exercise military power. This latter authority is directed, with the advice of the chairman of the Joint Chiefs of Staff, to the nine unified commands: Northern Command, European Command, Central Command, Southern Command, Pacific Command, Joint Forces Command, Strategic Command, Special Operations Command, and Transportation Command.

Northern Command oversees the defense of the continental United States, coordinates security and military relationships with Canada and Mexico, and directs military assistance to U.S. civil authorities.

The European Command covers more than 13 million square miles and includes 93 countries and territories, to encompass Iceland, Greenland, the Azores, more than half of the Atlantic Ocean, the Caspian Sea, and Russia. This territory extends from the North Cape of Norway, through the waters of the Baltic and Mediterranean seas, most of Europe, and parts of the Middle East to the Cape of Good Hope in South Africa.

Central Command oversees the balance of the Mid-East, parts of Africa and west Asia, and part of the Indian Ocean.

Southern Command guards U.S. interests in the southern hemisphere, including Central America, South America, and the Caribbean.

Pacific Command covers 50 percent of the Earth's surface including southwest Asia, Australia, and shares with U.S. Northern Command responsibility for Alaska.

Joint Forces Command is the "transformation laboratory" for the U.S. military, in this capacity it searches for promising alternative solutions for future operations through joint concept development and experimentation; defines enhancements to joint warfighting requirements; develops joint warfighting capabilities through joint training and solutions; and delivers joint forces and capabilities to warfighting commanders.

The Strategic and Space Commands merged in 2002 and are now known as the Strategic Command, which is responsible for controlling space, deterring attacks on the United States and its allies, launching and operating the satellites systems that support our forces worldwide, and, should deterrence fail, directing the use of our strategic forces.

Special Operations Command provides counter-paramilitary, counter-narcotics, guerilla, psychological warfare, civil education, and insurgency capabilities in support of U.S. national and international interests. Special Operations Command is responsible for special military support.

The Transportation Command provides air, land, and sea transportation for the Department of Defense in times of peace and war. It moves people and property around the world.

September 11, 2001: Day of Terror

"Today, our fellow citizens, our way of life, our very freedom came under attack in a series of deliberate and deadly terrorist acts. The victims were in airplanes, or in their offices; secretaries, businessmen and women, military and federal workers; moms and dads, friends and neighbors. Thousands of lives were suddenly ended by evil, despicable acts of terror," President George W. Bush said in his address to the nation on September 11, 2001.

Operation Enduring Freedom

"As the men and women of America's armed forces, you are the sharp sword of freedom. You fight without pause and complaint on foreign seas and in dangerous skies," Secretary of Defense Donald H. Rumsfeld said in a message to Department of Defense personnel on October 9, 2001.

The secretary and his team advise the president, who is commander in chief of the armed forces, in directing the war on international terrorism.

Our goals in Operation Enduring Freedom are to communicate that supporting terrorism carries a steep price; acquire intelligence; develop friendly relationships; eliminate terror operations; deny enemy access to offensive systems; and provide humanitarian relief.

On October 7, 2001, less than one month after America was attacked, the Armed Forces of the United States engaged international terrorism.

War on Terror: The Coalition

Citizens from more than eighty nations were killed on September 11, 2001.

The United States began building the coalition on September 12, 2001, and there are currently seventy nations supporting the global war on terrorism. To date, twenty-one nations have deployed more than sixteen thousand troops to the U.S. Central Command's region of responsibility. This coalition of the willing is working hard every day to defeat terrorism, wherever it may exist.

Coalition forces have made important contributions in the war against terrorism across the spectrum of operations. Particular contributions include, but are not limited to, providing vital intelligence, personnel, equipment, and assets for use on the ground, air, and sea. Coalition members also have provided liaison teams, participated in planning, provided bases, and granted over-flight permissions—as well as sizable contributions of humanitarian assistance.

Though there has been significant progress, the war on terror continues.

Progress in Afghanistan

• The Taliban regime is out of power and the al-Qaeda senior terrorist leadership is in disarray.

• Forty-nine schools are rebuilt, and thirty thousand boys and girls back in school.

• The children of Afghanistan have held their first Little League baseball game.

• Five hundred thousand metric tons of food delivered, enough to feed almost seven million Afghans.

The United States and its coalition allies have removed the dictatorship of terror from Afghanistan, where children are now free and eager to get back to school.

Afghanistan: Moving Forward

The International Security Assistance Force (ISAF) aids in developing Afghanistan's new security structures and assists with the reconstruction effort. It also helps to train the new Afghanistan National Army.

The war on terrorism in Afghanistan and across the globe continues.

Members of the coalition are helping the leadership in Afghanistan to assemble the ability to defend itself from terrorism and other threats to the national security.

Operation Iraqi Freedom

The United States and its coalition partners assist Iraq in developing a peaceful and representative government that protects the rights of all citizens.

As the central front in the global war on terror, success in Iraq is an essential element in the war against the ideology that breeds international terrorism. The ultimate victory will be achieved in stages, making steady progress in fighting terrorists and neutralizing the insurgency; meeting political milestones; building democratic institutions; standing up robust security forces to gather intelligence, destroy terrorist networks, and maintain security; and tackling key economic reforms to lay the foundation for a sound economy.

Homeland Security and Homeland Defense

The Department of Defense contributes to homeland security through its military missions overseas, homeland defense, and support to civil authorities. Ongoing military operations abroad have reduced the terrorist threat against the United States.

Homeland defense is the protection of U.S. sovereignty, territory, domestic population, and critical defense infrastructure against external threats and aggression, or other threats as directed by the president. The Department of Defense is responsible for homeland defense.

Homeland defense includes missions such as domestic air defense, maritime intercept operations, land-based defense of critical infrastructure and assets, and, when directed by the president or the secretary of defense, the protection of the United States and its territory from attack. The department recognizes that threats planned or inspired by "external" actors may materialize internally. The reference to "external threats" does not limit where or how attacks could be planned and executed. The department is prepared to conduct homeland defense missions whenever the president, exercising his constitutional authority as commander in chief, authorizes military actions.

Defense support of civil authorities, often referred to as civil support, is DOD support, including federal military forces, the department's career civilian and contractor personnel, and DOD agency and component assets, for domestic emergencies and for designated law enforcement and other activities. The Department of Defense provides defense support of civil authorities when directed to do so by the president or secretary of defense.

SELECT SOURCE MATERIALS

In writing this book I drew on a wide cross-section of research materials. Like the edifice the book is about, the subject is vast, with ties to a large assortment of topics ranging from biography to politics to military history to popular culture. At every turn I was challenged by the ever-present awareness that I was sailing through uncharted waters and needed, above all, to plot a true course. A wealth of documentary material was available from books, journals, and periodicals, and also via the Internet, but there seemed comparatively little that specifically addressed the plan for my book.

To continue with the sailing metaphor, the trick was to choose the guide stars to navigate by, while the difficulty lay in selecting those particular beacons that shed the surest light on the subject at hand, not such an easy task when confronted by a glut of information on a topic that often had a disconcerting way of defying easy interpretation.

The chronologically ordered bibliography of select source materials that follows is drawn from the most relevant of the texts I used in the course of my research.

BOOKS
Abbott, Tyler (Editor). *The Drew Pearson Diaries*. Holt, Rheinhardt, Winston. 1972.

Bernadotte, Count Folke. *The Curtain Falls*. Knopf. 1945.

Benjamin, Burton. *Fair Play*. Harper & Row. 1988.

Butcher, Harry C. *My Three Years with Eisenhower*. Simon & Schuster. 1946.

Cateau, Jeff and Michael Levin. *The Complete Idiot's Guide to The Pentagon*. Alpha Books. 2003.

Collins, Larry and Dominique Lapierre. *Is Paris Burning?* Simon & Schuster. 1965.

Commager, Henry Steele (Editor). *The Pocket History of the Second World War*. Pocket Books. 1945.

Editors of *Time* Magazine. *Desert Storm: The War in the Persian Gulf*. Time Books. 1991.

Eisenhower, Dwight D. *Crusade in Europe*. Doubleday. 1948.

Fishman, Jack. *My Darling Clementine: The Story of Lady Churchill*. David McKay Company. 1959.

Goldberg, Alfred. *The Pentagon: The First Fifty Years*. Washington, D.C., Historical Office, Office of the Secretary of Defense. 1992.

Haig, Alexander M., Jr. *Caveat*. Macmillan. 1984.

Historical Office, Office of the Secretary of Defense, and Joint History Office. *The Open House Collection: Documents from the Military Archives of Former Warsaw Pact Countries in the Library of Congress*. 2000.

Hogan, David W., Jr. *World War II Special Operations*. U.S. Government Printing Office. 1990.

Joint History Office. *The History of the Unified Command Plan 1946-1993*. 1995.

———. *The War Department from Root to Marshall*. 1998.

Kennedy, Robert F. *Thirteen Days: A Memoir of the Cuban Missile Crisis*. Signet. 1969.

Langsam, Walter Consuelo. *Documents and Readings in the History of Europe Since 1918*. Lippincott. 1951.

Lippmann, Walter. *U.S. Foreign Policy*. Pocket Books. 1943.

Mailer, Norman. *The Armies of the Night*. New American Library. 1968.

McNamara, Robert S. *In Retrospect*. Times Books. 1995.

Miller, Arthur S. *Presidential Power*. West Publishing Company. June, 1977.

Mosley, Leonard. *Dulles*. Dial Press. 1978.

New York Times. The Pentagon Papers. Bantam Books. 1971.

Orwell, George. *Coming Up for Air*. Harcourt, Brace & World. 1968

Powell, Colin L. *My American Journey*. Random House. 1995.

Rasor, Dina. *The Pentagon Underground*. New York Times Books. 1985.

Rhodes, Richard. *Dark Sun: The Making of the Hydrogen Bomb*. Simon & Schuster. 1995.

Richie, Alexandera. *Faust's Metropolis: A History of Berlin*. Carroll & Graf. 1998.

Roosevelt, James. *A Family Matter*. Simon & Schuster. 1980.

Ryan, Cornelius. *The Last Battle*. Popular Library. 1966.
Sheer, Robert. *With Enough Shovels: Reagan, Bush & Nuclear War*. Random House. 1982.
Sherwood, Robert E. *Roosevelt & Hopkins*. Universal Library. 1950.
Smith, Maj. Gen. Perry M., USAF (Ret.). *Assignment Pentagon*. Pergamon-Brassey's. 1989.
Triboro Bridge and Tunnel. *Spanning the Narrows*. 1964
Speer, Albert. *Inside the Third Reich*. Macmillan. 1970.
Terkel, Studs. *The Good War*. Ballantine Books. 1984.
Toffler, Alvin and Heidi. *War and Anti-War*. Little Brown. 1993.
Tully, Grace. *F.D.R., My Boss*. Scribners. 1949.
Woodward, Bob. *Plan of Attack*. Harper Collins. 2004.

ARTICLES AND REPORTS
"Alfred Goldberg Talks About the History of the Pentagon (Interview Transcript)." *Weekend Edition*. Saturday September 22, 2001.
"America Under Attack." *Newsweek*. September 14, 2001.
Barnett, Thomas P. M., "The Pentagon's New Map." *Esquire*. March 2003.
"Chaos Looms Over Soviets, Gates Says." *The New York Times*. December 11, 1991.
"Congress and Global Security: Inside the Pentagon." *Military Technology*. September 1990.
Controy, Sara Booth. "Foggy Bottom Brightens Up for A Celebration." *The Washington Post*. June 14, 1999.
"Defense Science Board Task Force Report. FY-1994-99 Future Years Defense Plan. May 1993.
Drury, Allen. "Inside the White House." *Look Magazine*. October 19, 1971.
"Ellsberg Talks: Why He Leaked the Pentagon Papers." *Look Magazine*. October 5, 1971.
"Excerpts from Pentagon's Plan: Prevent the Re-Emergence of a New Rival." *The New York Times*. March 8, 1992.
"Five-Star Pentagon." *Time*. January 8, 1945.
"The House of Brass." *Time*. July 2, 1951.

"Inside the 9/11 Investigation." *Newsweek*. March 29, 2004.

"Iran-Contra Report Says President Bears 'Ultimate Responsibility' for Wrongdoing." *The New York Times*. November 19, 1987.

"Khrushchev Remembers the Cuban Missile Crisis." *Life Magazine*. December 18, 1970.

"Khrushchev: The Red Riddle." *Look Magazine*. November 19, 1963

"The Might We Aimed at Cuba." *Life Magazine*. December 7, 1962.

National Defense Panel. "Transforming Defense." December 1997.

Nixon Center. "Between Friendship and Rivalry: China and America in the 21st Century." May 1988.

Office of the Deputy Under Secretary of Defense (Logistics). DOD Logistics Strategic Plan. August 1999.

Office of the Joint Chiefs of Staff. Joint Vision 2010. 1998.

Office of the Secretary of Defense. Conduct of the Persian Gulf War (COW). April 1992.

"The Organization Man." *Time*. January 13, 1958.

"Pentagon Imagines New Enemies To Fight in Post-Cold-War Era." *The New York Times*. February 17, 1992

"The Pentagon Project." *Civil Engineering Magazine*. June 2001.

"The Pentagon Report." *Civil Engineering Magazine*. February 2003.

"Pentagon Reports Improper Charges for Consultants." *The New York Times*. November 4, 1988.

"*Seven Days in May* . . . The Movie the Military Shunned." *Life Magazine*. January 23, 1956.

"Soviets Match U.S. On Nuclear Cuts on Strategic Warheads." *The New York Times*. October 6, 1991.

"Special Report." *U.S. News & World Report*. September 14, 2001.

"Thanks, General Groves." *The Washington Post*. October 19,1946.

"The Truman Memoirs: Volume II." *Life Magazine*. January 23, 1956.

"U.S. Fears Spread of Soviet Nuclear Weapons." *The New York Times*. December 16, 1991.

"Washington's Name Game (Editorial)." *The Cincinnati Post*. July 21, 2004.

White Theodore H. "In the Halls of Power: Part I." *Life Magazine*. June 9, 1967.

Yockelson, Mitchel. "The War Department: Keeper of Our Nation's Enemy Aliens During World War I." *Society for Military History*. April 1998.

INTERNET PUBLICATIONS (INCLUDES DOWNLOADED DOCUMENTS AND VISITED WEB PAGES)

The World Wide Web was also used as a research source, but exact publication data, including the names of authors and dates of first appearance, were often entirely lacking in the case of individual web pages. The list below is representative of the titles of some of the source materials downloaded or saved from websites. Publication dates are shown where available.

Construction Chronology & Historical Events for the Eisenhower Executive Office Building.

DoD 101: An Introductory Overview of the Department of Defense.

DOD Press Advisory. "Corridor Dedicated to 'Mayor of the Pentagon' ". May 27, 2004.

DOD News Briefing. June 5, 2004. "Vets Reflect on D-Day."

DOD Press Advisory. "Church Report on Iraqi Prison Abuse." March 10, 2005.

DOD News Briefing. March 11, 2005. "War on Terror is Transforming America's Military."

DOD New Briefing. June 4, 2005. "Transcript of Rumsfeld interview with CNN."

Engineer Memoirs: Major General Hugh J. Casey.

Headquarters Battalion Henderson Hall. BRAC document.

Historic Federal Buildings. The State Department.

Historical View of the EEOB—the 1800s.

Histories of the Secretaries of Defense.

Japanese War Planes Over San Francisco.

The Main Navy and Munitions Buildings. Naval Historical Center.

The Neutrality Act of 1937.

Rumsfeld Describes the Changing Face of War.
U.S. Army Chief of Staff Professional Reading List.
USACE Office of History Publication No. 34. Did You Know?
WW II and the Military, Congressional, Industrial Complex.

WEBSITES OF INTEREST
Army Corps of Engineers: www.hq.usace.army.mil
The Center for Military History Online: www.army.mil/cmh-pg/
Defenselink: www.defenselink.mil
Office of Air Force History: www.airforcehistory.hq.af.mil
Office of Naval History: www.history.navy.mil
The Pentagon Channel: www.pentagonchannel.mil
The Pentagon Library: www.hqda.army.mil/library
Truman Presidential Library: www.trumanlibrary.gov
U.S. Historical Documents Archive: www.ushda.gov
U.S. National Archives and Records Administration: www.nara.gov
The White House: www.whitehouse.gov

INDEX

INDEX